STEERING TO GLORY

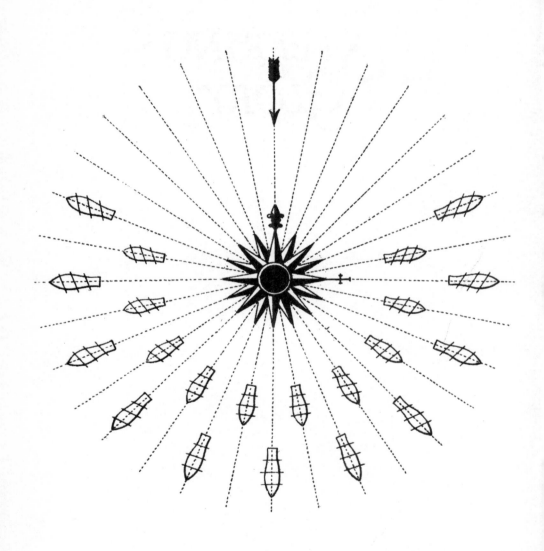

STEERING TO GLORY

A Day in the Life of a Ship of the Line

Nicholas Blake

CHATHAM PUBLISHING
LONDON

MBI PUBLISHING, MINNESOTA

For my family

Copyright © Nicholas Blake 2005

First published in Great Britain in 2005 by Chatham Publishing,
Lionel Leventhal Ltd, Park House, 1 Russell Gardens, London NW11 9NN

Distributed in the United States of America by
MBI Publishing Company
Galtier Plaza, Suite 200, 380 Jackson Street,
St Paul, MN 55101-3885, USA

British Library Cataloguing in Publication Data
Blake, Nicholas
    Steering to glory: a day in the life of a ship of the line
     1. Great Britain. Royal Navy – History – 18th century
     2. Great Britain. Royal Navy – Sea life – History – 18th century
     3. Great Britain. Royal Navy – History – 19th century
     4. Great Britain. Royal Navy – Sea life – History – 19th century
     5. Sailors – Great Britain – Social conditions - 18th century
     6. Sailors – Great Britain – Social conditions - 19th century
     7. Sailors – Great Britain – Social life and customs - 18th century
     8. Sailors – Great Britain – Social life and customs - 19th century
     9. Ships of the line - Great Britain – History - 18th century
    10. Ships of the line - Great Britain – History - 19th century
    I. Title
    359.00941' 09033

    ISBN-10: 1861761775

ISBN 1-86176-177-5

Typeset and designed by Roger Daniels
Printed and bound by CPD (Wales) Ebbw Vale

'A ship contains a set of *human* machinery, in which every man is a wheel, a band, or a crank, all moving with wonderful regularity and precision to the *will* of its machinist – the all-powerful captain.'

— Samuel Leech, in the *Macedonian*,
1810

'John Keller, prisoner: Was I drunk or sober on the afternoon of the 9th instant?
Answer: I cannot tell for I was drunk.'

— Andrew Phelim, private marine, on board the *Director*,
22 October 1798

'In the course of the passage he used to light his pipe, and sit over the hatchway, under which was 15 or 1600lb of Powder, which I desired him several times not to do.'

Shoubel Kelly, master's mate of the *Carnatic* (74),
3 February 1800

'"Have you not seen Mr Law [master of the *Gibraltar*, 80] very frequently drunk in his Cabin?"

"I believe Mr Law has at times taken a jovial glass, but particularly so, when he was engaged in a correspondence with the Admiralty, in respect to saving the remains of the *Boyne*, after she was blown up."'

George Smith, surgeon of the *Gibraltar*

A NOTE ON THE TEXT

Original material has been reproduced as faithfully as possible, with the following minor standardisations and exceptions: capitalisation is normally harmonised with modern practice; the long s is set as s; superscript is set as normal text, except where crucial to the meaning; underlining is set as italic; dash-length conforms to modern British practice; the various contractions of et cetera (*eg* '&co.') are replaced by etc. in holographs; money is expressed as £1 4s 8½d; the character for 'per' and 'as per', which is no longer available, is replaced by the word or words. Ship names are also all printed in italic. Modern printed material is reproduced faithfully (original material published by the Society for Nautical Research is modernised to the standard of the day).

Ships' guns are given in brackets after their names; these are the ratings given by David Lyon in his *Sailing Navy List*. Sources for details given in the foootnotes are included in the endnote to that paragraph.

CONTENTS

INTRODUCTION

In 1810, and for a generation to come, a ship-of-the-line was the most complex and sophisticated machine yet built: twenty-five miles of rigging and cables, weighing eighty-five tons, and fifteen miles of other ropes; 9,000 square yards of canvas, weighing eight and a half tons; a thousand tons of equipment and stores; and 640 boys, landmen, sailors and marines from perhaps twenty or thirty countries and twice that many land occupations and professions, with thirty-four named skilled naval trades, who themselves, with their chests and bedding, weighed sixty or seventy tons. This was all contained within a hull 167–176ft long and 46–50ft wide on the lower deck, and which was also home to licit and illicit women, children and livestock, from cows, pigs, goats and sheep to chicken, turkeys and even half a dozen geese smuggled into the midshipmen's berth. All this was to service an immensely powerful gun platform: a 74-gun ship had more firepower than Napoleon at Austerlitz, and on her quarterdeck alone had more than the British army's field guns for the invasion of Egypt in 1801, or Wellington's whole artillery train in the Peninsula in the summer of 1810. A great deal has been written about the battles the Royal Navy fought, and how by 1815 it had completed a naval Armageddon that ended 250 years of European maritime rivalry and smashed or confiscated the navies of Europe; much more has been published on the administration, technology and seamanship, and the social composition of the navy; the supply and victualling organisation has recently been given its proper attention: but although every book on 'Nelson's navy' shows how a typical day on board ship was supposed to have worked, none has attempted to show in detail, deck by deck and watch by watch, how it all fitted together – or occasionally failed to.[1]

This day in the life of a ship-of-the-line takes a fictitious 74-gun ship, the *Splendid*, and places her in a real situation on a real day in June 1810. She is in the

---

Mediterranean, having been detached from the fleet to victual and water at Mahon in Minorca, and returning with live cattle and other supplies. Admiral Collingwood, the popular and successful Commander-in-Chief of the Mediterranean Fleet, had died at sea that spring after finally being given permission to return home, and was succeeded by Sir Charles Cotton, who for the rest of the year, and into 1811, was 'essentially on the defensive' while blockading Toulon.[2]

Globally, in the summer of 1810 the Royal Navy was in a strong but by no means secure position, in command of the ocean but not yet able to destroy the French privateers in the Channel or the Danish gunboats in the Baltic, and not yet capable of the power-projection ashore that would win the war. In the largest action after Trafalgar, the squadron led by Sir John Duckworth in the *Superb* (74) had chased the Brest fleet to the West Indies and defeated it in February 1806, securing the Caribbean, and that year Martinique and San Domingo had been captured – in fact Britain had taken almost every colonial possession of France, her empire and her dependants: the only significant territories left were Mauritius, which fell in December, and the possessions of the Batavian Republic, which were taken by September 1811. The Cape of Good Hope had also been recaptured in 1806, in 1807 the Portuguese royal family and the Portuguese fleet had been safely removed to South America and the capital ships of the Danish fleet taken and removed to England, with most of the arsenal at Copenhagen, but Sweden had declared war on Britain and the Royal Navy maintained a large squadron in the Baltic. The navy had 664 cruisers in commission, including 108 ships-of-the-line, 79 of them the highly successful 74-gun ships, 133 frigates and 240 sloops, and had 140,000 men.

On the Continent, Napoleon had defeated Austria, releasing 140,000 men for the Peninsula, where 8,000 British and Portuguese troops were holding Cadiz against the French and where Massena, having taken the Spanish fortress of Ciudad Rodrigo, had crossed the Portuguese border only a few days before and was besieging the fortress of Almeida. Antwerp had been developed into a base that could hold forty sail-of-the-line and Napoleon was laying down, on average, a new ship-of-the-line each month throughout his empire, yet the failed attempt to raze Antwerp the previous autumn had been the greatest disaster of the war for Britain.

At home the 1808 and 1809 harvests had been bad, and 1810 looked no better; Napoleon had forbidden trade between his empire and Britain, though strategically he was prepared to exchange British gold for Continental wheat, and his Milan decrees declared that all neutral ships in British convoys were seizable by the navy or by privateers, which had taken 571 vessels in 1809 and would take 619 by the end of 1810.

British naval strategy throughout the wars was founded on the control of world trade routes – to secure her own trade and take the enemy's, especially and primarily the French – and to supply, support and project an army that was deployed or based in five continents. In the summer of 1810 the Admiralty had three priorities: to support the army in the Iberian Peninsula, supply Cadiz and harass the enemy from the coasts; to suppress the threat from the new fleets Napoleon was building by maintaining the blockades; and to hold the Mediterranean, where the navy was particularly concerned with the hostile fleet lying at Venice. Much of this activity was directed against fleets in being, fleets which in the event had little or no practical value: the new ships at Antwerp were largely obsolete, for example, and several that were built were too large to leave the dock. Most importantly there were no men to sail them; in 1810 Napoleon had not yet collected his sailors and sent them to die on the plains of Russia, but months or years of idleness in port did not make for skilled crews. As Admiral Sir Dudley Pound, then Commander A D P R Pound, observed a hundred years later, after the 'first great sweep' of the enemy's coast had produced a 'total bag' of '1 submarine sighted':

> … it would seem as if every day's delay in their coming out would tell against them because every day we remain at sea we are becoming a more efficient fighting force and our morale is improving whilst they as far as we know are laying in harbours with consequent demoralisation and lack of practice in handling their ships. It will I am sure be the same now as a hundred years ago, the Fleet waiting outside will have a far higher morale than the Fleet waiting inside … However the net result of the whole thing is that it is very dull work waiting for them to come out.[3]

It was dull work, perhaps, but never easy work, particularly off Brest – the most dangerous station for patrolling British ships, because with the wind at south-west or west-south-west it became a lee shore. John Boteler was a midshipman in the *Sceptre* (74) in February 1812:

> We had a hard gale from the south-west with a very heavy sea on from the poop at times, although as clear as possible, every now and then we could not see the masthead vanes of either of the squadrons – the sea as it came foaming above seemed as if it must break right over us, instead of which all at once it rolled beneath us. As we heavily rolled, our spare topsail yard, stowed outside the chains, was completely under water. At

last, in one of these lurches, we carried away the foretopmast and it took a long while to shift it.[4]

In the Mediterranean, Sir Charles Cotton, who had been successfully blockading the Tagus, had raised a Portuguese rebellion against the French and had, after protesting the terms of the Convention of Cintra that resulted from their defeat, negotiated with the admiral of the Russian squadron trapped there and arranged for his ships to be peacefully interned at Portsmouth, was fulfilling the requirements of the post of commander-in-chief, which needed 'not only an experienced seaman, but also an able statesman'. Toulon was under the command of Vice Admiral Allemand, with thirteen sail-of-the-line – one 130, two 120s, one 80 and nine 74s. The *Wagram* (130) was launched on 30 June, and the *Sceptre* (80), *Trident* (74) and a new 130-gun ship were on the stocks. Sir Charles had arrived off Toulon in the *San Josef* on 14 May and immediately issued a set of orders that essentially confirmed Collingwood's disposition of the fleet: the *Salsette*, with the *Frederickstein* and *Pylades*, was in the Archipelago, and communicating with the senior officer at Malta; *Magnificent* (74), with the *Montagu*, *Belle Poule*, *Leonidas*, *Kingfisher* and *Imogen*, off Corfu; *Eclair* between Maritimo and Cape Bon on the North African coast; *Active* and *Acorn* in the Adriatic, communicating with the squadron off Corfu; the *Seahorse*, *Pomone* and *Cephalus* cruising between Gaeta and Leghorn; *Trident*, *Paulina*, *Bustard*, *Elvin*, *Spider*, *Confounder*, *Theodoria* and *Ortenzia* off Malta; Rear Admiral Sir George Martin in the *Canopus* (80) with the *Spartan*, *Success*, *Volage*, *Espoir*, *Eyderen* and *Halcyon* off Palermo and the coast of Sicily; and the *Nautilus* sloop to carry dispatches and orders between them. Mahon, in Minorca, had been opened to British shipping in 1808 by the Spanish junta, and there was a naval victualler and a base where ships could resupply and collect and deliver despatches, but the main base for resupply, refitting and repair was still Gibraltar, where a tank containing 5,000 tons of water had been built. The main body of the fleet remained off Toulon, sailing in two columns with each ship two cables' lengths apart,* but gales in mid-July drove the flagship and most of the fleet eastward to Villefranche, leaving three 74s and a brig-sloop, under the command of Captain the Hon. Henry Blackwood, to watch the French. They chased an eastward-bound convoy into Bandol, about twelve miles west of Toulon, and on the 17th eight French sail-of-the-line and four frigates left port, and successfully rescued it. No

---

* The leading column was the *San Josef* (flag), *Tigre*, *Royal Sovereign*, *Sultan*, *Leviathan*, *Colossus*, *Repulse*, *Bombay* and *York*; the second column was the *Ajax*, *Fame*, *Warspite*, *Centaur*, *Ville de Paris*, *Victorious* and *Cumberland*.

damage was done to either side, and the French returned to port, but it caused a stir in the newspapers. On 31 August, with the fleet except the *Philomel* (18) and the *Repulse* (74) off Bandol, the Toulon fleet, led by the *Majesteux* (120), again came out, apparently with the intention of capturing the *Philomel*, but after a short night action were driven back into port. The French continued to build ships, but made no more attempts to leave port that year.[5]

The narrative of *Steering to Glory* takes place on 14 June, and follows in outline the real day of the *Conqueror* (74), which on 31 May had received orders from Sir Charles Cotton to resupply the fleet:

> You are hereby required and directed to proceed without loss of time in His Majesty's Ship under your command to Mahon for the purpose of replenishing her necessaries and water and refreshing the ship's company, which being done you are to lose no time in rejoining the squadron.
>
> You are to receive such empty casks as may be sent you from the different ships for the purpose of filling from the fountain at the head of the harbour at Mahon and bringing back to the different ships; and you are to place such casks in your hold in preference to your own, which are to be got up on deck if necessary to make room for them. As two transports will be sent into Mahon with empty casks from the ships here – you are to cause their filling to be particularly superintended and every care to be taken of such casks.
>
> And there being at Mahon 3 transports with troops for Cagliari and Palermo, in the event of any vessel arriving during your stay there, and bound to the eastwards, you will direct her commander to convoy the said transports to those places.[6]

This was a routine order, and that morning *Conqueror* distributed some of her stores to the *Leviathan*, *Colossus* and *Ville de Paris* (8,376lb of salt pork, 12,768lb of salt beef, 2,033lb of flour and seventy-eight bushels and four gallons of pease), and in the afternoon issued thirty tons of water, receiving in exchange 120 empty water butts from the *Ville de Paris*, *Colossus* and *Centaur*. (A great deal of a fleet's survivability on blockade was due to the management and distribution of stores, provisions and their containers, controlled from the flagship, and the ships' logs record hundreds of these transactions, accurate to the last pound of flour, half-piece of meat or barrel stave.) At 5pm she hoisted in the boats and made sail; at six the flagship was four miles distant and she recorded in her log, 'parted company with the fleet'. She arrived at Mahon without incident on the

A 74-gun ship getting under weigh.

3rd, where she moored in the harbour. There she repaired her copper and rigging, sent the *Halcyon* and *Redwing* sloops with the convoy to the east and took on board stores for herself and the fleet: 247½ tons of water; 5,398lb of fresh beef and thirty bullocks, 22,048lb of salt beef and 16,376lb of salt pork in seventy-one casks; 12,048lb of vegetables and greens; 57,929lb of other dried stores (1,140lb suet, 962lb currants, 282lb tobacco, 22,400lb bread, 50cwt 25lb sugar in lieu of oatmeal, 56cwt 12lb sugar in lieu of butter and 6,788lb rice in lieu of cheese); 220 bushels of pease; 4,642 gallons of wine; and 196 gallons of vinegar, returning the empty barrels, cases, bags and hoops. On the 12th she weighed anchor and sailed for the rendezvous, which she reached on the 15th to find the *Ville de Paris*, *Centaur*, *Tigre*, *Leviathan*, *York*, *Sultan*, *Ajax*, *Bombay*, *Repulse*, *Warspite*, *Colossus*, *Euryalus* and *Minstrel*. Next morning she returned forty butts of water (twenty tons) to the *Centaur*, thirty-nine to the *Ville de Paris* and thirty-seven to the *Colossus*, with the remains of three butts that had been damaged and one taken to pieces to repair the others. She sent three oxen and 400lb of vegetables to the *San Josef*, *Ville de Paris*, *Bombay* and *Repulse*, two oxen and 250lb of vegetables to the *York*, two oxen and 300lb of vegetables to the *Warspite* and one ox and 131lb of vegetables to the *Euryalus*. That afternoon the *York* parted company, having received orders to resupply at Mahon in her turn, with the additional caution that 'In watering the ship you will take care that a subaltern's party of marines attend at the watering place (with the previous permission of the Governor) in order to prevent the boat's crews from straggling, and particularly to prevent their purchasing the obnoxious spirit which has proved so serious in its effects on board ships lately at Mahon', and the *Splendid* resumed her station, the weather 'moderate and cloudy' and Cape Croupet NbE bearing '5 or 6 leagues'.[7]

All the events described as happening in the *Splendid* really happened, or at least are in the historical record, though only the weather and the shiphandling are taken from the *Conqueror*'s log, and no ship would really have experienced so much in a single day. The endnotes identify the real ships, places and times, supply the technical details and illustrate the key changes that allowed the navy to reach the sophistication of its techniques and practice that it had in 1810. Many of the members of the ship's company are drawn directly from accounts of real people, and they appear under their real names; those who are composed from several or many real people have fictitious names. The notes also give the real identities, and locate the real people in their ships.

Much of the information is found in the traditional sources such as published memoirs, captain's orders and the Admiralty's printed Regulations and Instructions, especially the most recent edition, that of 1808; these have the advantage of describing clearly and comprehensively, though not always without contradiction, what was meant to happen. Court-martial records are also used extensively. They provide an essential and unparalleled insight into what really happened on board ship, not so much through the events in question themselves, which are by definition out of the ordinary, but through the real and invaluably detailed accounts of who was where, when and why – and whether they were meant to be. Most interestingly they often record complete conversations; the only ones that typically show any sign of administrative censorship are those concerning sex (and not often then), and since witnesses were sentenced to a year or more in solitary confinement in the Marshalsea Prison for prevarication, they tend to be both full and direct. They are also close enough to modern English to be easily understandable, but possess a power of their own.

One of the most unexpected details of daily life that courts martial reveal was how time was observed on board ship. The published memoirs are full of references to bells to mark out time, and the first thing Jack Nastyface (who served between 1805 and 1811) tells his readers, once he is aboard his ship, is that the crew were divided into two watches, and that 'every half-hour is a bell, as the hour-glass is turned, and the messenger sent to strike the bell, which is generally fixed near the fore-hatchway.' This is very convincing, but all internal documents of the navy that record time use ordinary everyday clock time, and almost all witness statements in courts martial use clock time. In 1810 pocket watches were widely available in every town; a cheap one would cost three or four months' pay for an ordinary seaman, and would not be particularly accurate, but accuracy was not important when all watches were adjusted to the noon sight, a gold or silver watch was an essential purchase with prize money and they were excellent stores of value, both uniquely identifiable and tradable worldwide. Seamen often had them, therefore, and professional seamen often had several, and used them on board. A court martial in 1798 heard how a prisoner in the *Defiance* (74) was so troublesome that the sentry did not turn the glass and strike the bell; the master's mate had to step in and resume the sequence by reference to his pocket watch.[8]

Courts-martial accounts are also full of details of how men and boys dealt with and usually overcame the practical problems a ship-of-the-line threw at them, from overcrowding and anonymity to drunkenness and sexual predation, from finding space to keep clean and clothed to avoiding brutal petty officers. They also show how the officers tried – or, since these are court records, more often failed – to live in harmony, and in so doing reveal the expectations of the service, and the customs that divided those who belonged from those who simply aspired, such as the purser of the *Gibraltar* who fell out with the wardroom, was forbidden to use the lavatory and spent some weeks in his cabin in 'a distress'd state' before eventually court-martialling the wardroom for tyranny.

The court-martial minutes usually include the original documents either written by the prisoners (never 'the accused') in their own defence or throwing themselves on the mercy of the court. The defence statements are often laboured, with crossings-out and insertions, and many pages long; the pleas for mercy are often tiny squares of paper with barely literate handwriting. Sometimes the minutes include statements from character witnesses that are heart-breaking in their innocence and directness, and which would never have survived in any other context. Perhaps the best example is the letter written by Thomas Hubbard's mother in 1800. Hubbard was caught in the act of sodomy with George Hynes one night; it was a capital offence, four reliable witnesses had seen the act of penetration and death by hanging was the only possible sentence from a guilty verdict. Hynes denied the charge, but his character witness did not know him. Hubbard claimed he was drunk and knew nothing of what happened, even though Hynes was found 'under him, naked on his belly', which was a standard defence offered by desperate men, and he produced a letter from his mother, written before the trial, indeed before the act that would hang him, which was read out in court. It is difficult to see what he hoped to gain by it; perhaps he just wanted to show that he was supporting his mother and his ten brothers from his pay of £18 17s a year, not unreasonable in the circumstances. Sodomy cases were rare, but those invoking capital punishment were not, and there were hundreds of mothers in her position between 1793 and 1815. It is closely written, with almost no punctuation or capitalisation, on both sides of a piece of paper about 4½in by 6½in, and it still speaks directly, across 200 years, of the human cost of the victories the navy won.

Sept the 4

My dear chile it makes me very happy for to hear that you are save arrived to playmouth but o what happiness it wood be for me to see you once more your ten poor brothers join in love to you and is so happy to hear you are alive and well and poor things theay may well be happy for to hear of you for if it was not for what you alow me out of your pay we must all starve for provisions of all kind is so very dear that we can hardly live my dear i went to your master and he told me no he did not desire any thing of you at all but he is glad for to hear that you are so good to me and hopes that you will remain so and take care and save your money against you com home to your poor mother my dear child what you desired me to send you i must not send it your ant and couzens and all frends desires thir kind love to you and wishis you save hom again to me i have not heard any thing of your poor couzen harry since he sail out of playmouth witch is ever sence you went first abord the saint george and i be glad if you will let me know if the athemena should arrive thir before you leve it i heard of you by the paper but i do not hear any thing of him i hear that your couzen george is gone with is ridgment to waymouth on account of the royall family being thir so i have no more for to say now but my prays to god for to protect you all and send you all save hom to me again and soon

frome your loving mother tell death
sarah hubbard[9]

OUTLINE OF THE SHIP'S DAY

Middle watch: midnight to 4am
The watch on duty washes the weather decks; parties are detailed to work the pumps and ventilators to sweeten the ship and remove foul air.
The watch below is asleep on the lower deck, along with the officers in the wardroom and gunroom; a few men are drinking and smoking in the galley; the sentinels are at their posts and the master at arms patrols the ship.
Between three and four o'clock the captain begins his day, and the cook inspects the coppers.

Morning watch: 4am to 8am
The watch below comes on deck and holystones the waist, forecastle, quarterdeck and poop smooth, clean and white, then swabs them dry.
The watch on deck goes below; some go back to sleep, others wash, shave and prepare for the day: at 7.30 hammocks are piped up.
The cook lights the stove and brings water to the boil.
The officer of the watch reports the condition of the ship to the captain and the wardroom officers carry out their inspections – the gunner checks the guns and their lashings, the carpenter inspects the gratings, the hatches, the gunports and the boats, the boatswain inspects the rigging – and report to the captain at 7.30.
The wardroom and captain's cabin have breakfast.
Between 7.30 and 9 o'clock the purser's steward issues food on the orlop deck; the mess cooks collect it and take it to the cook in the galley.

Forenoon watch, 8am to noon
The ship's company has breakfast from 8 o'clock to half-past.
At 8.30 the marines mount guard on the quarterdeck, then from 9 o'clock they parade and from 10 to 11 practise drill and musketry.
At 8.30 the watch below goes on deck to work the ship and carry out any other duties; the watch above remains below to clean the lower and orlop decks, swab out the well and air the magazine, then between 9 o'clock and noon they carry out drills or exercise.
From 9.30 to 10.30 the surgeon inspects his patients in the sick bay then goes below to the cockpit to check his stores before reporting to the captain.
The captain is in his cabin with his routine work, and receiving reports from his officers; if there is no schoolmaster on board he gives lessons to the young gentlemen.

Between 11 and 11.30, on a punishment day the boatswain carries out punishment on defaulters, and on a divine service day the chaplain performs that office. At 11.30 the ship prepares for the noon sight.

Afternoon watch, noon to 4pm
The captain, master and any officers interested in navigation take the noon sight on the quarterdeck.
When noon is declared the men go below to their dinner, for which they are given an hour and a quarter, and receive the first half of the grog ration.
The wardroom dines at 1 o'clock, the captain at 2.
From a quarter past 2 until 4 o'clock the fresh water for the following day is got up from the hold; the casks are hoisted on deck, the water is stored in the tank, harness tubs and scuttlebutts and the empty casks are refilled with salt water or shaken (taken to pieces) and restowed in the hold.
At 1.30 on a washing day the watch below are piped to wash and mend clothes.

First and Second dog watches, 4pm to 8pm
At 4.30 the second half of the day's grog ration is served out.
Between 5 and 8 o'clock the mess cooks attend the purser's steward for the second half of the day's provisions and for necessaries such as candles.
Half an hour before sunset the ship beats to quarters: the ship clears for action, the ship's company assumes their action stations, the warrant officers check their equipment and the commissioned officers that all is in order and no one is missing or drunk, and when all is in order the retreat is beaten.
At 8 o'clock the ship's company are piped to supper.

First watch, 8pm to midnight
The master at arms patrols the ship to ensure lights and fires are out.
The watch below go to their hammocks.
At about nine o'clock the wardroom and the captain's cabin have supper.

Chapter 1

THE SHIP-OF-THE-LINE:
Its Organisation and Routine

'The wind was blowing strong, and we were more than an hour before we reached the frigate, which was lying at Spithead. My eyes during that time were fixed on twelve sail-of-the-line ready for sea. As I had never seen a line of battleship, I was much struck with their noble and imposing appearance, and I imagined everybody who served on board them must feel pride in belonging to them' – Frederick Hoffman, a new midshipman, October 1793.[1]

Robert Hay, a farmer's son from 'Kirkintilloch in the shire of Dunbarton' in west Scotland, joined the navy at Greenock, a port on the Clyde downriver from Glasgow, on 22 July 1803, aged thirteen and three-quarters, and was taken to Plymouth in a cutter. Three weeks later, after passing a medical examination, he was sent on board the *Salvador del Mundo*, a Spanish 112-gun three-decked line-of-battle ship captured in 1797 and now a stationary guardship moored in the bay. The ships of the sailing navy have often been described as a wooden world, with their own language, customs, even dress, but it is easy to forget the sheer physical impact a ship-of-the-line made on anyone seeing one for the first time. Three-decked ships, like the *Salvador del Mundo*, were built on the scale of cathedrals – a few feet narrower than Glasgow Cathedral, which they might have seen, but fifty or sixty feet longer, and more than twice as high. Before the industrial mills and factories, still a generation away, only castles and the largest dockyard buildings were massier, and for a farmer's son from Strathclyde this was probably the biggest man-made object he had ever seen. Add to that the shock of being thrown among 1,000 or 1,500 men and women from five continents and the experience was overwhelming. Even after years at sea in a 74-gun ship he was hardly able to give an adequate picture.[2]

From the description I had heard given during the passage, I had formed some idea of the appearance of a three deck ship, but I now find [*sic*] it fell far short of the reality … The noise and bustle and tumult which prevailed on board this ship astonished me. On the lower deck which was appropriated to the ships crew, almost every birth … was converted into a shop or warehouse where commodities of every description might be procured. Groceries, haberdashery goods, hardware, stationary and in fact almost everything that could be named as the necessaries or luxuries of life. Even spiritous liquors though strictly prohibited were to be had in abundance …

It would be difficult to give any adequate idea of the scenes these decks presented to any one who has not witnessed them. To the eye were presented complexions of every varied hue, and features of every cast, from the jetty face, flat nose, thick lips and frizzled hair of the African, to the more slender frame and milder features of the Asiatic. The rosy complexion of the English swain and the sallow features of the sun-burnt Portuguese. People of every proffession and of the most contrasted manners, from the brawny ploughman to the delicate fop. The decayed author and bankrupt merchant who had eluded their creditors. The apprentice who had eloped from servitude. The improvident and impoverished father who had abandoned his family and the smuggler and the swindler who had escaped by flight the vengeance of the laws. Costumes of the most various hues presented themselves from the Kilted Highlander to the quadruple breeched sons of Holland. From the shirtless sons of the British prison-house to the knuckle ruffles of the haughty Spaniard. From the gaudy and tinseled trappings of the dismissed footman to the rags and tatter of the city mendicant. Here, a group of half-starved and squalid wretches, not eating but devouring with rapacity their whole day's provisions at a single meal. There, a gang of sharpers at cards or dice swindling some unsuspecting booby out of his few remaining pence.

To the ear was addressed a hubbub little short of that which occured at Babel. Irish, Welsh, Dutch, Portuguese, Spanish, French, Swedish, Italian and all the provincial dialects which prevail between Landsend and John O' Groats, joined their discordant notes. While an occasional disciple of the Muses with his poetical effusions, and the sons of Thespis [actors] with their mutterings, execrations, songs, jests and laughter were every where heard. While the occasional rattle of the boatswains cane, the harsh voices of his mates blended with the shrill and penetrating sound of their whistles, served at once to strike terror into the mind and add confusion to the scene.[3]

This social and racial mix could be found in almost every ship in the navy. In the *Implacable* (74) in 1808 the crew came from thirty-two countries or islands:

English 285, Irish 130, Welsh 25, Isle of Man 6, Scots 29, Shetland 3, Orkneys 2, Guernsey 2, Canada 1, Jamaica 1, Trinidad 1, St. Domingo 2, St. Kitts 1, Martinique 1, Santa Cruz 1, Bermuda 1, Swedes 8, Danes 7, Prussians 8, Dutch 1, Germans 3, Corsica 1, Portuguese 5, Sicily 1, Minorca 1, Ragusa 1, Brazils 1, Spanish 2, Madeira 1, Americans 28, West Indies 2, Bengal 2. This statement does not include officers of any description, and may be considered applicable to every British ship with the exception that *very* few of them have *so many native subjects*.[4]

In the *St Domingo* (74), the seamen were from nineteen countries and fifty-five trades or occupations, including a calendarman, two fustian-cutters, an optician, a pipe-borer, an umbrella-maker and a violin-maker, and the marines were from ten countries and twenty-nine trades: they were aged from under twenty to fifty-two and sixty respectively. (The modal age was twenty-five to thirty and twenty to twenty-five respectively.) The crew of the *Bellerophon* (74), in a survey taken in 1805, included men who had been 'barbers, basketmakers, brushmakers, black-smiths, buttonmakers, cabinet makers, carters, farmers, glaziers, grooms, hatters, millers, plumbers, poulterers, shoemakers, snuffmakers, tallow chandlers, watch-makers, weavers and wheelwrights'; 174 had been merchant seamen (with eleven other sea- or watermen), and twenty had worked in the dockyards. Their average age was thirty.[5]

Strong agile men were valuable, and there was no guarantee that any of the foreigners in these ships could speak English. When the *Prompte* (20) arrived in

An Admiralty pattern anchor.

Yarmouth Roads in 1794 and came to anchor, the Marquis of Huntly, a passenger, went on shore in one of her boats.

> On his return, in coming along the pier (it being dark), came close to a man standing there and watching his boat. 'Come, my brave fellow,' said the Marquis, 'will you come along with me?' The poor fellow, a Swede, not understanding a word of English, foolishly enough went into the boat with him and was brought on board, and the Marquis returned to the transport quite forgetting the affair. Next day the man was seen standing on the forecastle, and no one knew who he was, so he was sent for on the quarterdeck, and being asked who he was, replied to every question, 'Orla hou,', which perhaps was 'I don't understand you.' To end the matter he was put on the ship's books by the name of 'Orla Hou' and stationed on the forecastle; and when I left the *Prompte*, near five years after, he was still in the ship and one of the best seamen on board, and had learnt to speak English as well as any one.[6]

❧

THE 74-GUN SHIP IN THE ROYAL NAVY

All ships in the navy were classified into one of six rates by the number of guns they were designed to carry. Line-of-battle ships were powerful enough to stand in the line of battle, and they comprised the first three rates. First Rates, with 100 or more guns on three gundecks, were the fleet flagships, but were too valuable to station outside the Channel and the Mediterranean Fleets, and with the exception of the *Victory* were not great sailers: there were only four available for most of the war (there were never more than seven). Second Rates had 98 guns on three decks; they were notoriously bad sailers, slow and leewardly, and they were often reserved for the flagships of the important colonial and Baltic expeditions, and on the crucial Leeward Island station, but since Trafalgar the Admiralty had favoured large two-deckers. Third Rates had 80, 74 or 64 guns, on two decks. The navy built four 80-gun ships-of-the-line; they were fast and weatherly, and the *Foudroyant* was 'the finest two-decker in the world', but they suffered from hogging problems (when the two ends of the ship's decks drooped lower than the midship part, and the keel and bottom arched upwards). The 74-gun ships, like the *Splendid*, were by far the most numerous and successful, although the 64-gun ship was most useful when shallow draught was an advantage; there were seven 64s on each side at the British–Dutch Battle of Camperdown in 1797 and three under Nelson at the Battle of Copenhagen in 1801, as well as two with him at Trafalgar.[7]

The classification of ships in the Royal Navy, 1793–1815[8]

			1793	1802, peace	1808
First Rates		100+ guns on 3 gundecks	850 men		837 men
Second Rates		98 or 90 guns on 3 gundecks	750	} 550	738
	Line-of-battle ships	84 guns on 2 gundecks	650		–
		80 guns on 2 gundecks	650		700
Third Rates		74 guns on 2 gundecks	600	} 500	640 or 590
		64 guns on 2 gundecks	500		491
Fourth Rates	_Below the line_	50 guns on 1 or 2 gundecks	350	320	343
		44 guns on 1 gundeck	300	214	294
		38 guns on 1 gundeck	280	200	284
Fifth Rates	_Frigates_	36 guns on 1 gundeck	270	190	264
		32 guns on 1 gundeck	220	180	244 or 216
		28 guns on 1 gundeck	200	150	195
Sixth Rates		24 guns on 1 gundeck	160	130	–
		22 or 20 guns on 1 gundeck	160		155*

The Royal Navy launched its first 74-gun ship-of-the-line, the _Culloden_, on 9 September 1747, at Deptford Dockyard, on the Thames. She was not a true 74, but a two-decked ship modified from the standard 1741 design for 80-gun three-decked ships, which were short, slow, unstable, undergunned and already obsolete. The following summer France began construction of a navy of sixty battleships and forty frigates, based on twenty-four very large two-decked 74-gun ships, carrying 38pdrs and 18pdrs; by December 1755 France had launched thirty-seven battleships, bringing the total in the navy to fifty-seven. That year the Surveyor of the Navy, Sir Joseph Allin, retired and was replaced by Thomas Slade and William Bately; in August 1755 Slade ordered the first two true Royal Navy 74s, the _Dublin_ and _Norfolk_, then in October the _Lenox_, _Mars_ and _Shrewsbury_, and in November the _Warspight_ (or _Warspite_) and _Resolution_. They were smaller than the French 74s, displacing 2,100–2,400 tonnes rather than 2,400–3,000, but were faster and more weatherly than the 80s they superseded, and the key characteristic that made them so valuable was already in place: like the French and Spanish 74s they were designed to defeat, they carried on their lower gundecks the heaviest guns in standard use and on their upper gundecks guns as large as or larger than those used in

---

* The figures for 1802 and 1808 include boys and the fictitious widow's men whose wages went to support real widows. Unrated ships and vessels, _ie_ ship-sloops and below, are not shown. The navy's lists continued to include the 60-gun ship but the Royal Navy in 1793 had none in commission, only a hulk and two receiving ships (for pressed men and volunteers) at Plymouth. Two 60-gun ships were captured during the war, and were used as a troopship/hospital ship/storeship and as a prison ship.

frigates. In the Royal Navy these were 32pdrs and 18pdrs, later 24pdrs; in the French navy, 36pdrs and 18pdrs, and in the Spanish navy 24pdrs and 18pdrs.[9] The 74-gun ship became central to the Royal Navy and to the navies of the other great powers from the 1760s until the end of the wars against Napoleon, when new construction techniques allowed much longer ships, because in a famous description it contained 'the properties of the First Rate and the frigate'.

> She will not shrink from an encounter with a First Rate on account of superior weight, nor abandon the chace of a frigate on account of swiftness. The union of these qualities has therefore, with justice, made the 74-gun ship the principal object of maritime attention, and given her so distinguished a pre-eminence in our line of battle.[10]

'Superior weight': although a 74 had only two gundecks to a First Rate's three, a well-designed 74 such as Slade's *Bellona*, launched in 1760, and whose physical form I have used for the *Splendid*, carried her lowest gundeck gunports 5ft 2in clear of the sea when victualled for Channel service (eight months) and 4ft 8in clear when victualled for far foreign (twelve months), while the First Rates often found their lowest deck unusable in blowing weather because the gunports were too close to the waves, leaving them only with their 24pdrs and 12pdrs. French and Spanish three-deckers carried 36pdrs on the lowest deck, but these were really too heavy for practical use and had a much slower rate of fire: on 28 May 1794 the *Bellerophon*, unsupported, engaged the 110-gun *Révolutionnaire* for an hour and a quarter and crippled her. 'On account of swiftness': the *Bellona* could sail from 11 to 12 knots either by or large, as fast as a frigate (though this speed was 'better than most' 74s, which could expect 8–10), and when well handled a 74 could outmanoeuvre a frigate, as when the *Northumberland* drove *L'Arianne* and *L'Andromaque* 44s onto the rocks near L'Orient in 1812.[11]

Including those in Ordinary (reserve), more than two hundred 74s served in the Royal Navy between 1755 and 1815; of the sixty-five in service in 1793, forty-one had been launched before the end of the American War of Independence in 1783. The sixty-five were all British-built except the *Courageux*, launched at Brest in 1753, and taken by the *Bellona* on 13 August 1761, and the *Pegase*, launched at Brest in 1781 and taken by the *Foudroyant* (80), herself originally taken from the French, on 21 April 1782. Of the ninety-five in service at the end of the war, only thirteen had been launched before 1793. There were many captures; those not fitted for sea were hulked as prison ships, victuallers, store ships and so on. Each ship took from three to five years to build (partly because of the practice of leav-

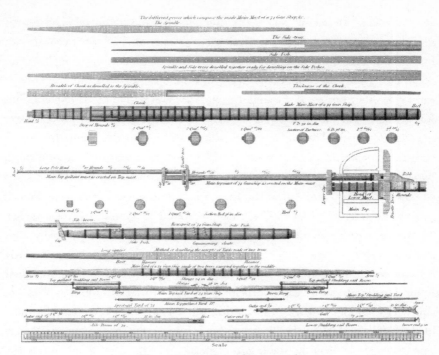

The construction of masts for a 74-gun ship.

ing ships 'in frame' before planking to weather the timbers and strengthen them –
unseasoned ships were damp and produced fatal vapours), used at least sixty acres
of English oak trees and cost about the same as two frigates.[12]

The original 74s are called Common Class (common because the most
numerous), and continued to be built until after the end of the wars with
Napoleon. Common Class 74s carried twenty-eight 32pdrs on the gundeck, and
twenty-eight 18pdrs on the upper deck if built in the British style and thirty if
built in the French, as well as an armed quarterdeck and forecastle (typically
fourteen and four 9pdrs, later replaced by carronades). They were 168–170ft long
at 1,600–1,650 measured tons, with a complement of 550 or 600 men.*

---

* Length for 74s is always length on the gundeck. The measurement was BOM (Builders' Old
Measurement), a formula used from 1667 to 1873 of the volume of the hull and therefore carrying
capacity, $(L \times B \times \frac{1}{2} B) \div 94$, where L = the length along the rabbet of the keel from the fore side of the
stem beneath the bowsprit to the after side of the sternpost, and B = maximum breadth. As Jan Glete
explains, it 'overestimated the size of sharply built small ships and underestimated the size of large ships
with fuller lines'; using half the breadth for the depth 'also underestimated narrow and deep-draughted
ships (primarily French prizes in British service)'. It remained in use because the Admiralty was
principally interested in ships as gun platforms, which this figure, since it measured internal volume
above the waterline, expressed well. There is no direct correlation with displacement tonnage: the
Commerce de Marseilles (120) was measured at 2,746⁷⁄₉₄ tons on her capture, but her load displacement
has been estimated (by Clowes) as 5,246 tons; the *Tigre* (74) at 1,886⁶⁷⁄₉₄ and 3,248; the *Loire* (40) at
1,100³¹⁄₉₄ and 1,479; and the *Bonne Citoyenne* (20) at 511¹⁄₉₄ and 546. Captain Bayntun measured the
Milford (74), 1,906³⁵⁄₉₄, as displacing 3,006 tons when victualled and stored for Channel service.

France, with her ally Spain, continued to outbuild the Royal Navy for the rest of the century, turning a British numerical superiority of 11 per cent in 1765 into a Franco-Spanish superiority of 34 per cent in 1790: even though France could not afford and Spain could not man the ships they were building, by the early 1790s they possessed the largest navies they ever had in the sailing era. This was certainly not the same as an effective superiority, and the Royal Navy was not defeated in the War of American Independence, but the Admiralty drew a clear lesson from the developments of that war: against four new 110-gun ships, two 80s, nine 74s and three 64s, the British launched six 74s and four 64s, or 22,000 tonnes displacement to the French 60,000 tonnes, and the new French ships were larger and faster still (averaging around 3,160 tonnes displacement). The difference is partly accounted for by the Royal Navy's needing as many ships as possible for the money rather than fewer very powerful ones, and partly because size was to some extent forced on the French by the failure of their foundry technology to keep pace with British improvements, so that a gun of equivalent power was made of metal from three furnaces, was weaker and more likely to split and had to be loaded with a less powerful charge; but the French ships were good sailers and stable gun platforms. The British response was a new kind of 74, the Large Class, still with the effective twenty-eight 32pdrs on the gundeck, but with 24pdrs on the upper deck (thirty in the British-designed ships and twenty-eight when using designs that were foreign or based on foreign plans). Two had been ordered as early as 1757, using the lines of the French *Invincible*, captured in 1747, but had been thought unnecessarily large; the new ships had new designs. The first was ordered on 10 January 1785, with two more on 17 January 1788, the same day as the 2,054-ton 80-gun *Foudroyant* and the 2,110-ton 98-gun *Dreadnought*, all intended to be faster and more seaworthy sailers. The first of these 74s were 176ft long, although some Large Class 74s were as long as 182ft 3in. They had a complement of 600 or 650 men, and were 1,850–1,900 measured tons. The ships were not launched until 1790, 1794, 1797, 1798 and 1801 respectively, but the Admiralty also ordered six 18pdr 74s launched before the Peace of Amiens that at 1,798–1,916 tons were rather larger than the normal Common Class ships, and also ordered larger frigates and sloops.[13]

Each Large Class 74 cost as much as 125 per cent of a Common Class; the natural-grown timber of the right size, particularly compass (curved) wood for the knees, was harder to find; and those longer than about 176ft, especially those longer than 180ft, began to hog, or break the curve of the sheer: ships whose upper decks carried 24pdrs, rather than the 18pdrs of the Common Class, had an extra gun weight of up to 11 tons 4cwt, or 19 per cent, and at least another 5¼ tons of shot. This was a serious problem: it reduced their speed and meant more time in dock for repairs and more pressure on dockyard resources. The *Kent*, for example, was 182ft 3in, lengthened 11ft during construction. Large Class 74s were often picked out as flagships, and she served as the flagship of Admiral Duncan in the 1799 expedition to Holland and of Rear Admiral Sir Richard Bickerton off Alexandria in 1801, but she eventually sagged 17in at each end, although she was not hulked until 1857 and not broken up until 1880. The longitudinal framing used in all the navies was not strong enough to support these lengths in 74s. The ships in French service had not had this problem, of course, because they were not intended to stay at sea in all weathers for months on end: they were built and fitted for the Mediterranean. The best solution was the system of diagonal bracing invented by Sir Robert Seppings, and in 1805 the *Kent* was used for its first successful adoption,* but in 1805 Sir Robert was plain Mr Seppings, master shipwright at Chatham, and his system was not used widely until after he was a junior surveyor of the navy, from 1813.[14]

The Admiralty experimented with fitting ships with guns that were of uniform 24pdr calibre but different sizes, carronades on the quarterdeck and forecastle, standard long guns on the gundeck and novel shorter guns on the upper deck designed by Captain Gover that weighed 33cwt each, rather than 47 or 50cwt for long guns. This was tried on several worn-out longer ships, including the *Hercule* of 1797, which had been taken by one of the most successful 32/24pdr Large Class 74s, the *Mars*, fulfilling exactly her intended blockade role in 1798, when she chased and trapped her off Brest on 21 April 1798, and from 9.25pm to 10.30pm fought her so close that 'the guns on the lower deck of each could not, as usual, be run out, but were obliged to be fired within board.' (Having taken her, the Royal Navy then spent £12,500 putting right the damage Captain Hood had done, before taking her into the service. Although only built in 1797, she was already rotten in 1807, and was broken up in 1810.) Unfortunately the Gover guns were not reliable when double-shotted, which was essential for effective British gunnery, and the experiment was not prolonged.[15]

The best-known advocate of smaller, cheaper ships that needed fewer men was Admiral Sir John Jervis, and his ideal 74 was the *Carnatic* of 1783, a 172ft 3in and 1,703²¹⁄₉₄ ton copy of the *Courageux*, taken in 1761. By the time he was First Lord of the Admiralty (as Earl St Vincent), from 1801 to 1804, the navy had already returned to building Common Class 74s, and since his verdict was for

---

* The Admiralty ordered her on 10 June 1795 and she was launched on 17 January 1798; she was a design modified from the *Valiant* of 1757 in turn based on the *Invincible*; captured in 1747, she was a major influence on the development of the larger 74s and had been given 24pdrs in 1755.

retrenchment he ordered no more. Those already being built were mostly 175ft, and the largest class of 74s built, called from their designers the Surveyors of the Navy class, which were thirty-nine ships launched from 22 March 1810 to 25 April 1815 (and five after the war), were 176ft 0in and 1,741^{17}⁄$_{94}$ tons, armed with twenty-eight 32pdrs and twenty-eight 18pdrs, so the smaller type was the more common for the rest of the war.[16]

The Royal Navy captured in total ten 74s from 1793 to 1801, and twenty-four from 1802 to 1815; of those fitted for sea, nine were the smaller type, and five the larger. One of the former, the *Implacable*, was launched at Rochefort in 1800 as the *Duguay-Trouin*; she was the last survivor of the prizes of the Napoleonic Wars and after attempts to preserve her in the dock now occupied by the *Cutty Sark* failed, she was scuttled in the Channel flying both the white ensign and the tricolour in 1949.

A TOUR OF THE SPLENDID 74-GUN SHIP

A visitor to the *Splendid* in the summer of 1810 would, like her officers, enter the ship by climbing an accommodation ladder immediately forward of the break of the quarterdeck; the steps were fixed to the ship's side, and ropes would be lowered to assist if he was important or senior enough. (There were also rope ladders suspended over the stern, one on each side, for the men to go down and come up, in and out of the boats generally lying there.) He would step off onto the gangway, which ran along the side of the ship in the waist; there was one each side, 3ft wide, and between the two stretched three booms on which the boats were stored. Looking down into the waist, which was 42ft long, he would see pens for the livestock – sheep pens forward and then cattle – and carcasses of bullocks triced up to the beams. Immediately aft was the mainmast, 36in thick here, and 186ft from the step in the hold to the topgallant cap. Running aft was the quarterdeck, 41ft long and 24ft wide, and terminated by the bulkhead behind which was the captain's accommodation – lobby and bedplace taking half the deck each, and the great cabin running the width of the ship with the gallery behind it. Just forward of this bulkhead was the mizzen mast, 21⅜in thick and 93ft 6in high, and forward of that was the double wheel, with the ropes leading below to the tiller, and its binnacle, containing two compasses, one each side, and a lantern. Above the captain's cabin was the poop. The part of the deck covered by the quarterdeck but not actually enclosed was the half deck; it was often used for storage, and was where malefactors were kept in irons, unless they were placed on the poop, where they could not talk to anyone or interfere in the ship's life. Forward was the forecastle, a deck 34ft long and 25ft wide. The chimney from the Brodie's stove could be seen 12ft forward of the rail, and 13ft forward of that was the foremast, 31¾in thick and 182ft 3in high. Eleven feet forward of that the deck dropped away at the beakhead bulkhead, and the area between it and the bowsprit was the head, part of the upper deck. The ship's sides and the waist were surrounded by rails, on which the hammocks were stored, protected by painted canvas covers.[17]

A ladder took the visitor down onto the upper deck at the waist. The mainmast had a hatch immediately after and before it, 7ft by 6ft and 8ft by 6ft, and forward of that a ladderway, 5ft by 6ft, leading forward to the lower deck. The upper deck was dominated by the two double capstans, and by the Brodie's stove under the forecastle; the galley where it stood had York stone flags, a bench, two harness casks for meat, and a preparation area. Forward of the stove was the sickbay, which took up the larboard half of the deck and encompassed one of the two roundhouses, which were enclosed toilets; the other was for petty officers. The beakhead bulkhead had two doors, and through them the men had access to the bowsprit, and the heads. The bowsprit was stepped on the deck below, and was 114ft long.

The after end of the upper deck was taken up by the wardroom, where the naval lieutenants, the marine officers, the master, the surgeon, the purser and the chaplain lived – their 'mess-room and common sitting room'. It was 19ft long, from the pantry forward to the rudder-head case aft, and the whole width of the ship (18ft at its widest, narrowing to 14ft at the rudder-head case aft). It had a full row of stern windows, cased and glazed, a quarter gallery each side aft (the larboard for the first lieutenant and the starboard for the others),* and a row of cabins each side. The four most senior lieutenants, the captain of marines and the master each had a cabin in the wardroom (the master had an additional cabin under the half deck next to the wheel for his charts and plans), the junior lieutenant, the two subalterns of marines and the chaplain had a cabin each on the lower deck, and the purser and the surgeon had their cabins on the orlop, next to the breadroom and the purser's steward's room, and the cockpit, respectively.[18]

Solid partitions had been abolished between the wardroom cabins by a warrant of June 1757, and to divide them from each other the *Splendid* had canvas curtains that could be rolled up in action, and stretched partitions that could be hooked up to the deck to divide them from the wardroom.[19]

---

* Brian Lavery's plans of the *Bellona* show the quarter galleries as 6ft wide at the stern, where the occupant sat, and 15ft long. Only one seat of ease is drawn in each, but a report of the defects of the *Tartar* (32), built in 1800–01, includes 'The cock in the starboard quarter gallery is leaking, and the seats [*sic*] want repairing'.

The wardroom was separated from the rest of the deck by a bulkhead, with a door at which stood a sentry with a lantern. Many ships had a cask of fresh water nearby, for the wardroom officers' use. For some this bulkhead had as much social importance as physical: Peter Cullen, newly appointed surgeon's mate in 1789, was shown his ship at Plymouth and told that the ship's company were on board a hulk while she was being repaired: he thought 'the idea of joining a *crew*, on board such a hulk, was truly disgusting'; but fortunately he knew the surgeon, was welcomed into the wardroom and found 'their free, familiar and disengaged manners, with their hilarity and joviality at table, made everything quite pleasant, and free from restraint, as if amongst old friends and acquaintances'. Until 1843 the master, the surgeon, the purser and the chaplain were still warrant officers, and so although they were wardroom officers by custom they had no right to wardroom status (the chaplain was not allowed to use the quarter gallery);* in a harmonious wardroom this was not an issue, but it was a delicate subject, and in a wardroom divided along a class fracture it was used to exclude unpopular officers.[20]

The table dominated the wardroom. It ran its whole length and was the focus of social life; it was rather uncivilised for an officer to eat privately in his cabin, certainly rude and antisocial for him to take all his meals there. The table was in fact three separate wainscot tables, each 6ft long when spread open, and joined together for dinner or used separately for supper, cards and so on.† As well as eating their meals in the wardroom, and lingering at table over their wine, the officers took their recreation there; there was a fire (in a stove), chairs and the pantry for their private stores, 'arranged to do the office of a sideboard', next to the door, with a cask of wine on the other side. The furniture in the ship was very substantial: the wainscot tables weighed 7¼cwt, and the small tables 4 cwt 3qrs

---

* A poem addressed to Cloacina, and attributed to William Falconer, begins:

'You who can grant, or can refuse, the pow'r
Low from the stern to drop the golden show'r,
When nature prompts, oh! patient deign to hear,
If not a parson's, yet a poet's pray'r!

Ere taught the deference to commissions due,
Presumptuous, I aspired to eat with you;
But now, the difference known 'twixt sea and shore,
That nightly happiness I ask no more.
An humbler boon, and of a different kind
(Grant, heav'n, it may a different answer find!)
Attends you now (excuse the rhyme to write);
'Tis, though I eat not with you, let me sh—e!'

† This was established in 1797, and applied to 'ward and mess rooms'. The tables were formerly of deals (pine). The 'beds' (upper frames) were 4ft 2in long; Fourth and Fifth Rates had two the same size, and Sixth Rates and downwards had one, 6ft long but with a bed of 4ft 0in.

12lb. There was just enough space between the table and the ship's side for an officer to walk for exercise in bad weather.[21]

The main ladder to the lower deck, which was where most of the men and marines lived and slept, was in the waist, with a smaller one forward of the wardroom. At the aft end of the lower deck was the gunroom, 28ft long and 40ft wide narrowing to 24ft. The gunner's cabin had been moved to the orlop deck in 1805, but the young gentlemen who had traditionally been in his care, the first-class volunteers, still messed there, and the junior lieutenant, the two subalterns of marines and the chaplain had their cabins there. Unlike in the wardroom there were no stern windows, and the tiller swept immediately under the deck above, so it was rather less comfortable. There was a sentinel at the door, as at the wardroom door; he was usually a marine.[22]

In the gunroom of the *Gloucester* (74) the chaplain had the starboard transom cabin (the aftermost), which he said was 'in shape, precisely, and in size, nearly the same as a grand piano-forte'; the junior lieutenant had the larboard, and there were also cabins for the captain's clerk, the pilot, and the two lieutenants of marines. 'Between us, from the stern to the mizzen-mast, a table was fixed, at which the clerk's assistants, ship's boys learning to read and write, etc., etc., were employed during the day; the uproar created by these literati, by the midshipmen, who were continually rambling and rioting in this gun-room, and by seamen perpetually passing and repassing, and stretching themselves out of the stern-ports (our only windows) was such as to render the act of writing a common letter, a matter of no small difficulty ... I read and wrote by what, at best, could scarcely be called twilight; and very frequently, even by the noon-tide of a summer-day, carried on these operations by candle light, or what by seamen is facetiously termed, a purser's moon.'[23]

Forward was the manger, not a space for animals but rather a strong coaming that protected the ship from water coming in from the hawseholes when the anchor cables were got on board. It had extra-large scuppers to let this water out, and was traditionally the last place of refuge for mutineers, or for those who wanted no part in a mutiny but could not get to the deck above.[24]

There was a ladderway to the orlop deck just forward of the gunroom door, and another forward of the mainmast; they were rather smaller, only 4ft square. The forward ladder was footed just before the entry to the storerooms, for the boatswain, with his pitch and tar room and the sail room, and the gunner and carpenter. Next to the gunner's store room was the filling room and the light room, where the light was kept behind glass while cartridges were filled. The aft ladder was footed at the after end of the cockpit, a kind of gunroom on the orlop

INBOARD PROFILE

1 Captain Edwards' cabin; his accommodation reaches as far forward as 1A, where the ship's wheel is sited.
2 Wardroom, which extends almost as far forward as the fourth gunport.
3 Gunroom.
4 Breadroom.
5 Powder room.
6 Step of the mizzenmast.
7 Spirit room.
8 After hold.
9 Mizzenmast.
10 Mainmast.
11 Foremast.
12 Main capstan.
13 Gundeck.
14 After cockpit.
15 Break of the quarterdeck.
16 Waist.
17 Pumps.
18 Fore jeer capstan.
19 Sail rooms.
20 Main hold.
21 Store rooms for the gunner, carpenter and boatswain.
22 Brodie's stove and its chimney.
23 Main magazine.
24 Filling room.
25 Light room.
26 Bowsprit.
27 Rudder.
28 Keel.
29 Shot lockers.
30 Well.

POOP

1 Captain's skylight.
2 Mizzenmast.

QUARTERDECK AND FORECASTLE

1 Quarter galleries.
2 Captain Edwards' great cabin.
3 His lobby, for daily business.
4 His bedroom.
5 Captain's clerk's cabin.
6 Master's sea cabin (for charts and equipment).
7 Ship's wheel.
8 Grating.
9 Ladderway.
10 Fourteen 9pdr long guns.
11 Mainmast.
12 Break of the quarterdeck. The area on the deck below this as far aft as 3 & 4 is the half deck.
13 Stairs to the waist, and entry to the ship.
14 Boom in the waist, for boat stowage (fore and aft) and for hanging beef carcasses.
15 Gangways.
16 Belfry.
17 Gratings above the galley.
18 Chimney for the Brodie's stove, with adjustable cowl.

19 Foremast.
20 Ladderway.
21 Four 9pdr long guns.
22 Catheads, from which the anchors are stowed.
23 & 24 Seats of ease and heads, accessed from the upper deck.
25 Bowsprit.

UPPER DECK

1 Wardroom.
2 Rudder-head case.
3 Master's cabin.
4 Wardroom quarter gallery.
5 First lieutenant's cabin.
6 First lieutenant's quarter gallery.
7 Cabins for the second, third and fourth lieutenants and the captain of marines.
8 Door, guarded on the forward side by a sentinel.
9 & 10 Wardroom's and captain's pantries, and mizzenmast.
11 Ladderway.
12 Gratings.
13 Capstans.
14 Twenty-eight 18pdr long guns.
15 Mainmast.
16 Brodie's stove, with a bench aft.
17 Cookroom.
18 Foremast.
19 Boatswain's cabin.

20 Carpenter's cabin.
21 Petty officers' roundhouse.
22 Sickbay roundhouse.
23 Beakhead bulkhead, with doors to the head.

GUN DECK

1 Gunroom.
2 Cabins for the junior lieutenant, the two subalterns of marines and the chaplain.
3 Rudder; the tiller extend forward into the gunroom.
4 Captain's storeroom.
5 Mizzenmast.
6 Ladderway.
7 Grating.
8 Capstans.
9 Mainmast.
10 & 11 After and main hatches.
12 Twenty-eight 32pdrs.
13 & 14 Scuttles for the powder room and gunner's store room.
15 Manger.

ORLOP

1 Breadroom.
2 & 3 Steward's room, where the provisions and supplies are issued, and his bedplace.
4 Purser's cabin.
5 Slop room.
6 Marines' slop room.
7 Wings.
8 Hatch to the after powder room.

9 & 10 Surgeon's cabin and dispensary.
11 Lieutenants' store room.
12 Mizzenmast.
13 & 14 Hatches for the fish and spirit room. This area is the cockpit.
15 & 16 After and main hatches.
17 Mainmast.
18 Sail room.
19 Fore hatch.
20 Block room.
21 Boatswain's store room.
22 Sail room.
23 Fore peak.
24 Gunner's store room.
25 Carpenter's store room.
26 Pitch and tar room.
27 Passages.

HOLD AND PLATFORMS

1 Magazine.
2 Shot lockers.
3 Wings.
4 Filling room.
5 Racks for filled cartridges.
6 & 7 Light room, with lights in glass-fronted compartments.
8 Well, with cisterns.
9 Shot lockers.
10 After powder room.
11 Light room.
12 Passage.

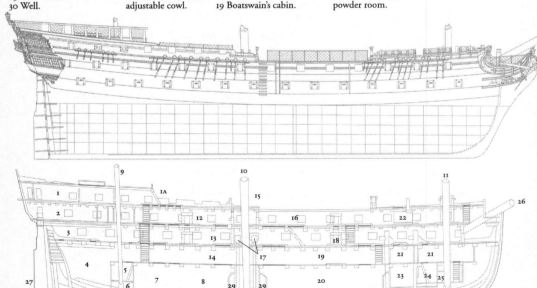

The Ship-of-the-Line

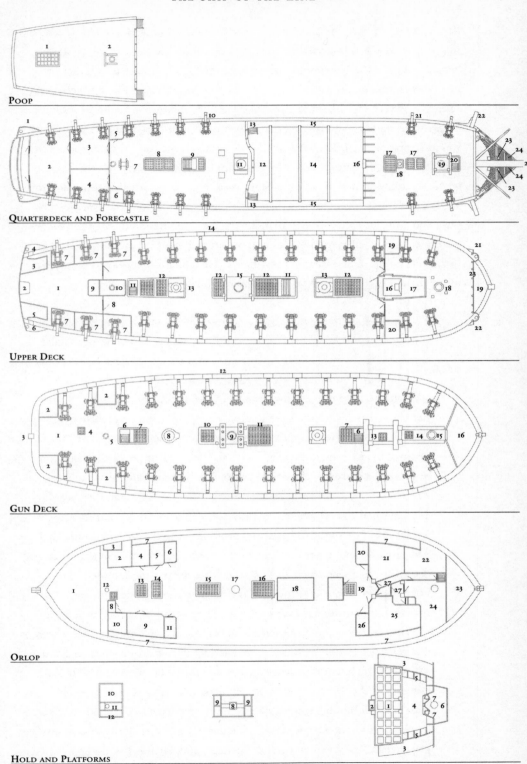

Poop

Quarterdeck and Forecastle

Upper Deck

Gun Deck

Orlop

Hold and Platforms

deck where the rest of the midshipmen, with the master's mates, messed. It can be imagined as the area bounded by the steward's room, the purser's cabin, the surgeon's cabin and the breadroom, 'where open daylight is almost as unknown as in one of the mines of Cornwall. The mids' farthing candles and the sentinel's dark, dismal, not very clean lanthorn just made a little more than darkness visible.'[25] There were traditionally two berths, larboard and starboard, and territorialism was as strong on the orlop as on the lower deck. 'In the early time of the guard-ships there was a board held by the midshipmen of the *Queen*, 98, the flagship, where the midshipmen of the other ships used to go to pass their examination for a blackguard' – it was notorious that 'in the starboard birth of the *Queen*'s cock-pit, young officers used formerly to pass a regular examination in *slang* and *black-guardism*', and when Frederick Hoffman was sent aboard her from the *Hannibal* in 1798 he found it an unnerving experience. He joined the starboard berth, 'one of the darkest holes of a cockpit I ever was yet in', with ten messmates.

> I was welcomed to the mess by the master's mate, who held in his hand a dirty, empty bottle, with a farthing candle lighted in the neck of it. 'Take care,' said he, 'you don't break your shins over the youngsters' chests.' 'Thank you,' said I; 'but I always thought a flag-ship's cockpit too well regulated to have chests athwartships.' 'Why, to tell you the truth,' replied he, 'those d—d youngsters are so often changing ships, being here to-day and promoted to-morrow, that it is impossible to keep either chests, mess, or them in anything like order. I wish they were all at the devil.' 'Amen,' responded a person in the berth, whose nose was looming out of a hazy darkness, 'for, d—n them,' he continued, 'they have eaten all the cheese and have had a good swig at my rum-bottle, but I'll lay a point to windward of them yet.' These two hard officers were both old standards. The last who spoke was the mate of the hold, and the other of the lower deck. One had seen thirty-five and the other thirty-nine summers. The hope of a lieutenant's commission they had given up in despair, and were now looking out for a master's warrant. They were both brought up in the merchant service, and had entered the Navy at the beginning of the war as quarter-masters, and by their steady conduct were made master's mates, a situation which requires some considerable tact. The greater portion of my hopeful brother officers were from eighteen to twenty years of age. Their toast in a full bumper of grog of an evening was usually, 'A bloody war and a sickly season.' Some few were gentlemanly, but the majority were every-day characters – when on deck doing little, and when below doing less. [26]

Abraham Crawford transferred to the *Royal George* (100) from the *Immortalité* (36), and thought 'those who had served chiefly in ships of the line, or passed much of their lives in guard ships … were well skilled in slang, and even their ordinary conversation was garnished and interlarded with a superabundance of oaths and obscenity', and when Frederic Chamier joined the *Fame* (74) from the *Salsette* (36) he wrote: 'I confess I did not much like the change, for in those days a certain stigma was attached to midshipmen who belonged to line-of-battle ships, while the midshipmen of frigates were the aristocracy of their profession'.[27]

The sails of a 74-gun ship: fore-and-aft sails (top), and square sails.

Chapter 2

WASHING THE WEATHER DECKS
Middle watch, midnight to 4am

QUARTERDECK, WAIST AND FORECASTLE

At eight bells in the first watch – midnight – the larboard watch were asleep, shoulder-to-shoulder, on the lower deck. The log recorded 'Fresh breezes and clear', wind west by north; the *Splendid* was sailing to rejoin the flagship, and was on the larboard tack, with Cape Mola distant eight leagues to the northwest. She had left Mahon two days earlier, having loaded 50 tons of provisions and 247½ tons of water for herself and the fleet, and though taken aback by a sudden squall in the harbour was making good time. Early in the evening of the 13th the wind had veered to the westward and she had taken in the lower and topmast stud-dingsails (the light sails used with fresh winds and smooth seas) that she had set in the afternoon. At 11pm she had ventured the larboard studdingsails, but at twelve carried away 'the short yard of the lower topmast studdingsail yard', which extended the sail at the foot. There was a heavy sea running, the ports were closed and the only light that reached the lower deck was from the marine sentinel's lantern at the gunroom door. On the deck above were crammed the bullocks she had bought at Mahon, and in the waist her own cattle and sheep. What little air came through the hatches smelled more of the farmyard than the sea, and in the summer heat the deck was stuffy and close. The *Splendid* was a well-regulated ship, and the bags for the men's clothes and belongings were strapped neatly to the sides, and their crockery, with the occasional picture, ornament or Minorcan souvenir, was stacked in the shelves between the ports. Like most ships-of-the-line in 1810 the *Splendid* was a two-watch ship. That meant no watch-keeping man slept for more than four hours at a time, and it meant also that when the watch below were woken by calls from the boatswain's mates they were fully dressed in their hammocks, except for their shoes, and ready to come on deck. They tied their hammocks to the beams and ran up to the upper deck through the hatches at the main mast and foremast, the boatswain's mates encouraging the stragglers and the reluctant, and then up to the poop, quarterdeck, gangways, forecastle, sides, head and main deck. Once the larboard watch were in their places on deck, the starboard watch were dismissed back down the hatchways to their hammocks to sleep for another four hours, and the larboard watch were formally mustered in their places, fore, waist and aft, and their names checked off. Then began the first work of the day – carried out without artificial light.[1]

In September 1797 Admiral St Vincent had ordered the ships of the Mediterranean Fleet to make sure that the decks were both washed and dried before daylight, so that they would be ready to 'seize that favourable moment to get under weigh, chase and fall suddenly upon an enemy', but in February 1801 Lord Keith issued a new general order to the fleet, noting that 'The custom of washing the decks of the ships of war in all climates in every temperature of the air, and on stated days, let the weather be what it may, having become almost universally prevalent to the destruction of the health and lives of valuable men', and 'prohibit[ing] its being done before sunrise, or even then, unless the weather has the appearance of continuing fair; and the men employed on this duty are always to pull off their shoes and stockings that their feet may not continue wet longer than may be necessary'. Dr Snipe, physician to the Mediterranean Fleet, argued strongly in 1803 that bare feet caused 'malignant sores', which were 'generally seated on parts, the greatest distance from the heart, where the circulation of the vital fluid is languid', but Dr Trotter controverted that in 1804, stating that

A 74 on the starboard tack with studdingsails set.

'it is a fact universally admitted that moisture [in wet clothes] is the chief predisposing cause to almost every malady with which a seaman is afflicted.'* The Admiralty's most recent Regulations and Instructions, of 1808, stated firmly that 'As cleanliness, dryness, and good air are essentially necessary to health, the captain is to exert his utmost endeavours to obtain them for the ship's company in as great a degree as possible. He is to give directions that the upper decks are washed very clean every morning'. The details were left to the captain, but the evidence is that Dr Trotter's view had prevailed and the men were bare-footed.[2]

Cleaning the weather decks was a two-stage evolution lasting well into the morning watch – washing was just the first. Under the supervision of the mate of the watch, the men were issued with brooms, scrubbing brushes and buckets, and in their bare feet scrubbed away the day's dirt while the petty officers oversaw them and handed about the buckets. The navy used single buckets, 7in deep, 11in wide at the top and 7in at the bottom, and double buckets, 9in deep, 16in wide at the top and 12in at the bottom. Brooms and brushes were also issued by the dockyard, and the *Splendid*'s establishment was 480 brooms a year.† The brooms were made of birch; single brooms were 10in or 12in in diameter at the band and double were 14in, both bound with three turns of strong withy, and had handles not less than 3ft long; according to the Board of Ordnance, birch brooms weighed 10lb each. The large brushes were 8in long, rectangular with trimmed corners, and had twelve rows of twenty-four sets of hog bristles. The *Spendid* wore out thirty to forty brooms each month, and brooming parties were sent ashore to cut broomstuff, usually myrtle, when the boats were sent for water. The dockyards also supplied iron-bound wooden buckets, sealed with pitch, and the *Splendid*'s sailmaker's crew made canvas ones, called draw-buckets, which were used to hoist seawater directly over the side.[3]

The mate of the watch superintended this duty; the forecastlemen washed the forecastle, the foretopmen pumped the water, the maintopmen washed one side of the quarterdeck, and the afterguard (which included the marines who

---

* He continued:

> Seamen are naturally indolent and filthy, and are merely infants as to discretion in everything that regards their health. They will assist in washing decks, and sit the whole day afterwards, though wet thereby, half way up their legs without shifting themselves, to the great injury to their health. They should therefore be compelled to put off their shoes and stockings, and roll up their trousers on those occasions, which will not only cause their feet to be dry and comfortable the rest of the day, but necessarily cause a degree of cleanliness which would otherwise be disregarded. The practice which has lately been adopted of having stoves with fires placed occasionally in those parts of the ship where the men reside, and in others subject to humidity, is of the utmost importance to the health of the people and should never be omitted in damp weather.

The tension between the benefits of cleanliness and the danger of the consequent dampness remained current to the end of the war.

† A Navy Board warrant of 1797 increased the establishment because of the 'very irregular and injurious practices' that 'have prevailed in order to obtain supplies of brooms for His Majts. Ships'.

were not sentinels) washed the other side and the main deck.[4]

The gunner's regular duty was to see that the shot was moved out of the lockers, though the weather prevented it that night, and that the guns, carriages and port sills were washed and dried; the carpenter's was to see the half-ports and gratings were cleaned and dried. The 'essential part of duty for the grand preservation of health' was to see that the heads were 'washed and scrubbed most perfectly clean', and this was the boatswain's duty. The work was done by the captain of the head and his mate, and two waisters. The boatswain also took care to see that the 'whole of the carved work of the head and stern be washed, sweeped and cleared of loose yarns, oakum and every kind of dirt, from the gunwale down to the waters edge'.[5]

The rail in the *Splendid*'s waist was 17ft above the waterline, and on the quarterdeck and poop from 23ft to 28ft, and much of the water used to wash the decks was brought up from the hold. At the step of the mainmast, the lowest point of the hold, was a 10ft by 8ft wooden chamber called the well, into which drained the waste water of the ship. The *Splendid* was fitted with two lead pipes running between the carlings in the orlop deck and through the hull that drew seawater into two cisterns in the well; this clean seawater was pumped up through elm pipes to the upper deck by members of the watch working at the winches.[†] The dirty water ran off the decks through the scuppers; there were six or seven on each deck in large ships, with spouts to take the water away from the ship; in one 74-gun ship of the 1780s (the *Bombay Castle*) the internal diameter was 4in. They were fixed in extra-thick planks called waterways, and from 1795 all two- and three-decked ships were given high coamings around the hatches to prevent water getting into the hold.[6]

The greatest collection of dirt was in the waist, where the livestock was penned. The *Splendid* was carrying sheep and cows: the cow pen was abaft the sheep pen under the booms, with a partition between. There was also the captain's hencoop, at the fore capstan, and his orders were that every morning it had to be shifted bodily aft, so that the dirt beneath it could be cleared away. Rabbits would have been an obvious supplement to the livestock, but although the *Victory* (100) was supplied with one 'rabbit coop', size unspecified, when fitted out as a flagship in May 1740, and the *Unité* (38) carried breeding pairs in summer 1808, examples are rare, presumably because of the difficulty of carrying green food for them.[7]

[†] Elm-tree pumps were the best for conveying water, and were traditionally made from solid tree trunks, growing hedgerow trees cut down for the purpose and bored out; making a 24ft pump was a week's work for two men. Navy contracts specified whole trees with two iron hoops, or one joining hoop if made of two elm trees, or six iron hoops if made of fir – allowed since 1807 if there was insufficient elm.

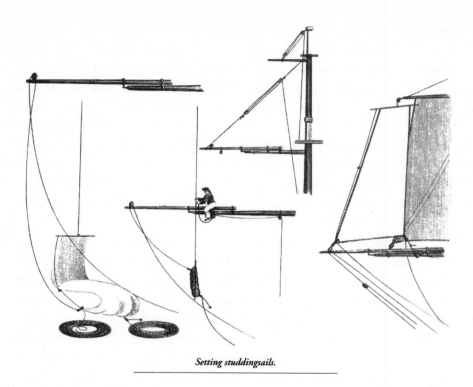

Setting studdingsails.

In the middle watch, the log recorded 'fresh breezes and clear' once more, and at 12.40 she set the lower topmast studdingsail that had been carried away at 12. The boom, about 30ft long and 6in in diameter, was hoisted by means of a guy reeved through a block on the spritsail yard and another through a block lashed to a timber head at the gangway; both were attached to the middle of the boom, and the former controlled the outer end and the latter the inner. A party of forecastlemen hauled out the fore guy and eased the after one, and the boom came across, while the sail, 30ft wide at the top, 38ft wide at the foot, 45ft deep and weighing more than 2cwt, was readied on deck. The sail was set to it, and as the outer halyards hoisted up the yard it came into place; finally the inner halyards stretched the head of the sail, 'sliding sideways like a curtain'.[8]

Meanwhile a party of waisters under the supervision of two of the gunner's crew were ordered to double-breach the guns to stop them moving as the ship heeled. About one o'clock, with them all secure, one of the seamen, James Carson, went up into the waist to make water through a piss dale 'where they belay the fore sheet' (between the fourth and fifth guns). There was a lantern on a shot box on the starboard side which gave light through the sheep pen, and one on the main hatchway grating, and in this glow he saw Robert Nelson, another seaman in his watch, come from the galley on the starboard side. Following him with his eyes he saw him 'cut the tackle fall of the third [weatherside] gun in the galley' then walk across the fore hatchway and back into the galley, where he messed, and where, unobserved, he cut through the tackle of the third starboard gun. Carson went to the gun and felt the tackle: 'there was only two strands cut'. Although, he said, 'I was uneasy in my mind' because 'it was not proper to keep the cutting of the fall a secret', he was afraid of three or four men who messed in the galley and who had been in disgrace, and when the watch was dismissed went below to his hammock, but found he 'could not sleep for fear of the gun getting loose' and went to a master's mate in the larboard wing berth. He immediately informed the officer of the watch, and Nelson was put into irons.[9]

Men confined in irons were under the care of the boatswain, who was responsible for discipline in the ship. In 1798, Samuel Sampson, the boatswain of the *Marlborough* (74), saw a prisoner strike a sentinel escorting him back from the heads: he told him 'if he did not go along he would shake his soul out'. The boatswain's notoriety for tyranny was founded in the third article of his instructions: 'He is to be very frequently upon deck in the day, and at all times both by day and night, when any duty shall require all hands being employed. He is, with his mates, to see that the men go quickly upon deck when called, and that, when there, they perform their duty with alacrity and without noise or confusion.' Their instruments were rattans (flexible canes of various sizes), rope's ends or sticks, and their use was called 'starting': Robert Wilson, who suffered under a tyrannical boatswain, wrote that in the *Unité* (38) the boatswain 'used a stick made of three canes marled together, which was called the Three Sisters'. He 'seldom used it of his own accord', though, and 'was not like the generality of boatswains in the service', who 'the moment they issue an order, follow it with a stripe, when scarcely the sound of the order has vibrated in the men's ears.' Some captains, like Lord Cranston in the *Bellerophon*, Cumby in the *Hyperion* and Pole in the *Colossus*, banned starting or all striking entirely, as did Campbell when he joined the *Unité*; some, like Keats in the *Superb*, limited its use: 'The boatswain and his mates conformable to the old custom of the service are to carry rattans, but they are to be used with discretion.'[10]

Jack Nastyface condemned it as 'torture' – 'Some of those men's backs have often been so bad from the effects of the starting system, that they have not been able to bear their jackets on for several days', and they had cuts on the face or head from warding off the blows – but his complaint was specifically against unreasonable and arbitrary discipline, especially in 'those ships whose captains give that power to his inferior officers,'[11] of which a typical example was seen in Collingwood's *Mediator* (44) in 1783:

the mate of our berth went up into the between decks, and calling one of the men, who was some time in coming, he found fault with him for his tardiness, and upon the man's making him some answer, began to beat him with a rope's end; the man ran forward and the mate after him, when the men in the between decks began to cry out shame and hiss, which made the mate pursue him the more; the man at last, however, got away.[12]

Most officers, at least publicly, deplored its use to excess but accepted its necessity. For example, when Martin Brooke, second lieutenant of the *Puissante* (74), a receiving ship at Portsmouth, was court-martialled on several charges including cruelty and oppression in 1797, Robert Duncomb, a seaman of the ship, testified that he was beaten with five or six strokes with a rattan because he 'did not bring fish for him'; Brooke argued that this charge was trivial, and he was acquitted on the grounds that the charges were litigious and ill-founded.[13] Admiral Lord Graves was asked to investigate the complaint of the crew of the *Venus* cutter, who said that Lieutenant Morgan often took them by the ear and hair and pummelled them, beat them with his trumpet or a broomstick, and once or twice with a heaver (a wooden bar used as a lever), and ruptured Henry Whiteman when he kicked him; Graves' decision was that the lieutenant was of a

> warm, hasty temper that cannot make allowances; and that kind of man who gives more offence, by an angry peevish manner than by doing any real injury; I said a great deal to the captain, and to Lieutenant Morgan, shewed how very improper that kind of hasty violence was, how unbecoming an office, to make himself the scourge and driver of a people; that whenever a stripe or two from a rattan was not sufficient, begged them to consider how much more exemplary, as well as effectual, it was to have the delinquent punished at the gangway; and to the lieutenant, by all means to endeavor to govern his passion, as never to kick a man or even strike him with what was large or heavy, or which carried the appearance of being capable of doing injury to any man by a blow.[14]

Likewise, Lieutenant James Gomm of the *Tickler* was complained of by his crew, who accused him of cruelty and oppression: the testimony of eight men that 'they themselves have all been beaten, more or less, by Lieut. Gomm personally on different occasions, with his fists, spy glass, speaking trumpet, and a colt [an 18in rope, knotted at one end] he was in the habit of carrying about with him', and which Gomm said was administered 'solely for … the negligence, or awkwardness of the men', was enough for him to be suspended. William Richardson belonged to the *London* in 1791, and 'did not altogether like their manner of discipline, for soon after I got on board we had to cat the anchor, and in running along with the foul, boatswains' mates were placed on each side, who kept thrashing away with their rattans on our backs, making no difference between those that pulled hard and those that did not'. It is an often-quoted passage; less often quoted is the conclusion of the episode: that summer the *London* paid off, and the ship's company 'subscribed two shillings apiece to buy Mr. Cooper, the boatswain, a silver call with a chain and plate, with a suitable inscription on it for his kindness to the ship's company, and a silver pint pot for his wife'.[15]

The kind of routine discipline the boatswains and their mates exercised is illustrated by two episodes, on board the *Marlborough* (74) in 1798 and the *Excellent* (74) in 1799. In the *Marlborough*, Lieutenant James Decardoux testified that at 5pm on 13 August, while he was officer of the watch, John Kearsley, a seaman, came aft and reported the theft of wine from his chest; having investigated and satisfied himself that Charles Moore, a seaman, was the thief, he had him put in irons on the poop, but the prisoner, by this time drunk, behaved very insultingly, saying he was no thief, and on the poop 'he stamped his foot upon deck and in a most contemptuous manner said he was never considered a thief by any person in the *Marlborough* before'. At 7pm he asked leave to go to the head, but on the way back he struck the sentinel escorting him. Samuel Sampson, the boatswain quoted above, was walking on the gangway when he saw the blow; he jumped down into the waist and secured Moore. The prisoner asked in court whether he was so drunk he did not know what he was doing; Sampson answered: 'Yes, you appeared so to me, and I am sure of it, seeing you drinking all day with the captain of the fore top, and I drove you on deck once.' The captain of the fore top, his defence witness, agreed they were drinking at 2pm, before their watch was called, and that though groggy that day he was generally a civil man. It did him no good; he was sentenced to 100 lashes round the fleet.[16] In the *Excellent*, Samuel Murray, boatswain's mate, said:

> In the first place the hands were turned up about ten o'clock in the forenoon near a fortnight since and part were employed in setting up the rigging the lieutenant told me to take the third watch of the waisters to strike down the beer & water into the hold which I did accordingly to his direction. [One of the men detailed to him, Patrick Gallahan,] happen'd at the time to be under the starboard gangway drinking small beer with another person; I told him 'twas better for him to come and attend to his

duty; to which he replied, 'I had no business with what he was doing there, and call'd me "a damn'd son of a bitch",' and made use of other abusive words which I cannot recollect.

Soon as the bell struck eight the commanding officer ordered to pipe to dinner, when [Gallahan] came to the grating home on the main hatchway and began his abusive language to me again by calling me a damn'd rascal; – I directly took hold of him by the left shoulder and bid him go down to his dinner; he immediately turn'd round and took me by the collar, and swung me across the grating; – I caught hold of the slings of the cask to save myself from falling into the hold; the middle grating being open all the way down; on which Mr. Barker a midshipman came and took the Prisoner aft to the commanding officer.

Prosecutor: Do you think the Prisoner intended to have throen you down into the hold, had you not caught the slings as you mention and saved yourself?

Answer: I do not know, *as he kept fast hold of me and did not let go his first grasp till I was upon my legs again.*[17]

When Samuel Mathews, boatswain of the *Quebec*, came on board the *Culloden* in September 1791 it was nearly his last act. John Rowe (1st), seaman of the *Culloden*, saw him walking by the capstan on the lower deck and said, 'Here is the bloody rogue coming.' He picked up a gun quoin and heaved it at the boatswain: when he saw him hit, he called out, 'Drop, you buggar.' 'The boatswain answered mildly, "My lad, I am not dropt yet." The court sentenced him to be hanged.'[18]

There was also a second set of officers to maintain discipline, the master at arms and his two corporals. In 1808 they were 'to prevent, or put an end to, all improper drinking, rioting, or other disturbances; and if any person shall presume to disobey his orders, and shall persist in his misconduct, he is to take him before the lieutenant of the watch' on the quarterdeck. On the afternoon of 15 December 1798, David Baillie, ship's corporal in the *Achille* (74), saw John Mackay, a seaman, and John Barr, a marine, fighting or wrestling under the forecastle; he called out 'Help, Marines!' Abraham Birtham or Beetham, another corporal, was sent to seize Mackay, and in taking hold of him struck Barr, and said 'he would mark him for his behaviour': after he had taken Mackay aft to the officer of the watch as ordered, he was put in irons by the first lieutenant. The captain examined him later and decided that 'if he had executed his duty with too much severity, he had already suffered an adequate punishment, especially as a petty officer, by being confined four nights in irons, during very severe weather', but Captain McNamara in command of the marine detachment sent him a letter desiring him to disrate the corporal and bring him to a court martial for drunkenness, which letter he forwarded to the Admiralty, requesting the Lords consider 'whether it be consistent with the discipline and necessary order of [the] service, that the captain of marines shall express his discontent upon the captain of the ship under whom he serves'. The Admiralty noted that Birtham need not have a court martial, 'having struck the man by mistake'.[19]

The master at arms had his own berth; in the Mediterranean Fleet under St Vincent it was directly opposite the fore hatchway on the lower deck. He was usually older than the typical ordinary able or ordinary seaman, and as likely as any other petty officer to take the opportunity to have a wife on board: the master at arms of the *Defiance* had his wife living aboard in the summer of 1798 while she was in Cawsand Bay, for example.[20]

The master at arms was also used for a variety of responsible jobs about the ship, acting as a senior sentinel. It followed naturally that he was also used as a kind of ship's policeman ashore. St Leger Beville, gunner of the *Valiant* (74), was absent from his ship without leave and after three days was found to be at home drunk; on the fourth day he told the lieutenant sent to fetch him 'he would not go on board the *Valiant* that Captain Harvey had used him very much unlike a gentleman and an officer and that he could never see him without it was at the point of his sword'. He was eventually carried to the ship after the lieutenant appeared with the master at arms, two soldiers and a corporal, and two constables called by the man of the house after Beville ran upstairs and broke a frame of windows.[21]

The post, and that of ship's corporal, could be filled by a marine NCO, an infantry NCO doing duty as a marine NCO or a former midshipman; although they were appointed by warrant the regulations directed that they were to be considered as petty officers, and could be rated or disrated by the captain, and consequently their social status was always below the 'true' warrant officers. When William Holsby, cook of the *Montagu* (74), was causing a disruption in the steward's room, as noted above, Lieutenant Harford warned him that he would send for the master at arms, to be told 'the master at arms had nothing to do with him he was a warrant officer'.[22] It made no difference, of course (he was caught by the same regulation, and was effectively a petty officer also), but the social distinction between the boatswain and the master at arms is neatly shown by this exchange in 1798:

Court: At the times you saw King and Pollington [two seamen suspected of theft] in the boatswain's cabin, was you ever invited in to take a glass of anything?

David Smith, master at arms: Never invited in, but I have had a glass of grog given me outside.[23]

Elsewhere on the decks, the ship's routine continued as it did in every watch. At the break of the quarterdeck the quartermaster was at the conn, directing the ship, with the helmsman at the weather side of the wheel and his assistant at the lee side carrying out his orders. Behind them was the marine sentry at the captain's cabin door, who turned the sand glass every half-hour and rang the bell. The lookout men were ranged at their stations, on the forecastle, the foremast head and the mainmast head, and on the quarter, gangways and catheads. The men on the quarters called out every quarter of an hour, and the mate of the watch walked round their posts to see they were alert. They were relieved once an hour. The officer and the mate of the watch were on the quarterdeck, and the midshipmen of the watch, 'tramping along the quarter-deck backwards and forwards, counting the half-hour bells with anxious weariness'.[24]

When she was in the Channel Fleet a few years before, the *Splendid* and the other ships of the line fished at night with a trawl net over the side, hung by a 9in hawser, rove through a block on the fore yardarm, and it was the last duty of the watch before it went below to haul it in. The procedure in the *Hydra* (38) while cruising off Havre de Grace in 1801 was described by William Mark: 'We trawled often and took plenty of fish. The trawl was made fast to the trawl-yard arm, that is to say, the line to which the trawl was fastened was rove through a tail block, the trawl itself being at the bottom of the sea, (we were near the shore on the coast of France). As soon as the trawl was properly let down, the main yard was filled and the ship was made to go ahead, drawing the trawl along the ground. We, in general, procured some flat fish, such as skate, plaice, etc., and also some oysters of a large size. This served as a diversion for in cruising off an enemy's coast there is but little to do'. Some smaller ships allowed their people 'to go at all times of the night fishing', and 'to exchange their provisions with the French fishing boats for fish', but this was not practical in a line-of-battle ship, especially when keeping station on blockade. In 1806, the ships had been ordered to return their nets and the twine issued for their maintenance into store and receive a seine net instead, and now the *Splendid* was hove to, 'main topsail to the mast' and 'the lee fore yard arm hauled aft', and the boatswain's mates piped a party to launch two boats, to leeward. They were stored in the booms, and hoisted by tackles from the main and fore yards.[25] When they were in the water and manned, the seine net was

laid carefully upon a grating placed across the stern of one of the ship's boats, with a rope of several fathoms long fastened to each end of it, so that the net thus placed is quite ready for use. When the boat leaves the ship, another generally goes with her, and the fishing party get away early in the morning, so as to arrive at the scene of action before day-light; here part of the men are landed who take with them one end of the rope that is fastened to the seine, and the boat then rows right off from the shore until the end of the net to which this rope is fastened is put into the water; then the boat alters her course alongshore until the other end of the net goes into the water, she then alters her course again, rowing right towards the shore where the men are landed with a second rope; by this direction of the boat a semi-circle is described by the net, and as soon as the men begin to haul upon the end of the rope, the net is drawn towards the shore.

During all this time a couple of men in one of the boats go to the back of the net, and keep beating the water with the oars and making all the noise they can to frighten the fish towards the shore, and prevent their jumping over the corks that float the net. As soon as the ends of the net are drawn on shore, some men go into the water, and keep treading down its foot-rope, to prevent the escape of the fish, that cannot now well get away without springing over it, or breaking through the meshes, which, unless a shark happens to be enclosed, they cannot well accomplish; but the shark by its endeavours to break through the net generally forces it up from the bottom, and then the small fish often get under and escape. The shark, however, most commonly, when he finds himself enclosed, will remain perfectly quiet until the net comes close to the shore, and then by one desperate effort rends the net asunder, gets away, and often drags a good piece of the net with him; but if he is perceived to be therein by the men in the boat at the back of the net at the time, which is generally known by the agitated movements of the other fish, they in such a case most commonly lift the foot rope off the ground, and let the shark escape. The fish caught are brought on board, and distributed to the officers and men as far as they go, and the next day the distribution begins where it left off the day before, by which partition the whole of the ship's company get a portion of the fish that are caught.[26]

The fish caught by the trawl net were kept alive in tubs of seawater, but it was impracticable to do so with seine-caught fish. Fish, whether caught, exchanged or bought, were by Admiralty regulation to be given to the sick first, in addition to their rations, and the Navy Board issued four to eight copper fish kettles for cooking them.[27]

The middle watch was also the time for the watch on deck to clean hammocks, bags and haversacks. Each man was expected to provide himself with a brush 'for scrubbing hammocks etc.' as part of his kit; seawater was hoisted into the waist, the canvas was scrubbed thoroughly, and then they were hung in the gantlines to dry. In 1804 Plymouth and Portsmouth dockyards complained of the excessive losses of hammocks and haversacks from gantlines 'when hanging up to dry after being scrubbed': in 1814 Plymouth took this to be a common fiction to obtain spare hammocks. Canvas was not cleaned on a washing day, however, and this was a washing day for the *Splendid*.[28]

At 3am all hands were turned up to reef the topsails. It was the third lieutenant's duty on deck, and he began by giving the order, 'Watch, single reef topsails!' First the halliards were let fly, which let the yard drop to the cap; as it came down the reef tackles were hauled taut. The weather tackle was rounded in first, to spill the wind from the sail, and the clew-lines hauled on to control it. When the yard was on the cap it was secured, and the men were sent up, with the order 'Way aloft, topmen! Take one reef in topsails!', climbing in the shrouds from the deck, or from the tops, where some of the larboard watch had been enjoying their leisure. To work on the yard they went out on the footropes, body straight and feet down and back; the first captain of the top led them to the weather yardarm, and the second captain secured the lee yardarm. The sail was fastened to the yard at the upper corners by small ropes called earings; the first captain hauled out the weather earing, and the men on the yard reached down and took the reef-points. On the order 'Haul out to windward!' they pulled the sail to the windward side, hauling on the reef points, soft rope as long as nearly twice the circumference of the yard, and the earing was passed twice around the yard. When it was secure the first captain held up his arm, which was the sign for 'Haul out to lee!'. The hand hauled the rest of the sail, helped by the wind, and the lee earing followed as the sail blew over. When the lee earing was secure the sail was slack; the men let go of the reef points and took in the sail in three or four folds, the last being the largest and covering the others, then secured them with reef knots. The captain of the top checked that all was secure and there were no granny knots. At the order 'Lay down from aloft!' they came off the yard and the hands on deck hauled on the yard until it was raised again.[29]

UPPER DECK

While most of the watch above were washing the decks, a party was working the
ventilators on the upper deck. The Admiralty had long been aware that the
breath and perspiration of so many men in a confined space filled the air with
'inelastic particles', breaking the 'spring of it' and therefore (since air was necessarily 'an elastic fluid', 'fitting and necessary to inflate the lungs') making it 'unfit
for respiration' and a principal cause of scurvy, and mechanical ventilation had
greatly improved the health of the fleet since the mid-eighteenth century. Admiral Collingwood when Commander-in-Chief of the Mediterranean Fleet had
written to Rear Admiral Purvis that 'I wish to impress on the minds of officers
what I have a firm conviction of myself, that though fresh beef and vegetables are
very good things, they are not of absolute necessity in the cure of scurvy and only
conduce to the removing it as they contain that air, which may as well be drawn
from the atmosphere in dry weather ... We got into this port [Syracuse] on the
6th, which is an excellent harbour but produces nothing for us but fresh water
and greens, so that we must go on with salt beef; but you know I have less alarm
about scurvy than most people; clean and dry ship and good air of the poop are
my specificks'. An early mechanical solution to the supply of fresh air had been
found in Sutton's pipes, which 'were led from the galley to the various decks', but
they were apparently not very effective, and were replaced by Hales' pumps,
introduced in 1757, which 'were operated by bellows and pumped air to each
deck'. Brodie's stoves, introduced in 1781, had a different arrangement for warm-
ing the sick, which carried off the foul air from the lower decks by convection
'through the fire of the boilers and by means of a pipe or funnel may be conveyed
to any part of the ship where the sick may be', using a 6in copper pipe. The
Admiralty had recently become interested in a new design, by Mr Lionel Lukin,
produced by George and Joseph Oliver at their 'Patent Ships Fire-Hearth,
Cabin-Stove & Anchor Manufactory' in Wapping. It was in two parts. The first
was a square trunk made of 1½in fir about 7in in internal diameter, which had a
cowl that could be turned to face the wind to draw fresh air into the hold, or
against the wind, to draw foul air out, using the difference in pressure. There
were four such trunks: as fitted in the *Berwick* (74), there were two before the
foremast, which went down on each side of the bowsprit through the boatswain's
storeroom to the limbers, and two aft of the steering wheel, which went through
the cockpit. Each had a valve at each deck. The second was an attachment fitted
to a ventilating stove that connected the hold with the weather decks and
worked on the principle of extraction, the warmed air rising and drawing the air
from below with it. Captain Otway of the *Ajax* (74) had reported that he could

'with certainty state' that the 'fire and mode of conveying air into the hold, pump well, and store rooms, has contributed much towards drying those places which were, on my taking command of this ship, extremely damp, from being built and enclosed with green wood', and the surgeon of the *Admiral Gambier* prison ship on her passage from England to New South Wales was sure that the reason there was not one man sick in the ship on arrival, though on departure 'we had upwards of fifty so bad with scurvy as not to be able to walk', was because of the ventilating stove. In 1810, however, it was being fitted in new two- and three-decked ships only, particularly to counteract the problem of damp new wood.[30]

The starboard watch were asleep; most were on the lower deck, but some were in the waist, to make the most of the cooler air – their hammocks were usually hung over the sheep pens, forward, so that they would not be disturbed in the middle watch – and under the half deck was also popular.[*] The men had come below after having had a watch of leisure; men were therefore going to the water casks that were immediately aft, and to get to the head they had to pass the galley (the companionway was in the waist) – few ships can have had leaking or overflowing tubs placed there to piss in, as the *Achille* (74) did in 1798. In the berthing plan adopted in 1799, forty men slung their hammocks in the galley itself. On the rest of the upper deck the petty officers were carrying out their duties: the carpenter's mates checked that the ports were well secured, and every half-hour the ship's corporals checked that only permitted lights were burning.[31]

Galley

The galley was forward, so that smoke would be carried away from the ship. Since breakfast for the men was not until 8am, the fire was not usually lit for most of the middle watch, but as the galley had a flagstone floor it sometimes had a little fire lit to make the cook's job easier in the morning, and was usually warm and dry, and even in the middle watch it was busy. It was the only place in the ship where the men were allowed to smoke, and there was at least one bench to sit on. Under Collingwood's leadership the *Splendid*'s ship's company had 'preserved the order of a regulated family rather than men merely kept in subjection by discipline', but in the troubled months after the failure of the Irish rising

---

[*] Some ships forbade sleeping on deck, others permitted it. Two men of the *Invincible* (74), in Port Royal harbour in July 1799, court-martialled for buggery after being caught in the same hammock, offered in their defence that they were intoxicated and that 'in a climate like this where it is common for men on board ship to lay about the decks, as they can make it most convenient to themselves, even when sober; how easy it may be for a man to be deceived in the conclusion he draws from the situation in which he finds two men in a high state of intoxication, without the least knowledge of their situation or actions' – both were sentenced to be hanged nonetheless.

in 1798 a group of Irishmen had formed themselves into the 'Smoaking Club', who went to the galley 'to smoke and keep themselves awake', talking in Irish whenever an Englishman came past. Henry Park, seaman, remembered: 'When I was asked to turn the watch up in the morning I went to the beer cask to take a drink of beer Derbyshire came out from under the forecastle and asked me to give him a drink I gave him the pot and he drank a toast, Bad Luck to the British Navy – God forgive me he says that is not a word that ought to be spoke at all times for it is enough to hang a man ... I believe he had been up all night in the galley – he looked stupid – he was neither drunk nor sober'.[32] Many other ships had similar problems.†

The galley area was washed at the same time as the decks, and the mate of the watch superintended this duty himself. Towards the end of the watch the cook inspected the funnel and the coppers, which had been cleaned the previous afternoon, and reported their state to the mate of the watch, who in turn came below, confirmed that they were properly clean and reported the same to the lieutenant of the watch.[33]

LOWER DECK

The rest of the starboard watch, about 220 men, were asleep on the lower deck, in hammocks stretched fore and aft between the (transverse) beams and carlines. For the safety of the ship, there was a marine sentry at the bitts (immediately forward of the fore hatchway), at the after hatchway and at the gunroom door. Each had a light in a lantern. Among them and moving about were the men woken to attend to their duties: the marines and seamen who had to serve as sentries, and the officers' servants who had to go to the wardroom door, collect a jug of fresh water and take it to the galley to be heated then return and prepare their masters' clothes.[34]

When the ports were closed, as they generally were in bad weather, sailing warships were very dark below decks. Almost no natural light came to the orlop deck, below the waterline, but the lower deck was almost equally dark. In the *Culloden* (74), at Spithead in December 1794, David Wallace, a seaman, was walking on the deck: a man told him to go below to the magazine; 'there were no lights', and 'it was by his voice I took it to be him'. Even with a light in a tin lantern, the gunner of the *Terrible* (74) could not distinguish any individual on the lower deck during the mutiny of 1795.[35]

---

† It was particularly acute in Cawsand Bay. The galley seems to have gained such a reputation as a place for skulkers and disaffected men to avoid their duty that in 1814 a report by a Committee of Sea Officers of Navy Board proposed that 'the fire hearth should face aft in line of battle ships that the people about the galley may be under the eye of the officers'. The proposal was not adopted.

Port lids were designed to make a weathertight seal with the side of the ship. In 1778 the Navy Board, in its perpetual campaign against damp below decks, had instructed the dockyards to begin fitting every port with a scuttle that had a sliding lid, and in 1782 staggered them in alternate ports; a secondary bene-fit was that it was now sometimes possible to distinguish a man by sight. The major innovation was that from 1809 a small piece of glass called an illuminator began to be added to the lower-deck ports of all two- and three-decked ships, which was found to supersede the use of candles. The *Splendid* was not fitted with this innovation, and her purser, like any purser of an older 74, expected to use 10lb of candles per day for all purposes in the ship. This is equivalent to 0.25oz per man, and it compares very unfavourably with figures for the maxi-mum winter consumption of candles for the army's barracks of 4oz for a cavalry-man and 2oz for an infantryman.[36]

ORLOP DECK

The orlop deck held storerooms forward and aft, and in the stern were cabins for the purser and surgeon and the cockpit for the midshipmen's berths. It was always dark – when the *Defiance* (74) was off West Capel in March 1812 it was so dark in the larboard wing, the passage between the storerooms and the ship's side, that a sentinel walking there after supper fell over two men having sex, even though he was carrying a lantern with a lit candle – and in the middle watch it was quiet, except for the master at arms doing his rounds, checking for forbid-den lights, which were common in cabins so far below. At 11pm Charles Kent, the surgeon's mate, had had a light in his berth in the cockpit, contrary to orders; the master at arms told him to put it out. He refused, and was summoned to officer of the watch on the quarterdeck, who repeated the order; he returned to his cabin and put the light out. At midnight the master at arms came past again, and Kent struck him down from behind with a broomstick, then grabbed his hair. They fell down on the coal-hole hatch, and the fight was only stopped by the surgeon coming from his cabin and a midshipman coming out of his ham-mock in the cockpit. Sitting in his cabin sitting waiting for his cut to be dressed, he told his friend, 'Oh, never mind, there will be nothing said about it tomor-row,' which he thought 'a very strange answer to give me upon so serious an occasion.' He was confined to his cabin until a court martial could be held.[37]

In the cockpit the midshipmen went back to sleep in their hammocks, but two of them had to turn out again at 3.30. They dressed, 'breakfasted on a roll and some jelly', and went on deck.[38]

HOLD

For seasick landmen on the lower deck, fresh air and the heads were up two sets of ladders: many who could not prevent themselves vomiting 'nor have the command of their legs to go upon the deck and do it over the gunnel of the ship ... empty themselves every way, either between decks or in the hold, to the great annoyance of all the rest of the crew'. The bottom of the hold was lined with 100 tons or so of shingle ballast, into which all the foul water of the ship drained. Not surprisingly, although the captain was also directed by the regulations to place 'proper centinels, or otherwise, to prevent people easing themselves in the hold, or throwing anything there that may occasion nastiness', the air was traditionally mephitic, foul and often fatal: on 6 March 1704, five of the carpenter's crew of the *Prince George* (90) went down into the well, 'just after pumping', and 'were taken up for dead, one of whom was quite suffocated, and the other four, though they came to themselves, were very sore and much convulsed'. William Hutchinson warned in his *Treatise on Practical Seamanship* published in 1777 that 'every seaman that does not know it should be told, that by his common breathing he fouls a gallon of air ... which becomes proportionably heavier as it becomes more foul, and loosing its circulating property it naturally descends to, and stagnates in the lowest vacancies, where it hastens to corruption every thing that is subject to decay, even the ship and her materials; and much more so the provisions, which must consequently make unhealthy ships.' From the 1750s ships had been supplied with ventilators in the hold to drive out the foul air. They were originally to be worked at least half an hour in each watch, and the times noted in the log, but records show they were used more and more frequently: in the *Splendid*, they were 'daily worked by the convalescents who are to be relieved every hour'. The hold was also aired by windsails, 'a sort of wide tube or funnel of canvas, employed to convey a stream of fresh air downward into the lower apartments of a ship. This machine is usually extended by large hoops situated in different parts of its heighth. It is set down perpendicularly through the hatches, being expanded at the lower end like the base of a cone; and having its upper part open on the side which is placed to windward, so as to receive the full current of the wind; which, entering the cavity, fills the tube, and rushes downwards into the lower regions of the ship. There are generally three or four of these in our capital ships of war, which, together with the ventilators, contribute greatly to preserve the health of the crew.' Boteler used them to steal fish from the tubs and send them below: 'we mids. used to have three fish hooks lashed back to back, and as we innocently leant against the carronade, would throw the hooks over our shoulders into the tub and very sure in a short time to pull out some fish or other. Then if a windsail was down the companion into the cockpit, the fish would be sent flapping below, and there would be somebody at hand to catch it.'[39]

With the foretopmen working at the pumps to get water on deck for washing it, Captain Edwards took the opportunity to sweeten the ship even more thoroughly. Each evening the *Splendid* let 16in of seawater into the well by means of a vertical pipe through the bottom, controlled by a stopcock of Captain Hamilton's invention, and in the morning watch the well was pumped dry by the boys and idlers (except the ship's cook and his mate). By the captain's orders, one man was stationed at the well and another at the cock, who were 'not to suffer a drop of [this rather dirty] water to overflow from the cistern into the well.' This conformed to the universal conviction that foul air brought disease: when the *Jupiter* (50) was suffering from a fever in 1781, 'the hand pump on the lee side' was worked 'night and day, and a run of water into the ship by the cock constantly just sufficient to prevent this hand pump from absolutely sucking. By this means the well, hold and every part must be perfectly sweet – no foul air can have rest'. This water was drained separately, into two cisterns on the gundeck and from there through tubes leading through gunports, one each side of the ship. These tubes, or dales, were very inconveniently arranged, but a better solution was not proposed until 1814.[40]

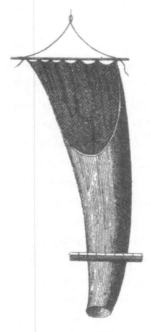

A windsail.

Chapter 3

HOLYSTONING THE WEATHER DECKS
Morning watch, 4am to 8am
(i) to six bells

QUARTERDECK, WAIST AND FORECASTLE

At eight bells in the middle watch (the beginning of the morning watch), the weather had worsened slightly, and the log recorded 'fresh breezes and squally'. The starboard watch was called from its sleep back on deck again; when they had relieved the larboard watch on deck, they began the second stage of cleaning the decks, by holystoning, washing and swabbing them clean, white and dry. The *Splendid's* holystone was a squared block of sandstone with a smooth flat base, weighing 130lb; iron rings were set in the top with ropes tied to it. The holystoning party wetted the deck with seawater, sprinkled sand over it, then dragged the holystone back and forth across the deck (against the grain), which sanded it clean; done properly, the deck came up gleaming, but it was exhausting work, even for the experienced. The holystone worked by forming a coarse paste with the water and sand that scoured away the surface of the deck, taking away any grime and decayed wood. The skill was to use enough water to wash or brush this away through the scuppers – with too little water the stone absorbed the dirt and wood dust, became slimy and polished, and slipped across the deck, with the danger of digging in a corner, and with too much water it skated across the deck. It was also essential not to let any metal remain above the deck, either loose pieces or fixtures that had been exposed by the holystoning: metal would cut a groove in the stone and the stone would score the deck. The *Splendid* carried 33 tons of sand for scrubbing decks.[1]

'To perform this work they kneel with their bare knees, rubbing the deck with a stone and the sand, the grit of which is often very injurious':

> Eight bells were struck, poor Jack awoke
> Before the dawn of day had broke,

And mustered round the capstan he
Picked up a holystone and bent the knee,
He bent his knee but not in prayer
But cursed the man who sent him there.[2]

Corners and hard to reach parts were scrubbed with smaller stones called bibles. James Anthony Gardner served in the *Edgar* (74) in the 1780s, when he suffered from his first lieutenant, John Yetts, who was 'a good sailor of the old school', but 'a devil for scrubbing the decks'. 'In the dead of winter we frequently had to shovel the snow from the quarter-deck, and take a spell, about half-past four in the morning, with the holystone and hand organs, while the water would freeze as soon as it was thrown on deck.'[3]

The wind still increased in strength, and the foretopmast studdingsails had to be taken in; in a strong breeze they would make the ship gripe, and carry weather helm. The forecastlemen were ordered to stretch the sheet aft, hauling in the inboard corner, while the outer halyards were lowered; as the tack to the weather corner was eased off the sail was pulled in over the nettings and gathered on the forecastle. The boom was swung fore and aft as the fore guy was eased off, and once safely inboard the sail was rolled up around it and stored against the mast. With that complete a second reef was taken in the topsails, and the order was given to strike the royal yards. They were the highest and lightest yards (the fore royal yard weighed 3qr 6lb, the main 1cwt 1qr 8lb, the mizzen 1qr 7lb), but still large – 30ft, 35ft and 23ft. Sending royal yards up and down was a manoeuvre practised in harbour, but at sea and at night it needed care. The yards were sent down the weather side of the mast, and a topman had to climb to the royal crosstrees, a platform made of five pieces of wood (three athwartships and two fore and aft) just large enough to stand on, 150ft or so above the waves, and another to the topgallant mast to secure the lower end of the yard as it swung down. The yard's descent was controlled by the halyards, which were untoggled and fixed to it, and by a tripping line, which was rigged to hold it as it began to be lowered, and whose free end was thrown to the weather side, abaft of the topsail and lower yards, and before the top. With the wind increasing the yards were sent all the way down to the deck, where they were secured on the booms. With the yards secured, the topgallant sails were now taken in, from aft forward; the halyards were let go, the weather brace (which controlled the lateral movement of the yard) rounded in (or hauled on) and the windward lower corner let go, which gathered the sail to leeward, and it was hauled in. With the topsails double-reefed, it was necessary to take in the jib. The halyards were let go, the

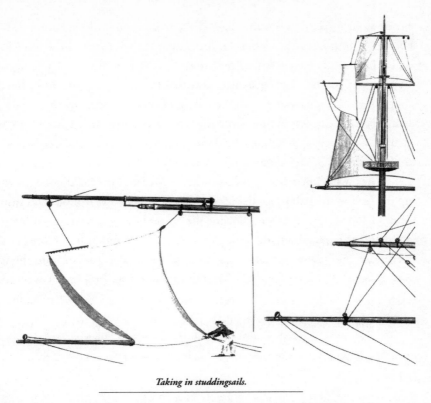

Taking in studdingsails.

down-hauler (which ran along the jibboom, through the fore corner, and to the top of the sail), hauled on while the sheet, to the inner lower corner, was eased off, and once the jib was on the boom the out-hauler was let go and the sail stowed away in the foretopmast staysail netting. The wind was now so fresh that the spanker was taken in as well.[4]

Cleaning the decks was at last completed at four bells, or six o'clock, but once the decks were completely clean they had to be dried, to prevent any danger to health from the damp. For this the men were given thrums (mops made from coarse wool or hemp yarn, issued by the dockyard) or swabs (a kind of long mop made on board from old and worn-out hammocks, canvas, rope, fearnought or buntin). The navy bore a rate of petty officer called a swabber or captain's swabber, paid as an able seaman, but it was obsolete; in the *Splendid* the duty was carried on by the men of the watch. She did have people told off as swab-washers, who took the swabs to the head, rinsed them in the sea and wrung them dry; one boy assigned to the job thought it was both hard labour and degrading, but professional seamen treated it like any other work.[5]

Once the decks were dry the after guard and mizzen topmen washed and cleaned 'the carved work of the stern frame, mizzen chains, mouldings, sides and bends as far forward as the after part of the main chains', the main topmen did the same 'to those chains and as far forward as the after part of the fore chains' and the forecastle men did the same 'from the after part of the fore chains to the figurehead', paying 'particular attention that no yarns or dirt are suffered to lodge or hang about underneath the railing of the head and bowsprit' – the last being particularly important because as the decks were dried the swabs were wrung in the head. Swabbing, final cleaning and restoring the decks to order took another hour and a half, until seven bells.[6]

Meanwhile, between 5 and 6am the steward and the butcher began to cut up the beef in the larboard wing of the waist. The 1808 Regulations and Instructions included a printed form showing the purser how to convert the slaughtered animals into regular beef and pork pieces. An ox head and heart counted as a 9lb piece, suet and tallow were put aside and the remainder was cut 'into the usual mess pieces', 4lb for beef and 2lb for pork (or as here for beef issued as pork).[7]

Form of Account of the Produce of Sheep or Oxen received and Slaughtered on board any of His Majesty's Ships.

An Account of Cattle received and killed on board His Majesty's Ship the
A   , between the   day of   , and the   day of   18

Time received.	From what Port or Ship.	Master or Purser's Names	No. of		When slaugh-tered.	No. of		Weight in Pounds.		Fresh Beef issued as		Mutton issued as		Suet Pounds	Tallow Pounds
			Oxen	Sheep		Oxen	Sheep	Oxen	Sheep	Beef Pieces	Pork Pieces	Beef Pieces	Pork Pieces		
18 February 2	Musquito Shore pur-chased by D E. Purser	} 6	10	18 Feb. 2	1	......	347	......	85	......	......	......	18	30		
					3	1	......	248	......	......	85	......	......	11	17
					9	1	......	360	......	85	......	......	......	19	35
					10	1	......	285	......	......	85	......	......	10	18
					16	1	......	354	......	84	......	......	......	20	58
					17	1	......	331	......	......	133	80	......	24	45
					23	..	5	......	254	......	......	......	......	......	
					24	..	5	......	226	......	......	......	80	......	
			6	10		6	10	1925	480	254	309	80	80	102	183

These are to certify, that the six oxen and ten sheep abovementioned, weighed viz. one thousand nine hundred and twenty five, and sheep, four hundred and eighty pounds; and were cut into three hundred and thirty four beef pieces, and three hundred and eighty three pork pieces, allowing nine pounds of beef for each ox head and heart, and three pounds of mutton for each sheep's head and pluck; and that the said oxen produced one hundred and two pounds of suet, and one hundred and eighty three pounds of tallow and no more, and that the same has been regularly entered in the Log Book.

Given under our hands on board the said Ship at Sea, the   day of
18

B. C. Captain.
M. N. Lieutenant.
H. I. Master.

(The weight in pounds is the beef produced, not the weight of the animal. It was not unusual for the log to record 'no suet or tallow'.)

The Regulations also supplied a 'Form for the Quarterly Account of the Receipt and Expenditure of Fresh Meat', which gives worked examples for the purser of how these six oxen, together with deliveries of fresh meat, should be recorded. It shows three interesting things. First, both the fresh meat and the freshly killed meat were issued at one piece to each two men borne and mustered, which matches the table of the 'daily proportion of provisions', in which every other day was a banyan, or meatless, day. Second, it is evident from the table above that if the meat had been cut accurately into 4lb and 2lb pieces there would have been 303lb unaccounted for; but the form shows that the pieces were cut to match the number of men borne, so that the 4lb beef pieces were on average 4lb 3oz, and the 2lb beef-for-pork pieces were 2lb 13oz (and the 303lb is accounted for). Third, these exemplary oxen were slaughtered so that the smaller ones could be issued on the pork days, but the Admiralty shows the purser what to do when this arrangement cannot be carried out: on the 17th the last ox is killed, producing 381lb pieces of beef-as-pork (at 2lb 14oz each); only 84 are needed, and the remainder go to the harness tub, which was used for meat intended for immediate consumption.* How this meat was distributed is not stated; perhaps it was given to the sick. In March the form shows the ship receiving three quarters of mutton, weighing 540lb, and this is divided in the same way: 74½ pieces issued as beef (3lb mutton equalled 4lb beef) and 74½ as pork (3lb mutton equalled 2lb pork), meaning that the actual weights issued were 4lb 13oz per beef piece and 2lb 7oz per pork piece. The Admiralty's fictitious ship sails from Jamaica in January, is off the Musquito shore in February, Madeira in early March and Plymouth at the end of the month; meat is issued within two days of delivery or slaughter in January and February, four days for the Madeiran meat, and two days at Plymouth. Records show that meat left over was cut into scuir or skewer pieces, which were issued to the men raw to cook themselves, although it is not clear how it was decided who received them. The rule for skewer pieces applied to salt meat as well as fresh. 'When the salt meat is cut up

* The harness tub or cask is rarely mentioned, but the *Director* (64) had one in 1796 ('Robert Willis, the Prisoner came by two or three times, pushed himself into our company and taking a shilling out of his pocket threw it on the harness cask and said give me what [liquor] you please for that shilling'), and in 1810 the *Rota* (38) had a larboard harness cask in the galley. According to Kenneth Kilby, in *The Cooper and his Trade* (London: J. Baker, 1971), p. 45, harness casks had hinged lids and were of 1, 1½, 2 and 3cwt capacity. Admiral Smyth distinguishes them clearly from the steep tubs, which were in the head and used for steeping salt meat (from June 1803 ships could be fitted with cisterns instead, on their captains' application); salt meat was also steeped by being towed in a net, though according to Captain Hall this was an 'abomination', 'a practice the men adopt, whenever they can' (he also says they tow bags of potatoes whenever they can, though the reason is less clear). Issuing fresh meat in portions greater than the standard allowance was permitted by the regulations: the purser was directed merely to take 'especial care at all times that no more fresh meat be received than the proper proportion, as nearly as may be, for the number of men actually mustered on board'.

on board ship by the petty officers, the captain and lieutenants are permitted to select whole pieces of 8 or 16lbs, for which they are charged 2 or 4lbs extra. The meat being then divided into messes, the remnants are cut into small pieces termed skewer pieces, and being free from bone, are charged ad lib. to those who take them' (so possibly the men charged them against their pay). When the system of pursery changed in 1813, the purser entered in his account the exact number of pieces produced by the slaughtered animals, 'previously adding to the beef one piece for every two pounds of suet yielded'.[8]

According to Jack Nastyface, the livers were fried with salt pork: when the *Revenge* (74) was detained in Torbay in 1811, on her way to Lisbon, it was

> a fine opportunity for our seamen to feast themselves on bullock's liver, or
> Torbay goose, as they call it; for this, fried with salt pork, makes not only
> a relishing, but a delicious meal for a mess: indeed, it has frequently
> occurred, that our captain would, when we were killing a bullock at sea,
> send orders to the butcher for his cook to be supplied with a plate of the
> liver, to be fried for his table ... we then often partook of this very
> excellent dish, as the livers were plentiful.[9]

As the work progressed the wind was blowing hard and the ship was heeling. In the pre-dawn light it was difficult for the butcher to cut the beef accurately, and it was taking longer than usual. The lieutenant on the quarterdeck went forward on the gangway, and as he recalled later, the beef

> was then all cut up except eight scuir pieces which remained to be
> completed. Observing some negligence on the part of the butcher, I
> desired him to make haste, who replied they had yet another scuir piece
> to make out of the pieces yet in a bag. The purser's steward at the same
> time saying there was one piece short, I reprimanded the butcher for his
> inattention and making so many scuir pieces, who answered that it was
> not his fault for he could no do better. I threatened to stop it from his
> allowance. He again replied that it was not his fault, he could do no
> better – or words to that effect. I observed John Parker, a seaman, pulling
> him by the elbow as if to prevent his making any reply to what I had said.
> The scuir pieces were then tying up in the net as is the custom in order to
> be counted into the bag as pieces. I observed Parker among a number of
> people who had assembled round whispering the serjeant of marines;
> suspecting him to be making observations on what had passed, I ordered

him and the serjeant of marines to come on the quarter deck. I then interrogated him as to his conversation with the serjeant and he said he was speaking to the serjeant about the beef I asked the serjeant what he had said to him; who told me that he affirmed that instead of their being one piece short, three more had been made from the carcass than ought to be ... I immediately took him to the gangway over the block and enquired how many double pieces there were. He said seventy five, which ought to make one hundred and fifty single pieces, instead of which if I counted the last bag I should find there were four more pieces in it than had been counted, as one hundred & sixteen single pieces had been counted to the cook, two double pieces and an half given to the officer, twenty-four pieces in that bag and eight scuir pieces on the block which made the eight scuir pieces that had been there first [*ie* 153 single pieces in all]. I consequently reprimanded him severely for not speaking to the officer who was attending it if he had observed any mistake in the counting the pieces, on which he replied that had he had tomorrow a small piece for his share he should have no satisfaction on bringing it to the officers, on which I ordered him into confinement.[10]

With the disturbance over, and the light improving, the butcher finished the work, the meat was distributed to the mess cooks, and taken to the galley.

The suet and tallow (hard fat from around the kidney), if present, were set aside and recorded in the purser's accounts for credit, along with the ox hides. There was a separate form to record ox hides, sheep skins and tallow returned into HM stores, or delivered to the boatswain if the ship was not in port (when the boatswain gave the purser a receipt for them). The total was periodically reckoned, recorded in the log, and countersigned by the master. Some of the hides were used on board: 'That part of a ship's rigging most liable to be chafed or rubbed is usually preserved by pieces of hide being securely sewn around it', wrote Captain Glascock, and the boatswain of the *Britannia* cut up three hides in hair on 19 September 1805 'to keep the rigging from chafing in different parts of the ship'; in the *Unité* (38), preparing to cut out the French frigates in Corfu, 'A platform was laid in the after hold made of bullock's hides for wounded men.' The captain's orders in the *Splendid* included one for preparing ox hides.[11]

Tow the hide over board as soon as the animal is skinn'd for 24 hours (soaking it in salt water will not answer). Then extend it on a taut stretch, and scrape very carefully from the hide all loose pieces of skin, blood and grease, and untill it is quite smooth, – keep it on the stretch for 3 or 4 days – the hide may then be hung up and will dry smooth and without shrinking and may be put below when quite dry, and no more smell will arise from it than from the dried hides with which we were supplied in England.[12]

Most, however, were either returned with the tallow for credit to the Agent Victualler who had supplied the cattle, or resold in the market, with any sheep skins. This was a small but important part of a ship-of-the-line's self-sufficiency as a local economy, and in August 1801 the *Caesar* (the flagship off Cadiz) created a signal, number 520, 'Hides & Tallow to be returned to the Ship denoted'. Tallow was also supplied to the fleet by the Navy Board for use as a lubricant: it was part of the boatswain's stores (a 74 was allowed 28lb), and pursers were allowed to transfer condemned butter to him to use as tallow. As noted above, some ships used it to make candles on board.[13]

As daylight approached the officer of the watch began to prepare to make sail, giving orders that the sails were trimmed, the topsail and topgallant sheets were hauled close home and the weather braces and running rigging were taut: if a strange vessel should be seen as dawn broke the *Splendid* would be ready.[14]

Captain's cabin

At daylight the officer of the watch walked along the half deck to the captain's cabin. Agreeable to custom and orders, he reported the condition of the ship and her course, and received his orders for the morning. The lieutenant entered the cabin after knocking at the lobby door; the formality of an older generation, when if an officer wanted to see the captain for a reason of his own he had to ring the bell for the captain's servant, send a written message desiring to speak to him, and go to his cabin on an answer being returned, had fallen out of use. Breakfast followed promptly: in the *Victory* (100) Nelson had taken his 'never later than six, and generally nearer to five o'clock', and a guest in summer 1805 wrote that they had 'tea, hot rolls, toast, cold tongue, etc.', which is much as they would have had on land. It was a long-standing naval tradition to have guests from the wardroom and cockpit to breakfast, and at Nelson's table 'A midshipman or two were always of the party; and I have known him during the middle watch to invite the little fellows to breakfast with him, when relieved. At table with them, he would enter into their boyish jokes, and be the most youthful of the party'. This was the custom of the service, 'along with the officer of the morning watch and the first lieutenant, who, in, many ships, is the constant guest of the captain, both at this meal and at dinner'. For Captain Foley in the *Britannia* (100), in the Mediterranean in the summer of 1796, breakfast was at eight, but he had two ladies aboard as guests, who kept land hours. Betsey Wynne, who married him, wrote that he kept 'an excellent good table his ship is a little town – you get all your [sic] desire in it', but for her sister Eugenia in the Neapolitan *Samnite* (74) in March 1798, breakfast was 'miserable' – 'a dish of coffee without milk and as much bread as would feed a bird'.[15]

The *Splendid* carried a heifer for the captain's milk, and the Brodie's stove supplied enough bread for the cabin and wardroom. The *Splendid* also had hen-coops at the foremost capstan; they were substantial constructions, weighing 6cwt. The French fleet under Suffren in Trincomalee harbour in 1783 (74s, five 64s, a 32-gun frigate, and prizes) sent its poultry ashore, 'as more likely to thrive upon land than stuffed up thickly in coops on board ... they were together in bundles of about a dozen ... about a thousand pair of fowls', and stuffed up thickly seems to have been RN procedure as well: as small a ship as Cook's *Endeavour* lost three or four dozen overboard in a gale in September 1768, and expense claims for conveying ambassadors and the like usually include poultry by the dozen.[†] Turkeys were also common in the Mediterranean. Captain Boteler, in command of the *Renegade* schooner, had an exchange of views with his poultry over how much freedom was proper for a hen in HM service: 'They had been confined in rather a small coop and I let a few out to stretch themselves: three directly flew overboard; it was nearly calm, a chicken takes time to drown and we out boat and picked them up; I then had all the others taken out and thrown overboard, with a rope yarn tied to a leg; none ever flew over after that.'[16]

UPPER DECK

Galley

Fresh water for the day's use was stored in two casks in the galley, one each side, and shortly after 4am the cook lit the fire in the galley stove, with a little water in the boilers. Hot fresh water was returned to the captain's and officers' servants for their masters to wash and shave with in their cabins, where they had washstands as they did on land. Between 7.30 and 9am the mess cooks arrived with the meat for that day's dinner.[17]

Wardroom

The captain's orders were that the boatswain, carpenter and gunner had to be on deck at daylight, 'to attend to their respective duties', so between 4 and 5am the

---

† The *Spartan*'s expenses in carrying the British and Spanish Ambassadors and suites from Malta to Trieste in April 1809 included four dozen fowls, one dozen pigeons, six turkeys, six geese, and three purchases of ducks, '2 dozen and 1 ducks', '1 duck' and '1 dozen Do.' Expenses in carrying the British Minister to the Ionian Republic in September included '8 Dozen of Fowls' and '12 Turkeys'.

boatswain, the only one of the three whose cabin was in the wardroom, washed, shaved and dressed. For an ordinary working day he wore the frock (undress) uniform, and for active work on board ship at sea he could wear a brown waist-coat and long blue trousers. In the Mediterranean, the *Splendid*'s officers pos-sessed enough personal linen to wear a clean shirt every day, but they only had one change of uniform coat.[18]

Once on deck, they began their morning inspections. The boatswain had charge of the sails and rigging, the cables and cordage and the anchors and boats, and he had to see that 'the forecastle, head, buoy, forechains etc. are thoroughly cleaned, rigging examined, ropes hauled taut and everything in its place.' The rigging was particularly important: the Admiralty regulations directed him 'to inspect into the state of the rigging' so that it could be repaired 'without loss of time', and to 'have ready at all times a sufficient number of mats, plats, knippers [nippers], points, and gaskets'; this was done after the decks were cleaned. The boatswain's mate went to 'the bowsprit end and to each mast head, to inspect the standing and running rigging and to report to the officer of the watch and to the boatswain of any ropes that may be misplace or badly rove, of rigging chafed, of seizings, strops or blocks or other defects wanting repair, that a remedy may be instantly applied. The carpenter's mate of the watch is to observe the same duty

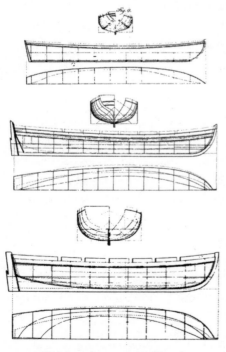

every morning and make the report to the officer of the watch and carpenter of the state of the masts, yards, tops etc.' Much of the time of any watch on deck was spent making and repairing rigging ready for repairing such wear and tear.[19]

The carpenter was responsible for the 'care and preservation' of the hull, masts, yards, bulkheads, cabins and boats: he had to see 'the gratings and coamings etc clean, half ports off or properly hauled in and every thing in his department in their proper places', as well as the masts and yards. The gratings over the ladderways were removed for the day, and all the grat-ings were lowered overboard and

Ship's boats: barge, cutter and launch. allowed to trail astern to wash them.

ABOVE: *Figures boarding a two-decker at anchor* (W. L. Wyllie). (NMM: PV1812)

PREVIOUS PAGE: *A Third Rate entering Port Mahon* (C. M. Powell). A 74-gun ship-of-the-line is hove to; her boat is carrying the captain ashore to the port buildings. After it was opened to British shipping in 1808 by Spanish rebel forces, Mahon, in Minorca, was essential to the Mediterranean Fleet for supplies. (Plate illustrations by courtesy of the National Maritime Museum, London: BHC1895)

ABOVE: *Gundeck of HMS Bellerophon* (H. Hodgson). Larboard side, looking forward. These 32pdr long guns are run out; in action they would be secured by a train tackle to the ringbolts near the centre of the deck. (NMM: PU6115)

BELOW: An 18pdr, run in, and its equipment: the *Splendid* carried twenty-eight 18pdrs, on her upper deck. The figures show the position of the gun crew in action. The salt boxes at the bottom of the picture contained the cartridges for ready use, and the cartridge box, which held two or three cartridges, was carried to and from the magazine by the boy. (NMM: D9880-1)

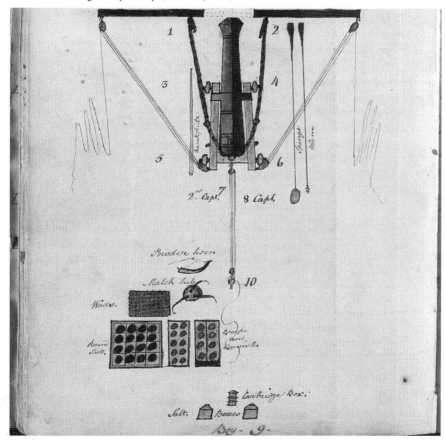

The captain's great cabin, ABOVE, and a gunroom cabin, BELOW. Although everything, including the bulkheads, was cleared away in action, captains' cabins could be quite luxurious. Captain Pasley in the *Jupiter* (50) had a couch in his, and off Fernando Noronha on 18 January 1782 he received a visit from eight Portuguese officers: 'They grew warm with licquor before the day was over, and not a little amorous; I never was so hugged and squeezed in my life, absolutely bit in extacy by the priest. *Beasts!* Three of them got so drunk that they could not go on shore at night: they spoiled all my couch and dirtied all my cabin. Dirty dogs! I ordered men to take them up, neck and heels, and *kennel* them on the wardroom floor.' Gunroom cabins were not cleared away, and small touches of comfort, such as curtains, were common, but the Revd Mangin's cabin in the *Gloucester* (74), shown here, was 'in shape, precisely, and in size, nearly the same as a grand piano-forte'. (NMM: PAD5857 and D7689/B)

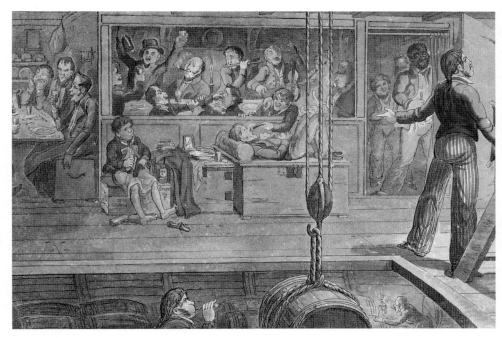

The midshipmen's berth. ABOVE: the starboard berth, after dinner. 'In the starboard birth of the *Queen's* cockpit, young officers used formerly to pass a regular examination in *slang* and *blackguardism*'. A barrel is being hoisted from the hold under the direction of the boatswain; the purser is recording it at bottom right: this is a butt, weighing half a ton. BELOW: apart from the formality of dress, little has changed in this print of 1821. The cockpit spirit continued at least until the First World War. (NMM: PAD4722 and PW3730)

A. Cockpit

F. Cockpit.

STOREROO

Hatch Way,

THE VEERING CABLE

LEFT: A diagrammatic representation of the disposition of the crew for weighing anchor. (NMM: D4802)

Two views of furling sails.
ABOVE: *A two-decker furling sails* (John Cantiloe), 1835. RIGHT: topgallant and standing jib.

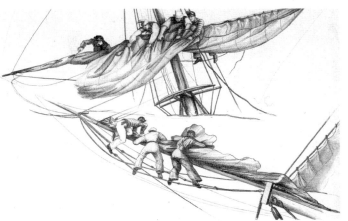

BELOW: Sailmaker ticketing hammocks. By 1810 the navy was battling shipboard disease by keeping the men warm and dry; each man was intended to have two hammocks, with a mattress and a blanket. The standard nominal width for a sleeping space was still 18in, though petty officers had more. (NMM: PT1992)

RIGHT: Heaving the lead from the windward chainwales. 'The hand-lead-line, which is usually 20 fathoms in length, is marked at every 2 or 3 fathoms; so that the depth of the water may be ascertained either in the day or night. At the depth of 2 and 4 fathoms, there are marks of black leather; at 5 fathom, there is a white rag; at 7, a red rag; at 10, black leather; at 13, black leather; at 15, a white rag; and at 17, a red ditto'. The leadsman 'proclaims the depth of the water in a kind of song resembling the cries of hawkers in a city' (Falconer's *Marine Dictionary*). At night or in fog the leadsman could find the depth by the texture of the different materials. (NMM: PW3758)

A B C D. The Dispensary, the remainder, accounted the Sick bay.

I K. — Mean height of the fore part of the Bay. 5 Ft. 9½ In.

A F. — 3 F. 3½. Breadth of the Drawers with their Partitions

A E. — 3 .. 9½. Height of D°. D°. to the Beams.

F G & H I, 1 .. 0. Breadth of each of those Pillastre's

B O. — 3 .. 5. Extremities of the Head Door with its Pillastres

P Q. — 3 .. 4. Width of the Roundhouse D° — D°.

E J, or c, d, 2 .. 0. Breadth of the Top of the Locker forward & height of Starb° Locker

J M. — 1 .. 11½. Depth of D° — D°.

K L. — 6 .. 0. Length of Partners round the Bowsprit

K Y. — 14 .. 0. Length from the bottom of the Lockers to the after part of the nearest Bulk head abaft the Dispensary

M N. — 10 .. 6. Length of the Deck from the foot of the Locker to the first turn of the Bulk head.

K D. — 9 .. 6½. Distance of the Foremost Locker from the Fore Topsail Sheet Bitts.

W D. — 0 .. 8. Distance between the After Locker jutting out forward & Topsail Sheet Bitts

W V. — 2 .. 10. Height of D° to the Top of the Table.

D T. — 5 .. 10½. Height of the After Lockers &c.

Z x. — 11 .. 6. Distance between the Bulk head & Side

Y, v. — 1 .. 8. } Parts of the Bulk heads —

n Y. — 1 .. 8. }

y z. — 3 .. 9½. Space between the Bulk head & Partners

z I. — 4 .. 4½. Breadth of the Partners.

C X. — 5 .. 2. Distance from the Fore part of the Bitts to the Bulk head.

o w. — 12 .. 6. Breadth of the after part of the Bay

N j. — 23 .. 0. Extreme breadth of the Bay

C D. — 5 .. 10½. Extremities of the Bitts.

l h. — 2 .. 3½. Breadth of the Head door or Window —

B N. — 2 .. 5. Height of the Head Window.

O h. — 3 .. 4½. Height of the Head Door.

p q. — 2 .. 3. Breadth of the Roundhouse Door

p r. — 4 .. 10½. Height of — D° — D°.

u t. — 2 .. 4. Height of the Open Locker for holding Vinegar & Water, from th[e]

s t. — 2 .. 8. Height of D°

t v. — 3 .. 3½. Breadth of D° —

R S. — 0 .. 10. Length & height of a small Locker

Z v. — 8 .. 6.

I i. — 3 .. 7½. Breadth of the Drawers with their partitions.

i B. — 0 .. 6. Breadth of the Pillastre between the Drawers & head Door —

E m. — 4 .. 3½. Length of the Top of the Locker

Drawer e. 1 .. 5. Wide: & of 0 .. 7¾. & g. 1 .. 13¼ & 9 Inches each in depth, the remainder a ascend decrease in depth, the uppermost bearing the same proportions in every part accepted which is only, 6½ Inches.

a b. — 1 .. 9. Height of the Table, to the Bottles.

C D X Y. Shot Locker round the Foremast, abaft the Bitts.

N°. 1. Door. 2 F. 8 in Wide entering the Dispensary. N°. 2. Door 2 F. 3 In. Wide ente[ring] the Sick Bay. N°. 3. Surgeons Table. 2 .. 8 from the Deck. 4 .. 4 Long & 3 .. 4½ Broad. N°. 4 Mates Table 1 .. 7 Broad. N°. 5. Sick Table. 8 Ft. 2 in long & 2 .. 9 Broad &, fixed upon the Cell[s] Foremost post 2 F. 4 in from the Deck. N°. 6 first Gun in the second Port of the Sick b[ay]

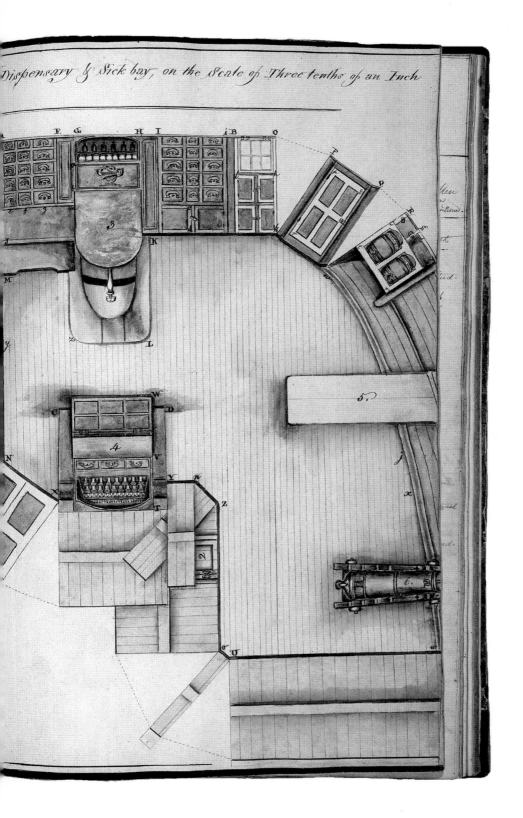

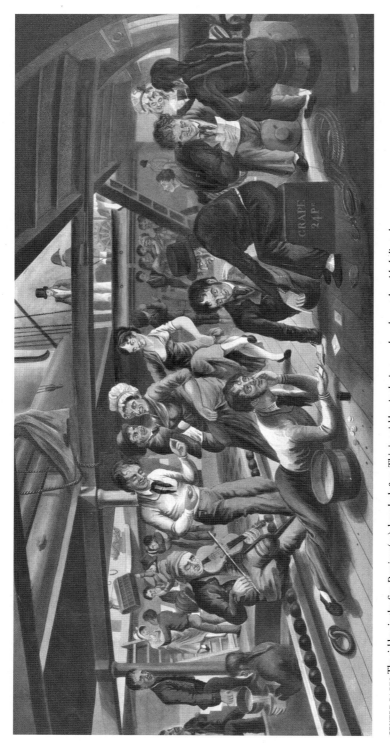

CENTRE PAGES The sickbay in the *San Domingo* (74), launched 1809. This is a sickbay in the improved modern style, with dedicated dispensary and roundhouse, whitewashed walls and separate examination tables for the surgeon (3) and surgeon's mate (4).

Below decks. The lower deck is engaging in the traditional pastimes, especially music-making, dancing and cards. Landsman Hay's tutor in the *Culloden* (74) 'could play at all-fours, at whist, at loo, at cribbage and at least a dozen of other games on the cards; he could play at fox and goose, at chequers, at backgammon, and I know what all besides.' (NMM: PAH7339)

Above decks. The military officer on the left has attracted the attention of the officer of the watch. In 1814, Sir Harry Smith, who travelled on board the *Royal Oak* (74) from the Gironde to America, wrote 'We soldiers had heard such accounts of the etiquette required in a man-of-war, the rigidity with which it was exacted, etc., that I was half afraid of doing wrong in anything I said or did'; but the officers 'welcomed me on board in such an honest and hospitable manner, that I soon discovered the etiquette consisted in nothing but a marked endeavour to make us all happy.' (NMM: PAD8486)

An amputation in the cockpit. By 1810 the surgeon's technique was very accomplished. The patient's limb was washed and shaved, two tourniquets applied, and the damaged part removed as fast as possible, then the tourniquets were removed, the blood vessels tied with waxed thread and the edges sewn together. In a survey taken after the Battle of Algiers in 1816, even though triage was not yet practised, surgeons who amputated immediately had a mortality rate of only a third. (NMM: PAD8484)

Four Marines eating pease. Unofficial and private cooking, both of ship's rations as here and privately bought food, was an essential part of the ship's life. (NMM: PT1993)

The galley fire on the upper deck, looking aft. Although later than 1810, this vividly conveys the way the galley was used for drinking, smoking and talking. (NMM: PAF5039)

OPPOSITE PAGE: *Steady Marines by the right dress. A sudden squall during drill.* The marines mounted guard on the quarterdeck each morning, then paraded and drilled. These are perhaps the 'awkward' men from the working party, and the men from the morning's guard who had made 'any mistake in his exercise or marching', and who were specially drilled. (NMM: PU0170)

A wardroom mess: the gentlemen are enjoying their wine after dinner. The height between decks is exaggerated. The hats are neatly hung and this wardroom is convivial, but in unhappy ships quarrels over the right to wear a hat in the wardroom led to several courts martial. (NMM: PAF8407)

Officers playing backgammon. After dinner, wrote the surgeon of the *Elizabeth* (74), 'the grog being finished, the remainder of my time till supper is spent variously in reading, writing, card-playing, backgammon, walking or conversation as humour leads', and the lieutenant of marines in the *Repulse* (74) made himself quite comfortable, with a sofa, backgammon table and curtains. (NMM: PAH4903)

A lower-deck scene. Professional seamen were predominantly literate; since the 1790s literacy, or at least functional literacy, was assumed for all ranks, and candles were issued daily. (NMM: PT2026)

OVERLEAF: The *Magnificent* (74), making sail after cutting her cables in a south-westerly gale, 1812. It was in the *Magnificent* that Captain Hayes escaped two enemy ships off Oleron in 1814 by club-hauling her off a reef with lower yards and topmasts struck: he kept the name 'Magnificent Hayes' as long as he lived, and it was by seamanship like this, the epitome of thousands of more everyday examples, that the Royal Navy drove the enemy from the seas by 1815. (NMM: X1520)

The half-ports were 'made of deal, and fitted to the slope of those ports which have no hanging lids. They have a hole cut in them for the gun to go through'; the lower half was hinged, and the upper half secured by lanyards.[20]

The *Splendid* had six boats: a ten-oared barge of 32ft, used for the captain's transport; a launch of 31ft, used for watering, but fitted with an 18pdr carronade ready 'at a moment's notice'; an eight-oared cutter of 28ft and two (six-oared) Deal cutters of 25ft, which were better sailers than the barge and launch and were used for anchor work and for carrying stores and passengers; and a four-oared Deal cutter or jolly boat of 18ft, which was used for fresh meat and known as the blood boat. The barge and launch were stowed fore and aft on booms across the waist, with the jolly boat stowed inside the launch. The two cutters were stowed from quarter davits, which were fitted on each side of the mizzen mast; all boats were hoisted in during the night, and in the morning watch the davits were raised until they were almost vertical so that the cutters were lashed tight against the mizzen shrouds, above the level of the carronades on the poop. All the boats except the launch were supplied with canvas covers. These all had to be checked, the boats for watertightness and the covers for security; when they wore out the covers were replaced on board with old canvas, and the boats were repaired and repainted as needed. This duty fell to the foretopmen, who swept the booms and kept them 'clean and clear of tackle falls, old rope, loose spars, spare oars, plank, bedding, clothes and linen, unless orders are given to air the bedding'.[21]

The gunner had to 'see the guns, gun carriages, slides, shot racks etc clean, guns square in the ports, all the people's arms in their places and everything in his charge in order', and he or his team also had to check the lashings at least once in each watch and report the same to the captain; the *Splendid*'s 18pdrs weighed 2 tons each and her 32pdrs 2¾ tons each, and a loose cannon in a running sea could be fatal to the ship. The guns were numbered so that on the upper and lower deck the foremost gun on the larboard side was no. 1 and the foremost gun on the starboard side was no. 28, and each gun had its own carriage, numbered to match (the guns and carriages on the larboard side of the ship were numbered and marked on their larboard sides, and the starboard guns on their starboard sides), 'by observing which rule, all the guns will fit their carriages, and stand a proper height from the sill of the ports', and it was the gunner's responsibility to make sure that whenever the guns were moved they were replaced correctly.[22] Guns, powder and small arms were supplied to the navy, and the army, by the Board of Ordnance, a separate military organisation with its headquarters in the Tower of London. But in 1813 the Ordnance Board, which supplied the navy's guns and their equipment, complained that excessive attention to scraping and polishing was rendering its stores useless:

> We have respectfully to represent to you, that in surveying the stores
> returned in an unserviceable state from His Majesty's ships, we have for
> some time past had occasion to notice that many of the articles have been
> rendered so in consequence of a practice which has latterly been very
> prevalent with the officers of His Majesty's navy, of scraping the wood
> and polishing the iron work of many of the stores they are supplied with,
> till they become so weak and reduced, as to be entirely useless: which not
> only creates a considerable expence in replacing them, but as several of
> the articles are weapons of defence, that are kept at hand to be in instant
> readiness, it appeared to us very probable they might be put into men's
> hands to defend their lives, or annoy their enemy, after they had been
> reduced to half their original strength by the practices alluded to ...
> Swords.—The guard and shield of the hilts being of plate iron, varnished
> black, is not sufficiently thick to allow being filed bright, without making
> them very weak in the first instance, and to keep them so, at sea, they
> must be so frequently cleaned with emery, or some other cutting
> materials, that they soon become no thicker in substance than tin ...
> Strong Pikes—By filing and polishing the iron work, it soon becomes
> weak, and gives way; and by scraping the wood work with pieces of glass
> bottle, etc. which on board some ships is done, very frequently to all the
> pikes that are kept in sight, the staves become so much reduced as to be
> unfit for weapons ...
> Spunge and Wadhook Staves—Are frequently rendered so weak by being
> scraped as abovementioned, as to become unserviceable.
> Pole Axes—By being polished and scraped as abovementioned, the
> handles become too weak for weapons, and so small in the gripe as to be
> easily wrenched out of the hand.
> Elevating Screws of Caronades [sic]—Should only be kept cleaned and
> oiled; but on board many ships, where not only the screw, but the shank
> and crop lever of it are kept bright and polished, and files [sic: filed], as
> also emery used for that purpose, the thread very soon becomes so much
> reduced as to run through the box, or female screw, and become useless.
> Caps for Elevating Screws—Are constantly returned unserviceable from
> being filed and polished.
> Traversing Bars for Caronades—The objecting to filing and polishing
> these articles, as also some others, does not arise from reducing their

substance, as they are sufficiently strong to admit its being done without injuring them, but the great consumption of the files, given to the gunner for use of the small arms only, which are worn out for this and similar purposes, render it desirable that the same should be discontinued.

At the same time the round shot was 'so corroded, from lying at the bottom of the shot lockers, that it can hardly be got into the long guns, and of course is unfit for the caronades where the windage is so much reduced'.[23]

This week the work of the gunner's team was particularly difficult because the *Splendid* had embarked sixty live bullocks for the fleet (along with twelve tons of onions and forty pipes of 'good and sound wine'). The bullocks were tied between the guns, with their heads towards the ship's sides and their tails towards the centre to make cleaning easier, and the butcher's team was detailed to take care of them. Captain Edwards' orders from the flag were that their fodder was to consist of 14lb straw, 1 pint oats and 1 pint bran per bullock per day, and to cost no more than 1s per head. One bullock had been killed that morning, and the *Splendid* expected to reach the fleet in four days with fifty-five alive for distribution.[24]

Half-deck
At half-past six, with the half-deck cleaned and dried, the master's mate called for the boatswain's mates to send four of the waisters to press the hay that was stored there; some of it was bags and some loose, and it was blowing about the ship. A machine called a jack-in-the-box, a large wooden screw turning in the upper part of a strong wooden box, was used to press it into bales, then it was taken below and stored in the breadroom, ready to be issued at the rate of 2lb per sheep per day.[25]

LOWER DECK
The carpenter had to 'visit daily all the parts of the ship, and see if the ports are well secured, and decks and sides be well caulked, and whether any thing gives way; and if the pumps are in good order', and after checking the upper deck he went below 'to examine the lower-deck ports, to see that they are properly lined; and when they are barred in, he and his mates are frequently to see that they are all properly secured.' The lower-deck ports were usually closed at sea, which meant that the deck was dark and airless, even in summer. For a generation each port had had cut in it an air scuttle with a sliding lid, and since 1809 a glass illuminator fitted in the scuttle. Although designed to allow fresh air rather than light into the ship, the scuttles did sometimes illuminate the darkness of the lower deck enough to distinguish a man by sight; the illuminators seem to have

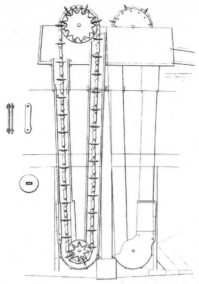

Chain pump (left: cutaway showing mechanism).

made little difference, and were frequently broken.[26]

Caulking was forcing oakum (old rope, untwisted) into the seams between the planks of a ship's sides and decks with caulker's chisels then sealed with hot pitch. The Royal Dockyards reckoned that a day's work of new caulking for one man was 60–55ft on the weather decks (of 2–3in plank), 36ft on the gundeck (of 3–2½in plank), and 30–13½ft on the topsides (of 3–9in plank), or for repair work 76ft on the decks, 60ft on the waterways and 69ft on the upper works. Since 1793 each ship had borne a caulker and since 1794 a caulker's mate, paid as a carpenter's mate of a Third Rate, so that 'the caulkers might be constantly employed under the directions of the carpenter'. The establishment of pitch was increased two years later, since 'if they do their duty [it] will occasion a much greater consumption of the said article than heretofore and the ships will not of course require much aid from the dock yards', and the caulkers were unique in having their tools supplied by the navy. Where caulking needed to be replaced at sea, the carpenter supplied oakum, which was now made on board – much of the routine work of the crew was entered into the log as 'working up junk'.[27]

On many occasions since 1793, the Navy Board had complained to the Admiralty that ships were not being maintained properly at sea:

> The Navy Board having represented to us, that when the defects of His Majesty's ships have been given in, on their arrival in port, it had been frequently observed that very trifling articles were wanted to be repaired; and they having therefore submitted, whether it might not be proper that directions should be given to the commanders of His Majesty's ships constantly to employ their carpenters crews and caulkers in making good such little defects as might occur, and for which materials are supplied for their sea store; which would not only save much expence to the public, but keep the ships in such a state, particularly in point of caulking, as to require much less assistance from the yards than they now do; observing

at the same time that caulkers were established on all H. M. ships in the hope that they would prove useful by being employ'd to stop the leaks in the decks at the moment they appear'd; whenever therefore any small defects (for which materials are supplied as aforesaid) shall be discovered on board the ship or vessel under your command, you are hereby required and directed to employ the carpenters' crew and caulkers belonging to her in making the same good, accordingly.[28]

The carpenter was accordingly to 'be attentive in observing that the oakum with which he supplies the caulker is of good quality, and that the caulker does his duty in a workmanlike manner', and the caulker to 'be very attentive in examining frequently the caulking of the ship's sides and decks, particularly in those parts where the seams are most likely to be opened, by the working of the ship.'[29]

The carpenter and his crew provided their own tools, although from 1804 the caulker's specialist tools were supplied, presumably because the carpenter's tools could be used to pursue his trade on land but the caulker's could not.* The carpenter was also unique in that he served ashore before receiving a warrant. Traditionally, carpenters were apprenticed to shipwrights in the dockyards and became ship's carpenters after several years as a shipwright; in autumn 1802 this was formalised to 'no new carpenters to be appointed who have not served a regular apprenticeship to a shipwright and then two years as carpenter's crew or carpenter's mate in a ship or vessel or in a dockyard', and in 1808 the second clause was changed to six months' experience as a carpenter's mate on board one or more ships of the navy. It was possible to be promoted from carpenter to assistant master shipwright or master shipwright in the dockyards, and back again: Provo Wallis was promoted from the *Eagle* to New York in 1778; Alexander Fall was carpenter of the *Ocean*, master shipwright at Antigua from 1759 to 1760, then carpenter of the *Suffolk* in 1763, and Andrew Anderson was carpenter of the *Dorsetshire*, master shipwright at Antigua 1760 to 1765, carpenter of the *Prince George* in 1766 and master shipwright at Antigua again from 1770 to 1779.[30]

The Navy Board periodically added to the stores and equipment in the carpenter's charge: when Brodie's stoves were introduced they belonged to him, for instance (though the wardroom stoves belonged to the purser), paint, oil, black varnish and brushes etc. for ships' sides and wales were in the carpenter's sea stores; when lightning conductors were established for ships on Foreign service they were issued to those ships that demanded them and charged to the carpenter;

---

* One set of caulker's tools comprised: irons sharp, 1; horsing, 1; meaking, 1; caulking, 1; crooked, 1; treenail, 1; spike, 1; horsing large with iron handles, 1; beetle, 1; caulking mallet, 1; ladle spout, 1; hook rove, 1.

and more obviously, carpenters of all ships on Channel and Foreign service were allowed 'Stuff & Nails' for the captain's sheep pen in 1788. The list of additional stores issued to the *Victory* when she became a flagship in 1755 included eight mahogany tables, with two mahogany chairs and two wainscot chairs, a mahogany close stool and five panes, eight bed screws, four brass handles, and two ketch locks for the admiral's bed and close stool, 300 yards of painted canvas for the admiral's cabin, bedplace, and state room, with 2,000 tacks, four cabin bells, seven curtain rods, twelve panes of ground glass, eighty feet of wainscot board and twenty deals, a canvas umbrella for the boat together with one set of awnings and curtains, fourteen dozen brooms, a salamander for firing salutes and five hencoops and a rabbit coop. The carpenter and his crew were also responsible for the fire engine: in the *Mars*, carpenters in the well were to let water into the ship to be pumped at the fire. (Ships had leather fire buckets until 1806, when the Navy Board instructed Chatham Dockyard, in response to its recommendation, to issue half the establishment as iron-bound wooden buckets.)[31]

The carpenter's cabin was established in 1757 'under the forecastle'; as separate sick berths were introduced into ships it was moved to the orlop deck, forward, next to his store room (the carpenter's cabin in the *Ça Ira* (80) had windows on the passageway side with curtains in them). The carpenter's storeroom in the *Bellona* (74) was approximately 19ft long and 14ft wide at its widest, and in the *Victory* 11ft by 14ft 6in. Some of the carpenter's work must have been done on deck but the logs merely record the fact, such as 'carpenters emply'd making a mizzen top mast' in the *York* (74), not the location, and where smaller work was done below decks is even less clear; John Major, carpenter of the *Vengeance*, was alleged in 1799 to have made a desk for his cabin from wainscoting belonging to the ship, implying that he did so secretly. Jeffrey de Raigersfeld said that during his time in the *Vestal* frigate, 'being always alive to any thing going on on board, I used to frequent the carpenter's bench, the armourer's bench, and forge'; he does not say where they were, but the carpenter's bench in the *Vanguard* in 1803 was, oddly, aft, near the spirit-room hatchway.[32]

'In ships of war, the cannon of the lower-decks are usually drawn into the ship during the course of an expedition at sea, unless when they are used in battle. They are secured by lowering the breech so as that the muzzle shall bear against the upper-edge of the port, after which the two parts of the breeching are firmly braced together by a rope which crosses them between the front of the carriage and the port; which operation is called *frapping* the breeching. The tackles are then securely fastened about it with several turns of the rope extended from the tackle and breeching, over the chase of the cannon.' In the morning

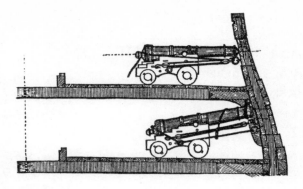

Guns and their tackles. The lower-deck gun is secured for sea.

watch the gunner's team made sure that all was secure, and that the ropes had not stretched.[33]

In the *Splendid*, hammocks were piped up at seven bells, so from about six bells there were men preparing for the day. Since 1782 the men had been supplied with canvas bags to keep their clothes in, issued by the pursers as slops, in lieu of chests in time of war (and from 1795 petty officers and seamen who wanted one had been issued with a haversack). All clothes had to be tidied into the hammocks or bags, and bowls, plates and cutlery into the garlands (hanging net bags) or shelves (the *Splendid* had recently received prize money, and 'every mess-place in the ship is ornamented with gold, according to their several tastes, at their own expense, and with some degree of uniformity in the shelves, broken by the little variety of their own paintings and ornaments; which, marking contented choice rather than the hand of power, the whole produces a very pleasing effect'). The master's mate, boatswain's mate and master at arms were 'very particular in seeing this order executed'.[34]

When this was complete, at seven bells the boatswain's mates piped 'Up hammocks'. In the *Splendid* the men were allowed seven minutes to take them up to their specified places on the weather deck and stow them in the hammock netting, where they were stowed during the day, for cleanliness and for protection against enemy fire in action. They were stored in painted hammock cloths or covers that folded 'completely round' the hammock and protected it from the wet.[35]

HOLD

Every evening the *Splendid* allowed 16in of seawater into her well, which mixed with any foul water draining through the ship; every morning it was pumped out again, and at six bells the carpenter checked that the well was dry, ready to report it to the captain.[36]

Chapter 4

BREAKFAST IN THE WARDROOM
Morning watch, 4am to 8am
(ii) to eight bells

QUARTERDECK, WAIST AND FORECASTLE

At seven bells the boatswain, carpenter and gunner came aft to the captain's cabin to report that everything in their charge was clean and in order. Once that was complete, they went below to the wardroom to breakfast.

The navy was certain that all this cleaning was essential for healthy ships and healthy crews. British visitors to foreign ships, especially those used to the Royal Navy, frequently commented on how dirty they were, with genuine disgust. Captain Pasley, for example, recorded on 22 May 1781: 'The Swedish boy we retook in the *Hinchinbrook* informs me that during the five or six weeks he was on board the *Artésien* the hammacoes were not once got up, neither the lower deck washed nor cleaned – dirty dogs.' In January 1783, William Hickey, by then an experienced traveller in England, the Continent and India, and a noted rake, was on board the 74-gun *Héros*, Admiral Suffren's flagship, in Trincomalee harbour: 'As I was passing through the steerage, along the main deck, I beheld such a scene of filth and dirt as I could not have believed had I not seen; it had more the appearance of an abominable pig-sty than the inside of a ship of the line bearing an admiral's flag, and this was very much the case with all the fleet except two, the *Vengeur* and *Flamand*, both of which were as neat and clean as any British ship of war.' When he went on board the *Superb*: 'I was equally surprised and pleased at the contrast between the main deck of the *Superb* and that of the *Heros*, the former being delightfully neat and clean throughout, the latter disgusting to behold from filth and dirt.' After the Revolution, Watkin Tench, a captured marine officer and prisoner of war, attempted to walk the quarterdeck of the *Marat* in 1794 but it was so greasy and slippery he found it 'impracticable'; he was assured by the captain that he made his men eat on deck 'to keep his ship clean', but the decks were not scraped or washed afterward – a 'curious improvement in the economy of a ship of war'.[1]

Waist

At 7.30 the *Splendid*'s main topsail split. This was a relatively common accident at sea, and the ship carried a spare; the hands were sent up into the shrouds and onto the yard to clew it up, by hauling on the clew lines, which ran through a block at the mast to the outer lower corners, gathering it in for repair.

Upper deck

Wardroom

Breakfast in the wardroom was essentially the same as the captain's, though it was dependent on the abilities of the caterer of the mess – one of the wardroom officers, who was elected by them for the duty and who collected a monthly subscription. At 7.30 a breakfast cloth was spread, and at 8.00 the officers, and their guest the mate of the morning watch, sat down to 'coffee, tea, as good rolls as ever were baked on shore, and what was more extraordinary, admirable fresh butter, toast, eggs, ham, sausages … ' This was rather better than a ship-of-the-line could normally provide, but the caterer had been able to resupply the wardroom pantry at Mahon.[2]

Watkin Tench was billeted in *Le Marat* (74), at Brest. He described life on board her in a letter he wrote to a friend at home that winter: the captain messed with the officers, which was forbidden but 'winked at' because it was so much cheaper, and they breakfasted 'every morning at nine o'clock on Gloucester cheese (taken out of an English prize), good brown bread, called pain d'egalité, which they bake on board, and a thin acid claret, of which the French drink very liberally'; the food was plentiful enough, but served in such a dirty state it would 'disgust a Hottentot.'[3]

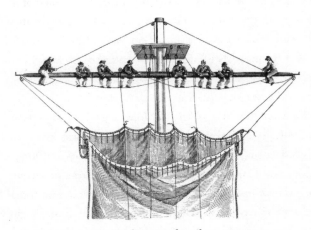

Bending a new foresail.

Chapter 5

DRILL, SLAUGHTER, PUNISHMENT AND THE SICK
Forenoon watch, 8am to noon

QUARTERDECK, WAIST AND FORECASTLE: ONE BELL TO SEVEN BELLS
Quarterdeck

At one bell in the forenoon watch the marine drummers 'beat the assemble, or drummers call'. The marine guard went to the quarterdeck, 'hair combed and tied', 'hands and face clean', and 'dress as much so as possible': 'it is expected that the men do appear with that cleanliness and exact regularity of dress which is maintained in a parade on shore; and for this purpose they are exempt from any other duty on the days they mount'. Once assembled on the quarterdeck they were drawn up. The marine commanding officer inspected them, and according to the captain's orders, 'After having seen that they are all properly dressed and accoutered, he will make the guard present arms and the drums and music will play the troop etc., after which march the sentinels, when they are relieved and the others marched in, face the guard to the right by a ruffle of the drum, and march once round the quarterdeck, the drums and fife playing a march, and deposit their arms in the stand.' Since today was a Tuesday, the guard remained on deck and were instructed in drill for an hour. The 'awkward men' in the working party were detailed off to the forecastle to drill under a sergeant for another hour.[1]

There is evidence that marines led very separate lives in the ship, even, contrary to the usual practice, when they filled some of the petty officers' roles. When John Jolly, a marine of the *Alexander* (74), was court-martialled for assaulting his officer on 30 June 1799 his corporal, James McDonough, testified that he did not know Captain Ball, the captain of the *Alexander*; but equally this could just signal how easy it was for anyone to live a circumscribed life among the hundreds of people who made up a ship-of-the-line: John Brightly alias John Brighty or Brighteye joined the *Bellerophon* (74) as John Brighty, sailor, when she commissioned in July 1790, but went ashore at Spithead in December and was marked as Run (*ie* a deserter): he then joined the marines as John Brightley and was sent to the *Ardent* then in May back to the *Bellerophon*, where he was recognised by W. Mitchell, captain's clerk, but 'he was sometime on board before we discovered him', even though he was Mitchell's assistant for three months in 1791. Admiral Patton, who was 'regarded as the highest authority on matters concerning the lower deck', argued that since marines were landmen assigning them positions of authority was 'completely overturning the natural order of things', and had no practical utility: 'Great part of these men never acquire what is called sea-legs and are therefore in a great measure useless in bad weather at sea. Let us now suppose the ship to have such a degree of motion as discomposes landmen and let us suppose the officers of this ship depending on the marines for protection from the irritated seamen; where is the security? In such a case, it is well known that three seamen are absolutely superior in force to ten landmen, whatever the colour of their coats or their state of discipline on shore.'[2]

After the prohibition on swearing, the regulation most frequently ignored was probably the requirement for divine service (twice a day, and a sermon on Sundays, in 1790; every Sunday, ship's duties and weather permitting, in 1808). In mid-century John Bulkeley, who sailed in the *Wager*, wrote 'The duty of publick prayer had been entirely neglected on board, though every seaman pays fourpence per month towards the support of a minister; yet devotion, in so solemn a manner, is so rarely perform'd, that I know but one instance of it during the many years I have belong'd to the navy'. In his day, and in 1790, the commanders of HM ships were required to 'take care' that divine service was performed twice a day and a sermon preached on Sundays; in 1808 the chaplain had his own section of the regulations, and he was directed to 'perform, with due solemnity, the duties of the Lord's Day, that the ship's company may be impressed with devotion'. In ships that performed it, it was held in the forenoon watch, as on land. In 1809 William Richardson belonged to the *Caesar* (74) on blockade; Rear Admiral Stopford joined her on 16 February 1809, and the 19th, 'Being a Sabbath day, a church was rigged out and divine service performed on board *Caesar* for the first time since I had belonged to her'; he was appointed to her on 16 April 1805.[3]

Throughout the eighteenth century, naval chaplains were in a difficult and anomalous position. Their sea pay was only 19s a lunar month, which was the same as an ordinary seaman, though since they were nominally warrant officers they had the standard compensation in lieu of one servant, at 19s gross or 17s 6d net per month; unless they had a private income, or were using the position as an opportunity for paid private travel, which was more likely in a frigate than a ship-of-the-line (especially in the Mediterranean), they actually expected to live off the allowance of a groat (4d) per man borne. (Chaplains to ships in Ordinary also received 1d every ten days provided it did not exceed 6d in any quarter from the men borne on the Extra and ropeyard lists.)[4] In a 74 of 600 men this gave the chaplain £130, making a respectable annual net pay of £140 8s 0d, suitable for an officer who messed in the wardroom, but when ships were below complement chaplains could suffer real hardship. Captain Smith of the *Hannibal* (74), 'at sea off Cape Francois', wrote to the Admiralty on 31 January 1797, concerning George Gunning, his chaplain:

> ... he is a gentleman of most exemplary character, and deserves every attention in my power to afford him. I beg leave to inform their Lordships that the *Hannibal* has been, upon an average, the last twelve months, 161 men short of complement, which reduces his pay £34 per annum [actually £34 12s 8d]. From the scarcity of stock upon this station of Cape Nicolas Mole, every article bears treble the price of its real value; so that in short the sum arising from the groates of the number of men victualled, does not afford a clergyman the means of existence.[5]

It is endorsed 'acquaint him that a new regulation has been made which will place the chaplains on a more advantageous footing than they formerly have been', but this new regulation has not been traced. N A M Rodger notes that many chaplains treated the position as a sinecure (as they would ashore), and quotes the anti-slave-trader Percival Stockdale, who had accompanied Admiral Byng's expedition to Minorca in 1756, writing in alarm in 1776 – 'When you were so good as to apply for me for this chaplainship, neither you nor I thought that in consequence of obtaining it I should be obliged to be near the ship or on board'[6] – but he was chaplain of the *Resolution* guardship in Ordinary, and the navy had difficulty enough keeping any of its warrant officers in Ordinary on board where their duty required them, and one might with equal propriety give the example of the letter the Admiralty received dated 4 March 1793 from the Reverend Edward Powell 'stating that he is nearly deaf and upwards of seventy years of age and praying that he may not be called on to serve but allowed the usual Pension, having served upwards of seven years.'[7]

In 1808 the captain was instructed that 'No ship is to go to sea without a chaplain, if a clergyman properly recommended and of good moral character be found desirous of being appointed to her'. His duties as expressed in the 1808

Regulations (they were not mentioned in 1790) were to hold divine service once a week, weather permitting, carefully adapting his 'discourses to the capacity of his hearers and the nature of their situation, that his instructions may be intelligible and beneficial to all who hear them'; but before this he was to instruct the young gentlemen put under his care by the captain, and all the boys, in the Christian religion, hearing them read and explaining the scriptures and catechism, with the help of 'an intelligent and well disposed person' appointed by the captain, to offer religious 'assistance and instruction' to any that desired it, and to visit the sick who asked for him and to attend the dying 'although they should not request it, to comfort or admonish them, as the state of their minds or other circumstances may require.' The principal article instructed him to conduct himself so that the ship's company might be inspired 'with reverence' for 'the sacred office' to which he was appointed, and it is interesting in this context that, even before this was formalised, when in summer 1758 Sergeant Grimes of the *Rippon* (60) saw John Blake 'with a goat between his legs … in motion, the same as if a man was acting with a woman', the first officer he acquainted was the chaplain.[8]

For Joseph Bates, pressed into the *Rodney* (74) in 1810, 'As a general thing, a chaplain was allowed for every large ship.'

> When the weather was pleasant, the quarter-deck was fitted with awnings, flags, benches, &c., for meeting. At 11 A.M., came the order from the officer of the deck, 'Strike six bells there!' 'yes sir.' 'Boatswain's mate!' 'Sir.' 'Call all hands to church! Hurry them up there!' These mates were required to carry a piece of rope in their pocket with which to start the sailors. Immediately their stentorian voices were heard sounding on the other decks, 'Away up to church there – every soul of you – and take your prayer books with you!' If any one felt disinclined to such a mode of worship, and attempted to evade the loud call to church, then look out for the men with the rope! When I was asked, 'Of what religion are you?' I replied, 'A Presbyterian.' But I was now given to understand that there was no religious toleration on board the king's war ships. 'Only one denomination here – away with you to church!' The officers, before taking their seats, unbuckled their swords and dirks, and piled them on the head of the capstan in the midst of the worshiping assembly, all ready to grasp them in a moment, if necessary, before the hour's service should close. When the benediction was pronounced, the officers clinched their side arms, and buckled them on for active service. The quarter-deck was

immediately cleared, and the floating bethel again became the same old weekly war ship for six days and twenty-three hours more. Respecting the church service, the chaplain, or in his absence, the captain, reads from the prayer book, and the officers and sailors respond. And when he read about the law of God, the loud response would fill the quarterdeck, 'O Lord, incline our hearts to keep thy law'. Poor, wicked, deluded souls! how little their hearts were inclined to keep the holy law of God, when almost every hour of the week, their tongues were employed in blaspheming his holy name; and at the same time learning and practicing the way and manner of shooting, slaying, and sinking to the bottom of the ocean, all that refused to surrender, and become their prisoners; or who dared to oppose, or array themselves in opposition to a proclamation of war issued from their good old Christian king.[9]

In 1812 the situation was revolutionised. Every ship from a First to a Fifth Rate was allowed a chaplain (though in practice few served in ships smaller than a Third Rate); his pay was increased to £11 10s od a month, with half-pay after eight years' sea service (with no more than six weeks' absence), of 5s per day (and if peace was declared, a pension 'proportionate to the term of service'), and he was guaranteed a cabin in the wardroom or gunroom, messing with the lieutenants. These changes were 'designed to attract a better type of man, such as Rev. Edward Mangin', who served in the *Gloucester* (74); but he found that 'nothing can possibly be more unsuitably or more awkwardly situated than a clergyman in a ship of war; every object around him is at variance with the sensibilities of a rational and enlightened mind'.[10]

Waist

The *Splendid* had received sixty bullocks at Mahon, and at nine o'clock a party under the ship's butcher began to slaughter one in the waist. The *Splendid* was fortunate: one of her idlers, George Price, had been pressed out of the *Walmer Castle* Indiaman; he had been a butcher in Southwark, had served as butcher in the *Walmer Castle*, though only for nine days before he was taken, and now, as he wrote home, 'I am Butcher On Board of the Ship But at the Same Time I have to Work in every Part of the Ship the same as every other Sailor'. The regulations directed this to be done in 'some convenient part of the ship, open to the view of the company', under the supervision of a lieutenant, the master and a mate, who were there to ensure a fair distribution.[11]

The bullocks bought by the navy in the Mediterranean weighed about

540lb each, yielding about 300lb of beef each. The plate 'Slaughter-Houses' in Payne's *Microcosm* of 1806 shows an ox being slaughtered. It is haltered 'previous to his being killed', then stunned with a poleaxe – 'the blow is instantly fatal. The noble animal drops on its knees, as if struck by a thunderbolt'– then skinned and bled. There was no guarantee of an expert slaughterman on board ship; if there was no George Price there must have been some improvisation. The carcasses were hung on capstan bars athwart the booms, to be cut up the following morning, even though, as Dr Trotter wrote, the meat was 'in these places exposed to the breath of the whole ship's company, and is often brushed by them as they pass. The sight is extremely disgusting.' Sentries were posted to protect it and prevent theft. In some ships it was customary for the butcher to be allowed a steak for cutting up the beef,* but not in the *Splendid*.[12]

The previous day Edward Berry had been punished with forty-eight lashes for drunkenness and striking Benjamin Sanford, Owen Sullivan with twenty-four lashes for being overboard at night and Edward Jones with sixteen lashes for absenting himself from the ship without leave (the last two offences committed at Mahon). The procedure for punishment was formalised and the same throughout the navy.[13]

> About eleven o'clock, or six bells [in the morning watch], when any of the men are in irons, or on the black list, the boatswain or mate are ordered to call all hands; the culprits are then brought forward by the master at arms, who is a warrant officer, and acts the part of Jack Ketch, when required: he likewise has the prisoners in his custody, until they are put in irons, under any charge. All hands being now mustered, the captain orders the man to strip; he is then seized to a grating by the wrists and knees; his crime is then mentioned, and the prisoner may plead, but, in nineteen cases out of twenty, he is flogged for the most trifling offence or neglect, such as not hearing the watch called at night, not doing any thing properly on deck or aloft, which he might happen to be sent to do, when, perhaps he has been

---

* According to Edward Overton, master of the *Gibraltar* (80), James Budd, the ship's butcher, was flogged for stealing steaks when cutting up the beef; while the sentence was in progress, Thomas Sharp the gunner's mate came forward and said that he heard the purser give Budd 'leave to take a beef steak & that it was customary in the service for the butcher to have a steak for cutting up the beef', and Budd was released after having received four lashes; but he also agreed that Captain Pakenham said 'that the Prisoner had made more confusion in the ship than all the rest of the people besides'. The purser's steward said he gave 'half or three quarters of a pound each butcher', but the butcher himself was unaware of the custom: 'I heard Samuel Dewitt one of the butchers say to you [the purser], that he had not had his breakfast & wanted to go away from the block to get it; you said it was customary for the butcher cutting up the meat, to have a steak'. The court satisfied itself that Budd was given leave to take one steak, but took steaks weighing 3–4lb and was therefore properly punished, and did not pursue the question of whether the custom was a genuine or universal one.

doing the best he could, and at the same time ignorant of having done wrong, until he is pounced on, and put in irons.[14]

The eighteenth-century Regulations clearly stated that 'No commander shall inflict any punishment upon a seaman, beyond twelve lashes upon his bare back with a cat of nine tails, according to the ancient practice of the sea', anything deserving greater punishment requiring an application for a court martial, but in the 1806 and 1808 editions the captain was not to punish 'with greater severity than the offence shall really deserve'. This again was consolidating common practice: not only did eighteenth-century captains not restrict themselves to twelve lashes, or serial punishments of twelve lashes for each of several offences committed or supposed to have been committed at the same time, they recorded them openly in their logs and official letters. When William Scott, captain of the *Niger* (32), received a letter from the Admiralty in May 1798 enclosing one from the ship's company 'complaining of the ill usage they receive' and requesting an explanation, for example, he immediately replied denying all the charges, saying that the men had disputed his order that the women leave the ship by 4pm and that he had given one of the men 'one dozen & eight lashes' for insolence and the ringleader 'three dozen & eight lashes' as an example and in order to suppress a potential mutiny. The Admiralty noted: 'acquaint him that their Lordships do not judge it necessary to bring him to a court martial under the circumstances he has related.'[15]

Joseph Nagle, when serving in the *St Lucia* brig, was accused of stealing the captain's Madeira and given a dozen lashes: 'After I was punished, the boatswain told me when I received to dozen more I would be a manawars man, and not before. The capt[ain] told me to do my duty as yousual.'[16]

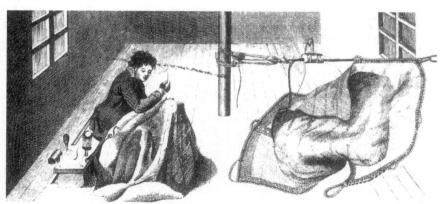

Sailmaker at work in a sail-loft; similar techniques were used at sea.

At 9.20 the officer of the watch ordered the main topsail to be set. This was a huge sail, 62ft at the head and 98ft at the foot, and 59ft deep. The topmen had to climb up the shrouds to the main top, about 130ft above the sea, loose the sail, which had been tightly reefed in, and kick it out and down; the sail was sheeted home (pulled to the ends of the yard) by easing on the clewlines while the sheet was hauled, and the topmen had to make sure the weather clew (lower corner) was home first. At 10.30 the third reef was taken in in the fore and mizzen topsails.[17]

Later in the morning the sailmakers were ordered to repair the fore and main top-gallant studdingsails that had carried away the evening before. The sailmaker was a war-rant officer classed as a petty officer; he reported to the boatswain, and had a mate and a crew of two. The main duty of the sail-maker's team was to keep the sails clean, dry and aired, 'and also constantly to attend all surveys and conversions of sail.'[18] These became increasingly common as blockade duty kept ships at sea for months and years,

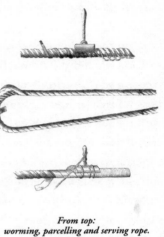

From top:
worming, parcelling and serving rope.

and the accounts of the Mediterranean Fleet in particular include many exam-ples of conversions, such as Captain Keats' note of the canvas, twine and other materials needed to convert a 74's fore topsail into a main topsail:

> to enlarge the sail canvas no. 2 – one hundred & forty-five yards.
> to reef bands canvas no. 2. – twelve yards
> to leech linings canvas no. 2 – six yards
> allowance for stepping canvas no. 5 – thirteen yards
> different cloths: top lining and belly bands no. 2 – six yards
> twine – twelve lb
> bolt rope of 5½ inch – nine fathoms[19]

The sailmaker ranked with the ropemaker; the Admiralty had continued problems with the supply of rope and cordage, and the Navy Board's instruc-tions to the dockyards alternately urged economy in its use and directions for forcing the contractors to make the ropes properly.[20] The situation was not helped by letters such as this from St Vincent of 6 October 1800 from the *Ville de Paris* in Torbay, complaining that the *Mars*'s cable was 'quite rotten', which he attributed to

the careless manner in which our ropemakers manufacture the cables, an allegation which holds good against the whole of our cordage, and unless there is an entire change of system in that branch, as well as every other in His Majesty's Dock yards, and wholesome laws enforced to govern the artificers by, the navy will be put to continued hazard, and the country ruined by incapacity, waste, idleness, corruption and every other vice.[21]

At the turn of the century English ships laden with hemp from Russia were embargoed, and the Admiralty consequently ordered the 'utmost frugality and œconomy'. Captain Keats in the *Superb* (74) therefore ordered that the boatswain must when shifting or reeving new rope (which must always be done with the master's knowledge and captain's permission) reuse unserviceable parts as 'luff and jigger tackle falls' etc.; and that when working up junk 'some of the bettermost yearns [*sic*] are to be drawn from each length, to be neatly knotted and put by in balls for making rope; the short shakings of junk and other broken yarns must be worked into matts & platts for the yards & cables', the remainder turned into oakum, and swabs made from worn hammocks and old canvas instead of junk; and to avoid confusion lists must be kept by the boatswain's yeoman and monthly returns submitted 'of all shifts and conversions, & of the quantity of rope, matts, platts, points, robands, gaskets, nippers & swabs that have been made since the last day of the preceding month.' This corresponds to a letter from St Vincent in the *Ville de Paris*, dated Torbay, 30 November 1800, in these terms, and which includes: 'The Commr. in Chief also strongly recommends that rope be made on *board* from junk, condemned hawsers, etc, for which purpose the necessary tools will be furnished from the dock yard, on demands being made for them by the respective boatswains, and the men employed will be regularly and well paid.* – By pursuing these methods, ships in the Mediterranean have performed the hardest services for upwards of three years with a less supply of cordage & stores, than is usually furnished for three months to ships in the Channel.' That winter, all ships of the

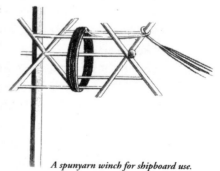

A spunyarn winch for shipboard use.

---

* Since 1798 this was 6d per day, good money when an ordinary seaman's pay was 9½d a day (or 10d per day in 1810), but it was paid with their wages, so not necessarily regularly.

Fifth Rate and upwards were supplied with a jack, hooks and sledges for reman-ufacturing cordage on board 'as fast as they can be procured', and coil of 1in and ¾in was removed from the carpenter's sea stores, 'as rope manufactured on board will do if ever it should be wanted'. By 1803, Nelson could write to the naval storekeeper in Malta to order eighty-four butts of hemp, to make 'small cordage, twine, etc.'; 'with respect to the making of rope, none under three-inch is neces-sary to be made for the line of battle ships, and we can make as far as four-inch … Our Master-Ropemaker is a child of thirteen years of age, and the best rope-maker in the fleet.'[22]

Captain's cabin

At nine o'clock the officer of the morning watch reported to the captain that all was clean and in its place on the gundeck and between decks.[23]

The captain's business of the day was similar in every ship-of-the-line. His most important daily record was the ship's log, but he was responsible for the pay, provisions, clothes and material supplies that passed through the ship, whether for her own use or the fleet's, and his records of consumption or dis-posal, or receipts for material remaining in store, had to delivered to his com-mander-in-chief to be forwarded to the Admiralty in London at various regular intervals. The 1808 regulations had an appendix that listed the twenty-three sets of papers required to pass a captain's accounts.

'Two log-books.' (Two copies of the captain's log.)
'Remarks on coasts, roads, etc. or a certificate none were made; signed by captain and master.' (A set of observations for the improvement of the commerce of the country and for HM service; it included making or correcting maps and charts and was supported by another book made by the master, which the captain was to 'correct, improve, or enlarge as far as his own observation shall enable him'. One copy was to be sent every six months, and another cumulative copy when he sent his log book.)
'Muster-books to be sent to the Commissioners of the Navy, at the expiration of every two months.'
'Slop-book, issues totalled, invoice account of DD men's clothes'. (The slop book recorded the issue of clothes and certain supplies (beds, blankets, etc.) for which a debit would be made against each man's pay, and the invoices were for slops sold to the ship's company belonging to men Discharged Dead.)
'Tickets, dead and remove, to be transmitted with the Muster-books.' (He

was required to demand from the Navy Board a number of blank printed discharge tickets, which were used when commissioned and warrant officers died or were discharged, and when 'petty officers, able seamen, ordinary landmen [*sic*], marines or boys were discharged unserviceable or sent away sick, or removed into any other ship'; he was also to send the Navy Board an account of the tickets issued, using another form, with the unused tickets or his successor's receipt for them.)

'Sick-book.'

'Copy of commission.'

'Receipt for a complete book left with Successor.'

'Gunner's, boatswain's, and carpenter's expenses, supplies, and returns. Orders and report of surveys.'

'Certificate of no back-stays shifted or top-masts lost.'

'Do. of no survey-book supplied.' (The survey books were the printed volumes of a ship's establishment of stores, one each for boatswain, gunner and carpenter.)

'Account of receipt and expenses, muster-paper, and tickets.' (This recorded the use of the printed forms that had to be demanded at the dockyard.)

'Vouchers for stores purchased.' (Captains buying stores for their ships who drew bills on the Commissioners of the Navy, again using a form supplied, had to obtain a certificate from the governor or consul, or in his absence two or three 'British merchants of the greatest consequence and repute', if there were none the respectable local merchants, that 'the bill is drawn at a rate of exchange as advantageous to the public as possible'; if they effected the purchase for him they were allowed a commission of up to 2.5 per cent.)

'Sailing qualities of the vessel, *if paid off.*'

'General account of provisions received and returned, as per form delivered from the Victualling Office.'

'Quarterly accounts to be sent to Commissioners of Victualling.'

'Certificate of the quantity of wine and spirits issued, if on home station.'

'Ditto [*ie* certificate] of complement and title page.' (The title page is not explained, but may be the page to be signed by the lieutenants so that their signatures could be compared to any certificates they submitted.)

'Ditto from purser to captain.' (This was a certificate of the money paid on the short allowance account (see no. 21), which the Victualling Board kept until it could be checked against the purser's account for the same period.)

'Orders and report of surveys on provisions.' (Food or drink found unfit for use after examination by the appropriate officers, with an account of how it was used or disposed of.)

'Vouchers for savings by ship's company, and of provisions purchased.' (The ship's company were paid every month, two months or quarter for bread, wine, spirits, beef, pork, sugar, butter and cheese that they had forgone or not been issued, at a rate fixed by the Admiralty. This was always in cash, in the local currency.)*

'An account of, or certificate of not, any cask shaken.' (Captains frequently shook, or dismantled, casks to make more room, but this caused great expense and inconvenience to the Victualling Board.)

'Letters to the Commissioners of Navy, Victualling, and Sick and Hurt, to grant certificates of no imprest outstanding.'[24]

When the ship paid off the captain had to submit five copies of the paybook, an open list, a slop book and three alphabets. This compares unfavourably with the thirty-two sets of records required for an entire regiment in 1812, namely fifteen for regimental details, seven for the quartermaster, six for the infantry companies, three for the surgeon and one for the paymaster: a regiment at full strength was a thousand men, and a ship-of-the-line's complement was from 590 to 837, but a ship was a vastly greater proportion of the nation's treasure. All these certificates and records had to be sent to London and accepted – and none of them 'will be dispensed with, except on the most satisfactory proof, that it was impracticable to obtain it',† each time the captain 'shall be removed from the command of a ship', or 'when he shall desire to receive his pay … which he may do at the end of every twelve calendar months'.[25] Francis Wilson had to transmit twenty-three books and papers for passing Captain Ball's accounts for 8 December 1796 to 31 December 1797:

---

* The savings and short allowance money was: bread, 1½d per lb; wine, 1s per gallon; spirits, 2s per gallon; beef, including flour etc., 1s 6d per 8lb piece; pork, 1s 2d per 4lb piece; sugar, 4d per lb; butter, 4d per lb; and cheese, 2d per lb. All these could be paid to individual messes, though not to individuals within a mess. Officers who did not draw their allowance of ship's provisions were also entitled to this payment, which may have been a significant source of income for some. Pease and oatmeal were only paid when the whole ship's company was at short allowance, and were paid at 3s per bushel for pease, and 6d per gallon for oatmeal. There was, of course, a form for this, which recorded the number of the mess, the quantities and value of the provisions and the date the money was paid, with a signature for its receipt.

† Despite the gravity of this warning, the Admiralty was known to be sympathetic. On 8 November 1810, the explorer Matthew Flinders, safely returned home after his imprisonment on the Isle de France, wrote that 'on examining into the state of my papers after the shipwreck of His Maj. armed vessel *Porpoise*, in which I was returning to England as a passenger in 1803, several were found to have been lost, and many others much shattered; [*sic*] the whole saved were afterwards taken from me by general De Caen, governor of the Isle of France; and when they were returned some years afterwards, the rats, I found, had gotten into the trunk and made nests of some of them. I transmitted the whole from the Isle of France in they then were; and now find that some of the papers necessary to the passing my accounts, as commander and purser of His Maj. Sloop *Investigator*, are wanting.' The Lords' response: 'Usual orders.'

the monthly book compleat to 31 December; quarterly accounts of provisions; general account of provisions; slop book compleat with invoices; an alphabet [the list that went with the pay book, recording the name and number of everyone in the ship]; boatswain's expenses; gunner's do.; carpenter's do.; boatswain's supplies and returns; gunner's do.; carpenter's do.; sick book; pay and sick ticket book; receipt and expences of [muster] paper; two journals; eleven reports of survey; two vouchers for surgeon's necessaries purchased; certificate of complement and title page; do. no shrouds or backstays shifted; do. from purser to captain; do. of no survey book lost by indecession [?]; do. of no new observations [of coasts and harbours]; letter to Victg. Board to certify no imprest [outstanding].[26]

In 1805 Captain Keats recorded the books and papers he had to submit to the Admiralty for passing his accounts in the *Superb* (74) between 1 May 1804 and 30 April 1805:

general account of provisions received & returned etc; two journals; slop book; sick book; ticket book; receipt & expence of muster paper etc; boatswain's expence, and supplies & returns; carpenter's expence, and supplies & returns; gunner's expence, and supplies & returns; one voucher for bullocks purchased at Algiers 17 June 1804; one voucher for the assignment of savings between the 8 February & 30 June 1804; one report of survey on water casks – condemned; one report of survey on ordnance stores – condemned; three reports of survey on running rigging & sails – condemned; one report of survey on boatswain's stores remaining on board prior to his leaving the ship; one report of survey on boatswain's stores remaining in my charge; one receipt for old canvas supplied to the carpenter; certificate relative to shrouds & backstays; certificate of complement & title page; certificate from purser; certificate of no remarks made on coasts; certificate of no stores being supplied to any merchant vessel; letter to Navy Board relative to imprest; letter to Victualling Board relative to imprest; letter to Board of Ordnance relative to imprest; alphabet.[27]

Next year it was even worse:

general account of provisions received & returned etc; slop book; boatswain's expense; boatswain's supplies; boatswain's returns; gunner's expense; gunner's supplies; gunner's returns; carpenter's expense;

carpenter's supplies; carpenter's returns; two logs from the 1st May 1806 to the 28 Febry 1807; sick book; ticket book; receipt and expence of paper; four cancelled sick tickets; one cancelled pay ticket; one report of survey on remains of provisions 28 July 1806; one report of survey on cheese condemned 17 September 1806; one report of survey on cheese & rice condemned 7 January 1806; one receipt for muster paper supplied *Kent*; one receipt for complete book delivered to successor; one receipt for tickets & muster paper etc delivered to successor; one voucher for payments of savings of provisions between the 6 September 1805 & 14 May 1806; one voucher for payment of savings of wine between 6 September 1805 & 14 February 1806; certificates from Mr F. Douglas & Mr S. Strut – pursers; certificates relative to shrouds & backstays; certificate of no casks being shook; certificate of complement & titlepage; certificate of no remarks on coats [*sic*] or harbours; certificate of no stores been supplied to merchant ships; certificate of no survey book from predecessor; letter to the Victualling Board relative to imprest; letter to the Navy Board relative to imprest; letter to the Board of Ordnance relative to imprest; alphabet.[28]

For all this work he officially bore only a clerk,* for whose every error and fraud he was officially accountable.[29]

Sending this library safely to London was an evolution in itself. Today there are formal procedures, and classified material is brought on board and taken ashore in sacks or bags, and once aboard ship is kept in a safe under the care of the Royal Marine lieutenant, but in the early nineteenth century a ship-of-the-line was self-sufficient and carried all the materials she needed, even for everyday details like this. Accordingly, Captain Edwards sent his clerk to the carpenter's cabin to ask him 'if he would be so good as to order a box to be made to send the captain's books home in order to pass his accounts.'[30]

UPPER DECK
Wardroom

Having drilled the marines, Captain Dymond came below to his cabin, where he was reading Sir Walter Scott's *Marmion*. The wardroom collectively possessed a

---

* 'I have a man to assist my clerk as is customary', borne as AB, wrote Admiral Barrington in 1771, but because this clerk's assistant was one of the shipboard roles carried out by men borne under another rate it is difficult to trace how widespread they were. Admiral's secretaries had, or at least were allowed, clerks; in 1804 they were restricted to one each, at £50 p.a., this salary to be paid by bills at the Navy Board, not paid as if they were on the ship's books.

library of 500 volumes, which were treated as common property and recorded in a book kept on the rudder-head. He had made himself quite comfortable, with a sofa, backgammon table and curtains,* but he was not enjoying the weather. Admiral Collingwood had been altogether too much of a blue-water sailor for his liking – he should be 'transformed into a fish, or a sea monster, for his delight is in gales of wind & buffeting about – worrying all the other admirals, captains & crews to death' – and the present squalls, with spars carried away and perpetual setting and taking in sails, were too strongly reminiscent of the winter storms.[31]

> So much for the comforts of a sea life – not anything else have I to speak of for every thing has been gloomy & every body sulky of late, & likely to continue so; if we get a few hours moderate weather, it but just affords us time to place our things to rights & talk a little together & then with the gale we take up a book or paper & sit in some snug corner to read & sulk. This sometimes happens the whole winter & off Brest or in the North Sea they enjoy 9 months of 12 blowing weather tho' not perhaps stormy & yet it is said by people who do not go to [sea] 'Dear me, if I had as much time on my hands as you all must have at sea I would *study* etc. etc.' In short for myself, I am fit for no earthly thing in blowing weather & the *little* time we get with being in harbour etc. I am glad to get a little relaxation & comfort, consequently no time for studies in particular & no *inclination either*, so I contend a sea life to be the most unprofitable of any except the *value* of our *services* to the country.[32]

Summer off Toulon was little better: in 1807 he had written home describing a gale very like the one that would blow Sir Charles Cotton's fleet off station in July and tempt the French out of harbour to rescue a convoy sheltering in Bandol. About eight in the evening,

> I had just crept out of my den, to have my bed made & was sitting at the table talking of the dreadful cruise we have had for some weeks past – & in fact I was so [dispirited] by remaining alone solitary & alarmed for the magazine, that I ventured out of my cabin to enjoy company, such as it was, – when a tremendous sea struck the stern … We were of course wet thro' & thro' – & my two subs, idle young men, were as usual sleeping on

---

* When he left the ship he gave his sofa, backgammon table and curtains 'etc.' to his friends in the wardroom, so he was probably better equipped than most; the captain of marines in the *Blenheim* slept in a hammock in 1794.

the window seats – their situation may easily be imagined & when got on their legs (for they were washed away as a cork would be in a mill-sluice) astonishment & dismay was depicted in each countenance & 'What's the matter, what's the matter?' was all they could say – for my part I could stay no longer, but instantly took off my clothes, made my servant rub me with flannels and went to bed, had some hot wine, but little sleep …[33]

Marine officers 'were on the whole poor men: often middle-class Irish and Scots, attracted to an honourable profession with low social and financial barriers to entry', and Dymond had written to his wife: 'I am perfectly solitary, and what is singular there is not one man on board whom I can make anything like a friend of – or converse with in a confidential way. They are all bachelors, men of fortune, or persons of a very different way of thinking from me. We have no ideas in common'. The proportion of marine officers living off their pay was greater than sea officers, and they shared prize money with the warrant officers (the captains of marines shared with the sea lieutenants); the regulations had to remind the wardroom that 'The Marine officers are upon all occasions to be treated, as well by the captain of the ship as by all other officers and people belonging to her, with the decency and regard due to the commissions they bear'. The junior marine officers lived in the gunroom but messed in the wardroom, and it was not unusual for marine officers to lead a life detached from the rest of the wardroom. Robert Wilson, who served in the *Unité* (40) between 1805 and 1808, wrote 'the lieutenants do not keep any watch except in urgent cases, such as prisoners on board, etc. They have nothing to do in regard of the naval manoeuvres of the ship. In short, they have the easiest life of any officer on board.'[34]

The marine officers were in command of the marine detachment; in the first decade of the war detachments from line regiments served in place of marines, both on board ship and in barracks to release marines for sea. There were early difficulties with using soldiers aboard ship; in particular, some of their officers maintained they were not subject to naval discipline, were disinclined to follow naval officers, objected to naval discipline being applied to soldiers and so on. The trouble came to a head on board the *Diadem* (64) in San Fiorenzo Bay, in 1795, when Lieutenant George Fitzgerald of the 69th Foot was court-martialled for behaving with contempt to Charles Tyler, captain of the ship, on 24 May. Fitzgerald denied the court's authority to prosecute an army officer except 'in cases of mutiny or crimes of such magnitude on board ship as require immediate investigation'; the court, which included Nelson, Young, Rowley and Hyde Parker, disagreed, found him guilty, dismissed him from the service and rendered him incapable of ever serving His Majesty, his heirs and successors, in any military capacity. When he arrived at Bastia he was ordered to rejoin his regiment; when the King confirmed the court martial he applied for trial by a military court. He was eventually reinstated on 20 January 1797 but retired on 2 November 1798. Meanwhile, on 24 October 1795 the War Office had issued a directive to soldiers setting out the state of discipline aboard ship; it included the rule that private soldiers who committed offences for which the navy authorised immediate punishment (*eg* flogging) might be so punished if their commanding officer concurred (if not they were to be disembarked and court-martialled), and on 28 October the Admiralty issued an additional article of war, stating that all forces embarked in ships of war or transports were under the command of the senior officer of the ship, and above him the commander of the fleet. All line-regiment detachments serving as marines had returned to their duty by 1798, but a few military units are found serving after that date, such as the Garrison of Gibraltar in the *Calpe* (14) in November 1801.[35]

The marine privates' main role in the routine life of the ship was to provide sentinels, and their NCOs' was to inspect and organise them, and sometimes to substitute as ship's corporals and the like. The officers' duties centred on supervising them and keeping them clean and orderly. In the *Blenheim* (98) in the Mediterranean in 1796 a subaltern was 'to visit all the marines' berths during the time of [their] dinner and to inspect the same during the afternoon, to see that order and regularity is preserved', and when Sir John Jervis was on board the officer of the guard was to parade the guard at half-past five o'clock, report to the commanding officer and dismiss them; in the *Mars* (74) in 1799 they were more particularly to be present in uniform 'at the reading of the Articles of War, all punishments and at prayers ... the exercise of the guns, loosing and furling sails', 'when all hands are called', attending the capstan when mooring or unmooring to 'suppress the absurd custom of huzzaing', to inspect the men of their commands frequently, especially 'during and after meal times to see that the men have every comfort, and their utensils clean and that no pretence may be made to leave them, or dirt or greens, about the decks afterwards', to be present when marines were ordered in boats and to accompany parties of more than twelve ashore and, untypically, to keep a watch at sea.[36]

Sickberth

After breakfast in the wardroom the surgeon went forward to the sickberth to examine his patients. Visiting the sick and wounded at least twice was one of the three daily tasks set out in the regulations; he also had to report to the captain every morning the condition of the men under his care, whether in the sick bay or elsewhere and to keep at least five separate journals and returns.[37]

The sickberth in the *Splendid*, which accommodated twenty-two men, was of the modern form: it was on the starboard side, and

> takes in the two foremost guns under the forecastle, and all that space from the ship's side to the fore-mast, so that it includes the round-house [toilet] and head-door, and also the midships, which was formerly occupied by a pig-stye. The head-door is converted into a sash-window, and occasionally into venetian blinds. Over the midships is a large sky-light, which gives a cheerful appearance to the whole, and in warm weather is thrown open, so as to cause a fresh current of air to pass through the ports and head-window. The walls of the sick-berth are [panels of deal]. The furniture consists of commodious benches and a settee for the weakly people to recline upon. Tubs and pails for washing, cooking vessels, with towels and clean canvas tablecloths, dishes, spoons, knives and forks, etc., complete the utensils, all of which are kept in fine order in concealed lockers within the sick berth. A canvas cot or two, with hospital bedding, neatly surrounded with white calico curtains, are kept for fractures or particular surgical cases. The utmost attention is paid to cleanliness and purity, which is easily done, as the round-house is often washed. In cold or damp weather a hanging-stove with clear embers is brought in and also when the deck is scrubbed.
>
> The space between the head-doors and under the sky-light is used as a dispensary and elegantly fitted with a desk; and along the head are ranged the drawers and bottles for present use, in a style of neatness that would do credit to the first apothecary's shop in London.[38]

There was a stove lit with 'clear-burning cinders', even in June, not for 'the comfortable warmth of the patients' but 'to prevent dampness and purify the air'. This account is given by her surgeon; it was inevitable, however, that because the sick-bay was immediately aft of the head, it took on an odour whenever the wind was unfavourable, and whenever it blew fresh, 'the sea', in the words of a visitor, 'defiled by a thousand horrible intermixtures', came into the sickbay and on occasion passed through it, 'augmenting most severely the misery of the patients', and adding to their 'writhings, sighs, and moans of acute pain', their 'pale countenance, which looks like resignation, but is despair; bandages soaked in blood and matter; the foetor of sores, and the vermin from which it is impossible to preserve the invalid entirely free'.[39]

For his morning inspection the surgeon examined the patients already in his care and those presenting to him, 'distinguishing such of them as are capable of going to quarters, doing day duty, acting as sentinels or other light work', and drawing up a list which was copied by his assistant. The list was given to the captain at 9.30, or as soon after as possible, and the copy to the officer of the watch.[40]

> I see my patients which takes up half an hour or an hour. From that to
> eleven generally read or write in my cabin, then take a walk on deck …
> After having stretched my limbs [to see] how we steer and how the wind
> blows, I come down to my cabin again and take up a book again till the
> drum beating 'The Roast Beef of Old England' warns me to dinner, of
> which I generally have a fore-feeling in my stomach.[41]

The surgeon was the warrant officer whose role changed the most visibly between 1793 and 1810. He was now supplied with medicines, instead of providing them himself, though he still brought his own instruments, and whereas in the eighteenth century it had been recommended that sick men remain with their messmates to be cared for, he now had a dedicated sick berth, but the most apparent change was in the new emphasis on fumigation. The surgeon of the *Blonde* (32) in 1793 examined the sick in the cockpit after breakfast, then after they had left fumigated it with a heated iron bar put into a bucket of tar, but the *Mars* in 1805 fumigated the whole ship, 'twice a week or oftener in damp weather by keeping fire in the [airing] stoves, by burning tar with a logger heat [head], or by firing small quantities of gunpowder made into squibs with vinegar, keeping the ports down and the hatches closed, or by firing a small quantity of strakings in one or more iron pots, and some trusty mates and midshipmen attending to the same.' Other agents used were brimstone and charcoal. This was entirely congruous with contemporary understanding of the pathology of bad air; in 1808 Captain Martin reported the loss of several men and the precarious state of others in the *Implacable* (74), caused by the easterly wind at Plymouth.[42]

Following success in defeating typhus in prison ships, receiving ships and hulks in the 1790s, a Select Committee of the House of Commons recommended in 1802 the nitrous acid process invented by Dr Smyth, and instructions for its use were included in the 1808 Regulations:

> Such a number of pipkins [small earthenware pots] as may be necessary,
> are to be two-thirds filled with sand previously heated. In this heated sand
> is to be inserted a gallypot [a small earthen glazed pot], into which is to

be poured one measure of concentrated vitriolic acid, (when it has acquired some degree of heat;) a measure of the pure nitre in powder, is then to be gradually added, and the mixture stirred with the glass spatula, until the vapour arises in considerable quantity. The pipkins are then to be carried to every part of the ship, where foul air is suspected to lodge.[43]

The vapour from three pipkins 'was in such quantity that a ward 57 feet by 20, and 10 feet 6 inches high, was filled with it' in fifteen minutes. The surgeon of the *Union* reported it 'destroys all the frowzy disagreeable smells arising from the emanations of many people being crowded together, and leaves the ship sweet for several hours after.'[44] The method used by James Glegg, surgeon of the *Defiance* (74) in 1798, was to hold

the pipkins under the hammocks of those with feverish symptoms; and at night, eight were carried about the decks when all hammocks and people were below; and this was attended with very little inconvenience to those in health ... [For] ulcers and foul sores I in general have a pot in fumigation, when I visit the sick in the cockpit, which I really think, independent of the utility of applying sores over it, tends to purify the air and dispel fætor; its smoak is particularly pleasant to me, and I often have it in my cabin when the sick are below.[45]

The nitrous acid process, according to the Select Committee, prevented 'the communication of the most virulent contagion', and was particularly useful aboard ship because 'it may be used in places the most crowded with sick, without injury to any class of patients'; and further, it 'not only prevents infection, but ... by improving the quality of the air, it facilitates respiration', and by 'infusing confidence into the minds of the nurses and other persons employed about the sick, tends to procure for them that assiduous attendance, which may either promote their recovery from the disease, or alleviate their sufferings under its continuance.'*

The committee was equally impressed by the acid's ability to treat ulcers, a particularly common and debilitating condition on board ship, not least because 'it has been frequently observed' that 'all the ulcers of patients in the same ward have on a sudden, and nearly at one and the same time, changed from apparently

---

* Both Lind and Trotter advised against it, but the committee was satisfied that they had made statistical and other mistakes in their presentations, and that Trotter's chemistry was faulty. All those who had tried it, including James M'Grigor, then surgeon of the 88th Regiment, recommended it. The French surgeons did not approve of it, and they burnt 'a few pounds of juniper berries daily in each hospital' instead.

an healthy to a foul, sloughing, or putrid state.' One of the testimonies it heard was Dr Snipe's, who on his appointment as surgeon of the *Sandwich* receiving ship at the Nore in March 1797 found 'a highly contagious fever raging in the ship' and of the 1,000–1,300 on board, he had a daily sick list of 80–130, of whom seven-eighths had the fever. 'The virulence of the contagion was such … until the nitrous fumigation was used, that the smallest scratch on the skin rapidly degenerated into an incurable ulcer, and the loss of muscular substance was so great, with caries of the adjacent bones, that a number of the patients lost their limbs, when they were sent to the hospital-ship at Sheerness.' The sick list diminished after a week to that of a line-of-battle ship. Daniel Stowell had an ulcer on his right leg, 'extending from the outer ancle [*sic*] across the anterior part of the tibia to the gastroenemius muscle, at which part it was four inches board and very deep, and discharged a thick ill-conditioned matter, which was very offensive: its length was rather more than ten inches.' After fumigation, it was cicatrized on 30 October, and he was sent to New South Wales.[46]

Medical supplies for the fleet were revised by Dr Trotter in 1794, who printed a comparative list for a 74's monthly allowance in his *Medicina Nautica* of 1804. For comparison the Navy Board's 'surgeon's necessaries for three months for 100 men', established in 1784, are given here.[47]

1784, 100 men		*Old Form 1794*		*New Form, 1794*		*Regulations, 1808, 100 men*	
brown sugar	24lb	lump sugar	48lb	finer new linen	12yds	new linen	6yds
rice	9	tea	1	Welch linen (bandages)	8	Welsh flannel	4
barley	9	currants	20	tea	8lb	tea	4½lb
Zante currants	10	rice	18	cocoa or coffee	12	sago	4
tamarinds	1.5	barley	18	sago	8	rice	8
mace	2	sago	10	rice	16	barley*	16
cinnamon	4	almonds	1½	barley	32	soft sugar	32
nutmegs	4	tamarinds	3	fine soft sugar	65	ginger	2oz
common sago	5	garlick	4	ginger	¼	saucepans	1
almonds	3	shallots	8oz	saucepans, strong	4	cannisters for sago	1
garlic	2	mace	2	canisters	2	ditto for tea	1
shallots	4 bushels	cinnamon	4	boxes	1		
new linen	6 yards	nutmegs	2				
saucepans	2	new linen	12yds				
box & card	1	saucepans	4				
pot for tamarinds	1	boxes	1				
bag for garlic	1	canisters	2				
a 5lb canister for sago							

* Replaced by macaroni in the Mediterranean, and arrowroot in the West Indies.

This was separate from the medicines and from the utensils supplied, which included soap, bedpans and urinals, spitting pots, tourniquets, spatulas, funnels and marble and metal mortars and pestles. The principal complaints, according to form no. 39, the weekly return of sick and wounded, were intermittent fevers, continued fevers, catarrhs, pneumonic inflammation, phthisis pulmonalis ('a disease of the lungs which is characterized by progressive consolidation of the pulmonary texture, and by the subsequent softening and disintegration of the consolidated tissue'), rheumatism, venereal disease, scurvy, ulcers and wounds and accidents; form no. 38, the surgeon's abstract of his service in a ship, also included fluxes.

A further important duty, not stated in the 1790 regulations but made explicit in the 1808 edition, was to 'inspect men newly recruited on board', 'not only very carefully to examine their persons, to discover whether they have any disease, or are in any other respect unfit for the service, but he is also to enquire very particularly in what situations they have been for some time past, that he may be able to judge whether there be any risque of their carrying an infectious disorder into the Ship, that if there be, proper precautions may be taken to prevent it.' This was matched by the regulations relating to the marines: 'none are to be sent or received on board, but such as of are age and strength fit for service ... and have no distemper upon them'; and if they were refused, the captain of the ship was 'strictly required' to return with them 'his reasons in writing under his hand'.[48]

BREAKFAST ON THE LOWER DECK
TO ONE BELL

At eight bells in the morning watch – the beginning of the forenoon watch – the boatswain's mates piped to breakfast. It was usual in the navy for the whole ship's company, sailors, marines and petty officers, to eat together in their berths, the work of the ship permitting, leaving only lookouts and sentinels on deck and on duty.

In 1810 the Royal Navy organised its ship's companies in three ways, as it had done for a generation: into watches (traditionally two, but sometimes three), messes and divisions. Once the men were berthed, that is assigned places to hang their hammocks, they were formed into messes: the berthing plan used by the navy included a 'form for messing the crew which makes the number of each man's mess become the number of his mess place'. In a ship-of-the-line, almost all the berths were between the guns, with the remainder along the centre, in the galley and in the cable tiers. Each berth had a table, made of deals (fir or spruce planks 9in wide, not more than 3in thick and at least 6ft long), nailed together; it swung down from the deck and was fitted with benches and stools. In a frigate it was usual to have one mess per table, but in a ship-of-the-line the tables were large enough to have two messes, one each side. Since the berth deck on a frigate was at the waterline it had no ports, and the tables could remain in place during the day and night,* but in a ship-of-the-line they were swung neatly to the deck above when not in use. The mess, a group of eight to twelve men, ate, slept and lived together. According to Captain Hall, 'A petty officer or leading man, who is styled captain of the mess, is at the head of each; and in a well-disciplined ship, he is in some manner responsible for the good conduct and cleanliness of the others. He also signs for [the receipt of] short allowance money, savings, and so on.' The captain of the mess was appointed by the first lieutenant or the captain. Each mess also had a cook, who did not actually cook but collected the food from the purser's steward each day, took it to the galley and supervised its distribution to the mess. This job was typically rotated around the mess – Captain Hall says daily. It was usual for marines and sailors to mess separately, and in some ships they were discouraged even from talking to each other, but examples can be found when they messed together, particularly when a marine was serving as a petty officer of the ship.[49]

Successful messes formed communities, and depended on each other even to preparing each other's corpses for burial. The importance of this sense of community is shown by the case of William Stiles, private marine, of the *Jupiter* (50), who in 1803 had a series of mad fits: William Goodson, the surgeon, noted that he was reported insensible on 16 January. He said, 'I found he had been slighted by his messmates and that he messed by himself. I thought it probable that this might have some effect on his mind which might wear off on his being taken into a proper mess, which I understood was done'; he slowly got better and 'appeared rational' by 10 February. In this foundation on eating and drinking together the messes directly mimicked the gunroom and wardroom, even to developing their own private antagonisms with other messes and naming themselves. In a deliberate reversal of this custom, four men who were in disgrace in the *Belliqueux* (64) in 1799 were made to mess in the galley and call themselves the Thieves' Mess, which was apparently a common practice; Anselm Griffiths, captain of the *Constance* (22) and *Leonidas* (38) frigates, had 'a drunken, a dirty, a blackguard and a thieves mess', and 'instead of being numbered, they were called by these names at the grog tub, the cook's coppers, etc, [which] had more effect than corporal punishment.'[50]

Watches and divisions were assigned by the first lieutenant; messes were

---

* The ship's corporal of the *Castor* in 1810, Solomon Nathan, was a sexual predator who preyed on boys, one of whom 'ran along under the tables' to escape him one night at nine or ten o'clock.

valued by the men because although they were put into one on joining the ship they could change at set intervals (usually each month). According to Captain Hall, 'the only perfectly free privilege which the interfering nature of our sea discipline allows to our sailors, is their choice of messmates', and the procedure was straightforward: the man gave 'timely intimation to the mate of the lower deck, and to the purser's steward, at the end of the month, to arrange his mess-book; no other sanction or form being necessary.' 'The captain, first lieutenant, and mate of the lower-deck, correct their mess-books every month from that of the purser's steward, to enable them to estimate the characters of the men who mess together, and in order to assist in referring to his associates when the conduct of any one is called into question.' It was possible for a man to join a mess without the knowledge of some of its members, so presumably the arrangement was made directly with the captain of the mess.[51]

Many officers thought an inside knowledge of the mess system was essential for a midshipman's education. In the *Mediator* (44), Captain Collingwood took on board a boy called Pennyman to oblige a relation, but he proved to be

quite a plague, a dirty lad without one good quality to set against a great many bad ones. He is the dirtiest, laziest boy in the ship, gets drunk, neglects his duty, learns no one thing, has been in every mess in the ship, and been turn'd out of them all. In his cups abuses the lieutenants and heeds my advice as much as he does theirs. He will never be an officer as long as he lives ... He's excluded by the other boys from their society and leads a miserable life by himself, and what to do with him I don't know.[52]

He had more success with Jeffrey de Raigersfeld, who wrote that Collingwood put him and another midshipman to mess with the men for three months, 'performing all the offices of the ship boys such as cooking the victuals, standing the rank at the ship's copper for the beef, burgoo and pease soup, and cleaning the mess platters': 'during those three months I gained more knowledge of the seamen's character, than in all the other ships I have since served in during the trials I have undergone in my profession.' When Collingwood was a vice admiral in the *Culloden*, in 1804, he gave Robert Hay and the other boys in the ship to 'the best seaman of the mess to which he belonged, with orders to look carefully after him, to teach him good behaviour, and all the little operations of seamanship.'[53]

Jack Nastyface recorded that in a line-of-battle ship

Nearly all the crew have [a hook-pot for boiling Scotch coffee and burgoo], a spoon, and a knife; for these are things indispensable: there are also basons, plates, &c. which are kept in each mess ... It sometimes happens that a lurch will dash all the crockery to pieces; they are then obliged to eat out of wooden or tin utensils, until they come into harbour, where they get another supply.[54]

Memoirs of those who served later in the war are more likely to mention finery in the men's messes. When the *Macedonian* was ordered to sea, having refitted at Plymouth, 'Most of the men laid out money in getting new clothing; some of it went to buy pictures, looking-glasses, crockery ware, &c to ornament our berths, so that they bore some resemblance to a cabin.'[55] This seems to have been more common in frigates, especially those with a stable company, than ships of the line, but when the ship's company of the *Blake* (74) received prize-money in 1812, they used it to improve their berths:

The prize-money has done the ship great credit, owing, perhaps, in some measure, to the power I have here of preventing the introduction of extra liquor. For, besides good clothing, every mess-place in the ship is ornamented with gold, according to their several tastes, at their own expense, and with some degree of uniformity in the shelves, broken by the little variety of their own paintings and ornaments; which, marking contented choice rather than the hand of power, the whole produces a very pleasing effect.[56]

The midshipmen's messes, on the orlop deck, were usually better equipped than the men's: Raigersfeld's mess in the *Mediator* had

a few pounds of tea and brown sugar, a couple of sacks of potatoes, and about sixty pounds of beef taken up from the purser, which was salted down and put into a small cask for to serve as fresh provisions during the voyage [from Spithead to the West Indies]: our spoons and plates were pewter, a dozen of knives and forks, two cooking kettles, a frying-pan, and a copper tea-kettle, these with a dozen tumbler glasses, two decanters, and a dozen teacups and saucers, of the old blue dragon fashion, with a tin teapot, some celery seeds and onions to make pea soup savoury, was all the stock midshipmen at that time thought of taking to sea; and this was stored in the lockers in the berth upon which we sat, and all within the old canvass screen [nailed to the beams].[57]

The usual allowance for breakfast on Monday, Wednesday and Friday was burgoo, which in the Royal Navy meant oatmeal boiled in water, sometimes sweetened with sugar or molasses (in 1806 the oatmeal ration had been halved and 6oz of sugar substituted). It was made by gradually adding water to oatmeal in the proportion of a quart to a pint, then boiling it for a quarter of an hour then adding a little salt, butter and sugar. James Durand was served burgoo as a prisoner of war and did not think much of it: 'The first sustenance I received on board ... was some boiled oat-meal without salt or butter or other seasoning. In America we ordinarily feed our swine better than this, but I was obliged to eat it to preserve life.' Burgoo was standard in the merchant service as well: William Richardson belonged to the *Forester*, from Cartagena to Philadelphia in 1786: 'On our passage our beef began to get short, and in order to make it hold out another mess was ordered for us for breakfast, which was oatmeal and flour boiled together like hasty pudding, and some wine poured on the top as a sub-stitute for butter: there was much grumbling at this at first, but in a few days we got reconciled to it, and liked nothing better.'[58]

There were various semi-formal substitutions: in the *Lion* in 1795, Lieu-tenant Pringle asked the captain 'if he approved of the ship's company having pease on Monday at dinner, in the room of the oatmeal for breakfast on the banyan [meatless] days, as was customary in many ships'; in the *Windsor Castle* in 1794, Lieutenant McKinley proposed and was given permission by Captain Cock to give the men 'water gruel for breakfast every morning instead of burgoo on the usual days, as being a more comfortable meal for them in my opinion', and the hands, on being turned up, agreed that they liked it, 'saying it was much better for them'. Lind recommended water-gruel in the morning, 'with a proper quantity of eschalot, onions, leeks, or garlic, boiled in it', instead of burgoo, as 'the proper antidote to the hurtful influences of cold and damp weather at sea'. On the East India station burgoo was replaced by rice, either boiled dry, or served slightly wet and known as congee; on the West India station it was replaced by cocoa in the 1780s, which became popular throughout the navy (Trotter thought cocoa much healthier). It also replaced rancid butter and cheese. The importance of the oatmeal from the navy's point of view was twofold: it was an effective way of supplying the men with a hot breakfast, and its acidity made it valuable in balancing the salt-meat diet (for example Lind argued in 1753 that bread is fermented, and so the 'glutinous viscidity and tena-cious oils ... are broken and subdued', making it 'adapted by its acescency [sour-ness] to correct a flesh diet', but biscuit is not, and 'will in too many cases afford too tenacious and viscid chyle'; the most acescent part of their diet was the burgoo, but the allowance was generally more than the men could use). It was not inspiring, particularly for the watch that had come off deck, and its absence does not seem to have been mourned.[59]

> Court: You say the ships company have never had their breakfast boiled from the 5th to 29th December [1807]. Did you ever hear them or any of them complain of their want of the hot breakfast?
> A: I did not.[60]

Sailors in the *Ganges* (74) in 1783 'would go to the steward and get a bowlful of oatmeal and make a cake of it and bake it in the hot ashes till it was done and sell it to the poor fellows [the soldiers she was transporting] for six mens allowance of wine, which was three pints'. An alternative was Scotch coffee, 'which is burnt bread boiled in some water, and sweetened with sugar. This is generally cooked in a hook-pot in the galley, where there is a range.'[61]

The men were permitted to store their biscuit in bags, and to exchange the dust (the crumbs) that collected for an equal weight of new biscuit in the afternoons: bread was popular with the goats, which came below and were treated as pets. John Blake was having breakfast one August morning on board the *Rippon* (60) when the goat came down to his berth: 'I gave her a piece of bread, and tye'd up the bag and hung it up, and then went to the larboard side and lay down under the gun, and the goat followed me, she was taking a piece of bread out of my pockett'. The *Swiftsure* (74) had Mrs Taffy, a Welsh nanny goat, who came to the wardroom each afternoon for her biscuit and grog – until one day in 1810, when the ship was off Halifax, Nova Scotia, she went into the wardroom and ate an officer's letters from home. She was banished for a month, until the affair was forgotten. The lieutenant had to wait eight months for copies of the letters. Bread bags were scrubbed clean at the same time as the hammocks.[62]

Tea and cocoa were also issued, as substitutions, at the rate of a quarter of a pound of tea or half a pound of cocoa for a pound of cheese. Since sugar was issued at the rate of 2oz a day on oatmeal days, and as a substitution at a pound for a pound of butter or two pounds of cheese, it was practicable for messes to save both tea and cocoa for breakfast.[63]

Cocoa came from the Caribbean and was very fashionable; tea was black tea imported from China by the East India Company (which supplied it free to its ships' companies), and which Sir Gilbert Blane thought entirely meritorious: 'Tea is an article universally grateful to the British population, and has to a certain degree supplanted intoxicating liquors', and he recommended its widespread use in the navy. He rejected the claim that 'its supposed relaxing property' 'unbraced' 'British nerves'. Some, particularly petty officers' messes, bought their own, and there are examples of seamen possessing teacups aboard ship.[64]

WASHING AND AIRING THE LOWER DECK
ONE BELL TO SIX BELLS

The ship's company was allowed half an hour for breakfast. Captain Troubridge, who commanded the *Culloden* (74) in the Mediterranean Fleet, set his men dancing every morning after breakfast, 'so that the exercise just keeps them in health', but in the *Splendid*, 'At half-past eight o'clock, or one-bell in the forenoon watch, the larboard [watch] goes on deck and the starboard remains below.' The current Admiralty regulations ordered the captain to give directions that the 'lower decks are washed as often as the weather will admit of their being properly dried'; and 'swept twice, at least, every day'. In the *Splendid* the lower deck was washed only on Saturdays, and only then if it could be properly dried; the heavy weather had prevented the lower-deck ports from being opened, and the regulations provided that it should be scrubbed with dry sand instead, and fires lit in the airing stoves supplied by Brodie. For a naval surgeon in 1810 this emphasis on driving out damp embodied the reaction against the persistent washing of the lower deck of the previous century. Dr Trotter wrote that 'we have often seen this baleful practice of washing decks persisted in, till the very planks became green with a vegitating substance, and appeared like the inside of a tank, or the bed of a pond', a custom that 'savoured equally of ignorance and cruelty', and extracts from surgeons' journals presented to the House of Commons select committee on nitrous acid show that by the end of the 1790s some ships, on the surgeon's advice, suspended washing the decks for months to preserve their companies' health, and used airing stoves or dry sand or both instead.* Congruent with this was the need to replace 'the foul air which lodges in ship's decks', named by Dr Trotter as the 'residuum of respiration' (*ie* nitrogen), with clean dry air as an antiscorbutic. In the orlop and storerooms it mixed with carbon dioxide rising from the well, and in the breadroom with 'putrefaction' from cheese, so that 'I consider the bread-room of a ship, from its present pent-up condition, the number of lights so frequently burning in it, and the noxious effluvia issuing from cheese, etc., as a species of volcano that is constantly throwing out pestifer-

---

* The *Formidable* (74) under the care of Mr Blair was healthy between October 1800 and January 1801, during which period 'no disease has particularly prevailed, and the complaints put on the list have been generally slight … The ship's decks were kept remarkably clean, but were seldom washed; fires were kept burning on the lower deck, as often as circumstances would admit'; the *Caesar* had an outbreak of typhus in January and February 1800, during which time 'no washing of the decks as usual was allowed, they were cleared [*sic*] by scraping and rubbing with dry sand'.

ous fumes to shorten and weaken life'.⁶⁵

The log of Captain Thomas Troubridge's *Culloden* for December 1794 and January 1795 typifies the belief in clean dry air. On 3 December, when she was at Spithead, the ship's company mutinied, believing her unsafe after an earlier grounding: the mutiny was suppressed on the 11th. The mutineers had remained below decks all that time, and the ship was immediately cleaned.

> 11 December 1794: 'got the cables on deck to clean the tiers washed ditto with vinegar and with hanging stoves … cleared hawse'
> 12 December 1794: 'cleared hawse and between deck with Brodies stoves Got the hawsers and stream cable on deck to clean out the tier'
> 15 and 20 December 1794: 'washed and aired between decks with Brodies stoves'
> 22, 23 and 24 December 1794: 'aired between decks with Brodies stoves'
> 26 December 1794: 'Empd. washing and cleaning the ship and between decks with Brodies stoves and hanging ditto'
> 30 December 1794: 'aired between decks with Brodies stoves'
> 31 December 1794: 'washed and aired between decks with Brodies stoves'
> 21 and 23 January 1795: 'aired between decks with Brodies Stoves'
> 26 January 1795: 'aired betwn. decks'
> 27 January 1795: 'Empd. washing and cleaning the ship'
> On 30 January she sailed for Torbay; on the 2nd the *Blonde* frigate tacked and dropped on board of her, carrying away her spanker boom.
> 3 February 1795: 'Employ'd washing and cleaning the ship'
> 4 February 1795, now in Torbay: 'aired between decks with Brodies stoves'
> 10 February 1795: 'Got the stream cable and hawsers on deck to clean the tier and wash it with vinegar, aired between decks with Brodies stoves.'
> On 15 February she sailed down Channel.⁶⁶

Just as the Mediterranean Fleet had changed its practices in washing the weather decks, so had there been a similar change from washing the lower deck early every day to only when necessary. In 1798 St Vincent had directed that his ships began at a quarter past eight in the morning, summer and winter, and 'this operation is to be performed, the decks swabbed and fire lighted [in the galley] by ten o'clock in the morning, at the latest',⁶⁷ but in 1801 Lord Keith changed this to:

> The lower deck is not to be washed oftener than once in fourteen days, unless the weather is dry, and immediately after washing stoves and fires

are to be lighted, and the men to be prevented from going below till the deck is quite dry. Wood or stone rubbers are to be used [instead], with which the decks are to be cleansed every day by their respective messes. Fires are never to be neglected when fuel can be procured, nor white washing with lime or vinegar, when time and circumstances admits [*sic*]. Smoke of pitch, sulphur or tobacco will be found to be salutary; and likewise and attention to the use of wind-sails; the opening of the doors of store rooms; the airing of beds and bags; the unlaying of gratings; and the keeping of the men on deck when the weather is fine.[68]

Airing stoves had been issued since 1783: they were portable iron machines that rested on a square frame, with a copper funnel; a new design by Brodie was introduced shortly afterwards whose description suggests it was intended to remain burning at night, when the air was most clogged with residuum. From 1793 ships were also issued with Moser and Jackson's fumigating lamps, which came with a tin japanned case to swing in. Since 1808 it had been part of the surgeon's instructions that when the lower-deck ports were not opened, and the 'breath and perspiration of the men sleeping below render the space between decks replete with moisture and noxious effluvia', he was to 'submit to the captain the propriety of keeping the ship as dry and sweet as circumstances will admit, for which purpose he is to recommend that iron pots or hanging stoves with burning cinders be carried between decks, into the well, and every other part of the ship where they can be placed with safety, where the air is stagnant and offensive from defect of ventilation.' Ships-of-the-line making full use of their allowance for their airing stoves were burning about a twentieth of their consumption of coals in the Channel Fleet, and in the Mediterranean Fleet about a fifteenth.[69]

The first task in the *Splendid* was to sweep the deck 'as completely as possible, from the extremity of the ship forward to the bulkhead of the gun room aft', under the direction of the mate of the watch, then the cabins of the gun-room. The watch then divided into several parties, some of whom went down to the orlop to clean thoroughly there. The newer procedure is described by Jack Nastyface: 'Here again the *holy-stones* or *hand-bibles* as they are called by the crew, are used, and sometimes iron scrapers. After the lower deck has been wetted with swabs, these scrapers are used to take the rough dirt off.' Falconer's description suggests the scrapers were very like a modern floor scraper; Professor Lewis believed the sand was heated.[70]

THE GUNNER IN THE MAGAZINE

The first and perhaps the most essential branch of the gunner's duty was to keep the powder rooms 'well secured, clean, and in right order', and to ensure that the powder was stored correctly. The standard barrels produced by the royal powder mills were copper- or hazel-hooped, and contained 75lb saltpetre, 15lb sulphur and 10lb charcoal; in 1805, copper-hooped barrels cost 7s 7d each and the ordinary hazel-hooped ones 4s 0d. Annual consumption by the navy was about 40,000 barrels, and that summer the country had 129,705 barrels in store. The 1790 Regulations directed that 'the powder in copper-hooped barrels be lodged in the ground tier, and last expended'; this article was dropped by 1808, but a new direction warned against allowing the gun-metal adzes to hit the copper, 'there being several instances of strong sparks of fire having been produced from the collision of a metal adze against a metal setter, or a copper hoop.' In 1808 he was told to turn the barrels 'once at least in every three months, to prevent the separation of the nitre [the saltpetre] from the other ingredients', a duty that would have seemed absurd in 1790, in the era of twelve-week cruises. Despite these instructions he was not allowed to go or to send anyone into the powder rooms without the captain's permission.[71]

The charge of powder traditionally used in long guns in action was 17lb for a 32lb shot, 11lb for a 24lb shot, 9lb for an 18lb shot and 6lb for a 12lb shot, progressively reduced to one-third the weight as the gun got hot. In September 1793 the proportions had been reduced for the Channel Fleet, and the accompanying instructions clearly show the detail and regulation of a gunner's life, and why when William Richardson was appointed acting gunner (against his will) in the *Prompte* (28) in September 1795 he studied the art of gunnery and learnt from his 'brother officers ... how to keep my books and make up my accounts of stores.'[72]

It is requested that the commanding officers of His Majestys [ships] will direct their respective gunners to enter in their expence books the day they receive this *new proportion of powder* that in passing their accounts at the Tower [of London: gunners were appointed by warrant from the Ordnance Board, not the Navy Board] the old proportion may be allowed for all expended before that time. As the powder measures on board the ships already fitted are calculated for the old allowance it is recommended to the gunners to weigh *one charge* of the new proportion and cut down *a case of wood* to contain the exact quantity which will serve as a measure until such time as they are supplied with *wooden cones* to fix in the bottoms of their present measures that will take up a space in them equal to the quantity of powder to be reduced which *cones* will be issued to them from any of the offices of ordnance on their application (with copper screws to fix them on) or with measures in which they are already fix'd in lieu of their others) [*sic*] as soon as a sufficient number can be provided for that purpose. The proportion for salutes and scaling may be ascertained by the above method of cutting down a case of wood to hold the proper quantity –

NB The allowance for *Exercise* & *Signals* to be the same as that for *Salutes*.[73]

In the spring of 1801 the Ordnance Board had begun issuing gunpowder made with charcoal that had been charred in cylindrical ovens, which was more powerful than the traditional powder because the charcoal burned more evenly than pit-burnt charcoal. The old powder was exchanged for the new, beginning with ships-of-the-line, and there were now two sorts of cartridge, with powder one-third the weight of the shot for firing one round, and one-quarter for firing

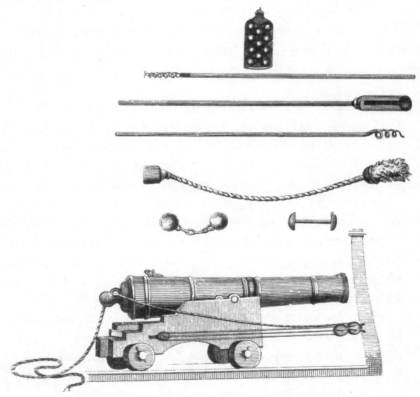

A long gun of 1810, its equipment and ammunition, including grapeshot (top) and bar- and chain-shot (just above the gun).

double-shotted. New measures were again supplied. From 1804 there were four sorts of powder, red long grain, white long grain, white long and white returned (recycled): the red LG was for distance shooting, the white LG or returned powder or white L for close fighting, and only returned or white L to be used for salutes and scaling. From 1808, ships on Foreign service received five-sevenths red LG, and on Channel service, four-sevenths. The charge was a third of the weight of the shot for single-shotted guns, and a quarter for double-shotted. Experiments conducted by the board had shown that a shot with a charge of one-third of powder at 2° elevation struck the target at first fall at 1,200 yards and upwards, and with one-fourth at 1,000 yards and upwards; double-shotted with one-fourth charge hit the target at 500 yards and upwards before the first fall, but the board 'recommended that the use of two shots for each round should be restrained as much as possible, it having appeared from various experiments which have been made with different natures [calibres] of Sea Service ordnance, that after firing twenty rounds repeatedly at only the interval of five minutes between each round, the gun has become so violently heated as to render it extremely hazardous to continue the firing at that rate.'[74]

The damage caused by increased sizes of roundshot was in proportion to the square of the diameter.[75] Experiments made in 1810 show its destructive power.

A butt of wood was constructed at 100 yards distance from the guns, 9 feet long, 6 feet high, and 5 feet 2 inches thick; it was made of sleepers of fir, 9 inches square, placed alternately horizontal and perpendicular, except two thicknesses of deal planks of 3 inches thick by 1 foot broad, placed one horizontally and the other perpendicularly; the butt was connected by five iron bars passing from front to rear, and by four bars passing from one end to the other. It was strongly shoared up behind by two deal planks of 4 inches thick, 1 foot broad, and 12 feet long, nailed to horizontal pieces placed in the ground; behind the butt were also placed two unserviceable 18 pounder garrison carriages run close to the butt, and with their hind trucks taken off.

The 24 pounder of 6½ feet [length] was fired double-shotted and at point blank, twenty-one times at this butt, with a charge of 4lbs ... On examining the butt it appeared much broken and ruined; ten of the balls had gone quite through to the average distance of 50 yards, many of the other shot were broken, one of the garrison gun-carriages moved back two feet, the iron trucks broken, and a capsquare knocked off to the distance of 50 yards, to which distance considerable splinters of the wood were driven. The iron bars which connected the butt were twisted and bent as if they had been of wire. The average penetration of such balls as did not go through the butt was about four feet, that is, one foot eight inches more than the thickness of a 74 gun ship near her lower-deck ports.[76]

The gunner kept accounts recording the expenditure or loss of all the stores and equipment under his command, and at midsummer and Christmas each year submitted an abstract to the captain, who audited them before the gunner sent them to the Ordnance Office. His routine tasks included checking the state of the guns, the muskets and the small arms; keeping the shot racks, the powder horns and the boxes of priming full; exposing the grapeshot to sun and wind, to prevent the bags getting mildewed; causing the iron pins of the blocks for gun-tackles 'to be knocked out, and to be oiled or greased', so that they did not rust from their exposure to sea water; and cutting spare cordage into breachings, tackles, muzzle lashings, port ropes and port tackle falls, according to an established table of dimensions.[77]

The guns were immensely heavy, the largest 32pdr weighing 5½cwt and the lightest 18pdr 27cwt, and establishing, checking and maintaining the breachings and tackles in good order was extremely important. Captain Glascock, who served in frigates and ships-of-the-line, wrote a *Naval Officer's Manual* in 1848, in which he described what happened when this was not done 'on board a ship of the line, scudding in a heavy gale of wind, homeward bound from Jamaica'.

The ship was a fast sailer, and, like most fast sailers, a 'heavy roller'. The preparatory pipe of 'Stand by hammocks!' had hardly escaped the lips of the boatswain, when the second master, rapidly ascending the quarterdeck ladder, motioned to the first lieutenant to stop the movement, exclaiming 'A lower deck gun adrift, Sir! Let me have two or three hammocks, and I'll endeavour to choke the trucks.' The hammocks were hastily thrown down the hatchways, when, after a heavy lurch had, with fearful force, propelled the gun back into its proper port, the second master succeeded in choking the aftertrucks, and the ship was immediately brought to the wind on that tack which left the unsecured gun on the *lee* side. Had it not been for the presence of mind and activity of this officer, the ship must have suffered serious, if not fatal, injuries.[78]

Lessons on the orlop deck

While the lower deck was swept, the captain of the foretop with a party of fore-topmen scraped and swept the fore cockpit, the captain of the maintop with maintopmen cleaned the main hatches and the afterguard and mizzen topmen cleaned the after cockpit and steward's room. When the orlop deck was completed the mate reported it to the officer of the watch, who then inspected the deck fore and aft.[79]

The *Splendid* bore a schoolmaster, 'a Christ's Hospital youth who is a skilful mathematician', and in the forenoon he instructed the midshipmen in the cockpit. Although 'many of the best captains for training youngsters were in frigates, and frigates, with continual cruising and activity, were the best schools of service', 'the very best man in the navy for training youth' was Captain Duckworth of the *Orion* (74). He was now Governor-General of Newfoundland, but by 1810 'captains were under growing pressure to take, and keep, young men who were not at all cut out for naval life', and the ship had a particularly pathetic example, a boy called Augustus. His brother Claude had been recommended by St Vincent to Captain Broughton of the *Penelope* (36) in 1802; he had been promoted lieutenant on 8 August 1806, and now his parents had sent Augustus out to the *Splendid* 'to be taken care of'.[80] Captain Edwards wrote home:

It hurts me very much. He is a good boy, but rotten, poor thing, with the evil [scrofula], and so blind that he cannot see across the table. I know the object of his parents is to get him made a Lieut't and have a pension on the naval establishment, but I will never make him. They know me little that expect it. My business is to look for officers capable of doing the duty of the service. When I find them, and find them gentlemen, I do not care who they belong to ... I think it is quite shocking, for he is blind of the left eye, and can see very little with the other. He is a good boy as can be, but totally unfit for the sea. I have recommended to his father to put him into the army. He appears to be much afflicted with scrophula, and consequently no chance of his ever being well. Unless he has a blister or an issue to make a sore, his eyes inflame. Sea provisions is death to him ... I am much hurt by their persisting to send that youth to sea, because his state of health totally unfits him for it, and his parents know it. He has very good sense, and the sweetest and most gentle disposition in the world. I was very much interested for him, and it was mixed with pity. I suppose they have adopted an opinion, that I am afraid is very general, that the outcasts of nature and of society, those who are unfit for community with fine land people, may do well at sea. They can only have in view to be clear of the trouble of him, for there is no chance of his ever being qualified for an officer ... I have recommended to his father to put him into the militia or some of the Volunteer Corps, where he can live on a vegetable diet, and his being blind will be of less consequence to the public, or to himself.[81]

He was also 'of any thing like education to fit him for his profession ... as entirely destitute as possible. Of the use of figures he has very little knowledge indeed, and as everything in our possession depends upon calculation and geo-metrical deductions, it is a misfortune that a youth should be so far advanced without his mind being called to a study so necessary. He is sensible of his defi-ciency in this respect, and as we have a very good school master, I hope his appli-cation will make up for lost time.' His messmate was a boy called William, who was not well educated either: 'it is a pity that so sensible a boy should not have been taught something. His education has not been careful.'* Worse, when he arrived off Cadiz in spring 1806 to join the ship it was discovered that he had had a rupture for three years, and was 'even without a truss or bandage for his relief': 'It is a great misfortune and had I known it before I certainly would have recom-mended him not to come to sea, for the natural effect of the sea air is to relax the body so that the complaint is worse at sea than on shore and it is much against his activity ... Ruptured people cannot serve at sea, and are generally discharged from the navy, for the very air of the sea is unfavourable to their complaint.' But he was supplied with a truss, prospered, and on 24 September Edwards wrote to his father: 'He has bathed three times a week which has done him infinite good and made him grow very tall': by June 1807, he 'grows strong and is very well'. The boys 'read history every morning alternately,† which is exceedingly conven-ient to both, for [Augustus] has weak eyes and William's voice is strengthened by reading aloud'.[82]

The position of schoolmaster aboard ship had recently improved. In 1790

---

* This was a continuing problem: William Hickey claimed that in the summer of 1756, when, aged seven, he was to go to sea in the *Burford* (74) as a midshipman with Lord Gambier, he could not read or write. He did not join the *Burford* because he disliked the idea of being forced to eat fat, and his father reverted to his original plan of making him a lawyer: consequently 'I was placed at a day school in Charles Street, St James's Square, for the purpose of learning to read and write'.

† Edwards wrote to Crespigny's father on 20 January 1806 about the kit he would need: 'his navigation books that he has been taught from – whether it is Robertson's Elements or Hamilton Moore; a quadrant and a case of instruments. For his reading, you will give him such books as you think proper and are least voluminous – a history of England, of Rome, and Greece, with Voyages or abridgement of them. But his baggage must be *light* – for the moment he enters a ship he must have no personal cares. All that relates to himself must be secondary – or nothing'.

the schoolmaster was to 'employ his time on board in instructing the voluntiers in writing, arithmetic, and the study of navigation, and in whatsoever may contribute to render them artists in that science', and the other 'youths of the ship' as the captain directed. Schoolmasters were only appointed to Third, Fourth and Fifth Rates, and their pay was the same as the midshipmen they were teaching, and with whom they lived and messed (though they received a bounty of £20 a year on production of a certificate from the captain of their diligence) – they were formally a warrant officer, but of an unusual kind; they had no right to mess in the wardroom, but the regulations for promotion to lieutenant of 1805 that closed off promotion from warrant officer allowed schoolmasters to apply. However, in 1808 there were two new clauses that showed the new focus on mathematics suitable for aspiring sea officers: 'He is not only to instruct them [now described as 'young gentlemen', *ie* everyone with the status of midshipman, whatever their formal rate] in mathematics, but is also to watch over their general conduct, and attend to their morals; and if he shall observe any disposition to immorality or debauchery, or any conduct unbecoming an officer and a gentleman, he is to represent it to the captain, that it may be immediately corrected as it shall deserve.' He was also instructed 'to assist any officers who may require him in any astronomical observations or calculations they may be desirous of making'. They were also allowed in all classes of ship. The position was still unattractive to many educated men – in the *Gloucester* (74) in 1812 the Reverend Mangin selected a member of the crew, who 'impressed everyone with respect, by his air of genteel and humble melancholy', and who was excused other duties, but in 1815 the schoolmaster was 'a clever seedy-looking creature, whose besetting sin was the love of grog; with very little trouble it floored him and then, I don't much like to record it, we used to grease his head and flour it' – and in 1812 qualified chaplains could also teach.[83]

PROVISIONS ON THE ORLOP DECK

Between half-past seven and nine in the morning the purser's steward and his assistant issued the day's provisions from the steward room, which was right aft on the orlop deck, next to the purser's cabin and forward of the breadroom. In the *Splendid*, like most ships, the cooper did the duty of assistant. This hour and a half allowed both watches to collect their food. The cook of each mess collected the day's biscuit, pease, butter and cheese and took what needed to be cooked to the galley in time for dinner at noon. Each mess had a number, and it has been suggested that each had a corresponding tagged net, and bag for a pudding day, which allowed the cook to identify its food when the mess cook came to collect it at noon.[84]

From time immemorial, pursers had received their dry and wet provisions at full measure but served them out having deducted an eighth for waste (except for flesh; and butter was issued at 12oz per lb, and cheese 9oz), though no formal statute or rule establishing this is known: Spencer, when First Lord, wrote that 'it does not, so far as we can discover, appear to have been originally authorised by any order, but to have been established by long custom.' One of the main demands of the fleet when it mutinied at Spithead in 1797 was for provisions to be issued at full measure: this was granted on 3 May, and the men were paid short allowance money until the new measuring equipment, made by the Navy Board, reached the ships.[85]

This was a significant development. The men of the *Saturn* thought the purser had taken the delay in supplying the new measures as an opportunity to defraud them, and court-martialled him, but he was saved by the purser of the *St Albans*, who testified that he did not know 'of any standard for trial of measures', and that pursers bought standard commercial measures and relied on the manu-facturer's accuracy.* Most pursers had several sets of measures for the different species (the Victualling Board noted that 'It is usual for provisions to be weighed on board ships with stilliards [steelyards], whereas they are weighed at the office with scales and weights, and which frequently causes a difference in the weight, the stilliards not being so correct', but did not issue weights and measures, even though Office of Stores records show them being delivered to the fleet for other uses): the purser of the *Sunderland* in 1758 had two sets of weights, one at 16oz to the pound, and one at 14oz, and his ruin came when he confused the two. The Navy Board's decision to issue new standard weights and measures is indicative of a new attitude to the care and distribution of government property while it was in its servants' hands that is seen in its decision a few years later to take over the supply of tobacco to the fleet and in the impeachment of Lord Melville for malversation in 1805. On 18 May 1797 the Admiralty issued an order detailing compensation for the abolition of the purser's eighths, and that it would pay when passing their accounts 'one ninth part (calculated at the credit prices) of

---

* Jonathan Edmunds, a captain of the forecastle, testified that although the ship's company did not complain of it, they suspected that the issue of wine at Gibraltar was short, compared to what he had been served in the *Powerful* and *Canada*, which he knew 'by the horn measure we drank out of in the berth which we had on board the *Powerful* and *Canada*, we found it short one horn-ful out of seven … when the new measures came to the ship [from the Victualling Office during her cruise].' The purser's first witness was Mr James Glencross, a druggist of Dock, who said: 'when I first went into business I purchased a set of measures from a tradesman of Dock which I supposed to be correct; to my great surprize and by chance I found about three months afterwards I found them incorrect the gallon measure was nearly a half pint short, the quart measure ½ a gill – some of the others were a little incorrect and one more than measure; but those short impressed my mind most.' The verdict was 'proved in part', but he was to make restitution in the usual manner only.

the several species of provisions issued by them to the crews of His Majesty's said ships as an indemnification of waste and leakage in lieu of the eighths', but in the 1806 Regulations it reverted to an eighth ('flesh excepted').[86]

The credit price was the price fixed by the Victualling Board for the provisions supplied to the purser and returned unused to store (always at a lower price than the fixed price they had been supplied at, for which he was the debtor). But he was also allowed to supply tobacco to the men (with the captain's permission) in quantities not exceeding 2lb per man per lunar month. He bought this at market price, but sold it at a rate fixed by the Navy Board, and since it was a private venture it was sold in 16oz pounds. The price established for sale to the men was initially 19d per lb, but by 1797 only 12d per lb; the pursers bought it for 4½d per lb at the beginning of the war, 'afterwards 5d and I now believe it is 6d per lb'; nonetheless demand from the fleet often made it extremely difficult to obtain, not least from 'the great shrinkage and length of time they [the pursers] remain unpaid for what may be issued, generally near three years and sometimes longer, by which a purser of a third rate has upon an average seldom less than £400 due to him for this article only and often a larger sum'; and in 1798, for example, the Admiralty received letters from the captains of the *Jason* 'that the purser refuses to purchase tobacco for the people, under a plea that he cannot afford to issue it at the price allowing' and of the *Garland* that the purser 'cannot get it put on board the ship for less than 10½d per lb a price which he thinks he cannot afford to pay'. In the 1808 Regulations, tobacco was given an entire chapter in the section 'Of the Provisions', and the first article stated 'Tobacco, for the use of the companies of His Majesty's ships and vessels, is in future to be provided and supplied by, and under the direction of, the Commissioners for Victualling His Majesty's Navy; and proper depots thereof will accordingly be made at the established Victualling Ports, both at home and abroad.' It was still limited to 2lb per man per month, but was now charged to the men at 1s 7d per lb: the purser was allowed a 'reasonable allowance' for waste and diminution of weight, and a commission of ten per cent (calculated by weight 'regularly issued') when passing his accounts.[87]

In 1808, 'For encouraging him to a faithful and zealous discharge of his duty', he also began to receive a commission when his accounts were passed, from 1¾d per gallon of beer to 1s 8d per 8lb piece of beef and 1s 3d per 4lb piece of pork to 6d per gallon of oatmeal.[88]

As well as being the officer 'entrusted with the keeping and distributing the provisions out to the ship's company',[89] he was responsible for the supply and care of 'coals, wood, turnery-ware [lathe-made goods such as spoons and bowls],

candles, lanthorns, and other necessaries',[90] slop clothes and beds (thin mat-
tresses). Preservation of stores was part of his responsibilities, and he had care of
'casks, tight or dry, iron-hoops, bags, and jars'. By custom the purser paid his
steward and the cooper extra, above their wages. He was allowed waste of cask
(compensation for damage, and for casks 'used for washing-tubs, steep-tubs, or
by the cook' or in the tops): from 7 December 1770 it was one tun of casks, two
iron hoops (for barrels) and three bread bags per hundred men victualled per
month, and from 1808 one tun of casks, three iron hoops, and four bags, plus
two bags per hundred men victualled per month 'after the ship shall have been
absent from a victualling port in England more than twelve months'. The form
provided in 1808 includes some examples of extra expense, which he was allowed
to claim if the certificate was counter-signed by the captain and master:

Spithead	Cut for match and top tubs per order of this day
At Sea	Making buckets with covers for the use of the sick per order 30th ultimo
Jamaica	Repairing 12 puncheons intended for a gang of rum casks
Martinique	Used for making two buoys, per order of the 12th instant
Musquito Shore	Repairing 32 gang casks, they being damaged by rafting
Hispaniola	Ditto and trimming 24 butts, 18 puncheons and 16 hogs heads
At Sea	Cut for match and top tubs (some of the old being destroyed) per order this day
Jamaica	Used in general repair of the remainder of the water casks, they being old and in bad condition as follows, viz. butts 101, puncheons 45, and hogsheads 60[91]

Deficiencies beyond the allowed waste were charged against his account, at casks,
£2 0s 0d per tun, iron hoops, £0 1s 0d each, bags £0 1s 6d each and oil jars £0 10s
6d each, for Channel service, and for Foreign service, 'the highest prices that
shall have been paid by the Crown during the period of his account.'[92]

For supplying turnery ware and the like he was paid necessary money,
which was 12d per man per month in extra petty warrant (harbour victualling)
and 14d in sea victualling, then in 1808 for ships whose complement exceeded
343 men, ½d per man per day. For these, he had to contract privately, which had

its own difficulties. First, he was only advanced a proportion of the money. The purser of the *Druid* (36, serving as a troopship), court-martialled for not supplying the ship with sufficient necessaries, was acquitted because he successfully demonstrated that he was unable to obtain enough credit for the 'extraordinary expence of necessaries, which must frequently arise in troop ships'. Second, the supplies were sometimes simply unavailable: Moses Hawker, the purser of the *Lion* (64), was court-martialled on the same charge; in his defence he said that in the neighbourhood of Deal there was no good wood for firing to be got, and all he could find was 'the refuse timber, of a sloop of war, that was then building at Sandwich', and was likewise acquitted. Third, he was only paid for necessaries used and recorded, and then at a price fixed by the Navy Board, regardless of the real price, with no compensation for loss from damage, wreck or enemy action. He had three other standard payments, adz money at 3s 4d per month for ships of 61 men or more for sea service only, drawage money at 4d per ton and lading or loading charge at 2s per month; these were replaced in 1808 by an annual allowance: for ships of 600–699 men, £20; 700–799, £22 10s; and 800 and upward, £25, with 6d per man per month for supernumeraries. There were also payments for the extra candles needed if the ship wore a flag or broad pendant and therefore lit top and poop lanterns. He was also paid 1s in the pound, originally for handling the sale of dead men's clothes, then for supplying all slop clothes and bedding.[93]

The system of pursery changed considerably on 4 November 1813, when purser's accounts now had to be made up and transmitted both quarterly and annually, and when the purser left the ship because of promotion, ill-health or dismissal; a number of anomalies and inconsistencies were removed, but the eighth was confirmed.[94]

The purser also had the care of officially supplied improving reading matter.

> To improve our mental faculties [in the *Rodney*, 74], when we had a few
> leisure moments from ship duty and naval tactics, we were furnished with
> a library of two choice books for every ten men. We had seventy of these
> libraries in all. The first book was an abridgment of the life of Lord
> Nelson, calculated to inspire the mind with deeds of valor, and the most
> summary way of disposing of an unyielding enemy. This, one of the ten
> men could read, when he had leisure, during the last six days of each
> week. The second was a small Church of England prayer book, for special
> use about one hour on the first day of the week.[95]

On 20 May 1812 the Admiralty ordered a New Testament and two prayer books to be issued to each mess, and on 18 March 1815, 'one copy of the New Testament, two Common Prayer Books, and two Psalters, to be allowed to each Mess on board a King's ship composed of Eight Men, and one Bible to Thirty-two Men'.[96]

FIRE IN THE HOLD

Once the orlop deck was clean the captain of the maintop and his party swabbed the well, which was now pumped dry. Forward, the magazine was aired.

> A gentle fire is to be kept by day in the magazine forward, during which time two tubs and four fire buckets filled with water are to be kept in it and swabs damped; – The fire engine hose pointed down [inserted: the engine filled with water] and great concern must be taken to prevent the fire being so brisk as to heat the stove or funnel so much as to endanger it's communicating fire.
>
> A midshipman, a corporal or master at arms, two marine centinels, and two gunners are to be constantly watching the fire in the magazine, are to be relieved every two hours & visited twice a watch at least by a lieut. & frequently by the gunner. the magazine must be frequently swept, the racks scrubbed, and all dust arising therefrom must be damped and very carefully taken up.[97]

GROG AND THE NOON SIGHT
SEVEN BELLS ON THE QUARTERDECK, WAIST AND FORECASTLE

At seven bells in the forenoon watch, 'the mate of the watch goes down to the master, and tells him what o'clock it is; upon which that officer, while he is getting his sextant ready, and looking at his own watch, to see how it agrees with the chronometer, asks the midshipman if the day be clear or thick, how the ship's head is, and what chance there is of his seeing the sun.'[98]

The master was the senior warrant officer in the ship, 'with but after' the lieutenants: he lived and messed in the wardroom but had a second cabin forward of the captain's accommodation for maps and charts, which were the tools of his trade and which he supplied himself. His principal concern was navigating the ship, under the direction of the captain, and he was specifically charged with this in the 1808 Regulations, and with giving the captain her position at noon, so his attendance on deck now was certainly the centre of his working day. His instructions directed him to see that master's mates attended the noon sight, and

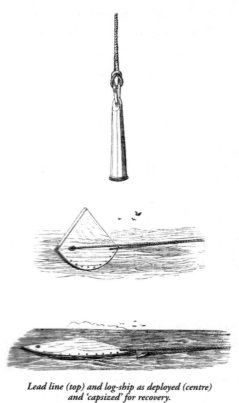

*Lead line (top) and log-ship as deployed (centre)
and 'capsized' for recovery.*

to 'encourage' commissioned and petty officers to take the observations at noon. He had long had responsibility for keep a journal that included observations of coasts and shoals, and in 1808 the article detailing these observations was correspondingly fuller, with a ten-page form provided by the Admiralty. He also had charge of the logbook, and oversaw the condition and maintenance of the sails, rigging and cables, compasses, glasses and log and lead lines. It followed that the master had to be present at the ship's fitting out, ensuring that her supplies, provisions and ballast were fit for the task and rejecting any that were not; to oversee the stowing of the hold, both for the trim of the ship and for the best storage and issue of the provisions; and to sign the boatswain's and carpenters' expenses.[99]

The master's questions to the midshipmen at 11.30 are

merely questions of curiosity; for whether it be a fine day or not, or whether there be any chance, or none at all, of seeing the sun, it is the same thing, or ought to be the same thing to him. By a rude inspection of the log board, the experienced eye of the master infers how much easting or westing the ship has made since noon of the day before, and, accordingly, he is prepared either to find the sun before or after the ship's time; that is, he judges whether to expect the moment of noon sooner or later than the watches shew.

So irregular, indeed, is the return of this period our noon afloat, that it is the custom, in most ships, not to turn the half-hour glass at 7 bells (½-past 11), because the interval between ½-past 11 and noon is seldom thirty minutes long – being sometimes fifteen, and sometimes forty-five minutes in duration. If, therefore, the sentry at the cabin door, who has charge of the glass, were to turn it at seven bells, and it were to be made noon when the sand had only half run out, what would he do? ...*

The master follows the mate of the watch to the quarter-deck; and if the sun be shining out distinctly, he glances his eye to one or the other gangway, from which it can generally be seen. If the ship's course be exactly south or exactly north, it is obvious that, to get the sun's altitude at noon, the observer must place himself either forward, over the bows, or abaft on the taffrail; but, in all other cases, or nearly all, the meridian altitude can be taken from the gangway. Most ships have a very convenient little recess at the after end of the waist hammock-netting, just over the gangway-steps, bounded, as the geography books would say, on the after side by the end of the quarter-deck bulwark, and on the foremost part by a board against which the hammocks rest. This snug corner, which is about 3 feet square, affords the officer of the watch the means of looking nearly right ahead or right astern ...

If the captain be one of the star-gazers of the ship, that is, if he takes any personal interest in, or charge of the navigation of the vessel under his command, he, of course, occupies this favourite spot, or observatory, in the gangway. Should any bold youth, therefore, have got there before him, the intruder leaps out of it in a great hurry, the instant the glitter of the captain's sextant is seen at the top of the ladder. I should have mentioned before, that every mid who has an instrument – whether it be a wooden

---

* ' ... as there are 360 degrees in the circuit of the globe, which revolves once in 24 hours, each degree of longitude must take four minutes to pass. Now, in those high latitudes where a degree of longitude – owing to the convergence of the meridians as they approach the poles – becomes only 30 or 40 miles in length, it will often happen to cruising ships that Monday may be half an hour longer than Sunday, and Tuesday, on the contrary, half an hour shorter. To make this plain, let us suppose the ship to have remained during Sunday on the same meridian – say she is in longitude 40° W., and in latitude 60 N. Her day will have lasted in this case exactly 24 hours, as if she had been in harbour. But if, at the beginning of the next day (Monday), she happens to start a chase in the western horizon, and during the pursuit runs due west, at the rate of about nine miles and a half an hour, she will make 225 miles westing in the course of the day. In the latitude of 60°, a degree of longitude contains only 30 miles; and as each degree is equal to four minutes, 225 miles, or seven degrees and a half, make 30 minutes difference of time, and the ship will now be in the longitude 47½ W. In other, and more popular words, as she will have run away from the sun seven degrees and a half of longitude, it will cost the sun thirty minutes' time to come up to the new meridian reached by the ship, further to the westward than the day before. The length of Monday (counting from noon on Sunday to noon on Monday) will therefore consist of 24 hours and a half.

Again, if it shall happen, just at twelve o'clock on Monday, when the sun is on the meridian of the ship, that a strange sail heaves in sight due East, and the ship starts off back again to the meridian of 40° W. at the same rate, it is clear she will now meet the sun, and anticipate the noon, by a portion of time nearly equal to that by which she had retarded that epoch on the previous day, by getting ahead of him. Her day, counted from one noon to the other, will now, of course, be only 23 hours and a half long. Thus, there will be one whole hour's difference between the length of Monday and Tuesday ...'
Traditionally, the nautical day in the Royal Navy had begun at noon, half a day behind civil time (so that the afternoon of 11 October 1804 at sea was the afternoon of 11 October on land, but at sea it was followed by the morning of 11 October and on land by the morning of the 12th); this had ceased by an order of 11 October 1805. Ships were supplied with a new form of log, and captains were to submit logs instead of journals.

quadrant, or a brass sextant – is required to muster on deck at seven bells, to look out for the sun. Of course, this is the grand period for comparison of notes; and much cheerful discussion goes on as to the merits of the different observers and instruments, methods of calculation, and all the crude slang of incipient information, in which half-informed folks delight to exhibit their knowledge – quite sure they know every thing.

In fine weather, accordingly, this is perhaps one of the pleasantest half-hours of the day. The good humour extends itself all over the ship; and mid-day being the dinner-time of the sailors, some of the most important steps preparatory to that ceremony are taken in this interval. The ship's cook, with his one arm (for he has seldom more – or if he have two arms, he has certainly only one leg), empties the coppers, by means of a monstrous fork, called his Tormentors, of the beef or pork which has been in preparation during the forenoon. He likewise allows the pease-soup to run off by a cock from another boiler into a huge tub, ready to receive it …

As the hour of noon approaches, the cooks of the messes may be seen coming up the fore and main hatchways, with their mess-kids in their hands, the hoops of which are kept as bright as silver, and the wood work as neat and as clean as the pail of the most tidy dairy-maid. The grog, also, is now mixed in a large tub, under the half-deck, by the quartermasters of the watch below, assisted by other leading and responsible men amongst the ship's company, closely superintended, of course, by the mate of the hold, to see that no liquor is abstracted, and also by the purser's steward, who regulates the exact quantity of spirits and of water to be measured out. The seamen whose next turn it is to take the wheel, or heave the lead, or who have to mount to the mast-head to look out, as well as the marines who are to be planted as sentries at noon, are allowed to take both their dinner and their grog beforehand. These persons are called 'seven-bell men,' from the hour at which they have their allowance served to them.[100]

The Regulations laid down that spirits had to be issued on the upper deck to prevent fire ('As Mr Male, first lieutenant of the Bellona, had been my old shipmate for some years, and now commanded the *Courageux*, I received from him several particulars which did not appear in the public accounts, more especially the very narrow escape he had from being burnt in the *Courageux*, the second night after her capture, when she was set on fire by some of our own people, in drawing off rum by candle light, and if he had not used the most desperate exertions by rolling himself in the flame and preventing its reaching the cask, they must inevitably have perished; but in this attempt he was considerably scorched, though he fortunately saved the ship'). The standard-issue rum was 'at least four times as strong as the "Navy" rum sold today', and to prevent drunkenness all spirits were to be mixed with 'a due proportion' of water. To prevent fraud a lieutenant and two other officers of the watch had to attend the issue. (Although the regulations are clear on mixing, the rum was served out 'raw' in the *Agamemnon* (64) in 1799,* and this is unlikely to be the only example.)[101]

A court martial in 1798 shows how this took place in the *Monarch* (74). Robert Nelson, a captain of the forecastle, accused the purser's steward of issuing grog for twenty men more than he mixed for, and the purser brought him to a court martial for doing so. Nelson's accusation was essentially that the purser's steward had defrauded the Victualling Board of twenty men's grog, and the charge he faced was effectively slandering the purser's steward, which meant the court had to enquire into the details of the issue that day – typically, there is no record of a court martial on the purser's steward for issuing grog for twenty men more than he mixed for.

The court learned that it was the custom in the ship for a quartermaster and a captain of the forecastle to attend the mixing of the grog, one to hold the pot and one to fill it with liquor. John Whiddon, the master, said the spirits put

---

* 'James Parkinson went up for the mess' grog, which was brought short one quart. Lawrence Henderson, the Prisoner, had the watch upon deck the same time. When he came down there was no grog for him: he was angry about it & said he would take Parkinson, the deceas'd, & the cooper aft [to complain to the officer of the watch]. Johnston, the Gunner's Yeoman, whose liquor was serv'd out to him raw, sent to borrow a gill measure, & he gave Lawrence Henderson, the Prisoner, his liquor to help keep peace & quietness.' Johnston went below 'between the hours of 4 and 5 o'clock in the afternoon', and 'I came into the berth, & I understood there had been a mistake in the serving & receiving of grog. I enquir'd who had not received their grog; they told me – every one but Lawrence Henderson. I said, "Never mind, Lawrence, I shall give you mine"; accordingly I did, a gill of rum, & he said he was satisfy'd. I understood by the conversation in the berth that Lawrence Henderson had threaten'd James Parkinson with the Ship's Steward with the quarterdeck to complain of them. Several words passed which I took but little notice of, seeing that James Parkinson was rather vex'd. I said to the Prisoner, "Lawrence, you have had your Grog, & are satisfy'd, and there was no occasion to make words about so trifling an affair." – Words ensued by both parties, which I gave no heed to, until Lawce Henderson, the Prisoner, started from his seat and said, "You are a parcel of disagreeable buggers altogether." The deceas'd [James Parkinson], more enrag'd, moving his hand as he spoke, the Prisoner said, "Don't point your finger to my face, or my nose" (applying his finger to his own at the same time), he was as good a man as the deceas'd in any respect, & would wish to know what the deceas'd could do, or show him. The deceas'd answer'd, "I could pull your nose, or haul you up the hatchway by the ears, you scoundrel;" and ask'd the Prisoner if he would try his manhood with him. The Prisoner answer'd in the affirmative, "Yes," – or I will. The deceas'd then, to the best of my knowledge, gave him, the Prisoner, a slap in the face. The Prisoner then having his knife open in his hand, thrust it into the left breast of the deceas'd. I started up, & seized the knife in the hand of the Prisoner, & said, "Are you mad; you have kill'd a man." As soon as I had secured the knife, I called for Parkinson, who had stepped backwards after he had been stabbed. The deceas'd came forward, & said, "Here, Johnston, I believe I am killed." Henderson's plea in mitigation – he had no defence – is particularly moving, but he was sentenced to death nonetheless.

into the grog tub were 'fourteen gallons a pint and a gill' (453 gills), the water was 'forty-three gallons one gill' (1,377 gills), and after all the men had had their allowance there was remaining in the tub 'about a quart' (8 gills); the court asked whether it was possible to serve grog to 600 men without there being a pint or two over or under, and he said it was not. The purser's steward said the number of men on the grog list on the day the accused was confined was 459, the spirits issued fourteen gallons, two pints, three gills (459 gills), the water forty-three gallons and one gill, the surplus one quart. (The court did not pursue the discrepancy in the amount of spirits issued; the steward's figures mean that every man on the grog list had had a pint of grog, made of one gill of rum mixed with three gills of water; the quart remaining means that each pint was $\frac{1}{459}$ short.) He claimed that Nelson came to the after cockpit to get his candles, was told they had been issued, and then alleged that the steward was wrong, and likewise in his account of his grog. Nelson's defence was that on the day in question he 'stood close alongside the steward and took the number of pints of grog that was served out to each mess, by desire of most of the ships company'; his total differed from the steward's, he acquainted the quarterdeck, and he was put in confinement. The court decided the charge against him was proved in part (a phrase very often found in court-martial verdicts), but in consideration of his long confinement (since 18 June), he was given only fifty lashes.[102]

It was forbidden to hoard, trade or sell unused alcohol. In some ships those who could not drink the full allowance without drunkenness were permitted to take part of the ration and be paid for the rest, but the eighteenth century was a hard-drinking age, and this regulation, as so many others, was frequently ignored: hoarding and trading were commonplace, and selling was not unknown, especially in the small town that was a receiving ship. Robert Wilson,

Sextant.

signalman in the *Unité*, remembered that 'So fond are seamen in general to liquor they would lose half a pint of liquor they would rather lose so much of their blood; yet it is odd to see how willingly they will part with their grog as payment for favours received, for sailors with all their faults are not void of the sense of gratitude'.[103]

Captain Hall's account continues:

Long before twelve o'clock, all these, and various other minor preparations, have been so completely made, that there is generally a remarkable stillness over the whole ship just before the important moment of noon arrives. The boatswain stands near the break of the forecastle, with his bright silver call, or whistle, in his hand, which ever and anon he places just at the tip of his lips, to blow out any crumbs which threaten to interfere with its melody, or to give a faint 'too-weet! too-weet!' as a preparatory note, to fix the attention of the boatswain's mates, who being, like their chief, provided with calls, station themselves at intervals along the main-deck, ready to give due accompaniment to their leader's tune.

The boatswain keeps his eye on the group of observers, and well knows when the 'sun is up,' by the stir which takes place amongst the astronomers, of by noticing the master working out his latitude with a pencil, on the ebony bar of his quadrant, or on the edge of the hammock-railing; though, if he be one of your modern, neat-handed navigators, he carries his little book for this purpose. In one way or another the latitude is computed, as soon as the master is satisfied the sun has reached his highest altitude in the heavens. He then walks aft to the officer of the watch, and reports 12 o'clock, communicating also the degrees and minutes of the latitude observed. The lieutenant proceeds to the captain, wherever he may be, and repeats that it is 12, and that so and so is the latitude. The same formal round of reports is gone through, even if the captain be on deck, and has heard every word spoken by the master, or even if he have himself assisted in making the observation.

The captain now says to the officer of the watch, 'Make it 12!'

The officer calls out to the mate of the watch, 'Make it 12!'

The mate – ready primed – sings out to the quarter-master, 'Strike 8 bells!'

And lastly, the hard-a-weather old quarter-master, stepping down the ladder, grunts out to the sentry at the cabin-door, 'Turn the glass and strike the bell!'*

By this time, the boatswain's call has been in his mouth for several minutes, his elbow in the air, and his little finger on the stop, ready to send forth the glad tidings of hearty meal. Not less ready or less eager are the groups of listeners seated at their snow-white deal tables below, or the crowd surrounding the coppers, with their mess-kids acting the part of drums to their impatient knuckles. At the first stroke of the bell, which, at this particular hour, is always sounded with peculiar vivacity, the officer of the watch exclaims to the boatswain, 'Pipe to dinner!'[104]

---

* The sand glass for timing the watch was half an hour; the navy also supplied hour, half-hour, half-minute, and quarter-minute glasses for use with the log.

Chapter 6

THE CAPTAIN DINES
Afternoon watch, noon to 4pm
(i) to four bells

QUARTERDECK, WAIST AND FORECASTLE
Dinner in the captain's cabin

According to the custom of the service, the captain dined later than the ward-room, at two. He dined alone, unless he chose to invite his officers. It was also a custom of the service for captains to take this duty, or opportunity, seriously, and cultivate an acquaintance with each officer in turn, though this acquaintance once established was not, apparently, developed by conversation: 'On the day of our sailing from England,' wrote the Reverend Mangin, new to the *Gloucester* (74), 'I dined, for the first time, with the captain, and was very kindly welcomed; but I took notice that the lieutenant of the watch, who also dined at the captain's table, scarcely spoke three words.' He spoke to the lieutenant that evening, and 'expressed some regret, saying that I concluded such sullen taciturnity must have arisen from some disagreement between the commander and his lieutenant: whereupon, I was undeceived and told with a laugh by my instructor that the parties were on the best possible terms – but that "it was not according to naval etiquette, to converse at the table of a captain of a man-of-war".'[1] It followed, therefore, that the captain resented a slight: Dillon recorded that 'On the 25th [July 1814] one of my marine officers, Lieut. [Edward] Capel, was discharged by his own request into the *Victorious*. That officer had, some time previously, refused to dine with me, and, as no reason or explanation ensued, he was not invited again … ' When he commanded the *Leopard* as a troopship, he embarked 450 men of the 5th Foot at Cork for the Peninsula.

> The instant the ship was fairly at sea, I sent an invitation to the colonel to dine with me. He declined it, and as he kept his distance, all intercourse between us ended. The army officers noticed his coolness and spoke to mine

on the subject. They coolly replied that 'our captain always has a reason for his conduct.' By the 27th [May 1812, eleven days later] we were near the land, making our way towards the Tagus. The colonel now requested an interview, and I was astonished to hear him launch out in a rhapsody of apologies for not having accepted my invitation. I listened patiently to all he had to say, and could only reply that I concluded he had had the worst time of it by keeping aloof; for if he had chosen to make himself agreeable my cabin would have been at his disposal: and that all his officers had in rotation been sufferers by his coolness. He had evidently mistaken his man. Explanations took place and he became an altered person. He had, I suspect, supposed that he was entitled to a great deal of consideration. But he was not captain of the ship. He found out his error late in the day, but we became friends and met again many years afterwards.[2]

In 1808 the captain's share of prize money was reduced from three-eighths of the value of the prize to two-eighths, and according to Captain Dillon this 'occasioned a universal feeling of dissatisfaction throughout the Navy ... the captains, generally speaking, left off keeping tables, as their pay would not admit of their doing so'. In 1810 he was offered a commission as acting commander of the *Bellerophon*, but declined because he was £200 out of pocket from his two previous acting commands. Sir Richard Bickerton told him, 'I advise you to accept that ship ... but do not keep a table. Mess with the officers in the ward room.' He did so: 'I had established myself in the ward room mess, which I found tolerably comfortable. The captain of marines was an old acquaintance of the last war: but there was a certain caution which I could not help feeling on the part of the officers. The captain is a different person to themselves in an official point of view, and the general tone of conversation was [not surprisingly] guarded.' Earlier in the war he had been sent with a flag of truce to the Dutch commodore in Helvoetsluys, and was sent on board a French frigate, *la Furieuse* (46): 'I became acquainted with their plans and arrangements. They were better paid than our naval officers. Table money was allowed them, and each individual in rotation received at the end of the week the overplus of that allowance: this in addition to their pay, which was quite distinct from their mess expenses, whereas with us our mess money absorbed the principal part of our pay. There was no regular breakfast. Everyone found his own just as it suited his convenience. There was always a very comfortable good dinner, which when ended, the officers would say "Voilà encore un dîner que les anglais n'auront pas."'. When fitting out the *Horatio* at Sheerness in March 1814, though, he returned to keeping a table. He lunched with Lord George Stuart, captain of the *Newcastle* (50), four years senior to him, who said, ' "All of us have given up the entertaining of young men who do not care about us. It's a mistaken notion. I have long left off blowing out their stomachs. I dine by myself, at considerably less expense, and I feel happier." To this I merely remarked that I was fully sensible to the feelings of my brother officers on the subject, but I could not as yet give up what had been so long an established custom, and that I should go on some time longer, as I had up to that period covered my expenses'.[3]

The great cabin in the *Splendid* was 12ft deep, and narrowing from 22ft wide forward to 19ft aft. The tables were 10ft long and dined twelve; Edwards had two sets of a dozen damask napkins and tablecloths to match. Earthenware and porcelain were widely available by 1810, replacing the pewter of an earlier generation, and he had a set of eighteen blue and white breakfast cups and saucers, another of eighteen blue and white cups and saucers, two creamware dinner services and a Wedgwood tray that contained four dishes with a small soup tureen in the middle. He also had four two-dozen sets of ordinary and cut-glass wine and champagne glasses. Apart from the Wedgwood tray the tableware was cheap and practical, and easily replaced;* of the breakfast set, three cups and six saucers were broken that summer, of the other set five cups and four saucers, as well as several plates, a fish drainer and twenty-eight wine glasses. He had a pantry, immediately forward of the mizzen mast on the upper deck, 10ft long and 6ft wide, to store all this and where his steward could prepare light meals.[4]

The admiral dined latest of all.

At two o'clock Sir Richard King, Captain Mitchell and all the other captains of the fleet were assembled on board the *Superb*, soon after which we sat down to a dinner so magnificent, and so capitally dressed, that it would not have discredited the cooks of the London, or any other equally celebrated tavern. Captain Mitchell who sat next to me at table asked me what I thought of Sir Edward [Hughes]'s fare, to which I answered I never had seen so splendid an entertainment, and had no idea such a one could have been produced on board a ship. 'Oh,' says my neighbour, 'our gallant Admiral likes good living, and always takes care to provide himself with a professed cook. Indeed, he usually has both a

---

* The previous December, the captain of the *Spartan* was ordered to carry the British and Spanish ambassadors and their suites from Malta to Trieste and laid in some stocks: as well as food and condiments he bought two dozen blue plates at £7 1s 0d, one dozen ditto soup at £3 3s 0d, six cups and saucers at £1 2s 6d, ten spoons and forks at £46 1s 9d a dozen teaspoons at £19 1s 0d, and a dozen knives at £8 0s 0d. (He also bought four toothbrushes at 3s 4d and four chamber pots at £2.)

French and an English cook. His present chief performer is of the former country, his English cook being killed in the last action, but notwithstanding this loss you will presently see one of John Bull's favourite dishes in all its glory,' and sure enough after two courses of all sorts of finery there were served up most admirable beefsteaks, smoking hot, and which to the eye and to the palate could not have been surpassed at Dolly's. A succession of these followed for half an hour, and I afterwards discovered that Sir Edward Hughes's nickname in the fleet was 'Hot-and-hot,' he being remarkably fond of, and always doing justice to, this truly English dish.

After a liberal allowance of the best French wines and madeira, and drinking nine public toasts, coffee was served. At dusk the party broke up, the different commanders repairing to their respective ships ...[5]

This was in 1783. Dinner was simpler, and later, on board the *Victory*:

At two o'clock, a band of music plays till within a quarter of three, when the drum beats the tune called *The Roast Beef of Old England* to announce the Admiral's dinner, which is served up exactly at three o'clock and which generally consists of three courses and a dessert of the choicest fruit, together with three or four of the best wines, champagne and claret not excepted. If a person does not feel himself perfectly at ease, it must be his fault ... Coffee and liqueurs close the dinner at about half-past four, or five o'clock, after which the company generally walk the deck, where the band of music plays for nearly an hour.[6]

If keeping a table was important to Captain Dillon, it was essential to flag officers. The Admiralty paid them table money when they applied for their wages, 20s a day until January 1806 then 30s thereafter. Nelson had simple tastes in food, and when he embarked in the *Vanguard* in March 1798 he chose a cook from the ship's company and subscribed with the wardroom for supplies (he paid £1 19s 0d a month): the caterer bought 'sugar, tripe, rice, cheeses and oysters' and 420 bottles of wine, and for livestock 'sheep, pigs, geese, ducks and fowls'. When St Vincent became Commander-in-Chief of the Channel Fleet in 1806, flying his flag in the *Hibernia* (110), he had not been to sea since 1801 and he spent more than £700 on 'food and drink, livestock, tableware, cooking utensils, furniture, carriage and boat hire'. When he joined her on 8 March, his stores included a range of spices and seasonings, such as ketchup, curry powder, cayenne, 'Quins Sauce', lemon pickle, chilli and tarragon vinegar, Harvey's sauce, mushrooms, French olives, capers, mixed pickles and essence of anchovies. He returned on 23 June, and spent 'much less ... principally on live-stock, fresh vegetables, and summer fruits': 'cherries, raspberries, currants and [four gallons of] gooseberries'. His kitchen equipment for preparing food included two cook's knives and a steel, a rolling pin, a turnip scoop, a ragout spoon, a poaching fork, a chopper, sugar and halibut nippers, oyster pincers and two tin funnels; equipment for making food on board included two tartlet pans, one round and one oval pudding mould, a box of pastry cutters, two dozen patty pans and two sausage fillers. An admiral's table had diaper and damask table-cloths, and silver spoons, or a complete set of silver cutlery, and plate was popu-lar with City guilds rewarding success in action.[7]

A dinner for ten, given for Rear Admiral Digby, in the *Prince George* (90) on the American station, on Tuesday 14 August 1781.[8]

Turtle

R' ducks

kedny beans	beat butter	Potatos
Pallets		sweet meat torts
Tongue	Limen pudding	Fowl brown sous
sweet meat Torts		muton strokes
carits & cabiges	beat butter	Abbocore*

Fish

R' mutton

Water

The log recorded that at noon the *Splendid* was in 41° 31' N, 5° 32' E, Cape Sicié bearing N12°E ninety-six miles, with the wind NbW, still fresh breezes but now accompanied by a swell from the northward. At 2pm the order was given to get up the water for the following day.[†] This was the duty of the forecastlemen, and the 1808 Regulations made it clear that recording the use of water, like beer and

---

* Abbocore is albacore, a species of tuna.

† Of all the essential daily tasks, hoisting the water from the hold is probably the least documented. The 1808 Regulations instructed the master not to permit 'more to be hoisted up in a day than the quantity allowed to be used', in the section about economical use of stores, with no directions on procedure or frequency. The captain's orders for the *Indefatigable* in 1812 included 'the water for the day (if other duty will permit) is got up every afternoon at three o'clock', which implies that it was an everyday evolution, but the order ends 'The mate is to acquaint the first lieutenant and master some days before water is wanted to be got at hand or any material alteration in the hold'.

firing, were the master's responsibility, since their stowage materially affected the ship's ability to stay at sea. The Regulations and Instructions ordered the captain to direct the master to report to him weekly the quantity of water used and remaining, and ordered the master to report to the captain daily the same information, while the purser was directed to obtain witnessed and certified receipts for water purchased while abroad; the purser was required to account for water used both by volume and by weight.[9]

In 1810 the water on board was still stored in wooden barrels in the hold. Ships-of-the-line stored the water with the beer in three tiers of progressively smaller barrels, with the lowest (the ground tier) bedded into the shingle ballast for stability. By 1810 it had become routine to use all three tiers to extend the time spent on station,[10] though it was a laborious and time-consuming job:

> the decks of a man-of-war, in consequence … of getting at her daily
> supply, bore a greater resemblance (pending the operation) to a wholesale
> cooperage than a battery, from the quantity of empty cases with which
> they were unavoidably lumbered. This frequently caused the greatest
> confusion, by constantly impeding the performance of important
> evolutions; such as 'making sail in chase', or clearing suddenly for action.[11]

Water could be started and pumped out directly in the hold, but the 1808 Regulations ordered the master not to permit it without 'particular directions from the captain'. The standard procedure was to sway the barrels and casks out of the hold and draw off the water on deck, where the casks were held in place by the water whip stay tackle ('two light tackles rigged as "yard" and "stay"'), which removed them from the hold – a water leaguer was only 4ft 10in long, with a maximum diameter of 3ft 3in – and the water was started 'upon deck from the bung-holes' into measured containers. It has been suggested that once on deck the barrels were put in rigid stands while the water was tapped off. When the King visited the *Hydra*, off Weymouth, he requested a glass of beer and 'a barrel was hoisted up and, being lowered on the fife-rail at the front of the quarterdeck and tapped, he had a tumbler presented to him', which perhaps indicates the usual practice. A marine vocabulary of 1805 stated that the scuttlebutt, the cask for daily drinking water, was lashed upon the deck, and it is possible to infer that this was standard for all casks, but unfortunately the word used in contemporary accounts for this process is 'started', which merely means emptied. Spirits were directed to be hoisted, however, and during the Egyptian expedition of 1800, troops carried in the *Duke of York* transport demanded more water and when refused took it: 'A soldier officer … said they wanted 5 butts and should have it, and no thanks, and immediately ordered the hatches to be forced, which was done by his orders and a butt of water forced therefrom at 8 p.m. or thereabouts', showing that casks as big as a butt were hoisted up full; Sir Gilbert Blane attributed most of the navy's hernias to 'the severe strains to which men are exposed in removing water casks from the hold for daily use at sea'. The obvious alternative is that the casks were pumped out on deck: the *Dreadnought* (60) had pumps in casks on deck in February 1758, for example, and pumping had several obvious advantages – it was quick, the cask was stable and the sediment could be left behind. However, the description and the time of day suggest this was a cask for drinking water (the ship was in the Caribbean), and the device that made this procedure obsolete, Truscott's force pump, was valued not least because 'the power of this pump will draw a cask quite out'.[12]

In 1811 Lieutenant George Truscott invented his new pump while in the *Dryad*. On 8 June he wrote to the Admiralty:

Sir

I have to beg you will do me the honor of laying before their Lordships, an invention which Captain Galwey has had the goodness to admit of my trying onboard the *Dryad* – and which I trust will be of the greatest benefit to His Majesty's Service.

Seeing the trouble, and lumber, ships are thrown in from getting up their water, induced me last cruise to beg Captain Galwey to admit of my trying the force pump in the well, on the orlop deck with leaden pipes conducted round the hold, to throw the water on the quarterdeck, which after a trial of nearly six weeks, during which time we have had several gales, I have found to answer, not leaving half a gallon in the casks, and a puncheon [72 gallons] pumped out in twelve minutes.

The pipe is connected about every six, or eight feet, by leather's about a foot in length, the tube which goes into the casks being also of leather, with a led [sic] elbow, and tubes within to hinder it from closing, by the present suction. The small tank on the quarterdeck contains about thirty gallons, which the Messenger boy fills in five minutes.

I beg leave to also mention, independent of the labour which is avoided, the very great expense it would be saving of in casks – for rarely does a ship, from her being obliged to get her water up, arrive in port, but what is found to get supplied with new casks, her own being destroyed by the hoops being knocked off, which breaches the chimes. In gales of wind the great difficulty of getting up the water, besides the numerous incidents occasioned thereby, all which may be obviated by the trifling expense of thirty five pounds.

I have now sir, to beg pardon of their Lordships for trespassing so long on their time, but should they think if worthy of their notice, I am certain Captain Galwey would feel great pleasure to give their Lordships every information they may require. I am sir
Your Most Obedient
Humble Servant[13]

Their lordships did think it worthy, and wrote to Captain Galwey, asking him 'to state his opinion of the utility of the invention.'

Captain Galwey's reply is dated *Dryad* at sea, 8 July 1811:

Gentlemen
In answer to your letter desiring to be acquainted how the plan which Lieut. George Truscott of the *Dryad*, invented for conveying the water from the casks in the hold to the ships tank, I am to acquaint you that it has succeeded extremely well, and it is in my oppinion one of the most satisfactory and useful contrivances, which have been tryed on board His Majesty's Ships – A forced pump fixed inside the pump well door, with a leaden pipe leads upward to the tank, and the same kind of pipe in length about six feet, connected together with stout leather hoses in the hold, according to the distance of the casks to be got at, either forward or in the wings, with the power of this pump will draw a cask quite out – This mode of getting at our water has been in use about two months in the *Dryad*, and I have found it to answer so well, with the alteration and amendments which have been made from time to time, that I have entirely done away with the large tank on the main deck, and only use the small one before the main mast on the quarterdeck, which contains about thirty gallons of water, filling it occasionally from the cask in the hold, which one of the smallest boys in the ship do with the greatest ease.

The method I have thus described for getting up the water on board a man of war, has much in my opinion to recommend it, instead of the whole afternoon being taken up rousing casks upon deck, and knocking them to pieces, heaving them up by the bungholes out of the hold, deranging the whole ship and lumbering up the decks with empty casks, and often employing the whole watch on this service when the [sic] might by this useful method being put in practice be very much more practically employed on other duties, which they are very often wanted for, and it is amongst the reasons which in my opinion make the mode I have thus described the more desirable to have established throughout the Service ... [14]

It was tested in *Malta* and *Bulwark*, and adopted in 1812. (The mention of tanks on deck is another problem; the *Culloden* certainly had one, which she filled with seawater to keep turtles in, and the *Castor* had one in 1810, but little more is known.) [15]

Drinking water for the ship's company was supplied in a scuttlebutt, 'a cask having a square piece sawn out of its bilge and lashed upon the deck'. It was traditionally 'scuttled' by having a square piece cut out of it through which the seamen drew water with a mug, but in the *Splendid* in the Mediterranean the supply was limited: there were casks on the quarterdeck, in the waist and at the wardroom door but they were fitted with cocks. There was a marine sentinel at the each one, whose orders were 'to allow the ship's company to drink as much water as they desire at the butt, but on no account to allow water to be taken away from it by any person, without orders from the quarterdeck delivered to him by a non-commissioned officer.' (This distinction seems to have been typical: Captain Pasley recorded his relief when on 16 March 1780, between the Cape Verde Islands and the Cape of Good Hope, the *Sybil* (28) experienced 'a heavy and uncommon fall of rain; on the coast of Guinea only I recollect to have seen it equalled. Filled several tons of water which, altho' we are not in immedeate want, enables me to give a larger allowance of this necessary element to the seamen, than which nothing contributes more to their health in long southern voyages. The men drink when, and as much as, they please – restrained only in carrying away more than one pint each for breakfast'.) Whenever possible, drinking water was supplied from rainwater, collected in the poop and quarterdeck awnings.* The navy bought water scoops, made of beech, with a 2ft 4in handle and a bowl 1ft 6in long, 9in wide and 2½in deep, which may have been intended for use at the scuttlebutt. Private drinking water was possibly common for officers: Nelson carried supplies of Bristol water to mix with his wine after dinner ('He never exceeded four glasses of wine after dinner, and seldom drank three; and even those were diluted with either Bristol or common water'), and

---

* For the value of rainwater in preserving health in southern voyages, see Captain Carteret's account of his voyage in the *Swallow*; he made an awning out of wood and the canvas supplied for a floor cloth for his cabin, and used it to collect rainwater, which he served out to the people mixed with spirit of vitriol, both for drinking and for mixing with the grog – the spirit of vitriol presumably because its acidity would be antiscorbutic.

when William Hickey sailed home from India in 1807 in the *Castle Eden* India-man he took with him thirty dozen bottles of water, 'which during the voyage home proved far more valuable than the wine, being a much scarcer commodity to get good', and which gave him and his fellow passengers an ample supply when the ship ran short. It was also carried by the passengers in the *Charlton* Indiaman in 1799; Mrs Ranken brought three hampers and found after her voyage (19 June to 7 November) that she and her husband had four bottles left, even though she gave half away to a friend who had brought none, 'for good water on board of ship is much scarcer than wine'. Some petty officers kept water in their berths, but whether it was private or ship's is not clear.[16]

As well as fresh water supplied for drinking, some fresh-water washing was allowed, but most of the daily supply was used for boiling the men's dinner. Wednesday was a beef-issued-as-pork day in the *Splendid*, so the cook needed 270 gallons, weighing 1 ton 3cwt 2qr 18lb 10oz, for the meat (had the ship been on salt meat the same would have been needed to steep it).[17] Water consumption was a perennial problem for the Admiralty, the Navy Board, ship's captains and admirals in command of a fleet. All ships could resupply themselves by sending watering parties in boats, but this was rarely possible except on a neutral or friendly coast. In the second half of the eighteenth century the Navy Board took as standard an issue of 180 tons to ships of 80, 90 and 100 guns, and 170 tons to 74-gun ships, but actual use clearly varied considerably: the *Victory* used three tons (648 gallons) a day in the Mediterranean in summer 1797; St Vincent expected the *Montague* (74) to use two tons (432 gallons) a day in August 1800 off Brest; *Culloden* (74), fitting out in Bombay harbour, 1805, used two and a half to three tons a day. A solution was Osbridge's machine for rendering sweet the stinking water from the casks, and for a generation, all ships had been directed to carry one. It worked by repeatedly splitting a stream of water into drops, and Dr Blane described it favourably in his *Observations on Diseases Incident to Seamen*, noting that 'It is a machine deservedly in common use, and the working it is a moderate and salutary exercise to men in fair weather'. There seem to be no ship-board references to its use, but records in the Office of Bills show that the navy was paying between £1 13s 0d and £1 7s 6d for 'tin machines for purifying stink-ing water' 'as demanded', which may be for these machines.* All ship's stoves

---

* The machine was 'made of plated sheet-iron, with several flat-bottomed trays placed one above the other, with a space between. The bottom of each tray is pierced like a collender [*sic*], so that, with the aid of a machine-driven pump, the water from the bottom of the usual drinking casks on deck is raised six feet high to the topmost collender; it is then filtered through this in large drops, and falls from tray to tray in an increasingly fine rain, until it is down again in the cask, to be continuously raised once more and dropped many times'.

could be fitted with distilling equipment to convert seawater to pure water for the use of the sick but again their use is rarely mentioned. The *Intrepid* (64) carried a distilling machine on her voyage to the West Indies in 1772 that gave ten to thirteen gallons an hour, and Lamb fitted an apparatus to his new stove that produced twenty to twenty-five gallons of fresh water per hour when tried in the *Trusty* (50), without using extra fuel, and her captain reported that 'the coppers boil in one-third less time than by any mode before employed', but it is not clear whether any ships routinely distilled water. That the equipment was not always fitted is shown, for example, by Captain Pasley in the *Sybil* (28), who on 12 February 1780 opened his sealed orders off the Lizard and found he was to sail to the Cape of Good Hope; he regretted not being told of his destination before he left England, because 'I would have added to my water; carried no beer; and floored my ship between decks with casks, however fatal to my ship's company. At the yard they refused to fix my coppers for the distillation of salt water, so that resource is denied me'. (Some East India Company ships carried portable stills, or distilling apparatus, but for the livestock.)[18]

The Victualling Board allowed pursers to claim waste of cask at the rate of one tun per hundred men per month, and estimated water cask at 'Three tuns to one hundred men a month, in regard to the great decay of the ground tier, and shaking the cask, and setting them up again'. This included casks used for 'washing-tubs, steep-tubs, or by the cook'. The Regulations noted: 'The very great demand for beer and water casks at the out ports, making it extremely difficult, more especially in time of war, to raise and fit them fast enough, and the expense attending the same being very great; and as both the difficulty and expense would be materially lessened if the beer and water casks on board ships employed in Home or Channel service were not to be shaken, all commanders of His Majesty's ships so employed are hereby most strictly required, never to suffer the empty beer or water casks to be shaken unless in cases of absolute necessity; and when such necessity shall arise, to give particular orders that the casks be very carefully taken to pieces, and the staves and heading marked and packed in such a manner as shall enable the cooper to set them up again';[19] even at the eastern end of the Mediterranean, Collingwood was well supplied, but he had complained of their misuse:

> A great number of casks come out in every victualler, more I believe than
> the current consumption, so that I cannot account for the defective
> nature of them. I am afraid it sometimes happens that casks are shook,
> for the convenience of making room, as I remember it was in one ship,

and that those good staves are not selected, but thrown indiscriminately with the bad into the ship which receives old stores: the most strict injunctions must be given against shaking any water casks. Empty wine pipes, white washed within, with hot lime, which destroys the acid, make very good casks for the transports upper tier, of which each ship should take a proportion and start. I need not observe to you, my dear sir, the necessity of practising whatever can be devised for promoting the economical use of casks, and every thing else, because I know you feel the necessity of it as I do, at a time when the difficulty of obtaining supplies to the extent they are wanted every day increases.[20]

The navy made whitewash (limewash) with seawater; it could be prepared and stored on board (the *Splendid* carried 8cwt), and the Mediterranean Fleet carried ready-made stocks (for example, in the approach to the enemy fleet at Trafalgar, Nelson noticed that 'the enemy had iron hoops round their masts painted black; orders were issued by signal to whitewash those of his fleet, that in the event of all the ensigns being shot away, his ships might be distinguished by their white masts and hoops'). Because it contained lime, it was particularly useful for the sick bay, and for general cleanliness; the *York* (74), moored in Port Mahon harbour in June 1810, whitewashed her lower and orlop decks, and the white-painted lower decks of the *Mars* under Captain Lloyd had 'the cheerful look of a drawing-room'. However, there was no standard practice for handling and storing water casks in 1810.* If not reused, the proper procedure for empty casks was to be stowed, sent ashore or filled with seawater (to maintain the ship's trim).[21]

Watering at sea or on shore was carried out by the ship's boats. In January 1802 Keats issued instructions for the watering parties of the *Superb* at Tetuan that serve as a model for all such:

The officer charged with the watering party on shore from the *Superb*, is

---

* Dr Snipe, Physician to the Mediterranean Fleet, recommended charring the inside of the casks annually, as the East India Company did. 'Water unless it is very pure indeed, produces a slimy matter which adheres firmly to the inside of casks, and cannot be separated by common rinsing', and charring them worked because the 'pores of the wood are so effectually shut, that the staves cannot absorb the water which very soon rots them. When ships are first fitted out there can be no excuse for not carefully charring the casks. It is very little additional expense or trouble, and in the end it would be a considerable saving to the Crown.

'The waste of the human species in hot climates are [*sic*] almost invariably occasioned by bad water, and more particularly seamen. The East India Company have of late charred all their water casks, and fluxes which formerly carried off one half of their crews, also the troops they carried out, is [*sic*] a disease now scarcely known on their ships ...

'By putting a portion of lime into each water cask when full it in a great measure preserves the water sweet, and effectively destroys all *animalculae* which often generate into a species of maggot.'

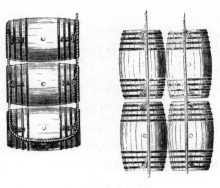

Methods of 'rafting' casks.

desired to occupy as convenient a situation as circumstances will allow for watering, but separate from any other ship, & particular attention must be had to prevent his Cask being mixed with other ship's [*sic*]. He is to take care that the cask are handled gently, are well rinsed, & when full, to be well bunged, & whether sent off in boats or by raft, that they are slung & stowed bung up – He is to cause the cooper to examine each cask, & to mark the initials S.B. or the ship's name on the stave next the bung stave of any that may be found without mark – He is to take great care that no boats are sent off overloaded, especially if they are taking extra men on board; – and that the launch under most favourable circumstances of weather, do never take in more than 18 [*sic*] butts – No boat should be allowed to lay on the beach, but at a grapnel, or on their oars, & the petty officers & crews not allowed to stray from them: – When there is a brooming party employed, the broomstuff may be sent off in such small quantities in the boats as not to render it inconvenient to row. – A look out is to be kept on the ship for signals, & early notice is to be given when in want of empty cask, of boats to take off rafts, & also at such times as the surf may be found to rise suddenly, or to such a degree as to render it impracticable to water – When the party returns on board, great care is to be taken not to leave any buckets, funnels, hoses, rope, strands of yarns, etc., etc., on shore; and at all such times that cask are left, they should be carefully rolled above high water mark, placed in rows together, bung up, & in a distinct & separate place from that of the cask of any other ship, & their numbers should be mentioned to the officer of the Moorish guard.[22]

The launch was the best type of boat for this evolution. It had less sheer and a squarer midsection than other ship's boats, it was usually cutter-rigged (with mizzen sails from 1803), and from 1783 was equipped to row double-banked, with fourteen men, a midshipman and a coxswain. In 1804 the Admiralty decided that 'Launches at present supplied to ships are not properly calculated for watering them', and new launches of First and Second Rates should floor fourteen butts, and Third Rates' should floor twelve butts. The butts were rowed to a river or spring, rinsed and filled, and rowed or towed back to the ship.[23] Jeffrey de Raigersfeld described the process of filling butts at Dominica:

> The casks were landed from the boats and rolled to a deep part of the river, filled and bunged up; they were then rolled down again into the salt water, when the men floated them, and fastening them one to the other, they were towed on board, and as the wind blew off shore, the boats were soon alongside the ship, which was at anchor between two and three miles off shore, in nearly sixty fathoms water, so very clear that the anchor could be seen distinctly lying at the bottom.[24]

When a whole fleet came to water the local inhabitants made the most of the opportunity, as they did at Cagliari in 1805:

> Monday April 1st 1805: everything being in readiness to receive the water, all the boats proceeded on shore with casks, etc., and in a short time tents were pitched, guards stationed, triangles [lifting frames] erected and the whole shore looked like a camp and a fair united; hundreds of the natives flocked down bringing quantities of provisions, animals, vegetables, fruit, etc., which of course met with a most welcome reception from 12,000 men, with plenty of money, and no means for two years before of spending it, so that these ships were all loaded with these luxuries ...
>
> Never was a place better adapted for watering a fleet: the boldness of the shore admits the ships to approach within a few hundred yards[,] and about a dozen paces from the sea shore is a delightful river, divided only by a bank from the sea, and empties itself into it; it is a running serpentine stream from the interior, of course very clear. The boats are ranged along close to shore, the casks rolled over to the river, and when filled by one party, are returned to the boats, hoisted in by the triangles and rowed to the ships, and so return. The tents pitched on shore are for the guards who attend these proceedings, and pass the day in the most delightful manner, as the shore, especially the banks of the river, is

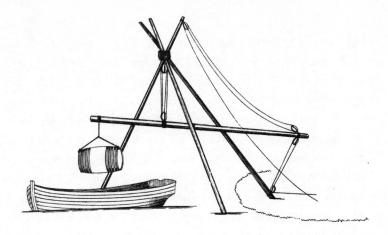

The use of a 'triangle' for hoisting casks into a boat.

covered with flowers, in the midst of which they pitch a tent, and their friends dine with them, their dinner dressed after the fashion of the gipsies etc. In this manner is a fleet of 15 ships completed with water for 12,000 men for 4 months and in the space of 2 days and some hours.[25]

James Anthony Gardner used the opportunity of watering near Carthage to do a little sightseeing and had to be rescued from the Turks, and watering parties remained the most popular opportunity for desertion throughout the war.[26] William Saunders, a seaman of the *Arrogant* (74), was in a watering party near Goa.

I went on shore with Mr Cochrine on the 25 of January [1798] To fill & Load a lighter of water, which by Mr Cochrine's Orders we helped To Do & when we hal [*sic*] Almost Done. Mr Dalrimple Came on Shore & Reliev'd Mr Cochrine, when we had Loaded the Lighter, we Asked Mr Dalrimple Leave to go to the top of the hill To Get some Todey [*sic*]. He Gave Us Leave & we promised him that we would be back in Ten Minutes if there was Any there – When we Came To the Top of the Hill. The black people Told Us that they had None there, but there was some Tody [*sic*] & Arrack about one Mile from That, we Imediatly Mustered Up all our Money & found it To Amount To Two Pagodas = we then proceeded To A Dutchmans house were [*sic*] we Got Evrything wich we could wish for & our not being on shore for sometime before Induced Us To Stop Longer that what we should have Done, we found ourselves so Comfortable Situated that we was Determined Not To Come on Board Untill our small sum was Exhausted, Lett the Consiquence be what it would, on the 26 in the Morning we Came Down upon the Beech which was About twenty Yards from the Dutchmans House, we Could Not see the Lighter at the Watering Place. – Therefore we concluded that She went on Board without Us. We Returned to Dutchmans were [*sic*] we Remained until the Next Morning, our Money being then All Gone but one Rupee, we Took our Leaves of the Dutchmans & proceeded towards the Garrson [*sic*] in order To Get Aboat [*sic*] To Come on Board Imediatly on our way we met with three of our women & Laurince Courtney & two or three boys = They Told Us There was No boat then One [*sic*] Shore Neither Did They Expect any Untill Near Night, we told them by that time our Mony would be Quite Gone & then we would Go on Board with them, we Imediatly went into a house Close by the Roadside were [*sic*] we remained untill Near 3 Oclock = when there Came A party of Soldiers into the house they said they was in Search of three Men Belonging To the Arrogant, they Asked us if we belonged to that ship = we told them we did = the Corpl. Imediatly puld a piece of paper out of his pockett and Gave it To Us To Read: which we did & found it To be our Description they asked us if we was the persons therein mentioned = we Told them we was & was willing To Go with them were Ever they pleased

He was delivered to the ship by the guard on shore on the 28th; he was confined but there being so little chance of ships meeting together to constitute a court martial he was liberated, but deserted on 19 March and was brought back from the guard house at Goa on the 25th. He was sentenced to 200 lashes round the fleet and all pay due mulcted in favour of Greenwich Hospital. It is not stated why the other two men were not tried.[27]

Watering parties on tropical shores were issued with Peruvian bark as a specific against malaria morning and evening, a drachm of Peruvian bark in half a gill of sound wine and another half-gill immediately afterwards (making sure it was 'some of the best of the wine supplied for the ship's use'), repeated on their return in the evening.[28]

The best English river water was generally held to be from the Thames – for the Cadiz expedition of 1701 the hospital ships were stocked with Thames water brought specially to Portsmouth[29] – but after fifty years of industrialisation it had become less than ideal. Joseph Bates was a seaman in the *Fanny* merchantman of New York when she filled her casks in 1807:

When we hauled out of the dock into the river Thames, and commenced filling our water-casks for our homeward voyage with the river water that was passing us, finding its way to the great ocean, I thought, how could a person drink such filthy water. Streaks of green, yellow, and red muddy water, mixed up with the filth of thousands of shipping, and scum and filth of a great portion of the city of London. After a few days it becomes settled and clear, unless it is stirred up from the bottom of the water casks.

Four years later he was an impressed sailor in the *Rodney* (74) in the Mediterranean:

we were emptying out all our old stock of fresh water; the ground tier was full of the same river water from the Thames, only a little further down from London, and had been bunged up tight for about two years. On starting the bung and applying our lighted candle, it would blaze up a foot high, like the burning of strong brandy. Before stirring it up from the bottom, some of the clear was exhibited among the officers in glass tumblers, and pronounced to be the purest and best of water, only about two years from London. I admit that it looked clear and tasted good, but from my former knowledge of its origin, I confess I had a little rather quench my thirst from some of the pure springs from the Green Mountains of Vermont, or granite hills in New Hampshire.[30]

Ships that came to the English dockyards for water were by the end of the war supplied by the Victualling Board's ships, lighters and boats, an improvement on the original arrangement by which ships sent their own boats. Captain Sir Hyde Parker, for example, commanding at Portsmouth, complained to the Admiralty in January 1793 that

at this season of the year it is impossible for the ships to keep their proportion of water complete by means of their own boats; and that the launches employed on that service are frequently detained on shore in bad weather, the boats damaged and the crews of them forced to sleep on board some of the ships in the harbour without their bedding, a circumstance of such inconvenience and hardship to the men as tends more to induce their deserting the service than perhaps any other.[31]

In foreign harbours pumps, tanks and other machines could be made use of. St Michael's Road in the Azores had three cocks: 'Two of the three cocks which are for the supply of the inhabitants were given up to us by day and the other at night – and on an average a butt could be filled from each of these cocks in 15 or 16 minutes.' Minorca did not offer much water, and Gibraltar, where 'in some seasons' 'water has been of as much value as wine' was historically ill-provided: 'the flow of water into the tanks and well is so slow that they will not produce more than forty-two tons a day exclusive of the supply required by the frigates [*Dolphin* and *Flora*]', complained Captain Ball of the *Alexander* (74) in 1797.[32] In March 1802 Captain Keats in the *Superb* was obliged to investigate reports of a fight between his watering party and a Portuguese frigate there. He concluded that

on Lieut. Butler's arrival at the watering place with the *Superb*'s launch, he found the Portuguese Commodore's launch at the outer part of the stage occupying two cocks, and as the *Superb*'s drew too much water to occupy the cocks further in, which, without inconvenience or delay could be done by the Portuguese launch from her light draught of water, and with the advantage of filling both boats at the same time, Lieut. Butler assures me (and his testimony is corroborated by the mate & pateroon of his boat, & particularly by Mr Gale mate of the *Cesar*, who was present and saw the transaction) that he represented to the Portuguese officer the advantage such a movement would be of to him & civilly asked him to shift his boat, to which he would not consent; after repeating his request in vain, Lieut. Butler acknowledges he ordered the Portuguese boat's sternfast to be cast off – that the painter was not cut by our people [as alleged] seems unquestionable from three several testimonies, all of which say they heard Mr Butler particularly *forbid* it's [sic] being cut: – The mates of the *Cesar* & *Superb* declare, and also Lieut. Butler, that no indecent or uncivil expression was made use of by him; – on the contrary they all represent the Portuguese officer as high and seemingly uncivil in his language & in proof of his being of a very unaccommodating disposition, Mr Gale prior to the arrival of the *Superb*'s boat had civilly requested him to move his boat a very small distance ahead, which without any *hindrance*, delay or inconvenience to the Portuguese would have enabled Mr Gale to make use of a third cock inoccupied [sic] by the Portuguese, but which he would not consent to do. – The Portuguese officer on Lieut. Butler's having order'd his sternfast to be cast off for the reason I have stated, made use of some Language which they considered threatening, which induced three of his men to draw offensive weapons, & produced some recriminatory Language from the Seamen of both Boats ...

Had the Portuguese Officer been guided by the same spirit of accommodation & conciliation which I trust the *Superb*'s was, no cause would have existed for offence. I am at all events concerned any has, & conformable to your wish (& I am sure my own Inclination) shall renew my directions to the officers of all denominations [commissioned, warrant, and petty], to conduct themselves on all occasions with great civility & attention to the Portuguese.[33]

Gibraltar had recently been upgraded, however. In the autumn of 1797, St Vincent having represented that 'the springs being frequently drained and that the men of war find it tedious to fill their casks', Commissioner Inglefield proposed a reservoir of four tanks ('to secure a portion of the water in case of accident'), to be filled by both summer and winter rain, and in 1803 an underground brick-lined bomb-proof tank or reservoir was completed, 200ft long, 60ft wide and 17ft high, and supplied by rainwater both from the hillsides and from the neighbouring buildings between October and May. The four chambers meant it could be 'made useful in the progress of building it', when full it held 10,462 butts, or about 5,000 tons, of water, and supplied '25 sail-of-the-line and some frigates' in the three dry months, filling their launches 'by pipes and hoses'.[34]

In the early part of the war the squadron in the western Mediterranean got much of its water from the river at Mazara Bay, a few miles to the eastward of Tetuan, despite the fact that the governor had to be continually bribed or conciliated – Keats, who was frequently sent to water for the fleet, was convinced that 'the impediments we meet may be traced to the intrigues of our enemies'.[35] When Spain had re-entered the war on the British side, Mahon was opened again.

Once back at the ship the water had to be brought on board and stowed in the hold. The casks were filled or refilled on deck and swung directly into the hold; this was the job of the waisters, the relatively unskilled men who were not trusted to go aloft, under the direction of a lieutenant, and the stowage was the duty of the mates of the hold, under the supervision of the master. Above the leaguers in the ground tier were two more tiers of progressively smaller casks: in order, they were butts, puncheons, hogsheads, barrels and half-hogsheads, wedged to keep them stable, with barrels or half-hogsheads using up any gaps:[36] and in July 1800 St Vincent issued a general order that expressed his surprise that when the ships under his command [of the Channel Fleet] go into port for the express purpose of filling up with water, there is the smallest space in the hold left unoccupied; and he requires in future that every possible means be used to stow, even to a barrel, and no pretence of 'room to stow away chests' or other accommodation, at the whim of the master or mates of the hold, will be admitted.[37]

By 1810 ships had become accomplished at resupplying with water at sea from ships of the fleet or from transports, though the biggest barrel used was the half-ton butt, containing 108 beer gallons, and it was a time-consuming business. On 9 July 1810, for example, the *Tigre* (74) rendezvoused with a transport in 42° 34' 39"N and 6° 12' 29"E, about thirty-one miles south of Cape Sicié, and at about 8am, in fine weather began getting her water. In the afternoon, 'moderate winds and fine weather', the *Sultan* (74) joined and gave the *Tigre* six sheep, one bullock and forty-three bags of vegetables, to add to the three bags of onions she had received from the transport. At the same time she broached four casks of beef and four of pork, forty-two and eighty-four pieces each. (The *Sultan*, meanwhile, spent the afternoon supplying the fleet with six bullocks, seventy-two sheep and twenty-three tons of water.) At 4pm she received from the *Colossus* (74) seven casks of beef, twenty-nine of pork and one of beer, and fifty bags of bread, and at 4pm got the launch in. At 4am the next day, 'light airs and fine weather', the boats returned to the transport for more water, and at 8am, 'nearly calm', she received forty butts of her own from the *York* (74) that had been filled at Mahon, 'two of them stove and shook nearly all leaked out and several others more than ¼ leaked out'. Before noon she had got thirty-three of her own butts and seventy-three puncheons from the transport and filled 158 butts (seventy-nine tons) in the hold and returned 227 empty butts, and in the afternoon, 'light winds and fine weather', returned the empty puncheons to the transport and sent on board twenty-one of her own butts to be filled at Mahon.[38]

The introduction of Truscott's pump meant that casks could remain in position throughout a cruise, and in 1814 iron tanks began to replace casks. They were made to measure for each ship and placed directly on the riders, the shingle ballast no longer being needed.[39]

UPPER DECK

As soon as noon was declared the officer of the watch ordered the boatswain to pipe to dinner. The mess cooks had been waiting in order according to the number of their mess, and the cook and his assistant had prepared two tubs, one with each mess's net of meat and net of vegetables, the other with the pudding bags. The cook, like most ship's cooks, 'was not over and above stocked with learning' and he had prepared the steward's list of messes by 'making a mark with a pin on the paper opposite the number of the messes' the raw meat had been issued out to. The moment the boatswain piped to dinner was long anticipated, and the notes were 'nearly drowned next instant in the rattle of tubs and kettles, the voice of the ship's cook and his mates bawling out the numbers of the messes, as well as by the sound of feet tramping along the decks and down the ladders with the steaming, ample store of provisions.'[40]

Dinner in the wardroom

The wardroom in the *Splendid* dined at one o'clock. It was the main meal of the day (lunch was still rather modish), and all the wardroom officers attended except the officer of the watch. The wardroom table in ships-of-the-line ran fore-and-aft; it comprised three smaller tables and when they were joined together it was very substantial. When the wardroom was at dinner, the table had a president at its head and a vice-president at its foot (in the *Splendid* the presidency was changed each week), and each officer had his servant to each chair: 'It was now my object to see that no officer surpassed my master in a well-brushed coat, in the brilliancy of his boots and shoes, and in the neatness and order of his cabin; to appear, which his kindness enabled me to do, clean and tidy at the back of his chair at dinner, and to take care that if he missed his share of the good things going at the ward-room table, it would be no fault of mine', wrote Landsman Hay.[41]

In the reign of George III, dinner, both on land and at sea, was according to the 'French service'. 'For each course the table was covered with a large number of different dishes of varying sizes according to the positions they occupied' – recipe books of the period are full of diagrams of table arrangements. 'At each end there was a large tureen of soup, one thick and one thin. When the guests had drunk a polite bowlful, the tureens were removed and their place was filled with splendid roasts, beef or venison, and a large fish: these were carved and cut up by the host and hostess' – in the service, by the president and vice-president of the mess. 'To all the other dishes, people helped their neighbours and themselves.' The several dishes placed on the table together for each course were sweet, savoury or sometimes both; a remove was a smaller dish changed while the course remained, sometimes with a contrasting dish. Examples are recorded, in plan form, in the table book of John Gulivar, steward to Rear Admiral Robert Digby, commander-in-chief on the American station aboard the

Royal George (98) (p. 127). The arrangement could assume great importance: General Sir Alured Clarke, Commander-in-Chief Bengal in 1797, for example, 'could not bear to see any dish removed from one part of the table to another, nor any person to attempt carving what stood before him until the whole course was completely set out and arranged'. These were 'peculiarities that gave great offence to some of his guests', but when William Holmes, chaplain of the *America* (64), took the joint from the vice-president at dinner with the intention of helping himself he was court-martialled for scandalous behaviour. (He was also alleged to have put a dog on the supper table, and to have made a number of frivolous or groundless complaints.[42]

Conversation was inevitably limited. William Hickey, in the *Plassey* Indiaman, noted that 'The effect of [the surf at Madras], and the numerous incidents that happen from it, is generally the topic of conversation the first fortnight of a voyage out', George Parsons remembered that 'the master's tale [of his shipwreck] was a standing dish in our gunroom, and came with the wine on the dinner-table daily' and William Dillon had the *Horatio* (38) 'disfigured in her painting to make her look like a foreign man of war, and occasionally boarded a craft under the expectation of obtaining some information, however small', just to have 'something to talk about when alone in the midst of the ocean'. Many wardrooms banned discussion of certain topics, especially their professional duties: Ralph Beaver, first lieutenant in the *Barfleur* (90) in 1799, even banned the delivery of a letter on naval business and the officer had to receive it on the quarterdeck, but in this he seems to have been excessively formal.[43]

The wardroom officers' supplies usually comprised both the food, drink and livestock purchased collectively for the mess and their own private supplies. The usual impression is that the officer chosen caterer of the mess was responsible for these purchases, but in the *Splendid* the purser acted as agent; he was frequently on shore buying supplies for the fleet, often in very large quantities, and it was becoming increasingly common.[44]

The wardroom generally broke up around three or half-past, after sitting over their wine – Major Wybourn of the marines greatly enjoyed a dinner given in Sicily, but noted 'after dinner came a most elegant service of every fruit of the Country and choice wines, but their custom is to break up after the third or fourth glass, not quite according with John Bull's notion',* and the abstemious

---

* On the evening the *Blanche* (32) anchored in Leghorn Bay after arriving from England in 1796, the officers 'all sat down to drink to see who could get drunk first. After they were drunk they were riotous between themselves. Mr Cowan jump'd up out of his chair and came out of the gunroom door and knocked [the sentry] down. After that he threw the oil bottle into the gunroom, and beat the chairs, glasses and bottles about the place, calling out for Charley Sawyer, a man fucking buggar, and swore he would kill him'.

Nelson could only 'bear' five glasses of wine on the anniversary of the Nile – but much later if it was a special occasion or if guests were present.[45]

In 1812 Wybourn gave a birthday dinner in the *Marlborough* (74), off Harwich:

> My birthday commenced & finished with great mirth, gaiety & happiness, tho' no previous plan. A large party of 14 ladies & several gentlemen came on board to see the ship. I escorted them & having put dinner back an hour & increased it to *double* the quantity, made them all stay, to their inexpressible delight, not one of them having seen a military or naval society before & when they saw a room full of servants with 25 or 30 covers as bright as silver, with tables covered with plate & china, they stared in wonder at each other. We made the men very *happy*, before they parted & the ladies were gratified with a dance on the quarterdeck, our excellent band was also a great treat. ... The day passed off to the satisfaction of everyone & the party went off by moonlight, escorted by several officers to bring the boats back.[46]

Even towards the end of a voyage across the Atlantic the *Marlborough* assembled an impressive New Year spread:

> The day commenced with lovely weather, & a fair wind. We have now traversed an immense expanse of water, upwards of 2,000 miles without seeing an individual object on the surface of the sea. Gave a very grand Gala & kept it up as on Xmas Day, as no idea of a [?] dinner, after so long a voyage can be imagined. I will merely enumerate the articles, as I myself gave the steward, and which, as we shortly expect to see Bermuda, we launched out in, certainly extravagantly: — excellent soup, salt fish, saddle mutton, round of beef, leg of roast pork, giblet pie, a curry, a couple of boiled fowls, a ham, couple of roast ducks, a turkey, raspberry pudding. plum duff, pumpkin pie & the remainder of our old Port wine (11 years) with excellent Madeira & sherry – nor do I believe a London tavern cd. have dressed a better dinner. Conviviality & harmony subsisted till one o'clock, songs, glees, etc., the remaining half of the Mids dined with us.[47]

The *Marlborough*'s band was not unusual; professional and semi-professional music had been an essential part of daily life for many officers since at least the 1790s. The *Macedonian* had a band collected by John S Carden, 'composed of Frenchmen, Italians and Germans, taken by the Portuguese from a French vessel. These musicians consented to serve, on condition of being excused from fighting, and on a pledge of exemption from being flogged. They used to play to the captain during his dinner hour; the party to be amused usually consisting of the captain and one or two invited guests from the ward-room; except on Sundays, when he chose to honor the ward-room with his august presence'; when the *Macedonian* was captured by the *United States* they shipped with Decatur. In the summer of 1796, the seventeen-year-old Betsey Wynne, a guest aboard the *Goliath* (74) in the Mediterranean, recorded 'I was much delighted this evening' when the *Courageous* joined company: 'There is a famous band of musick on board of her and all night they played the most charming tunes ... the flutes and bugle horns made a most delightful effect', and when Rear Admiral Stopford 'came on board and hoisted his flag on board the *Caesar*', in Basque Roads in 1809, he brought with him 'two lieutenants, a captain of marines, a chaplain, a secretary and his clerk, two master's mates, nine midshipmen, his coxswain and a band, and two live bullocks, which were very acceptable, as we have not tasted fresh beef this long time.'[48]

LOWER DECK

Dinner

The noon dinner hour was for the men and boys, marines and petty officers. They were summoned together by the boatswain and his mates, who gave a 'long and various piping'. They ate in their messes in their berths, at deal tables that swung down from the deck. They supplied their own utensils: cutlery was a spoon made of wood, tin or horn and a sharp all-purpose knife; tableware was plates, typically square lipped oak trays 11¾in on a side, and bowls, usually wood; some examples recovered from the *Invincible* are elm, 11¾in across. For beer there were mugs and tankards; *Invincible* examples include a mug and a tankard 6in and 6½in tall, made of twelve lignum-vitae staves bound with string; the tankard has a lid with a carved oak tree. Horn mugs were also used. (The *Invincible* (74) was the ex-French *Invincible*, captured in 1747, that began the Large Class 74s. She was wrecked on the Dean Sand near Portsmouth in February 1758.) By 1810 china was common; cups were owned for tea, and a marine berth in the *London* had a white basin for wine in 1800.* For general use there were kids, small wooden tubs, that could carry food or drink.[49]

---

* 'The Prisoner was in his birth at the foremost capstan, after dinner he was asleep, and he slept for a considerable time with his hands under his head, untill the wine was served out – One of his messmates poured him out a pint of wine, in a white bason – the Prisoner he woke, and drank some of the wine and poured the rest into a kid. He went then as centinel, at the after ladder, and seemed quite stupid.'

Both the eighteenth-century stoves and the Brodie's stove that replaced them had capacities based on half a gallon per man of the complement, in two boilers,[50] so that the whole complement could eat together, with the exception of the seven-bell men, but men who were still at work when dinner was piped – especially waisters and idlers, who were not worked by watches – went without, unless their messmates saved it for them or they could find an opportunity to cook their skewer pieces or private stores. Dr Trotter thought that boat's crews suffered particularly in this respect, and were 'generally ragged as well as sickly', because they sold their clothes 'to buy food, on account of their being unnecessarily kept on shore, to the loss of their regular meals with the rest of the ship's company'; the captain's orders in the *Splendid* guarded against this particularly, directing that 'the commanding officer will, when situation, weather and service permits, send a boat for them, one after breakfast, another before their dinner hour and one to be on board by sunset', unless 'from the appearance of the weather' there 'is risk of their not returning.'[51]

Today was Tuesday, and so a beef day: each man was allowed a piece or pieces weighing 2lb before cooking. The standard-issue salt meat was always boiled (skewer meat and private stocks were cooked privately), and when beef was issued half of it could be replaced by 'a proportion of flour, raisins, or suet' to make suet puddings; but this was only for the first four months' victualling of a cruise, and the *Splendid* had been out two years. When fresh meat was issued the men were also given vegetables – the regulations stated 'roots and greens', leaving it to the captain or purser to buy whatever was available locally, always remembering that the expense was not to exceed the value of the pease saved. Onions were most popular, being antiscorbutic and full of flavour whether cooked or raw. Cabbages, leeks and potatoes were widespread when available; St Vincent thought carrots were 'far the best root for taking to sea'; and in the Mediterranean, pumpkins were very useful for both flesh and seeds.[52]

The dried vegetable issued was pease, half a pint per man on pork days (Sundays and Thursdays) and on banyan days (Wednesdays and Fridays). It is not clear whether these were whole green or split yellow: accounts exist of both, and most probably the green were made into soup and the yellow boiled in a cloth. When fresh vegetables were issued the pease was served on Monday, and the oatmeal that would have been their dinner served at breakfast.[53]

The eighteenth-century navy had a suspicion of fresh fruit, particularly unfamiliar ones such as 'that mischievous and dangerous fruit, the pineapple', and fruit was forbidden to be sold, but by 1808 long experience of blockade had shown its necessity, and the Regulations omit the clause. The *Splendid*'s great cabin had 'grapes clustered' and 'oranges in nettings hung thick' 'with peaches and nectarines', and when the *Macedonian* lay at Lisbon, 'our ship was well supplied with fruits from the shore. Large bunches of delicious grapes, abundance of sweet oranges, water-melons, chestnuts, and also a bountiful supply of gigantic onions, of peculiar flavour, enabled our crew to gratify their palates in true English style.'[54]

By the captain's order dinner lasted an hour and a quarter. One historian has wondered whether the men 'ate their meat dinners hot', because of the time taken to serve the food; but a letter by the captain of the *Acasta* (40) reporting the benefits of installing gratings between the quarterdeck and forecastle when she was in the West Indies included the fact that when the ship's company turned in at night the gundeck was 'comparatively cool and comfortable', 'not having been heated during the day by hot provisions & the exhalations of the people'. The *Splendid* was not a silent ship, but many were, and in these ships especially dinner was the most important time of the day that the men had to themselves. Conscientious captains therefore often made it part of their orders that they were not to be disturbed at meals. Thoughtless or uncaring officers frequently did break in on this private time: the maintopmen in the *Rodney* were 'immediately ordered from their dinner hour to appear on the quarterdeck' because a pair of wet trousers had been found 'in a concealed place behind the main-topsail', and while the butcher of the *America* was at dinner the chaplain summoned him and 'abused him, for not feeding the sheep properly ... he convinced the [chaplain] that they had more than they could eat – the chaplain appeared very angry what reply he (the butcher) made him, which was, that he could feed sheep as well as the [chaplain] could'.[55]

The noon dinner hour included the members of the midshipmen's berth, who were officially ratings; but though ratings, they were expected to maintain the standards of officers, which meant keeping a mess. The *Splendid* had sixteen midshipmen, and they had laid in supplies: 'we sent for our stock of tea, sugar and other groceries for the voyage; they were brought on board and deposited in the bottom of a sort of buffet at the end of a berth, the upper part serving for the mess utensils, cups, plates, dishes, glasses, etc.' Off the Maddalena Islands a friendly captain had sent a boat: it 'contained one of the most acceptable presents, I will answer for it, that ever was made to mortal – it was truly manna to starved people – being no less than a famous fat goose, a huge leg of pork, and a bag of potatoes!' Unfortunately, in the recent storm the sea had got in and destroyed it all, and they were reduced to ship's food.[56]

By this time too the Reefer's Mess
Of course had come to dire distress,
As usual each gradation known
From Grub galore, to the King's own;
The Murphies all being eaten too,
They could not even sport a stew;
To 'save the pieces,' was no joke,
For all their Staffordshire was broke;—
As for their Cookery, John, we're sure,
Was now a perfect Connoisseur—
Salt Junk and Pork, Pillaws of Rice,
Lob's Cowse [sic], Dog's Body, and Sea-pies,
Pea-coffee, Hurryhush, and Chowder,
Fresh Waster tasting of Gunpowder,
(Which Seamen say's the best with Rum)
Were all familiar now become—
And tho' he did not drink his quartern,
He'd eat boiled pork like any Spartan,
Nay seldom could he find enough
They said 'to choak his bloody luff.'[57]

While the ship's company ate the ship's day continued, with the seven-bell men, the sentinels, lookouts and helmsmen on deck, and they needed to eat; there were also men who had been given skewer pieces and men with their own supplies: unofficial or private cooking was clearly an essential part of the ship's life. A Brodie's stove was supplied with stewing stoves, each with two grates (100- and 90-gun ships seven; 84 and 80, six; 74 and 64, five), and as a court-martial in the *Bellerophon* shows, it was not unusual.[58] James Fennigan, sergeant of marines, was on trial for striking the gunner's servant, quarrelling with and using insolent and improper expressions to the gunner, and catching hold of his coat and jostling against him in a mutinous manner. His account was as follows:

on the eleventh of this month, I sent one of my messmates to the galley to dress some beefsteaks; some duty calling him away I went thither myself in order to dress them. I had not been in the galley many minutes when the gunner's son came there, and inquired who the person was that took his father's tea kettle off the fire; some person made answer it was the doctor; the gunner's son immidiately [sic] went away, and returned with the gunner's servant, who said it was I, James Finnigan, that took the kittle [*sic*] off the fire, I answer'd I did not, he told me I was a lyar. I then gave the boy a push from the fire, both the boys then went away and fetched the gunner who immidiately siezed [*sic*] me by the collar calling me scoundrel and rascall, 'How dare you take off my kettle.' I replied I did not take it off and would thank him to use better language, he desired me to take off my pan immediately. I replyed there was nothing on the fire before I put it on, and apprehended he had no authority to order me to take it off, he immidiately pushed me and my frying pan out of the galley and told me he would take me aft on the quarterdeck. I replyed I would go aft immidiately and beged [*sic*] of him not to use me ill he then dragged me to the fore capstern, and then let me loose calling me scoundrel and rascal. I answered I was neither and would acquaint Captain Campbell (commanding officer of the party of Marines on board the *Bellerophon*) of his behaviour to me, he expressed himself Thus. 'Damn you and your Captain Campbell do you think I value either of you?' and immediately went into the wardroom and acquainted Mr Launder the Commanding Officer of the misunderstanding between us ...

Fennigan was sentenced to be reduced to private marine and ineligible for promotion for six months from that day's date.[59]

In the *Defiance* (74) it was the spark for mutiny. John McKenna, wardroom steward, testified that

On the 19th of August I went forward for Lieut. Williams dinner who had been officer of the afternoon watch, and found the wardroom cook, ships corporal and a great many others disputing at the cook's table. On the cook's seeing me he told me the ship's corporal had thrown a bucket of water and spoil'd the meat [a leg of mutton] he then spoke to the ship's corporal to let me have 5 minutes to dish Lieut. Williams dinner, upon this [six of the alleged mutineers] came to me, and swore that they had as much right to the fire as he had and would not give him a minute longer ... there should be equality in the ship ... they then turned round to the ship's corporal and said some words to him when immediately he hove two buckets of water over the fire. The corporal swore that he had no right to it, and would not stop a moment longer. I was advised by the servants who were with me to go aft on the quarterdeck and make a complaint which I did, but Mr Williams was gone below, I then went down to look for the master at arms and found him sleeping on his chest, I told his wife, who was setting [*sic*] in the birth, that I had something to say to him, when she immediately woke him.[60]

For petty and warrant officers living aboard with their wives, of course, private cooking must have been normal: certainly William Richardson, gunner in the *Tromp*, expected them to have their own cooking utensils: 'No officer in shifting from ship to ship has more bother than a warrant officer; he has not only his chests [*sic*] and bedding to lug about but also his cabin furniture, cooking utensils, and if he has his wife with him so much the worse'.[61]

The ship's company of the *Blake* (74) received prize money in 1812, and when her captain went round the ship on Sunday 23 December her captain 'was amused' to see

a whole sheep roasting in the galley, stuffed with potatoes and onions. It seems the mess to which this belonged had bought it, like many others, for a Christmas dinner; but it being agreed that there was no certainty of what might happen in the intervening time, they determined 'to have a good *blow-out* while they were all stout and hearty.[62]

Chapter 7

WASHING CLOTHES AND REEFING TOPSAILS
Afternoon watch, noon to 4pm
(ii) four bells to eight bells

WAIST

In the early afternoon the wind was still blowing strongly, and at three bells in the afternoon watch, or 1.30pm, the watch below were piped to wash and mend clothes,* to take advantage of the breeze.[1] Joseph Bates was an American pressed into the navy and turned over into the *Splendid*, and he found the simple impracticability of washing 700 men's clothes in two hours twice each week without order or regulation to sum up for him everything he hated about the navy.

> In the mild seasons, the sailor's uniform was white duck frocks and trowsers, and straw hats. The discipline was to muster all hands at nine o'clock in the morning, and if our dress was reported soiled or unclean, then all such were doomed to have their names put on the 'black list,' and

---

* There was no regulation of the frequency and method of washing men's clothes, and the practice varied widely. In the *Expedition* fireship it was Saturday morning, in the *Glory* (98) it was Thursday night, in the *Mars* (74) it was Monday and Friday morning, in the *Indefatigable* (38) it was Tuesday, Thursday and Saturday afternoon, and so on. Ships washing clothes in the morning usually did so before or while the decks were cleaned, and it seems likely that they were more likely to use cold water or sea water, while those waiting until the afternoon more often used hot; in ships in port or in hulks, certain nights were often given over to washing. It is also possible to infer that ships of the line were more likely to wash at sea than frigates. Bates actually served in the Mediterranean in the *Rodney* (74), where 'about two hours before daylight once a week, all hands (about 700) called on the upper decks to wash and scrub clothes'; I have made the *Splendid* a more efficiently run ship, and assumed only the watch below was called to wash clothes, which is more usual, but frustration arising from inefficiently organised washing sessions was common. The cause of the mutiny in the *Glory* was the bad handling of washing night: on or about the evening of Thursday 9 August, 'after enquiring at the coppers [in the galley] if that was washing night, and being answered it was', one man said, ' "Damn and bugger the ship and washing too – that he had never any thing but suds since he belonged to her" – After which he said – "If the ship's company were all of his mind, he'd have water whenever he pleased without asking any one for it" … The water was just going to be served out by the cook and his mate.' According to the cook he said: 'damn and bugger the ship and the washing too for he'd had no water since he came to the ship nothing but suds which he had got from one and another'. He was found guilty, but was only given 100 lashes, so perhaps the court was sympathetic.

required to do all kinds of scouring brass, iron, and filthy work, in addition to their stated duty, depriving them of their allotted time for rest and sleep in their morning watch below. There was no punishment more dreaded and disgraceful to which we were daily liable.

If sufficient changes of dress had been allowed us, and sufficient time to wash and dry the same, it would have been a great pleasure, and also a benefit to us, to have appeared daily with unsoiled white dress on, notwithstanding the dirty work we had to perform. I do not remember of ever being allowed more than three suits at one time to make changes, and then only one day in the week to cleanse them ... Not more than three-quarters of these could be accommodated to do this work for themselves at a time; but no matter ... at the expiration of the two hours, all washed clothes were ordered to be hung on the clothes-lines immediately. Some would say, I have not been able to get water nor a place to wash mine yet. 'I can't help that! clear out your clothes ... 'Orders were most strict, that whoever should be found drying his clothes at any other but this time in the wash-day, should be punished.

To avoid detection and punishment, I have scrubbed my trowsers early in the morning, and put them on and dried them. Not liking this method, I ventured at one time to hang up my wet trowsers in a concealed place behind the main-topsail: but the sail was ordered to be furled in a hurry, and the lieutenant discovered them. The main top men (about fifty) were immediately ordered from their dinner hour to appear on the quarterdeck. 'All here, sir,' said the under officer that mustered us. 'Very well, whose trowsers are these found hanging in the main top?' I stepped forward from the ranks, and said, 'They are mine, sir.' 'Yours, are they? you ——!' and when he had finished cursing me, he asked me how they came there? 'I hung them there to dry, sir.' 'You —— —— see how I will hang you, directly. Go down to your dinner, the rest of you,' said he, 'and call the chief boatswain's mate up here.' Up he came in great haste from his dinner. 'Have you got a rope's end in your pocket?' He began to feel, and said, 'No, sir.' 'Then away down below directly and get one, and give that fellow there one of the —— floggings he ever had.' 'Yes, sir, bear a hand.'

Thus far I had escaped all his threats of punishment, from my first introduction into the ship. I had often applied for more clothes to enable me to muster with a clean dress, but had been refused. I expected now, according to his threats, that he would wreak his vengeance on me by having the flesh cut off my back for attempting to have a clean dress, when he knew I could not have it without venturing some way as I had done.

While thoughts of the injustice of this matter were rapidly passing through my mind, he cried out, 'Where is that fellow with the rope? why don't he hurry up here?' At this instant he was heard rushing up from below. The lieutenant stopped short and turned to me, saying, 'If you don't want one of the —— floggings you ever had, do you run.' I looked at him to see if he was in earnest. The under officer, who seemed to feel the injustice of my case, repeated, 'Run!' The lieutenant cried to the man with the rope, 'Give it to him!' 'Aye, aye, sir.' I bounded forward, and by the time he reached the head of the ship, I was over the bow, getting a position to receive him near down by the water, on the ship's bobstays. He saw at a glance it would require his utmost skill to perform his pleasing task there. He therefore commanded me to come up to him. 'No,' said I, 'if you want me, come here.'

In this position, the Devil, the enemy of all righteousness, tempted me to seek a summary redress of my grievances, viz., if he followed me and persisted in inflicting on me the threatened punishment, to grasp him and plunge into the water. Of the many that stood above looking on, none spake to me, that I remember, but my pursuer. To the best of my memory, I remained in this position more than an hour. To the wonder of myself and others, the lieutenant issued no orders respecting me, neither questioned me afterward, only the next morning I learned that I was numbered with the black-list men for about six months.[2]

After the cook and his mates had served and eaten dinner, they had put water on to boil. This was fresh water from the hold – the navy only used salt water for washing when on short allowance. The purser had issued soap to the men, at 1s per pound, and they scrubbed with their brushes. In 1813 an admiral openly admitted that a fleet 'was compelled' to have 'a few women to wash and mend, etc.', but most people washed their own clothes, or formed arrangements with their messmates. A line was strung between the masts to dry clothes,[3] and for Basil Hall, a midshipman in the *Leander*, nothing could have been more natural than the lieutenant's opinion:

It was a positive order, and a very proper one, that no clothes should be hung up to dry except on the clothes' lines, or in the weather rigging, and even there only by permission of the officer in charge of that part of the ship. Every one, of course, is aware that nothing is considered so sluttish as hanging clothes below the gunwale, and especially on the davits or guys of the quarter boats. But all the poop middies who have tried to keep these ropes clear of shirts and jackets, know that it is not very easy to exact obedience to these orders. In all well-regulated ships, however, these apparently small matters are found to contribute to the maintenance of uniformity and good order. They form the tracery or fringe, as it were – the ornamental parts of discipline – which, if properly attended to, generally imply that the more substantial requisites are not neglected …

Of course, therefore, as soon as I was placed in command of the poop [as a midshipman], I waged fierce war against the wet shirts of the sailors, or the still more frequent abomination of the well-pipe-clayed trousers of the marines, who naturally affect that part of the ship, and are seldom seen forward amongst the seamen. All experience shews, however, that there is no due proportion between the difficulty of getting a trifling order obeyed, and that of accomplishing a great affair. People are apt to forget, that the obligation of obedience does not always turn upon the greater or less importance of the measure commanded, but upon the distinctness of the injunction. At all events, the unhappy poop-mids of my day were in hot water, almost every morning, about this petty affair, which the men, to our great plague, were exceedingly slow to take up, without more severe punishments than the first lieutenant was generally disposed to inflict. 'It is entirely owing to your negligence, young gentlemen,' said he to us one day, 'that these wet things are so continually hung up, to the disgrace of the poop. If you would only contrive to keep your sleepy eyes open, and look about you, instead of snoosing in the hammock netting, with the fly of the ensign wrapped about you, the men would never think of hanging up their clothes in such improper places.'[4]

If some accounts are to be believed, the decks of a man of war were the scene of a battle between men trying to wash and dry their clothes and officers trying to stop them; the boatswain of the *Volage* (22), accused of having attempted to commit a crime 'unnatural and detestable', claimed, rather desperately, that the boys testifying against him were lying, because they were lazy and disobedient, often getting a thrashing for 'washing when it was not washing days, and towing their cloaths, with the running rigging'. The men were encouraged to sew their names or numbers into their clothes to prevent confusion and theft, and in July

Capstan showing one capstan bar manned.

the captain's log of the *Sultan* (74) recorded that 'every man is to have a sufficient number of knittles for his washed clothes in the rigging any man found with rope yard stops will be flogged they will also be punished severely if they cut their knittles or leave them in the rigging every officer is to promulgate this order.' (The first ship in the Royal Navy with dedicated drying facilities was the *Warrior*, which had a drying room on the orlop deck fitted in 1862: a stove burning 80lb of coal dried 120 hammocks or 320 items of clothing in five hours.)[5]

Many men, like Bates, resorted to private washing, and it is clear that opportunities were much greater in a ship-of-the-line than in a frigate, especially in port. In 1798 the signalmen on watch in the *Queen* (98) were washing their clothes while on duty one night, and in 1796 the people in the *Director*, a lazaretto in the Medway, washed with hot water in the galley – or rather their wives did. Ships near land also made much more opportunity of washing ashore than they thought of recording: the ship's company of the *Ardent* (64) landed on the Baltic island of Romsø one night in May 1809 'to wash clothes and gather fire-wood overnight', but the fact is only noted because they were surprised by Danish soldiers who killed one of them and took several prisoners. Private washing at sea also occurred, but it is usually only heard of in the margins of other stories, such as the fight that broke out in the galley of the *Valiant* (74) between five and six o'clock in the afternoon on Thursday 16 July 1812, when she was with the blockading fleet off the Scheldt.[6]

The amount of clothing likely to be possessed by each man varied considerably, as can be seen from these three examples of captain's order books, and for comparison the 'List of Necessaries, to be provided for the Foot Soldier, out of his Pay, and Allowances, *as Occasion may require*, in the Course of the Year', issued in 1792.[7]

Captain Edward Riou, *Amazon*, 1799	Captain George Duff, *Mars*, 1805	Captain John Fyffe, *Indefatigable*, 1812	Foot soldier, 1792
blue jacket, outside, with yellow buttons: 2	two blue outside jackets	two dress jackets	one pair of black gaiters
Guernsey waistcoat, blue striped: 3	two inside jackets	two working ditto	two pair of shoes
trousers, white duck, pairs: 3	four shirts	two dress pairs of trousers	one pair of stockings, or two pair of socks
ditto blue cloth, pairs: 2	one frock	two working ditto	two shirts
banyans, white duck: 2	two pair breeches or drawers	two dress waistcoats	a foraging cap
drawers, flannel: 1	three pair of white trowsers	two working ditto	a knapsack [every six years]
shirts, striped cotton: 4	one pair of blue do	two Guernsey frocks	a clothes-brush [every two years]
silk handkerchiefs, black: 2	two pair of shoes	one dress hat	worsted mitts
stockings, worsted, pairs: 3	three pair of stockings	one working ditto	a powdering bag, and puff [every three years]
hat, round, small brim: 2	two hats or Dutch caps	two dress neckcloths	two combs
	one black silk handkerchief	two working ditto	grease, and powder for the hair
		four shirts	one pair of black cloth gaiters
		four pair of stockings	one pair of breeches, besides the ammunition pair
		two pair of shoes	one hair leather
		two pair of drawers	
		one pair of trousers and frock for dirty work	
		great coat	

These lengthy lists are borne out in practice. John Broid, a seaman of the *Rota* (38), for example, was robbed in 1810 of a bag containing two shirts, two blue jackets, three pair of blue trousers and two pair of white, two handkerchiefs, three pair of shoes, five pair of stockings, one red and one blue waistcoat and a red comforter, and John de Cruize, supernumerary seaman of the *Namure*, said that while he was in confinement the marine guarding him offered him eight pints of wine for a pair of his blue trousers. De Cruize replied that he wanted fourteen, to which the marine helpfully said he was 'going to be hung and as I had so many clothes advised me to part with them.'[8]

The Regulations of 1808 provided marines on their first coming on board with 'two checquered shirts' and a uniform each year of a red cloth coat, with white cloth waistcoat and breeches, one shirt, with one black stock, one pair of stockings (to sergeants only), one pair of shoes and a hat', but they were expected to supply their own undress clothes, which were to be sold at the mast when they died.[9]

Hammocks, beds and blankets were all washable. Although the Navy

Board treated washed beds as second-rate and not to be issued for long voyages, when the captain of the *Mars* on the advice of his surgeon threw overboard the beds and blankets belonging to the wounded after a battle, the Admiralty said he should have known that washing the blankets would have rendered them 'as serviceable as when new', and charged the same against his wages.[10]

Leech, who served in the smart frigate *Macedonian*, noted 'As great attention to cleanliness, in frequently changing their linen, is observed among naval officers, a good washerwoman is considered quite a desideratum', and there is a surprising amount of surviving detail about this essential part of daily life, from which it seems officers rarely, if ever, washed their clothes on board. No memoir is complete without the story of the day the author sailed with his clean linen still ashore, for example, and Major Wybourn of the marines, serving in the *Isis* off the Helder, had to go without clean clothes in November 1799, writing 'having quitted the place so precipitately I, as well as the rest, left most of my things behind, and what we have we are afraid of trusting to be washed as we are in hourly expectation of sailing, so that after wearing a shirt a week and putting it away, it comes in its turn to be worn again', though Captain Dillon, when in command of the *Leopard* (troopship), probably went further than most in securing the recovery of his washing in November 1812, off Algiers: he had sent it ashore while waiting for bullocks, but after it was done his trunks were seized by the Custom House officers. He collected the vice-consul, Mr Sedgovitch, and called on the Bey, but no promise of its return was forthcoming: 'At last, Mr Sedgovitch told him in my name and behalf that, if he would not liberate the trunks, I should in a couple of hours bring my ship abreast of the town, and lay it about his ears with a few broadsides.' The promise was given and he collected his linen. Even when blockading Cadiz in 1797, the officers of the *Centaur* (74) had their washing done in the town, and the version told, or embellished, by Basil Hall, confirms that for an officer cleanliness was the product of a large wardrobe: in spring 1809 the *Endymion* (44) was off the coast of Spain, supporting the local junta against the French. 'The officers, as usual, sent their clothes on shore to be washed. It so chanced, that the captain's stock, from being much the largest, had not been sent back at the time of the last French incursion, though most of the officers' things had been received. The captain, naturally enough, gave his linen up as lost; and was even ashamed to ask about it, seeing that the inhabitants were not only burnt out of house and home, but had been stripped of very [*sic*] thing they possessed in the world. His Spanish laundress, however, by loading her children's shoulders, and her own, with the half-washed linen, just as the French were entering the town, contrived not only to carry the clothes away safely, but to hide them in a cave near the beach. Meanwhile, her house, and every article belonging to herself, was burned. Nevertheless, after the French retired, she managed to get the linen properly done up, and, having brought it all on board, quietly counted it out, piece by piece – never seeming to imagine she had done anything remarkable, or that she was entitled to make a greater demand than the bare price of the labour!'[11]

Midshipmen were officially gentlemen, and in this respect they seem to have behaved as their seniors, despite the obvious problems, and no midshipman's memoir is complete without a story typified by the anecdote told twice by George Parsons, who had to refuse an invitation to dinner from Nelson because he had no clean shirt, 'and my messmates are in the same plight'. He was aboard the *Foudroyant* (80), and the dinner was to celebrate the anniversary of the Nile. Nelson told him he might 'dine in any shirt, but must celebrate the anniversary of that glorious and unprecedented victory at his table at three o'clock that day.' (He also had no clean shirt when Nelson invited him to a dinner for the anniversary of Cape St Vincent.)[12] The *Renown* (74) cruised in the Mediterranean from June 1803 to July 1804 without going into port to refit, which caused her midshipmen some difficulty.

> There was a small village about seven or eight miles off, at one of the Magdalen [Maddalena] islands, where some few got their linen washed, but most of us in the fleet were put to our shifts to get that necessary comfort (clean linen) accomplished.
>
> These long cruises used to put our wits sadly to the test for an appearance of a bit of white linen above our black cravats, particularly when we had to answer the signal for a midshipman [to attend] on board the flagship.
>
> Soap was almost – indeed, I might say, quite – as scarce an article as clean shirts and stockings. It was a common thing in those days of real hard service to turn shirts and stockings inside out, and make them do a little more duty. Sometimes we used to search our clothes-bag to see 'if one good turn deserved another.' These expedients, added to reefed stockings, made us appear sufficiently dandified to go and answer the signal. Borrowing those articles that had been washed on shore – if such a thing was left amongst one of us – was quite out of the question, for we knew the day of repayment was very far off …
>
> Previous to the Spanish war we were sent by his lordship, in the *Renown*, to the Bay of Rosas, in Catalonia, to procure bullocks and

oranges for the fleet, where we remained long enough to have our clothes washed – a luxury we stood much in need of.[13]

Life was evidently no easier in Indiamen: three days into the *Charlton*'s voyage to India in 1799, the cadets were 'already very badly off – bread and beer were both done, what water they had for drinking very indifferent and none allowed them to wash but what the ocean afforded … how they continue to be so decently dressed surprizes me for the steerage is also their shaving shop and it being but a passage is only lighted accidentally by the cabin doors being open, for all the light which comes from the companion stairs and the hatchway is just enough to make darkness visible!'[14]

The *Gorgon* storeship sent the washing ashore with the women of the ship:

We came to an anchor in a bay [21 April 1796] within the town and found the *Blanch* Frigate laying there. At this time the Corsekons were troublesome to the English. Abreast of where we lay was a large stone building with a high wall around it and a run of fresh water running past it into the bay. The wimen went on shore to this creek to wash for the officers and men, but we had to send all the marines on shore to guard them of they would of taken all the clothes from [them].

The marines was paraded in a file abreast the house. Our first leut't and a midshipman went with there fusees into the next field to shoot some birds. The Cosecans ware laying in ambush in sight of us on board. One Cossican came to them and took both their guns from them, and showing them the men that ware laying ready with their rifels to fire at them if they resisted and then walked off with there guns and left them to come on b[oar]d empty handed. As soon as the wimen and marines got on b[oar]d they got into the large stone house, up stairs and begin to fire at us upon deck which made it dangerous to walk the deck till the capt[ain] ordered the six pounder on the forecastle to be got ready, and we board the house and walls and nocked one corner of the house entierly away. They then thought it time to leave the house and not trouble us any more.[15]

Washing officers' necessaries on board was not unheard-of, however, as shown by events in the *Lion* (above).

Lists of linen embarked by various officers include Hoffman's twenty new shirts as a midshipman, Commodore Cornwallis' dying in 1798 in possession of eighteen and Colonel Bayly's embarking with the 12th Foot in the *Melville Castle* Indiaman in 1796 with eighteen only to find that 'at least six dozen were almost indispensable' for the 204-day journey from St Helen's to Madras.[16]

This practical fact helps to explain William Hickey's amazement at Admiral Suffren's dress when he went to pay his complements on board the *Heros* (74) at Trincomalee in January 1783. He was shown into the cabin, but Suffren was busy writing:

> He received me with the most engaging attention and politeness, and, pointing to a chair, desired I should be seated until he finished some matters of business that required dispatch ... Of course, I did so, and this afforded me an opportunity of observing his extraordinary dress and figure. In appearance he looked much more like a fat, vulgar English butcher than a Frenchman of consequence; in height he was about five feet five inches, very corpulent, scarce any hair upon the crown of his head, the sides and back tolerably thick. Although quite grey he wore neither powder nor pomatum, nor any curl, having a short cue of three or four inches tied with a piece of old spun-yarn. He was in slippers, or, rather, a pair of old shoes, the straps being cut off, blue cloth breeches unbuttoned at the knees, cotton or thread stockings (none of the cleanest) hanging about his legs, no waistcoat or cravat, a coarse linen shirt entirely wet with perspiration, open at the neck, the sleeves being rolled up above his elbows as if just going to wash his hands and arms; indeed I concluded in my own mind that he had been broken in upon and interrupted whilst at his toilette, but afterwards ascertained that he always appeared as above described during the morning.

The next day he visited Suffren again, and found him 'exactly in the same deshabille as on the previous day'; after a conversation dinner was announced, 'whereupon he retired to his stateroom, from whence he in five minutes returned dressed in a blue jacket of thin coast cloth, his shirt collar buttoned, with a black stock on. He had also pulled up his stockings, buttoned his breeches knees, and put on shoes instead of slippers.' Suffren, however, was notoriously 'slovenly and foul-mouthed': Hickey, homeward bound from India in the *Castle Eden* Indiaman in 1807, learnt from his previous voyages and took 'an immense stock of linen of every description'.[17]

At 2.30pm the watch was called to set main topgallant sails, and at 3pm to set the jib and spanker again. At 4pm the log recorded 'Ditto weather',[18] and

James Mitchell, a seaman of the starboard watch, went to the main top, where he found his friend Mason lying on a studding sail. He lay down with his head against Mason's leg and they continued their conversation. After a few minutes John Jameson came into the top. He was known in the ship as a quarrelsome man, even when sober, but he had been drinking with the captain of the foretop, and was drunk. He began to pull Mitchell about, asking him questions, until Mitchell 'desired him to let me alone'.

Mason sat up and said, 'Who don't you leave Mitchell alone, and not trouble your head with those that don't concern themselves with you?'

Jameson turned to him and said, 'Who the hell are you?'

'I am a man.'

'What am I?'

'You are acting like a boy.'

'Yes,' said Jameson, 'you are a play-acting bugger, but you shan't come your play acting tricks over me!'

'I am, and I can act a play that would astonish you.'

'I am but a short time in the top and you wish to impose on me!'

'I do not.'

'Do you want to fight? There is room enough in the top, come—'

'I will not fight in the top, but if you want to fight come down below and I will have it out.'

Jameson then said, 'I will not, there is room enough in the top,' and hit Mitchell, knocking him down against the mizzen topgallant staysail.

'Is that what you are up to—' and Mason and he fought on the larboard side of the top. Jameson chased Mason round the mast and hit him in the mouth, making it bleed; they stripped off their jackets and began to fight. Jameson knocked Mason down in the fore part of the top, and struck him after he was down; Mitchell said, 'That was not fair, and if you strike him so again I will strike you.' This gave Mason time to get up, and they fought four or five rounds, about fifteen minutes; Mason was twenty-two and Jameson only a year older, but he began to tire, and said, 'I will give it in for the present, and fight you another time.' Mason was about to shake hands with him when two men watching the fight, John McCarty and Stephen Bools, shouted, 'Don't give it in, fight it on through!' He swung at Mason but missed, and Mason's blow sent him straight through the lubber's hole. With the heel of the ship, he fell into the sea. The cry was instantly raised, and a capstan bar thrown to him. When he saw that Jameson had fallen, Mason collapsed on the studding sail 'and cried, and said he would never fight another battle as long as he lived.'[19]

A 74 launching a boat from the quarter davits to rescue a man overboard.

The jolly boat was immediately launched over the lee gunwale, with the lieutenant and three men; the ship was brought to; in the swell from the northward Jameson could not at first be seen, but then the lieutenant caught sight of his white shirt and the boat pulled strongly towards him. The surgeon's assistant had been called and was waiting at the rail. A whip had been rove with the standing part made fast, the boat secured it to Jameson's body, and as soon as he was aboard he was carried down to the sick bay, with his head lowered to empty his stomach of seawater. The fire was ready in the sick bay, and dry clothes had been warmed in preparation. Jameson was stripped of his wet clothes and placed on a bench in front of it with his head still downwards. The surgeon, Mr Binding, rubbed his belly, chest and stomach with the warm clothes while his assistant chafed his legs and arms with hard coarse clothes, and together they shook and rolled him about. After two minutes there was no response, and Mr Binding proceeded to cut the temporal artery. He took a quart of blood, then bound the artery and placed moist tobacco in Jameson's mouth, which was known to encourage vomiting from the irritation it caused to the throat and stomach. The assistant then turned to alternately pressing and dilatating Jameson's ribs, and after a particularly firm compression of his stomach Jameson suddenly choked, spat out the tobacco and began to move, though weakly.[20]

In the waist, the recently killed bullock was hanging on a capstan bar athwart the skids, and with the motion of the ship, the neck touched the deck. With the events on deck, the purser thought the lieutenant was not attending to the carcass. He approached him and said, 'Sir, the beef is dragging about the deck.' The lieutenant had already had occasion to speak to the purser, who had been standing on the gangway talking to the captain's coxswain and some of the cutter's crew while the topsails were reefed, interrupting the duty of the ship, and told him to go to the quarterdeck out of the way. Now he replied that he would attend to it when the duty was completed, and if the purser would wait until the watch was called and make a complaint in the proper way on the quarterdeck it would be attended to.[21]

At three o'clock a marine sergeant assembled the 'awkward' men from the working party, and the men from the morning's guard who had made 'any mistake in his exercise or marching', on the forecastle and drilled them for an hour.[22]

Chapter 8

WRANGLESOME AND QUARRELSOME
First and second dog watches, 4pm to 8pm

QUARTERDECK, WAIST AND FORECASTLE

After the watch was called the third lieutenant sent a messenger to the purser and asked him about the complaint he had made. He said that he had spoken to the butchers, and that it could not be remedied, as the bullock was triced up as high as they could get it, and it was that that he had been attending to when turned off the gangway, and now supposed that he was forbidden to go on the main deck to attend the fresh beef. The lieutenant reminded him that when he was on the gangway he had been talking and laughing with the men, not attending to the beef.

At that the purser grew rather warm and said, in what was later alleged to be a contemptuous manner, 'It is as much my business to take care of His Majesty's beef, as it is yours to take care of His Majesty's ship.'

'It is my duty to take care of both, and I conceive you treat me with great disrespect, and if you utter those words again, I shall confine you.'

'I have a right to speak, and will speak!'

The purser spoke in such a high tone of voice that the chaplain had come off the poop to hear, but the lieutenant would not be drawn, and went forward on the gangway. There the matter rested that afternoon.[1]

Captain's cabin

In his cabin, Captain Edwards was writing to his wife. About a week earlier he had received 'a petition from the gentlemen of the cockpit, requesting to be allowed to perform the tragedy of Douglas, with the pantomime of Harlequin and the Miller; and last night a ticket was sent to me, with a bill of the play. The performance to commence at 5 o'clock. What think you of all these fine doings? It is an innocent amusement, much better than being idle and drinking.' By

1810, theatricals in ships on blockade had become an accepted part of shipboard life – usually the latest West End successes (though not with thirty or so head of cattle on board). In 1811 Private Wheeler took this for granted: 'When we were at sea, when the weather permitted the amusements went on the same as at anchor. Once a week a play would be performed by some of the officers and men. On those occasions a theatre would be errected as it were by magic. The scenery displayed the skill of the artist and the manner some of the characters were sustained would have drawn bursts of applause from a London audience.' In the summer of 1812 Sir Thomas Byam Martin entertained an admiral and his party of ten on board the *Aboukir* (74) off Anholt: 'in the evening a play was got up which for neatness, good scenery, excellence of dresses and good acting was never surpassed at Portsmouth or Plymouth. One or two of the characters, particularly Wingle in the Bee-hive, would have been applauded at Covent Garden. The whole thing was as much superior to that which you saw on board the *Saturn* as the London performance is to the country. But I am ashamed to think of the expense the officers and midshipmen must have been at in buying up the best part of the stock at the Deal Theatre.' Not all ships welcomed play-acting and theatricals; as already seen, when Rear Admiral Stopford came on board the *Caesar* (80) in February 1809 he brought a band, but although 'A play was acted on board the *Revenge* called "All the World's a Stage," and several of us went on board to see it, the Admiral among the rest, which gave much satisfaction', in the *Caesar* 'we never had diversion of any kind to cheer us up during the many weary dull nights we had passed on this station.'[2]

Beating to quarters

The *Splendid* beat to quarters half an hour before sunset in a drill that rehearsed clearing for action with an enemy. 'The officers are to see their respective quarters clear for action, guns supplied with the proper implements, arms in their places and clean and everything in readiness.' This included checking that the lanterns were 'regularly arranged', and that the candles in them were matched, which was the purser's duty. 'They are then to muster the men and report to me if any of them are drunk or missing. The people are then to be piped up to stand by their hammocks [in the hammock netting, see p. 71] and when stationed the boatswain and one of his mates to pipe them down.' The ceremony ended by beating the retreat. In company, sunset was declared from the flagship; 'the officer of the watch reports to the captain that the sun is down, drums and fifes beat off a second time and the guard and sentinels are mustered.'[3]

This evening custom was performed in most ships by 1810. There had been

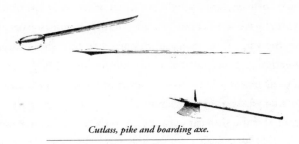

Cutlass, pike and boarding axe.

a 'slow increase in formality in naval life' in the second half of the eighteenth century, and beating to quarters seems to have become established in the 1790s. When Lieutenant Harry Humphries of the *Centaur* (74) was late on deck one evening in 1798 he was court-martialled for negligence in the performance of his duty; the court heard that the *Centaur* was 'accustomed to' do so 'each evening', and when St Vincent, in command of the fleet, read the court-martial minutes he issued an order that stressed the need for officers' expedition in this, 'the most important branch of their duty', and in the following year the marines aboard the *Princess Royal* (98) beat the retreat, ending the ceremony, every day before 5pm.[4]

The reference to reporting men missing is perhaps surprising in a ship at sea, and it was a formality in a well-worked-up ship such as the *Splendid*; but while some men would have been known and recognised, for good or bad, throughout a ship, the contemporary accounts contain many instances of men who made no impression on their ship's company and were effectively invisible. It was very possible, for example, for a man to be sent to work under a petty or warrant officer he did not know, with men he had not seen before. A man would know his messmates, but not necessarily the mess across the gangway, or the men hoisting in the boat while he was scrubbing the decks: when the mutiny in the *Culloden* started the mutineers unshipped the ladders at the hatchways, so John Johnston 2nd, who said he was not a mutineer, went aft to the gunroom, hoping to get out of the gunroom port to get on deck, 'but I found several men there, wanted to know who I was and where I was going'. The *Royal Yeoman* troopship in 1808 had two parades a day, morning and evening in forage caps and sidearms; while at sea the morning parade was for cleanliness, the afternoon was merely a roll-call, 'as in a transport crowded with troops, a man might fall overboard, and not be missed for some days, without such arrangement.' The advantage of knowing a man was lost overboard for four hours rather than forty is not altogether clear.[5]

As well as a formal ceremony that signalled the end of the day, and reminding the men and officers that theirs was a life that required continual attendance to their duty, this gave the captain yet another opportunity of ensuring that all was well with the ship. The boatswain reported to him that everything was 'in readiness for action', and in particular that 'all the shroud and topsail-sheet stoppers' were in their places – these were lengths of hawser with a stopper or a similar knot and a lanyard so that they could be secured to any parted shroud, and would be essential if the ship came to action in the night. The carpenter checked that the main and lower deck gratings and tarpaulins were in their places, and that battens and tarpaulins were ready at hand if the weather required it; and the gunner reported that enough shot plugs and caps were to hand if the ship met an enemy in the night.[6]

The gunner, and his assistants the armourer and gunsmith, were appointed by warrants from the Ordnance Board. The second branch of his duty was 'to teach the sailors the exercise of the cannon'. The 1790 Regulations allowed six charges of powder per man for small arms, once a week for the first two months and once a month thereafter, and 4lb of musket shot 'for them all once a fortnight'; and five charges of powder and five of shot per month, for exercising the upper-deck guns. In the 1806 and 1808 Regulations, the captain was directed to train all the men, in batches, until 'the whole of the ship's company are become expert', and also to train them in the use of the cutlass and half-pike, 'in the various modes of boarding the ship of an enemy and of repelling the attacks of boarders'. (The cutlass was used particularly in boarding, and the half-pike, 'A small pike, having a shaft of about half the length of the full-sized one', in repelling boarders.) The batches were 150 men in First Rates, 120 in Second Rates, 100 in Third Rates of 74 and upwards and eighty in 64s: the same number of men were to be trained particularly in operations on shore. This consolidated good practice: in the *Mars* under Captain Duff, known for the quality of her small-arms training, 'a convenient proportion' was 'exercised during one hour at least every day', 'especially in sponging, loading and priming the great guns with dexterity', 'and the small arm men in the loading and firing exercise'. At sea, every Tuesday, Wednesday, Thursday and Saturday the officer of the watch exercised the men of his quarters, with the mate and midshipmen of the watch and the gunner, 'six at least at a time, between ten and half-past eleven'. The allowance of powder and ball was therefore greatly increased.[7]

[The gunner] is to supply, at such times as the captain shall direct, ammunition for the guns and musketry, not exceeding in each month, for six months after the guns are first received on board, one charge of powder and one round shot for one third of the number of the upper deck guns, in ships of two or three decks; or one fourth for ships of one deck; and twelve charges of musket cartridges with ball, and twenty-four without ball, for each man of one third part of the seamen of the ship's company, and for all the marines; not exceeding, after the first six months, one half that quantity for the guns, or muskets.[8]

In an average-sized fully-manned 74, this produced an average of sixteen rounds of ball cartridge per training man per month followed by eight rounds per man per month. The captain's version of this article, however, directed him to require from the gunner ball cartridge equal to half the number of the seamen, or twenty-five and thirteen rounds respectively. Both figures were much more than the allowance for practice and exercise in the army at this time.[9]

The final branch was salutes. They occupied a whole chapter of the Regulations and Instructions, from admirals and commanders-in-chief, who were saluted with seventeen guns, and returned fifteen to flag officers and thirteen to captains, to the salutes for officers who died on active service: for a flag officer, his flag was lowered to half-mast until he was buried, and minute guns fired not exceeding twenty-five by every ship beginning when the corpse was put in the sea or carried ashore, for a captain, the same, but with pendant, and twenty guns, and for a lieutenant, who received three volleys of musketry from his ship at his funeral.[10] The need to establish appropriate marks of respect, and the importance naval officers placed on it, is well illustrated by the visit of the *Peterell* (16) to Corfu in October 1796 in search of a privateer. Her captain went ashore to present his compliments to the governor, and found that she was the first Royal Navy ship to visit.

After the usual questions upon occasions of this kind were answered, and we had been presented with chocolate in a very superior style, his Excellency desired to know whether or not I meant to salute the garrison. I told him I most readily would salute upon his giving me his honour an equal number of guns should be returned from the garrison, but that otherwise I was not at liberty to fire a gun. He replied that it had been for ever the custom at Corfu to return to ships of all nations one gun less, and he hoped that I would not break in upon an established rule from which there yet had not, nor could he permit, any deviation.

'Your Excellency must pardon me,' says I, 'if you have a proof of one now. His Britannic Majesty's ships of war, by the express command of his

Majesty himself, never fire a gun more than is returned from any power under Heaven, and I should think myself highly culpable was I knowingly to burn a grain more, much less to act so derogatory to the great character of the British navy as to fire a gun in addition to what his Majesty's ship under my command received.'[11]

The governor was persuaded, and sent the keys to two boxes to the opera that night.

Lower deck

Grog and supper for the men

At one bell, the second half of the day's ration of grog was served out to the watch on deck and to the watch below. The watch below could take it to their berths – it was a popular time when off duty to take care of belongings and to wash – but the watch on deck had orders not to leave their posts.

Supper was piped at eight bells. It was a small meal: in the *Splendid*, bread, cheese and olive oil. Like dinner, it was eaten by all the ship's company together, except those on deck. For tired, hungry men, with a pint of grog inside them, especially if they came below to a lower deck with the ports closed, a flashpoint could be reached all too quickly.[12] William Thomas, a marine of the *Duncan* (74), dropped dead on Saturday 11 July; it was suspected that the cause of death was a blow and violent throw from Richard Potter, another marine. At the ensuing court martial, Isaac Ridley, private marine, was asked to relate what passed between the prisoner and the deceased on the evening in question.

'I was standing in the gangway on the lower deck near their berth, on the larboard side, and the deceased shoved in pass [*sic*] the Prisoner into his berth, the Prisoner rose up and wanted to know of the deceased if he wanted to be master of the berth; the Prisoner struck at the deceased, which did not hit him, but he made another blow at him and struck him in the belly, and said he would let the deceased know that he should not be master of that berth, as he had got the wrong person to deal with; the stool was laying on the gun tackle, and the deceased leant his head over it, when the water began to run out of his mouth, and put his hand on his belly and changed colour, and appeared to be in distress. – as he rose his head up, he turned round and asked the Prisoner, what he meant by striking him that way, and the decease [*sic*] pressed forward to come out of the berth; the prisoner catched hold of the deceased by the shoulder and threw him out of the berth, and his neck fell upon my foot. I directly took hold of him and helped him up, and he went off as far as the after ladder, as I understood, to make his complaint to the serjeant major. he made a very distressful noise at this time, and turned to come back and the water continuing to run off his stomach, as he came back towards our berth, he made a stagger towards me, and claped his hand upon William White, and sung out a number of times I am killed, and for me to unbutton his stock immediately. I unbuckled the stock as quick as possible, in the mean time he held on by White, and vomited directly the stock was unbuttoned, and then he staggered towards our berth, and staggered backwards again to the capstan and fell and vomited by the capstan directly he fell he was then taken hold of and taken to the berth, and made water directly his head was held up, and the assistant surgeon was sent for, and immediately afterwards the deceased was taken into the sick bay, by order of the surgeon, and that is all I known [sic].'

The court asked: 'Have you frequently seen the deceased and the Prisoner scuffle or quarrel?'

Answer. 'No. Thomas told me at the end of month that he wanted to come out of the mess as Potter was always down upon him, that he wanted to come into Corporal Morrison's mess that I am in; I told him I had nothing to do with it, he must speak to Corporal Morrison, which I believe he did, nothing more passed between us.'[13]

On 21 March 1800, William Collins, a marine of the 35th company serving on board the *Prince*, was troublesome all day, and his discontent came to a head at supper:

On the 21st I saw him very wranglesome and quarrelsome amongst his comrades and struck one of them on which I immediately went and parted them and told the Prisoner to sit down and be quiet or I would immediately take him on the quarterdeck [to make a complaint to the officer of the watch]. The Prisoner sat down in his birth some considerable time and he was quarrelling again in the galley I went and made him sit down again This was in the morning about ten o'clock. In the evening between four and five o'clock I saw the Prisoner quarelling along with his messmate who was sitting down in his birth the prisoner struck him in the flace [sic] I told him to leave off and on my giving him a shove he said he would serve me in the same manner I took and immediately shoved him to take him aft on the quarterdeck he immediately squared his yards to strike me – he said he would not go aft without I went and complained of him – Serjt. McWilliams desired me to go aft and complain of him – I went aft and complained of him I took him upon the quarterdeck afterwards and complained of him to the lieutenant.[14]

McWilliams said: 'he seized me by the leg with his two hands and bit me by the calf of the leg I told him if he would not let me go I should stamp on him with my other foot, getting a little more assistance we took him to the quarterdeck.' One of the defence witnesses, John Hendry, a private marine, said that most of this quarrelling was just play:

> He was skylarking* with his messmate but whether they came to anger or not I do not know he was walking about in the gangway and Serjt. Burt said, 'What capers are you going on with now' – he took and put his hand to the back of the Prisoner's neck and gave him a shove and said go along aft – the Prisoner said, 'Go and complain of me and then I'll go' – then he got him as far as the entring port and the Prisoner made a round turn and was coming back again and as he was coming back again Serjeant Williams [sic] struck him.

He was sentenced to 200 lashes round the fleet nonetheless.

One well-attested way to prevent drunken fights after supper was to encourage exercise. In 1811 Captain Griffiths published his *Observations on Some Points of Seamanship*, in which he disapproved of interrupting the short period for the men's recreation:

> It has frequently been remarked that men do not dance and play as they used to do. Are they sufficiently and judiciously encouraged in it? In some ships they cannot have the fiddler without asking for him. This seems almost putting a negative on dancing, for their dislike to come aft [to ask

---

* Although skylarking is usually taken in the sense given by Burney in his *Marine Dictionary*, 'a term used by seamen, to denote wanton play about the rigging, and tops, or in any part of the ship, particularly by the youngsters', here the court established the witness meant 'quarrelling or fighting', a sense prefiguring that in Admiral Smyth, 'of late the term has denoted frolicsome mischief, which is not confined to boys, unless three score and ten includes them'. In the court-martial of John Whittorne, carpenter of the *Zebra*, on board the *Haerlem*, at the Nore, 3 August 1798, 'for drunkenness and insolence, making use of daring and provoking language, setting His Majesty's service at defiance, and saying he did not care a damn for it, and by his conduct affording an example of mutiny and sedition', skylarking means 'fencing with his fists'.

permission] is I think great; and then when have they to dance? The only time appears from supper to quarters. Yet this is a period constantly interfered with, with reefing, exercising guns etc. I do think time might be found enough in the day for the exercise, and as to reefing every night, whether necessary or not, [it] has always appeared to me to be a very trivial business. Even reefs are let out merely to take them in again. I cannot view it as an evolution which merits the stress and consequence that is attached to it. Can it require that perpetual practice it has? If you wish to see your crew playful and dancing, let the fiddlers be up invariably from five to eight in the afternoon, and except getting down the hammocks do not unnecessarily interfere with them. I think I would then vouch for nearly as much amusement as formerly. If not previously inclined to dance, the music will set them a-going provided you do not interfere. I have frequently when I have seen them amused put off reefing till after eight o'clock and then it was done with the watch only, and when piping the hammocks down would have upset what was going on among them, would have allowed them to be taken down as they were disengaged.[15]

With her fleet stores aboard and the bullocks restless in the close heat of the upper deck there was no opportunity that night to indulge the men with music, which had become both fashionable and popular, especially in ships-of-the-line condemned to blockade duty. Even the dour St Vincent had had one, with twenty-six musicians, although delight in it was not universal. One member of the *Splendid*'s band 'joined the musicians thinking it easier to play an instrument in the ship's band than to do ship's duty. There was a first rate instructor and for three weeks … my chief work was blowing on a flute. Gradually I gained some proficiency at it. The captain now purchased new instruments equal to a full band. I learned the claronet.' In the *Culloden*'s voyage to India, in 1804–5, Robert Hay recorded that in the evenings 'the instrument of black Bob, the fiddler, was in almost constant requisition, giving spirit to the evolutions of those who were disposed to trip it a little on the light fantastic toe.' 'They never seemed to dance with any spirit unless they had an old black to fiddle to them … He is a most curious fellow and cannot play on his instrument unless it be accompanied by his voice, or rather his throat, which makes a rumbling noise, growing louder and louder as the longer he fiddles, so that at the last his own sounds are much stronger than those of his catgut …' The *Merlin* sloop had a semi-official band; the men, with the captain's permission, subscribed to buy 'musical instruments such as fiddle, fife, or bagpipe, and a keg of liquor to splice the mainbrace with' in

1788. The band was less than wholly welcome in the *Minotaur* (80) in Cawsand Bay in 1803: it rehearsed 'under the direction of the sergeant, in the captain's cabin twice a day, and a horrible confusion of unmusical sounds they made for more than six weeks. The skipper was in his glory, and everyone else was amazed. Some of my messmates prayed for them heartily, particularly the first lieutenant, who thought the captain musically mad. The mids declared they never would be respectable enough to be called a band, but they would be bad enough to be called a banditti, as they looked more like brigands than musicians'.[16]

In the *Revenge* (74), on passage to Lisbon with five companies of the 51st Foot in 1811, Private Wheeler wrote home that

> Two evenings each week is devoted to amusement, then the boatswain's
> mates, with their pipes summons 'All hands to play.' In a moment the
> scene is truly animating. The crew instantly distribute themselves, some
> dancing to a fiddle, others to a fife. Those who are fond of the
> marvellous, group together between two guns and listen to some frightful
> tale of ghost and gobblin, another party listens to some weather beaten
> tar who 'spins a yarn' of past events, until his hearers sides are almost
> cracked with laughter. Again is to be found a select party immortalizing
> the heroes of gone by days by singing songs to the memory of Duncan,
> Howe, Vincent, and the immortal Nelson, while others whose souls are
> more refined are singing praises to the GOD of Battles. Thus my time is
> passed in the midst of health, pleasure and contentment.[17]

Wheeler had 'formed a very unfavourable opinion of the navy' while in the *Impetueuse* in 1809, and commented on the marked difference in the *Revenge*: 'A short time on board this ship has in a great measure corrected that opinion'.[18]

For the *Splendid* the weather had eased slightly, and at 5pm, the log recorded, she took out the third reefs in the fore and mizzen topsails and at 5.30 set the fore and mizzen topgallant sails. A squally night and two hours off duty for the larboard watch meant that many were in their hammocks below. 'It is ridiculous [comical] to hear the sailors lie and sing in their hammocks of an evening. They chant the most dismal ditties in the world and the words be ever so merry, yet the tune is one and the same, namely "Admiral Hosier's Ghost".' Perhaps the most famous of these dismal chanters was Billy Culmer, well known as the oldest midshipman in the fleet; he had belonged to the *Buffalo* (60), and in the *Barfleur* he would 'upon all occasions when sea fights were spoken of' sing a song 'in honour of his old ship' in a voice 'as melodious as that of the raven'.† Others preferred the printed story – 'In one place might be seen a sailor sitting on a gun reading to his shipmates, others reading to themselves'; in summer 1810 William Smith enjoyed *Roderick Random* so much he borrowed a copy of *Humphry Clinker* without asking and was flogged for robbery – or teaching their messmates to read and write. Others still played cards. Landsman Hay's tutor in the *Culloden* 'could play at all-fours, at whist, at loo, at cribbage and at least a dozen of other games on the cards; he could play at fox and goose, at chequers, at backgammon, and I know what all besides', and 'whenever spare time permitted', in the *Renown* (74), the midshipmen's evenings 'were spent in the amusements afforded by the old games of cribbage, loo, draughts and able wackets, which is a kind of forfeit played with cards, where each player is subject, for every mistake, to one or more blows with a knotted handkerchief on the palm of the hand.'[19] Barnet Hughes, a private marine, had been a card player in the *London*:

> Serjeant Perkins and a messmate of his came over from the starboard to the larboard side of the deck, just by where I mess, and I heard him challenge a mess just opposite me, (any two of them that were in it) that he and his messmate, would play them for a quantity of grog at cards – they refused to play and I replied, 'I did not care, to have a game with him for a shilling or sixpence at all fours,' and accordingly we played three or four games – and I won. During the play he (the Serjeant) frequently got up to strike me, and clenched his fist and put it to my cheek. When I had won all the money that he had got about him, he said, 'Come, cut the cards.' 'Not till the money is down,' I said – Serjeant Perkins immediately said, 'Damn your eyes, you son of a bitch – I'll knock your damned head off. Do you misdoubt my words?' And he went and got more money – We played then three or four games more, and he won all his money back – I told him I was glad of it, and that I would play no more – he said, 'Damn your eyes, I'll do for you before tomorrow night,' and accordingly on the next day, when I went centinel, he came to me and said to me, 'Well, Hughes you are drunk,' – I answered, 'I am not,' – and he replied, 'Damn your eyes you are, and I will have you relieved.' – He sent for a corporal and had me relieved, and the moment

---

† Billy Culmer had less famous rivals; in May 1799 Thomas Bassington, the boatswain of the *Conquerant* hulk, was court-martialled for embezzlement and sentenced to serve before the mast in one of HM ships; he had thirty-three years' service, and a large family, and in consequence of an appeal from his wife to the Lords of the Admiralty was promoted to midshipman before the year was out.

the bayonet was out of my hand, he struck me on my face, and knock'd me down – the back part of my head against a shot locker which rendered me senseless – and I do not recollect any thing that passed afterwards.[20]

ORLOP DECK

Provisions were issued in the first dog watch, and this was also the time for exchanging spoiled provisions, bread in particular – the Navy Board was obsessed with keeping bread (biscuit) aired to preserve it, even venting windsails to the breadroom; it was stored in 1 cwt canvas bags, rather than airtight containers, and so a great deal of it crumbled to dust.* The bread room was right aft on the orlop deck, and the food was exchanged at the purser's storeroom, which was just forward of it on the larboard side.[21] It was normally the job of the purser's steward, nicknamed Jack-in-the-Dust, and today William Patterson, the boatswain's mate, found that the bread bag for his mess had so much bread dust in it he could not fit the next allowance in. Accordingly he went below to have it exchanged, but was refused, and so went aft to the quarterdeck to make a complaint in the proper manner. Thomas Lawless, a midshipman present on deck, saw what happened next. Patterson entered a complaint against the purser's steward's refusing to change his bread dust. Mr Symons, the midshipman on duty, went into the wardroom and acquainted Lieutenant Grey of it. Lieutenant Grey came on the quarterdeck and asked Patterson the reason the purser's steward objected changing his bread dust.

Patterson said, 'Sir, I went down to get my bread, oil, and cheese this evening to the steward room and asked the purser's steward to sift the bread dust or change it and give me good bread in the room of it, he told me he would not and abused me.'

Lieutenant Grey took the bag in his hand and looked at the bread dust and afterwards went into the cabin and informed the captain. Captain Edwards then came and asked Patterson what was his complaint.

Patterson said, 'Sir, I went down to get my bread, oil and cheese to the steward room and asked the steward if he would change my bread dust, and could not take any bread up if he did not change it, as my bag would not hold it, he told me he could not change it then.'

Captain Edwards asked where the purser's steward was.

---

* If figures supplied for the *Merlin* sloop for 1788 are typical, a ship 'produced' on average about half a pound of dust per man per calendar month. According to Mr Acheson, the *Merlin*'s master, usable condemned dust was given to the livestock.

Patterson said, 'He is in his cot.'

Lieutenant Grey asked, 'A purser's steward in his cot?'

Captain Edwards said, 'He is allowed a cabin. Send for the steward.'

He did not come up but Robert Richards the steward's mate came on the quarterdeck. Captain Edwards asked him if he refused changing the bread dust. He said he did not remember refusing to do it.

Lieutenant Grey took up the bag and asked Captain Edwards to put his hand into the bag two or three times, and said there was villainy and rascality going on in the steward room in serving the ship's company, asking, 'Is this fit for any of his Majesty's subjects to eat?'

Captain Edwards said he was upon his duty and asked Lieutenant Grey to walk on the other side of the deck.

Lieutenant Grey replied, 'Which side shall I walk on, will you wish me to walk on this side or the other?'

Captain Edwards said, 'Where you please.'

Lieutenant Grey said since he had been a lieutenant he was never ordered to walk on any particular part of the deck.

Captain Edwards asked Patterson how many servings he had got that bread dust in; Patterson answered in three weeks' servings. Captain Edwards asked the steward's mate if he had not particular days for changing the bread dust. He said yes. Captain Edwards asked him if this was the day to change the bread dust. He said yes again. Captain Edwards asked him if this was the day. The steward's mate said it was not. Captain Edwards then desired the boatswain's mate to take his bag and go away.

Lieutenant Grey laid hold of the bag and said, 'As second in command of this ship give me leave to let the bag remain.' The purser's steward was sent for, he did not come up – soon after the purser came on the quarterdeck and spoke to Captain Edwards, but what he said could not be heard. Lieutenant Grey walked to the other side of the deck, and told Lawless, 'I have been in the service twenty-five years and never saw a British seaman come aft with such bread as this.' Fortunately Captain Edwards had remained temperate and chosen to over-look Grey's asking him to put his hand into the bag (or as William Symons, the midshipman on duty, remembered it, 'Do Captain Edwards be so kind as to frust [sic] your hand into the bag and see if this is proper for one of his Majesty's subjects') and Lieutenant Grey had not raised his hand to his superior officer. Grey left the deck a few minutes later.[21]

When the routine of serving provisions followed supper, there were inevitably occasions when tempers got inflamed. On evening in the winter of

1796/97 a quarrel broke out between the cook and the steward of the *Montagu* (74) that drew in the steward's wife and the cook's mate. William Pocock, surgeon's mate, gave his version of events as follows. That day,

Futtock shrouds.

> near 6 in the evening Lieutenant Harford came down visiting around the ship as usual, and came into our birth in the cockpit the starboard side, and we heard a great noise between the pursers steward and the prisoner, and then we told Lieutenant Harford of it. He went out and followed him, when he came to the door of the stewards' room, he ask'd what was the matter, the cook (the Prisoner) persisted and made more noise, and said he was come after his provisions. Lieutenant Harford then told him to come out of the steward's room. The Prisoner then said he would not come out as he was a warrant officer, and he would see the ship's company righted, he told him a second time to come out, and when he told him a third time, he did come out. Lieutenant Harford then ask'd him, if there was not to be a little respect shown to a first lieutenant of a 74 gun ship, such as pulling off hat or cap. The Prisoner said No! not there unless it was on the quarter deck the lieutenant then sent for the master at arms. The Prisoner said the master at arms had no business with him that he was come to draw the ship's provisions, he then stamped his wooden leg with very great force, very near Lieutenant Harford's toes, when the master at arms came, Lieutenant Harford told the master at arms that the cook was his prisoner. Not to put him in irons as he shewed pity upon him having a wooden leg – when the master at arms & Prisoner were going up the ladder the Prisoner said if he was called to account in the morning he knew who kill'd the pig and that he would raise the ship's company, as he had seen the transaction that had been carried on in this ship.

According to the purser's steward, the dispute was about provisions that had been lost from the ship's coppers. One of the cook's mates, Michael Cruise, had accompanied him below:

> The Prisoner said we must have 24 gallons of oatmeal – the steward's wife told the cook he must not have oatmeal to sell for grog. so then the steward called the prisoner a damn'd liar the stewards wife said the cook

was a old villain then the steward wanted to fight with the prisoner. Then Lieutenant Harford came down and order'd silence, and said what do you do here. The prisoner then said, 'Sir I'm come for my provisions,' Lieutenant Harford then said, 'Come out of the stewards room,' the prisoner answered, 'Very well, sir!' Lieutenant Harford said, 'You are to give the provisions to the cook's mate.' So I took my bag of provisions up and went to the galley. The prisoner then said to Lieutenant Harford he had been 16 years a cook and never sold oatmeal for grog.

The cook's hasty words and refusal to pull off his cap had already condemned him: the verdict was that the charge of mutinous and seditious language was proved, but in view of his service and loss of leg, to be broke as cook of the *Montague* and to receive fifty lashes.[22]

QUARTERDECK, WAIST AND FORECASTLE

The starboard watch returned to the deck. For some who experienced it the naval life was one without freedom – Troubridge is famous for declaring, 'Whenever I see a fellow look as if he was thinking, I say that's mutiny', and Captain Browne, of the 23rd Regiment, found that on board the *Diadem* (64) it was forbidden to 'assemble in groups of more than two on the deck' – but one evening pastime, inevitably almost unrecorded, was walking on deck, to clear their heads after drinking or to talk over private matters.[23]

At 6.15pm the *Splendid* carried away the two after mizzen futtock shrouds, which secured the lower dead-eyes and futtock-plates of the topmast rigging to a band about three feet lower down around the mast. Shrouds were always rigged in pairs, and without the futtock shrouds passing the mechanical strain of the topmast to the mast below, the whole mizzen mast was endangered, and they were immediately replaced from the boatswain's stores.[24]

At 7pm she took in the topgallant sails again, calling the watch on deck, but the weather grew worse and at 8pm, with the log recording squalls, she took in the jib and spanker.[25]

Taking in the jib.

Chapter 9

SUPPER IN THE WARDROOM
First watch, 8pm to midnight

Supper for the officers

Supper in the wardroom was a lighter meal than dinner, taken between the evening gun and about nine or ten o'clock. Since the galley stove had been out since mid-afternoon, this was the opportunity for the mess to bring forward its private stock of cold and preserved meat, together with its pickles, tracklements and preserves. Supper was also less formal than dinner, though for an officer to be 'sitting at the table without coat, waistcoat, or handkerchief round his neck, and his shirt collar open' was still 'very improper'. An officer coming off duty could expect the supper table to be laid even if other officers had finished eating and were playing cards. An important indicator was the tablecloth, since the removal of the cloth signified the end of the meal and the arrival of the wine – that is to say, the port, rather than the everyday wine.[1]

Accounts of evenings spent in the wardrooms of ships of the line reveal that the officers treated it rather like a club room, with parties forming in various groups by the fire, at the table, on the lockers and at the rudder head, to talk, drink, play cards and so on. The surgeon of the *Gibraltar* said that he did not notice the lieutenants burning Mr Parke's hand with a poker: 'I was sitting in the after part of the wardroom at that time, either playing a rubber of whist, or reading, but not attending at that moment to what was passing at the fire side.'[2]

Night watch

Once the evening gun had sounded it was the duty of the master at arms to patrol the ship, 'particularly about the cable tiers, the cock-pit, and the store-rooms', to see that there were no lights burning.[3]

Lower deck: berthing and cleanliness

The formal procedure in the Royal Navy was that each boy, man, marine, petty officer and marine non-commissioned officer in a ship had a hammock (and a spare) and a place allocated for it to be hung at night that corresponded to the part of the ship in which his duty lay. In ships of the line, most hammocks were hung on the lower deck; on the upper deck the wardroom occupied the after-most 40ft, and forward of that was the main capstan and the waist, leaving only the galley area forward, where a small number were usually assigned places. Although the men could traditionally choose and form their own messes, the berthing plan was fixed: it was usually created by the captain or more often the first lieutenant when the ship was fitting out. For most of the war the plan for arranging the hammocks that was used was that drawn up by Daniel Ross, master of the *Vengeance* (74). In his scheme, battens were fixed across the width of the ship 3ft apart: since the standard nominal width allowed per man was 18in and the hammocks were suspended from clews that gathered the ends into a tri-angle, this allowed the hammocks to interlock like a honeycomb. The *Vengeance*, like most 74s, had twenty-two beams (inclusive) between the manger forward and the gunroom aft, but they were not equidistant, so Ross's plan directed that 'the length from the manger to the gunroom [be] divided into tiers of six feet, excepting the first, which should be nine' (because of the narrowness of the bows), and the battens nailed or screwed to the beams or athwartships carlines as appropriate. Each tier had two messes, one inside (nearer the gunports), and one outside, and there were seven messes amidships. The inside messes were given to petty officers such as the captains of the tops, the captain's coxswain and the master at arms, who had 28in width; seamen, landmen and marines had 14in, idlers and boys, 16in, and midshipmen, 20in. The larboard and starboard watches were berthed alternately, so each man would have the space of his oppo-site number when he was on deck. Arranging the tiers in regular 6ft intervals meant that some men had to sleep above a gun, and Ross reminded the reader that 'room must be left for the petty officers in the most convenient spaces between the guns', and to 'make allowance for the muzzles of guns, particularly in low ships'; 'the lower-deck guns were usually kept housed and secured when at sea', and when secured the muzzles were meant to touch just above the port, which in a ship-of-the-line typically gave a clearance of a little less than 30in to the deck above and 18in to the beam, and double that when the guns were run out. Space was also gained by hanging the hammocks at different heights or even in layers,[4] and a fight that broke out in the *Excellent* (74), while she was on the Jamaica station, shows how tension over the apparently simple arrangement of hammocks could become unmanageable. Thomas Burrows, a marine, shared a berth with Charles Coleman, a seaman.

> The first beginning of the quarrell was Burrow's hammock was quite low from any of the rest in the Birth – the Prisoner [Coleman] said then, if he hung in the birth as he had done before, he should make him hang higher or otherwise lower him down – Burrows going over to the other side of the table – he fell upon the Prisoner, who shoved him up – Burrows was in liquor. The Prisoner asked him if he wanted any thing, and Burrows said he did not care whether or not – the Prisoner gave him a shove and told him to stay off him – Burrows catched him by the collar and dragged him out of the birth, and said he would take him to Serjeant Monday – the Prisoner said he would stand it no longer – the Prisoner let go his right hand, and struck at him several times – the man fell, and when I looked the Prisoners shirt was torn.[5]

This court martial also indicates that the usual arrangement shown in berthing plans, with the marines sleeping between the officers and men and discouraged from messing with them, was not always followed in practice. Ross's plan was readily convertible to other ships, and in 1799 it was directed to be adopted in all ships built or repaired in the royal dockyards. Some berths, apparently those of certain petty officers, had canvas screens fitted.[6]

The navy followed the best contemporary medical advice, and encouraged fresh air to flow through ships. Ships-of-the-line could sail with their lower-deck ports as little as 18in above the waterline, and so they frequently spent days with the gunports closed. To help air flow every gundeck port of all two-deck ships had an air scuttle cut in it.[7]

The hammocks were made of canvas, and supplied by the dockyards. In the eighteenth century the men had one hammock each, but the Channel Fleet found after the winter of 1793/94 that the high incidence of sickness 'may have been caused in part, by the dampness of the men's hammocks after washing them' and spares were supplied. The conflict between the benefits of cleanliness and the evils of damp lasted as long as the war, but by 1810 the emphasis was on keeping the men warm and dry. A standard-issue hammock came with a 'bed', a thin mattress 5ft 10in long and 2ft 1in wide, made either of rags or 'sweet clean light flocks' (woollen refuse, 'on no account to be filled with shank wool'), or of goat hair. Hair beds were superior; washed beds were available, but were issued at half price, and usually given to ships on home service. Beds were intended to be issued with one blanket each, and although contracts in 1788 included one pillow per bed and in 1790s one bolster 1ft 9in long and 1ft 2in wide, in 1803 they were declared unnecessary (the seamen were allowed to supply their own if desired). According to Captain Hall, 'a pair of sheets may or may not be added'; Dr Trotter, in 1804, wrote 'they sleep without sheeting'. Blankets were 6ft 10in long and 5ft 4½in wide; flock beds weighed 12lb and the blanket 4lb 2oz.[8]

The size of hammocks varied. Deptford Dockyard, which always held the largest store for the fleet, was buying hammocks 7ft 0in long and 2ft 4in wide from 1784 to 1792 and perhaps later;* in his plan Ross assumed they were 6ft long, and in June 1806 that became the fixed size: 'to be 6 feet long and 4ft 2ins wide when tabled [hemmed]'. In October they were reduced to 5ft 10in long, and in 1814 made smaller again – 'at present they are so unnecessarily large that every man finds it convenient to reef his hammock at least eight inches' – and were to be 5ft 6in long, and there was a new smaller issue for boys, at 4ft 10in. The War Office reckoned a bale of fifty 6ft hammocks weighed 7cwt 2qr 6lb, and eight beds complete weighed 11cwt for single and 17cwt for double. It was usual to sleep with the head forward. Double hammocks were also supplied, for offices and petty officers, with two clews at each end, but since the 1790s ships had often carried cots instead.[9]

Ross directed that 'each tier be marked off in large characters' with a code for the number and location of the hammock, and Samuel Leech, who joined the *Macedonian* (38) in 1810, states: 'Below, the beams are all marked; each hammock is marked with a corresponding number, and in the darkest night, a sailor will go unhesitatingly to his hammock.' The *Macedonian* was brand-new and even from launch was considered a smart frigate, and the navy had been at war since 1793; in well-worked-up, well-disciplined and well-led ships this scene of order was probably normal, particularly late in the war. But in many ships, particularly ships-of-the-line and especially three-decked ships, it was not. It was usual for the petty officers of the watch to have lanterns lit below decks at night, for example, and William James, a seaman accused of theft while in the *Director* (64), was able to prove an alibi for himself by establishing that when he came below he asked a ship's corporal 'to be so good as to light me to my hammock'. It was all too easy for a drunk or tired man to find himself out of place; men also took every opportunity to hang their hammocks where they could get some room or privacy, slept in them with their wives and lost their way entirely. There were even a few men of low character who had no hammock or berth at all, and wandered their ships. William White, boatswain's mate of the *Trident* (64), said

---

* A document enclosed with the volume suggests there were six patterns in use in the 1790s.

in a court martial in 1802: 'On Tuesday the 4th May, 'twixt the hours of 8 & 10 pm, I saw Jas. Holland the prisoner slew [*sic*] the mess table that was in my birth into the side. I thought it only was to make a birth for himself to sleep for the night as he had no hammock.' The court asked, 'Do you mean to say the Prisoner Holland had no hammock with him at the time, or that he had no hammock in the ship?', and he answered: 'He had no hammock slung in the ship these 4 years he has an old hammock which he carries about with him to cover him wherever he pitches his lodging for the night.'[10] The confusion that was possible among hundreds of tired, drunk men is typified by these scenes, in the *Marlborough* (74) at Hamoaze in the winter of 1794, and the *Terrible* (74) in May 1798:

'On Wednesday night the 24th Inst. the Prisoner [William Read] and his Wife were going to their hammock and were quarreling Mr Pardoe [William Pardoe, midshipman] desired them to be silent They continued still making a noise, he threatened to turn them out of the tier, and sent for the master at arms'.

Thomas Ball, master at arms, told Read to be quiet. 'He had nothing to say at this time, but was undressing himself and going to bed. I saw the Prisoner into bed and his wife undressed to go to bed with him, on which I went on deck again, and left them very quiet. A few minutes after Mr Pardoe sent for me again, and ordered me to see the Prisoner's hammock upon deck – The Prisoner said he would take his hammock upon deck – With that his wife wanted to persuade him to keep his hammock down, but he said he [remainder cut off].

Thomas Roach, gunner's crew: 'I was in the best bower tier and I turned out when I heard the noise, which happened with (the Prisr.) his girl – She being down in Mr Cenullins [?] cabbin and the Prisoner could not get her to come to bed – and he fetched her out by force and got her down to his berth in the sheet tier – He then wanted her to go to bed and she wou'd not go, without his beating of her – She began to make a noise, and Mr Pardoe said he would not have such noise there but that the Prisoner should go out of the tier with his hammock ... To the best of my opinion all the gentlemen were in liquor; as one of them, a Mr Stoker [captain's clerk – Roach did not know where he messed] lost his way in going aft, I found him in the carpenter's mate's birth [which was] between decks on the starboard side. After the noise I went there to get a pot to fetch some beer, where I found Mr Stoker sitting on a chest, he said, "I believe I've lost my way," but I made him no answer.'[11]

Lieutenant Robert Parry of the *Terrible*:

On the evening of the 1st of May last, about ten o'clock, I was going on
the quarterdeck to leave the necessary orders for the morning, and heard a
violent noise on the forecastle & in the waist; i went down into the waist
to know the cause of the disturbance, & perceived 40 or 50 of the ship's
company, many of them intoxicated round the beer cask, and the beer
swimming about. I order'd them all down to their hammocks, which very
few of them complied with, for a considerable time, being so extremely
drunk I found it necessary to give orders to plug the beer up. The uproar
or noise rather encreased than otherwise, which brought Lieutenants Hill
& Chivers out of the wardroom, and we obliged most of the people to go
off the deck. I then went on the quarterdeck and shortly after heard the
noise increase again in the waist, upon which I desired Mr Mackie, mate
of the watch, to go down into the waist and see the cause of the
disturbance. Mr Mackie soon after came on the quarter deck (with Mr
Chapman a midshipman) and told me that Thomas Dundas had knock'd
him down. I immediately called the master-at-arms and went into the
waist and had Thomas Dundas put in irons under the half-deck. Whilst
putting in irons, or just after, the Prisoner said – He'd be damned if he
would not knock any one in the ship down that struck him. I told him to
be very cautious of what he said, which seemed to have little or no weight
with him; – he continued noisy & riotous, but I do not recollect any
other speeches which he made.

Read was acquitted, but Dundas was sentenced to 200 lashes around the
fleet.[12] There were also a few rapists and paedophiles, such as Carol Manning,
seaman of the *Tremendous*, who made a habit of climbing into the wrong hammock.

On the night of the 6th instant between the hours of nine and ten I felt
the Prisoner's hand underneath my bed cloaths, feeling over different
parts of my body. I then moved myself and he drew his hand away. I fell
into a dose of sleep and shortly after that I awoke. I heard Robert
Thompson who lay next to me say to the Prisoner what business had you
in Hammond's hammock. The Prisoner made no reply but turned into

his own hammock. I then fell asleep again and about ten minutes or a quarter of an hour after that, the Prisoner came to my Hammock again and pulled the cloathes off from me which awoke me: I was then lying on my side with my back toward him. He got in close alongside of me and got the shirt up above the small of my back: I then felt his yard in between my thighs – I started and hove him out of my hammock directly into his own, which was close alongside. I called him a dirty scoundrel and told him he was no man, he was a beast. He said he was a man. I then told him he was a disgrace to mankind. He then asked if I imagined he wanted to bugger me. I then turned out of my hammock and hauled him out of his. He seized me by the hair and struck me. I then called for the Master at Arms and hove him out from between the guns into the gangway. I told the Master at Arms to take him away, for alongside of me he should not stay any longer. The Master at Arms went up and reported him on the quarterdeck.

Hammond did not report the previous occurrence because Manning was drunk, and next morning, when sober, apologised and said he would not do it again. Manning was sentenced to 200 lashes around the fleet, mulcting of four years' pay, towing around the squadron with a halter around his neck, and turning on shore with ignominy.[13]

Arrangements were also less formal in port, particularly in fine weather, when men took the opportunity to escape the stifling heat below. In the *Prince* (90) in the summer of 1798, for example, hammocks were hung over the foremost sheep pen in the waist, under the half deck and under the forecastle, and in the tropics and West Indies many preferred to sleep on deck, though this was usually forbidden. In receiving ships it was often impracticable to assign berths, and people hung their hammocks were they could, or spread their blanket on the deck. William Taylor, a supernumerary boy of the second class belonging to the *Namure*, said in summer 1810 that he had never had a proper berth in the ship, but generally slept in the after cockpit, but was turned out when the clerk, evidently his friend or protector, left the ship. He hung his hammock up on the half deck one Sunday night but when he came to bed a few hours later the hammock had been lowered down and he slept half on his bed and half on the deck. A supernumerary seaman laid his bed alongside and Taylor woke up 'with his privates in my bottom'.[14]

Eugenia Wynne, who had spent some time as a guest of the Mediterranean Fleet, was given a passage in the Neapolitan *Samnite* (74), and recorded in her diary for 8 May 1798 'I walked on the deck paved by the filthy bodies of the sailors, who to my astonishment are allowed to lie down and sleep there until the lieutenant's voice rouses them from their indolent rest'.[15]

In the eighteenth century ship's companies had tended to be organised into two or three divisions, with an officer appointed to each 'to inspect into and regulate their conduct, to discipline and form them', which would prevent them remaining 'a disorderly mob', 'sottish, slovenly, and lazy', apt to 'form cabals, and spirit each other up to insolence and mutiny'. The 1790 regulations only required the captain to quarter them, *ie* to assign them an action station when the ship beat to quarters, but in 1806 and 1808 he was to divide all the ship's company except the marines into as many divisions as there were lieutenants, with an equal number in each, and drawn equally from the different stations in the ship. The master's mates and midshipmen were distributed equally to them, and each had a subdivision. The lieutenants were 'to attend at all their exercises; to examine into the state of their clothes and bedding; to see that they keep themselves as clean as the duty of the ship will admit; to prevent swearing, drunkenness, and every other immorality'; and to ensure the subdivisions were equally well attended. Those who were found to be 'ignorant, idle, dirty or profligate' were to be reported to the captain, so that they could be 'instructed, exercised or punished, as circumstances may require'. The marines were similarly divided into divisions commanded by subalterns, though there were no subdivisions. At sea, they worked with the afterguard, except those who were sentries. The lieutenant's instructions reinforced the emphasis on cleanliness, adjuring him to see that they 'keep their persons clean by washing themselves frequently', and specified that he was to 'observe attentively the progress they make in their various duties as seamen', giving them exercises as appropriate.[16]

The first ship in the Royal Navy to have dedicated washing facilities for all hands was the *Penelope* armoured corvette, laid down 4 September 1865, launched 18 June 1867 and completed 27 June 1868. Dr Lind, in his 1779 *Essay on the Most Effectual Means of Preserving the Health of Seamen in the Royal Navy*, had rather optimistically advocated cold baths 'either in tubs under the fore-castle, or to dip in the sea, early in the morning', 'in warm weather, and in hot countries', advising that 'the fibres' were thereby 'braced and invigorated', and certainly the boys in the *Macedonian* washed themselves 'in a large tub provided for the purpose on the main deck' while the deck was being washed, holystoned and swabbed during her cruise from Lisbon during the Peninsular War, but baths for the men existed only in the sick bay. Sea-bathing was popular by 1810 – James R Durand, a petty officer of the USS *Constitution*, recorded an order given off Sicily in 1805, 'all hands were called to go into the water to wash', and the *York* (74), moored in Port Mahon harbour in June 1810, recorded in her log 'allowed ships co. to bathe' – but accounts of it in the Royal Navy suggest it was for the enjoyment of swimming, not for cleanliness.[17]

Robert Wilson, who served as signalman in the *Unité* in 1805, gave an account of his duties that ended 'a signalman must always keep himself clean and decent', but accounts of how the ship's company kept themselves clean, or even how clean they kept themselves, are at best scattered. Since no formal place was appointed for it, the men washed themselves in their berths: this can be assumed partly because it was one practice stopped by the surgeon of the *Princess Royal* when she was infected with a fever in spring 1801, to maintain cleanliness between decks. The forenoon watch seems to have been typical: for example, 'On December the 31st [1797] between the hours of nine and ten in the morning, the ship's company [of the *Adamant* (50)] were cleaning themselves', and when John Stirling, a midshipman of the *Leviathan* (74), was sent for on deck just before noon on 1 January 1814, he had been 'naked, washing himself'. The lieutenant's instructions in the 1808 Regulations were merely to 'see that they are at all times as clean as the duties of the ship will allow', 'and particularly that they keep their persons clean by washing themselves frequently'; once every few days or once a week seems likely for men in good health: the unsuccessful mutineers in the *Defiance* (74), for example, were confined in the coal hold, and while they were given exercise and fresh air on the poop every day, they were only brought up to the gunroom 'to wash and clean' themselves 'a few days after being confined'. Truly verminous men, those who had become offensive to their messmates, were reported to the quarterdeck and dealt with. In the summer of 1810, one sailor in the *Sceptre* who was 'filthy about his person, easing himself on the lower deck, [and] losing his clothes', and showing other signs of unsociable attitudes towards public cleanliness, was scrubbed and shaved in the head and his frock was thrown overboard. He was perhaps more typical of the outsider who failed to adapt to naval life, and who therefore threatened the safety of the ship; he was described as a black man, 'a stupid and lazy fellow', and his crimes included throwing away a broom he was given and refusing to use it, although he was shown how to by a messmate, another black man. A marine aboard HMS *Nereus* in 1810 was demented and doubly incontinent; his messmates were ordered to 'have him wash'd every morning when the decks were washed; afterwards to wipe him dry with his blanket & dress him or see him dress'd or put in his hammock'; on one occasion they scrubbed him with a birch broom, though not vigorously enough to break the skin. (The master, who brought the case, testified that 'The last time

I saw him scrubb'd I saw great marks of violence on his sides back and posteriors the skin was off in several places, apparently to me by scrubbing', but the surgeon said 'his death was not occasioned by any means used by the Prisoner [Lieutenant William Fynmore RM], it being brought on by a collection on the brain which caused an occasional derangement and ultimately brought him to his grave', and he saw no signs of violence, 'except blisters and excoriation from laying in his own excrement and urine, which our utmost attention was not able to prevent.' The court decided that the accusation of cruelty was not proved further than Lieutenant Fynmore's having struck the marine.)[18]

By the 1790s cleanliness had been recognised as one of the modern weapons against fever, the great killer of men confined on board ship, and men were being washed in receiving ships before they joined a ship, and on admittance to the sick bay in ships in service. This was not necessarily in hot water, though. On volunteering, William Mark and a friend were taken on board the *Boreas* in the Thames and were examined by the surgeon and his mates then 'warm baths were prepared, and all were bathed and washed with soap', the surgeons of the *Formidable* (74) and the *Belleisle* (74) in 1800 and 1801 dealt with an attack of contagion partly by washing their patients on their admission to the sick berth 'with soap and tepid water' and 'warm water with soap'. Nor was it necessarily frequent; the surgeon of the *Belleisle* stated that his patients were 'again washed before they were discharged and allowed to mix with the ship's company', and Captain Dillon, who claimed to have cured seventy men of boils with warm salt-water baths in 1814, wrote that 'Every precaution, as well as decency', was observed, suggesting the procedure was still unfamiliar. (In the sea-bathing in the *Constitution* noted above, one of the men, who swam to a ship's buoy, was wearing a thin cotton shirt.)[19]

The men were clean-shaven but had long hair, which they wore in a queue (pigtail), as did soldiers. The navy recognised the ship's barber as a petty officer, though he was paid the same as a seaman, and there is an example from the *Defiance* of a man being shaved: John McKenna was 'between the hours of 11 and 12 o'clock [am or pm is not stated] sitting down in Roach's berth the starboard side before the pump dill to get shaved'.[20]

Officers washed and shaved in their cabins, with fresh water heated in the galley and brought by their servants. Unless their servant was particularly skilled, they shaved themselves. Captains had enough room for baths; Captain Pakenham had one in the *Merlin* sloop in 1788, and Captain Pasley mentioned a 'bathing tub' in the *Jupiter* (50) in 1782, which he filled with seawater, apparently cold; he found it 'extremely refreshing altho' salt water has not that salutary effect on my constitution that fresh water has, which braces while the other relaxes – a very different effect, I believe, to what it has on the generality of mankind.' St Vincent, touring Portsmouth Dockyard in 1802, 'observed a patent apparatus for a water closet, which I desired might be fixed in the quarter gallery which [Admiral Sir Henry] Digby had turned into a bath'. The frequency with which they bathed is hard to discover: the regulations stress the importance of appearing clean at all times, from which one might infer that officers needed reminding; they also stress the importance of appearing in uniform, and it is known that most officers appeared in uniform or its acceptable working alternative most of the time. Hoffmann, appointed to a sloop in the Downs, wrote that the captain's cabin was 'a complete den full of smoke and dirt'; his 'linen was the colour of chocolate, his beard had I presumed, a month's growth.' Dr Maturin's deliberate frowstiness, intended to show his lack of connection to naval propriety, is almost certainly correct.[21]

On 10 February 1811 James Costragan was caught 'pissing out of the top', and received a dozen lashes on the 17th for filthiness; associated with 'walking the deck' and 'taking the air' is the freedom men had to go to the head while on duty. On the evening of 8 December 1797, William McCloud, seaman of the *Ganges*, then in Yarmouth Roads, was 'out in the head looking at the weather about 8 or 10 minutes between 9 and 10 oClock' during his watch on deck;[22] William Jordan, a marine of the *Brunswick* (74), would not leave his post: John Cod, seaman, said that

> We were at Cape Nicolas Mole, I do not recollect the day of the month, it was after dinner, I was in the head doing my business, the Prisoner was centinel on the grating, he made water over the head, and 'twas flying right in our faces, John Fordham (I believe) told him not to do it, as it was very disagreeable – The Prisoner answered, if we did not like it we might help it, that none of it came near any of us. I replied, if you say so, you are a liar, he then pushed the fixed bayonet at my head which entered my hat, and drew a little blood.

His neighbour was John Fordham:

> John Cod and myself was sitting on a seat each in the head. The Prisoner was making water (and the ship being head to wind) it came in our faces. I told him that was no place to piss, he then said, 'You be damned,' it is nothing to you, it did not come near you. John Cod & I replied if you

say so, you are a liar – with that he [Jordan] up with the fixed bayonet and stab'd John Cod in the head and said, 'If you do not like it you may help it.'

Jordan said he acted in self-defence, and it was his first ship: he had 'imbibed (perhaps too strictly for the duty of a ship) the principles of a soldier ... I only acted as in former service I was taught to do.'[23]

The seats Cod and Fordham were sitting on were either open or partly enclosed like a wing-backed chair; a 74 typically had two on each side. Larger ships-of-the-line had a row of three or four seats; the *Victory* had six. Brian Lavery notes that 'few ships had as many as one seat for a hundred men', and that 'other areas, such as the lee chains, were still used'. William Richardson records the lonely death of a marine of the *Caesar*, off Lisbon on 12 April 1811: 'At midnight a marine was found in the ship's head quite dead; it was supposed he had fallen and struck his temple against something.' The lee side was preferred, for practicality and comfort; in April 1810 a man was washed out of the weather side of the heads of the *Gibraltar* (80), but fortunately a boat was lowered in time to rescue him.[24]

Their very public nature is shown in this account of the unpleasant experience of John Jones, captain's steward of the *Hermione* and now belonging to the *Puissant*, as he passed under the bows of the *Royal William* (100, hulked as a receiving ship) on 30 July 1800. He had given evidence before a court martial held for the trial of one of the mutineers of the *Hermione*, who was hanged, and as he

passed the *Gladiator* under her bows, a woman on the starboard side of the forecastle called out there goes bloody Jack Catch [Ketch], belonging to the *Hermione*, you bloody buggar you hung the man the other day, if ever I catch you on shore I will have your life taken from you, she still kept calling after me as far as I could hear her I ordered the waterman to turn back to take me alongside the *Gladiator*, when I got alongside her I asked for liberty to speak to the commanding officer and the officer of the watch told me to come on board when I came on board I related every thing to him how the woman had served me, he got a candle and lanthorn and went to search for the woman, but she could not be found I came up again, and went down into the wherry, and was going away, and [Thomas Nelson, supernumerary seaman] was sitting down on the top of the head chock forward, and said you buggar who are you going to hang now, that is the bloody buggar belonging to the *Hermione* who hangs all the men, you buggar if I had my will of you I'd hang you, I'd make a swab of you upon the beach he still kept abusing me as far as I could hear him, as I was passing along to go on shore I could not understand what he was then saying but he kept his eyes on me all the time.[25]

Nelson was sentenced to lose all the pay and wages due to him, and to two years' solitary confinement. Ships-of-the-line also had a roundhouse for the petty officers on the larboard side. Access was via a door on the upper (main) deck.

Oakum was used, though not necessarily exclusively: while the *Trusty* (50) was in dock, said John Owen Wigley, midshipman, 'I was leaning on the rail with another gentleman in the ship and I saw [William Jacobs, seaman] walking off as if he was coming from the taphouse. I jumped down and ran after him, and when I got to the place where I saw him I lost sight of him, in a little while after I saw him walking down towards the necessary house I called after him, and asked him where he was going to, he told me he was going to the necessary and he showed me some oakum he had in his hand for that purpose'.[26]

Petty officers on duty were usually in charge of a gang and therefore had to be formally relieved, as shown in this slightly incoherent account by William Franks, seaman of the *Brunswick*, two years later, after Thomas Thompson fell overboard:

> About 7 o'clock [in the evening of 2 March 1799], Thos. Thompson came to relieve Jones the boatswains mate, after Thompson came to relieve him, the Prisoner [Lieutenant James Oades Lys] asked him who sent him there, Thompson answered he came to relieve Jones to go to the head, the Prisoner called Jones to come back again to the gangway, after Jones came, the Prisoner told Thompson to go away, he did not want him there, Thompson did not go, and he began to grumble, the Prisoner asked, what do you say, Thompson said he did not want to go, he did not want to be relieved, after some words the Prisoner told him to go away – he went to the head = [*sic*] The Prisoner sent to call him back again, when he came he told him to lay hold of the tackle fall with the rest. Thompson came back again upon the gangway, I saw him tumble down, and he fell overboard. I endeavoured to lay hold of his foot, but was too late. The Prisoner called for a lanthorn, and said a man was fallen overboard – several people with lanthorns were looking for him. One of the seamen named Jno. Liverbourne said he would not see him. – The

Prisoner desired they would look everywhere – he called for the jolly boat, and desired them immediately to look if they could see and find the man, they remained some little time and returned and said they could not find him. The Prisoner asked if the man was drunk or sober – nobody answered.[27]

When the sickberth had been moved under the forecastle it had acquired the starboard roundhouse for the sick; in 1806 the Navy Board had decided that all ships that had sick berths could have a water closet in the roundhouse, on the captain's application.[28]

Ships were also provided with piss-dales, lead basins with tubes passing out through the ship's side,[29] which appear to be what Isaac Western was using in 1795: 'While in Cawsand Bay three or four days before we sailed I turned out of my hammock at 11 o'clock at night and went on deck to make water I heard a great noise of people under the starboard galley I went up the starboard gangway and made water then I laid down on the gangway.'[30] But in the *Achille* (74), at least, there were also tubs in the galley: 'The galley was wet; the people go into the galley to piss, where tubs are placed for them … but the benches were perfectly dry, and also the flagstones', according to Richard Cunningham, boatswain's mate.[31]

QUARTERDECK, WAIST AND FORECASTLE

At midnight the ship wore, to get her on the starboard tack. This was a major evolution; she had been on the larboard tack since 5pm on the 12th, but tacking in squally weather presented 'danger to the masts from the pressure of the sails when aback, as they are then supported only by the stays', and 'the mainsail was extremely dangerous in this kind of weather if it flew aback hard against the

Four stages in wearing a ship.

mainmast and shroud. If that happened, it would defy almost all efforts to run it up in its gear'. Wearing the ship, when the ship 'went about stern to wind', was much safer and always succeeded, with little loss to leeward. The watch on deck went to their stations. As explained by Darcy Lever, in his *Young Sea Officer's Sheet Anchor*:

> When every thing is ready, the mizzen topsail and cross jack yards are squared, the main tack and bowline eased off, and the *weather* clew-garnet hauled up [to bring up the lower corner, because this way 'the sail naturally flies to leeward and keeps full']: the main sheet is then eased off, the *lee* clew-garnet hauled up, and the buntlines and leechlines [which brought the foot of the sail upwards and forwards, and to the mast, respectively]: the main and main topsail yards are squared, and the helm put a-weather.
>
> As she falls off [from the wind], the fore bowline is let go [releasing the weather edge of the sail], the fore sheet eased off, and the weather or larboard braces gathered in forward [allowing the weather ends of the yards to swing to leeward]; when she is before the wind, the starboard tacks are got on board, and the main sheet hauled aft; but the weather braces are kept in forward. When the main tack is difficult to be got down, a luff-tackle is hooked to the lower bowline cringle, or to a lizard spliced into the bowline bridle for the purpose: as she comes to [and has nearly come round onto the new tack], the helm is eased, that she may not fly up too rapidly, the fore sheet is hauled flat aft, the yards braced sharp up, the bowlines hauled, the weather braces set taught, and the rolling tackles [which confined the yard] shifted to the starboard side, and the geer coiled up.[32]

This was not quite all for that night; she also took in the third reef in the mizzen topsail and, the log records,

> At 1.15 in 3rd Reef the main, & Close Reefed the Fore & Mizon Topsails
> At 2.30 Wore Ship at 4 Fresh Breezes & Clear
> Strong Breezes. At 4.40 Split the Fore Topsail, unbent it and bent another. At 5 Cape Sicié N½W 10 Leagues. Set Mainsail. 6.30 Set Foretopsails.
> At 8.30 Out 3rd Reefs the Topsails & made Sail at 9.30 saw the Fleet NNW.

At 12 that night she recorded:

> *San Josef* with the Fleet in Co. Consisting of *Ville de Paris*, *Centaur*, *Tigre*,
> *Leviathan*, *York*, *Sultan*, *Ajax*, *Bombay*, *Repulse*, *Warspite*, *Colossus*,
> *Euryalus*, and *Minstrel*.

Next morning, in 'light airs inclinable to calm', she began 'hoisting up water for the fleet', and that afternoon the *York* set off to Mahon in her turn to continue the task of keeping the fleet on blockade.[33]

APPENDIX 1
Ships' Complements

GUNNER

1790	First Rate	Second Rate	Third Rate
Gunner	1	1	1
Gunner's mate	4	4	2
Yeoman of the Powder Room[1]	2	2	2
Quarter Gunner	one to every four guns		
Armourer	1	1	1
Gunsmith	1	1	–

1810	First Rate	Second Rate	Third Rate				
			738 men	719 men	640 men	590 men	491 men
Gunner	1	1	1	1	1	1	1
Gunner's mate	4	4	4	2	2	2	2
Yeoman of the Powder Room	2	2	2	2	2	2	2
Quarter Gunner	25	23	21	20	20	18	16
Armourer	1	1	1	1	1	1	1
Armourer's mates[2]	2	2	2	2	2	2	2
Gunsmith	1	1	1	–	–	–	–

BOATSWAIN

1790	First Rate	Second Rate	Third Rate
Boatswain	1	1	1
Boatswain's mate	4	4	2
Yeoman of the Sheets	4	4	2
Coxswain	1	1	1
Master Sailmaker	1	1	1
Sailmaker's mate	1	1	1
Sailmaker's crew	2	2	2

1810	First Rate	Second Rate	Third Rate				
			738 men	719 men	640 men	590 men	491 men
Boatswain	1	1	1	1	1	1	1
Boatswain's mate	4	4	4	3	2	2	2
Yeoman of the Sheets	4	4	4	4	4	4	4
Coxswain	1	1	1	1	1	1	1
Sailmaker	1	1	1	1	1	1	1
Sailmaker's mate	1	1	1	1	1	1	1
Sailmaker's crew	2	2	2	2	2	2	2

CARPENTER

1790	First Rate	Second Rate	Third Rate
Carpenter	1	1	1
Carpenter's mate	2	2	2
Carpenter's crew	12	10	8

1810	First Rate	Second Rate	Third Rate				
			738 men	719 men	640 men	590 men	491 men
Boatswain	1	1	1	1	1	1	1
Boatswain's mate	4	4	4	3	2	2	2
Yeoman of the Sheets	4	4	4	4	4	4	4
Coxswain	1	1	1	1	1	1	1
Sailmaker	1	1	1	1	1	1	1
Sailmaker's mate	1	1	1	1	1	1	1
Sailmaker's crew	2	2	2	2	2	2	2

SURGEON

1790	First Rate	Second Rate	Third Rate
Surgeon	1	1	1
Surgeon's first mate			
Surgeon's second mate	5	4	3
Surgeon's third, fourth and fifth mate			

1810	First Rate	Second Rate	Third Rate				
			738 men	719 men	640 men	590 men	491 men
Surgeon	1	1	1	1	1	1	1
Assistant surgeons	3	3	2	2	2	2	2

PURSER

1790	First Rate	Second Rate	Third Rate
Purser	1	1	1
Steward	1	1	1
Steward's mate	1	1	1

1810	First Rate	Second Rate	Third Rate				
			738 men	719 men	640 men	590 men	491 men
Purser	1	1	1	1	1	1	1
Steward	1	1	1	1	1	1	1
Steward's mate	1	1	1	1	1	1	1

MARINES

	First Rate	Second Rate	Third Rate		
			80 guns	74 guns	64 guns
1795					
Captain	1	1		1	1
Subaltern	2	2		2	1
Sergeant	4	2		2	2
Corporal	4	3		3	2
Drummer	2	1		1	1
Private	100	70		70	50
Total	113	79		79	57
1810					
Captain	1	1	1	1	1
Subaltern	3	3	2	2	2
Sergeant	4	3	3	3	2
Corporal	4	3	3	2	2
Drummer	2	2	2	2	1[3]
Private	156	138	139	115	82
Total	170	138	150	125	90

APPENDIX 2
Light and Darkness in a Ship-of-the-Line

The authors of at least two published reminiscences of sea life used Milton's description of the flames of hell, 'darkness visible', to record their astonishment at the lack of light on board ship. From these and other narratives quoted in the text it seems clear that when the ports were closed the gundecks of a ship-of-the-line were usually very dark. On Boxing Day 1798 John Higgs, second lieutenant of the *Druid*, reported to the captain that there were no candles on board the ship. The purser was sent for and desired Higgs to look below, where he saw three or four. The purser asked him, 'Do you not see there are enough, and did you not answer quite an illumination?' This was not poetic exaggeration: it was true by day as well as by night, even in midsummer, although the introduction of illuminators in 1809 improved the situation.[1]

A vivid demonstration of this darkness visible as it was experienced mid-century, before the introduction of sliding scuttles and illuminators in the gun-port lids, is provided by this account by Sergeant Grimes, a marine in the *Rippon* (60), of what happened one day in August 1758, while the ship was at Black-stakes, in the Thames estuary:

As I was getting up the 1st instant about ten o'clock in the morning I heard a noise on the other side of the gun, I looked to see what it was it being dark and the ports not hauled up, only in the second port from me there was a wedge which occasioned a little light, I observed the Prisoner (with a goat between his legs) kneeling on his left knee and standing upon his right leg, I saw him full in motion, the same as if a man was acting with a woman. I beheld him for some time till I recollected that it was proper to have a witness on such occasion. Corporal Mansfield being nearest to me, I got up without speaking and took him by the arm & so shewed him the Prisoner continuing in the same affair as before, and I said to Mansfield, I take you as a witness of what you see. Immediately the Prisoner let the goat go and fell down upon his side, which seemed to me as if he was going to make his escape. I immediately told the Corporal to go round the gun and stop him because I was not sure who he was, and found him to be the said John Blake the Prisoner. I immediately lighted a candle keeping the Prisoner in my eye at the same time, I then examined him and found his breeches down, I called him a Vile wretch, and went immediately and acquainted the Chaplain of it, and he owned before the Chaplain in my hearing that he was guilty of the act of buggery with the goat.[2]

Corporal Mansfield stated in court that he did not see the alleged motion, and when Grimes was questioned about this he said:

> The corporal being doing something in the next birth where the light was, and coming out of the light could not see so plain as me who had been looking in the dark some time, and moreover I gave but little time for the moment he came I pointed to the Prisoner and told the corporal, I take you for witness, then the Prisoner immediately let the goat go and fell down upon his side.

This is more than 'darkish', or 'duskish', Grimes's reason for not seeing Blake withdraw from the goat, and although Blake was sentenced to death the court must have had its doubts, because he was discharged from the *Rippon* that October.[3]

After sunset, of course, it was equally dark on deck, if there was no moon. When the *Courageuse* (32) was in Port Mahon harbour, Minorca, on 21 August 1799, a prisoner was making a disturbance under the half deck at about 8.30pm, but the sergeant of marines on duty had to use a lantern to see whether the lock around his leg was broken or not, and when Captain Dillon of the *Leopard* troopship came on deck one night off Algiers, 'the effect of candlelight still operating upon my eyes, I could not distinguish any object (on the quarter-deck). I had not made more than three or four paces, when I came into contact with an individual and demanded who he was. No answer being made, I began to handle him. Judge then of my surprise when I beheld a white turban close to my face.'[4]

Artificial light on board ship was provided by tallow, wax or spermaceti candles and by oil lanterns, but something as mundane as how they were used and in what quantities is very rarely recorded, except when they contributed to a fire on board.

The fire risk from naked lights with so much flammable material in the ship was obvious, and the regulations directed that the captain be 'extremely attentive in taking every possible precaution against fire': no candles were allowed in the magazine, the warrant officers' storerooms, the orlop or the cable tiers except in 'good lanthorns', and he was 'strictly to enjoin the officers not to read in bed by the light of either lamps or candles; nor to leave any light in their cabins without having some person to attend it.' Fourteen ships were lost to the navy from fire between 1793 and 1815,* but this was yet another regulation that was routinely ignored. In the *Success* (32), in February 1799, for example, William Lamb was corporal of marines: 'There were orders for the centries whenever the captain rung his bell to take a light and see what he wanted; there were no orders to go into the gun room, no farther than to give a gentleman a light when he put out a candle at the gun room door.' The *Ça Ira* (80) caught fire because of the carelessness of a servant and a bottle of 'combustible stuff' kept in the carpenter's cabin. His servant was making the bed when his candle went out, and since the boatswain had said he would beat him 'if he ever came nigh his cabin again' and there were people in the purser's steward's cabin, he took a match to the carpenter's bottle. The match broke, so he tried a second; it would not light. He stirred the bottle with a fork, and 'putting in the third match it lighted and I lighted the candle, and put the box with the combustible stuff on the shelf from whence I had taken it.' He made the bed, put the candle on the table, shut the door, sat outside it, and then the carpenter came back and noticed the smoke – the 'combustible stuff' had been put back next to a heap of oakum, which ignited.[5]

Fortunately, their use and misuse were the subjects of several courts martial of pursers for failing to supply necessaries, in which extensive and detailed evidence was presented. On 30 and 31 May 1798, Robert Dale, the purser of the *Lion* (64), was court-martialled for 'calling her commanding officer a scoundrel and not supplying her with pease and necessaries': one of those necessaries was candles, and the minutes of the trial list in some detail her consumption. However, it is probably unsafe to take the *Lion* as typical, since she seems to have been a very profligate ship (according to Dale, the officers 'were two nights in the week washing all night', and when Moses Hawker, her purser in the summer of 1795, was also court-martialled for not supplying the ship with sufficient necessaries her first lieutenant admitted she kept her fires lit from 4 or 5am to 9pm), but the trial is useful not least because the purser's defence was based on his statement of the typical use in his experience.[6]

According to the *Lion*'s log for 1797 and 1798, on 27 December she was moored at Spithead (and had been at Portsmouth since 8 October); on 10 April she weighed anchor and sailed west in company with the *Prince, Edgar, Marl-*

---

* 1794: *Ardent* (64), April, off Corsica; *Impétueux* (74), 24 August, Portsmouth. 1795: *Boyne* (98), 1 May, Spithead. 1796: *Ça Ira*, burnt and exploded, 11 April, San Fiorenzo Bay; *Amphion* (32), burnt and exploded, 22 September, Hamoaze; *Cormorant* (18), burnt and exploded, 24 December, Port au Prince, San Domingo. 1798: *Resistance* (44), burnt and exploded, 24 July, Straits of Banca. 1800: *Queen Charlotte* (100), burnt and exploded, 17 March, off Leghorn. 1801: *Iphigenia* (troopship), July, Alexandria. 1804: *Hindostan* (storeship), 2 April, Rosas Bay. 1806: *Dover* (troopship), August, Woolwich. 1807: *Ajax* (74), burnt, 11 February, off Tenedos, Mediterranean. 1808: *Unique* (18), 31 May, Basse Terre, Guadeloupe. 1813: *Captain* (74), 22 March, Hamoaze. The French lost two.

borough and *Success,* and arrived at Beerhaven on the 13th; on 10 May she sailed for the Mediterranean with the squadron, arriving off Cadiz on the 25th, where she remained on the 31st.[7] Dale's evidence was that from 27 December 1797 to 7 April/16 July [*sic*] 1798, he supplied her with 1,878lb of candles, 'which with oil constantly supplied for bittacles and centinels & other services, at a fair calculation of 10lb/day, ought to have lasted 187 days [to 11 October] ... instead of which the Expenditure was so great as 18lb/day to the 5th day of July', with boatswains' mates being issued four candles each, gunners' mates and yeomen the same '& so on with inferiors down to the lowest man in the ship': 3–4lb 'expended, wasted or made away with in the tiers' on getting under way, and in one instance 'between 5&6lbs being burnt at one heaving up', a waste that was out of his power to guard against.

His steward, Samuel Rickards, testified that between 1 January and 10 April she took on 700–800lb, and on that day, when she sailed from Cawsand Bay for Beerhaven, she had 395lb of candles. (The ship's company had therefore used, or perhaps hoarded or sold, 30–40lb per day at this point.) She took on 520lb 8oz more at Beerhaven. Questioned by the purser, he said that he thought the expenditure excessive for a ship of her class, particularly since there was oil in the ship for the bittacles and sentinels, and stated that the expenditure of candles since 9 April was 10–12lb/day, 'exclusive of oil', and that on 31 May she had 4cwt left. The supply since the *Lion* left Cawsand Bay was six mould candles per week to the captain's steward, two long moulds and one dip per day to the wardroom steward and twenty-four dips at ten to the pound for the cockpit daily; this was less than the usual supply for the wardroom but not the cockpit. The petty officers had 5lb per day, tens and cutts. (Dips were the cheaper sort of candles, made by repeatedly dipping wicks into hot coarse tallow; moulds were the better sort, made by pouring tallow made from mutton or ox suet, beeswax or spermaceti (or a mixture) into tin moulds; tens were tallow candles weighing ten to the pound.) A similar court martial, of the purser of the *Druid* (36) in 1799, suggests that warrant and commissioned officers were usually issued mould candles for their cabins: the master said he had sometimes 'had two mould candles in the course of the night, but another night when I reported it to Capt Abthorp, he put out one of his own mould candles, and desired me to put one out in the gun room, which I did, and I had one in my own cabin.' Her consumption, as a troopship, was five boxes for four months.[8]

Using Rickards' answer it is possible to deduce that the moulds weighed 3oz each, and this agrees with some contemporary figures supplied by the purser's accounts in the *Victory* (100): on 22 April 1797 he was issuing wax candles to the wardroom mess table at five per night. At that date he had on board 2,165 candles weighing 440lb (about 3.2oz each) and 707 weighing 109lb (2.4oz each). The *Victory*'s wardroom was at its maximum 37ft 5in long and 21ft 10in, with seven cabins, so if five candles were needed per night the *Lion*'s wardroom's low consumption is put in context. For comparison, the Commissioner at Chatham Dockyard was issued wax candles from time to time not exceeding 6lb per year. The cockpit's twenty-four dips can perhaps be accounted for by the claim that the midshipmen in the *Edgar* (74) cooked steaks over candles in their berth.[9]

On 24 December 1798 Walter Burke, purser of the *Powerful* (74), was court-martialled for writing a letter to Captain Drury of the *Powerful* 'complaining of a wasteful expenditure of necessaries, he not having any just grounds for so doing, and by his exaggerated misrepresentations in the said letter, reflecting on his, Captain Drurys, conduct in the regulations of His Majesty's Ship under his command, and expressly imputing to him a disobedience of my [Sir Roger Curtis's] orders, dated 6th May and 17th August last, directing the utmost frugality in the consumption of fuel and candles'. This court martial means that figures also survive for ships-of-the-line in the Mediterranean Fleet in 1798, since the letter, dated 4 October, states that the consumption of candles in the ship is 14–15lb per day, 'almost *one third* more than any ship in our squadron of a 74 make the representation of their daily expence' (the commodore having directed the purser of the *Leviathan* to regulate her use at 8lb per day). Further, he states that when fitting out at Portsmouth he supplied 120 new lanterns in addition to those already in the ship and exclusive of signal lanterns, but 'from the very wanton, and distructive waste of these articles, they are mostly reduced useless and unfit for service', even though the armourer's mates had repaired them where possible while supplies of horn etc. lasted, 'because all the boys, & men also, must have lanthorns (besides the real duty of the ship) on any frivolous excuse, and take no care whatever of them so that my steward and his assistance [*sic*] have to be gathering them up daily in the wings and thro' the ship, most of them destroyed and broke and unfit for use – all of these articles are so hard to be replaced or procured in our present situation and the ill consequences arising from the want of them in a man of war, particularly when they cannot be procured or replaced'.[10]

The figures for barracks established in 1795 offer a useful comparison. They are for the maximum weekly delivery per room; one room was occupied by a captain, or one subaltern of cavalry or two of infantry, or eight troopers or twelve NCOs and privates, and each room had one candlestick. An officers' mess had two rooms.[11]

Cavalry	November to March inclusive	2lb 8oz
Infantry	November to March inclusive	1lb 4oz
Cavalry	April, September, October	2lb
Infantry	April, September, October	1lb
Cavalry	May, June, July, August	1lb 8oz
Infantry	May, June, July, August	12oz
Lights in passages and galleries, 1lb per lantern per week, 1 September to 1 May		

The design complement of the *Powerful* was 550/600, which is 0.4oz per man per day, so on this basis she was very frugal compared to the cavalry's allowance of 4oz and the infantry's of 2oz.[12]

The officers' consumption in all ships was disproportionately great, but even the gunroom and wardroom were often dimly lit. Captain Dillon relates how he was invited to dinner in the gunroom of the *Horatio* off Margate Sands in December 1816: 'Having the shade over my eyes, I could not see well, and as the day was dark, the gun room had a very sombre appearance.' During the meal he calumniated against the pilot, whom he considered would have wrecked the ship had he not overridden him: the words 'had scarcely escaped my lips when I heard the motion of a chair trailing away from the table, and the person who occupied it instantly left the gun room. "Who's that?" I asked. "It's the Pilot, sir." '[13]

A printed stores list issued at Rochefort and found in the *Mutine* (18) when she was captured in June 1797 shows her consumption to date, in French pounds (to convert French pounds to British, add one-twelfth). 'Chandelles' are wax candles, and 'bougies' the cheaper tallow candles or tapers.[14]

	Maître d'Equipage [boatswain] (chandelles)	Chef de Timonerie [master] (bougies)	Maître Cannonier [gunner] (chandelles)	Maître Cannonier [gunner] (bougies)
Nivôse [21 Dec to 19 Jan]	20	–	1	–
Pluviôse [20 Jan to 18 Feb]	23	–	½	–
Ventôse [19 Feb to 20 Mar]	18	–	1	–
Germinal [21 Mar to 19 Apr]	17	2	½	1
Floréal [20 Apr to 19 May]	29	3	1	–
Prairial [20 May to 18 Jun]	16½	4	½	–
Messidor [19 Jun to 18 Jul]	15	4	½	–
Thermidor [19 Jul to 17 Aug]	2	2	½	–
Fructidor [18 Aug to 16 Sep]	18	5	½	–

Admiralty documents include a series of printed forms in which the dock-yards gave an account of ship's drafts at their fitting out, and these include an entry for candles. The dockyard clerks recorded the weight of candles on board, and occasionally the number of boxes, but not the number of candles, and though the clerks at Plymouth usually issued candles in boxes of 1cwt each, no direct correlation can be drawn between the figures given and the consumption on board, since it is not stated whether the ship is to deliver some of the candles to the squadron she is joining, nor whether she received all she demanded before she sailed. For example, the *Tremendous* (74) and the *Bellerophon* (74) both left Sheerness on Channel Service in the quarter ending 15 July 1793, the *Tremendous* with 200 men and the *Bellerophon* with about the same, but the *Tremendous* had 6cwt of candles and the *Bellerophon* 11cwt, and four ships are recorded as sailing with no candles at all, while the *Temeraire* (98) left Sheerness on 23 June 1799 for the Channel Fleet with 3 tons 5cwt on board, as well as 125 chord of wood and forty-four chaldrons of coal, and from Portsmouth in the quarter ending 15 April 1800 with the same amounts, though she had 599 men on board on the first occasion and 750 on the second, her coal being 270 days' consumption for a Third Rate and her wood 1,140 days. Figures for the *Formidable* (74) suggest that dockyard candles weighed 1lb each, but since the *Ramillies* (74) sailed from Ply-mouth on 23 April 1799 with sixteen boxes weighing 16cwt 1qr 16lb, and the *Ter-rible* (74) likewise on 8 April 1799 with sixteen boxes weighing 16cwt, not exactly so (tare of cask is recorded separately).

Totals recorded certainly rise as the war progresses and ships stay on station longer, and most of the forms also record the complement, so it can be calculated that of those ships in the quarters ending 9 July 1792 and 25 October 1802 inclu-sive, those sailing for Channel Service with complements below that of a line-of-battle ship (*ie* 493 or fewer men) carried 6lb 4oz per man and for Foreign Service 6lb 13oz, and those with 494 or more sailed with 3lb 10z and 4lb 12oz respectively, and all ships and vessels for which figures are recorded in this period carried an average weight per ship of 10 cwt 1lb. Channel Service was eight months' and Foreign Service twelve, from which it can be deduced that the average figures per man borne per day were 0.412oz, 0.299oz, 0.202oz and 0.208oz respectively. This apparently paradoxical result is perhaps explained by the supposition that ships in the Channel Fleet were principally resupplied with food and drink, while those on Foreign Service were expected to buy supplies of all species locally. The purser was allowed for candles, lanterns and other necessaries (coals, wood, turn-ery ware, etc.) 'a halfpenny per man a-day' in a ship-of-the-line.[15]

Candles used aboard ship were supplied by the dockyards when fitting out

(Navy Board records include contracts in the 1780s for tallow candles 9–9½in long and seven to the pound), or bought by the purser from commercial suppliers during a cruise, but some ships made their own. Those that slaughtered their own animals usually had tallow as a by-product, and the correct procedure was either to return it for credit to the agent victualler with the cured ox hides as the opportunity arose or to distribute it to other ships, but tallow-candle-making was a standard winter farmyard task and the temptation, and the available skills, must have been familiar to many ships. Nonetheless, it was dangerous, and in 1807 Captain Keats had to censure the captain of the *Penelope* for having done so: 'Pursers should recollect that that they are amenable in every sense to a court martial for a false report of the necessaries on board, and however desirous interested individuals may be to subject a ship to a necessity of making candles on board [in this case from 100cwt of tallow] – still it is an expedient that should never be resorted to but in cases of absolute necessity, which seldom occur.'[16]

Pursers must have had a rule of thumb when buying candles, or even a formula, but it is also difficult to discover from the sources how long one candle lasted. In 1798, the sentinel at the cabin door in the *America* made a complaint that his candles would not last the night; the first lieutenant reported that he 'immediately sent for the pursers steward, and desired of him what number of candles were usually issued to the centinels, he answered they had I think 6 cutts, and 2 short candles, or else if longer candles a lesser number but upon enquiring how long each candle was to burn, I found that less then that quantity would be sufficient to burn the whole night'; William Miller, corporal of marines, drew '3 of 8 to the lb in winter, and 2 in summer, for the centinel at the cabin door and 6 cutts in the winter & 5 in the summer for the wardroom & gunroom doors [and] 3 to each corporal, the same to the serjeant, except that he had a longer for his birth. The sentinels never complained that this was insufficient.' In the *Druid* (36), 3lb of small candles and three mould candles was 'nearly enough to serve all night'; in the *Warspite* in 1814 the ship's candles lasted 'two hours and longer'.[17]

No regulations concerning the distribution of candles seem to have survived. Robert Dale's defence was not very articulate – he lost, and was dismissed the *Lion* – but his miscalculation seems to have arisen from the unexpectedly heavy use of candles by petty officers '& so on with inferiors down to the lowest man in the ship', which was by the order of the captain. N A M Rodger concluded that literacy was common among seamen in the Georgian navy, and that professional seamen were 'predominantly literate', giving an example of men off duty reading in their hammocks; whether or not the *Lion*'s lower-deck consumption was because she was an unusually literate ship cannot be stated, but by the 1790s literacy, or at least functional literacy, was be assumed, certainly among petty officers, and candles seem to have been available for them. Sergeant Grimes had one in the *Rippon*, though he had to take it to the nearest midshipman's berth to get it lit, but in the *America* in 1798 Sergeant Sleffito reserved some of the marines' issue in his berth against the long winter nights. Robert Nelson, captain of the forecastle of the *Monarch*, messed with Thomas Hare, captain of one of the tops, and in June 1798 asked the purser's steward for his two candles; the implication is that his berth had two candles per day.

Several court-martial minutes reveal men wandering about the ship with naked lights and sticking them against beams, both directly forbidden by the regulations. These trials are particularly useful because prosecutions often depended on identity, and the court was keen to establish exactly how much light was available to a witness and what its source was.[18] Charles Bellion, for example, lost his hammock in the *Atlas* (90) one evening in May 1797. He went looking for it, and found more than he expected:

> On the 1st of May last between 8 and 9 o'clock in the evening I was
> looking for my hammock under the forecastle between the funnels of the
> copper & the foremast when I discovered the prisoners Duckworth and
> Simpson in the act of sodomy with both their breeches down. I stood
> there for some little time and they both went into the head door the
> larboard side and Simpson went out of the starboard head door the
> Drummer Duckworth came in of the larboard side.
> Court: How long did you remain there?
> A: About a quarter of an hour with my eyes fix'd on the prisoners with a
> lighted candle in my hand.[19]

The dispute in the *Warspite* was about the alleged theft of a candle:

> the Prisoner came with one of the lanthorns in his hand holding it up to
> me, I thought there was something amiss, and so I asked him what was
> the matter; he said he wanted a fresh candle as that was burnt out; I said
> it is impossible that the candle is already burnt out, it is hardly 10
> minutes since I lighted it, and they will burn two hours and longer, upon
> this I went into the wing and while passing out of the small passage from
> the cockpit, the Prisoner followed me, I said to him, 'You have cut the
> top of the candle and put it in the socket to make me believe the candle is
> burnt out,' upon which he called me a liar; coming upon the fore grating

he said in a loud voice to the people, 'Here, this old fellow of a liar says I cut the candle,' upon which I took my hand and struck him upon his mouth saying you d–d 'rascal' [*sic*] hold your tongue, at the same time I received a blow upon my face from the Prisoner with his fist.[20]

The regulations forbade naked candles because of the fire risk, and lanterns were supplied. A contract survives in the Admiralty records for lanterns to be issued to the dockyards for use in fitting out ships. It lists fixed and hand lanterns for the various rates of ship, and gives the dimensions and prices.[21]

	Dimensions			
	Height Ft In	Diameter Ft In	Number of panes in each square	£ s d
Horn'd Hand Lanthorns	1 2	0 7 bottom	Per Dozen	1 14 0
Tin Plates White Double*			"	0 7 0
Single			"	0 4 0
Double & Single wrot. on Galley's Bread andCook Rooms for Workmanship			"	0 0 6
Copper Powder Room Lights with 5 Sides, 2 Light & 3 Dark, 2 Panes in each light	2 9	1 8½	2	3 6
Do.	2 2½	1 4	2	2 4
Do. Storeroom triangular 2 sides light & 1 Dark 4 Panes in each light	1 8	0 11	4	4 2 5
Subject to an abatement of £27 10s per cent for Poop & Top Lanthorns and £35 for Copper Store and Powder Room Lanthorns				

Ordnance Board tonnage books record that there were thirty-two Muscovy lanterns to the ton, eighty ordinary, and 216 dark; according to Captain Boyntun, who weighed everything in the *Milford* (74) in 1810, hand lanterns were 5lb each.[22]

The master list of stores to be supplied to ships before they were launched for most of this period was issued on 23 October 1771, revised and updated periodically: in a letter of 3 December 1794 the Admiralty said it was intended for all ships except flagships, and ships going to the East Indies or remote parts, and described it as a book. Unfortunately it seems to have been lost, but there is a smaller list of stores for ships in Ordinary dated 3 December 1784 that includes items to be supplied to ships as they are fitted for sea, and hand lanterns are on the boatswain's list. Towards the end of the war the Admiralty issued printed forms: boatswain's stores for a 74-gun ship included three hand lanterns, or five if she was stored for eighteen months, and for the carpenter, three or six hand lanterns, three powder-room lanterns with lead cisterns, five storeroom lanterns and a poop lantern (three if not a private ship). In 1815 this became three hand lanterns for home service and six for foreign, one top lantern and one crank

---

* These were fixed to the ship's side adjacent to where the lantern hung, when the ship was fitted out.

lantern.† The lanterns for the general use of the ship were supplied by the purser: the *Victory*, for example, bought four dozen on 3 June 1796, 200 on 4 December, and forty-eight on 5 December, some of which must have been for the fleet. Oil lanterns burnt seal or rape oil.[23]

Shortly after the war ended the Admiralty made two revisions to its issue of lanterns: it informed the Navy Board that

> Having taken into consideration the very inferior light exhibited in the night signals of His Majesty's ships; and having determined that this most important branch of the naval service shall be put on a new and better footing; we do hereby desire and direct you to advertize for specimens of the best description of lanthorns either for oil or candle, and as encouragement to ingenious men, to offer a premium or premiums of moderate amount (of which you will be the best judges) for the best and second best specimens

and when ready sent for trial; and it decided that magazines were to be lit by oil lanterns, in ships of the line according to the plan of the *Scarborough* and in frigates after that of the *Nautilus*. The oil was to be supplied by the Navy Board, not the purser, and to be best spermaceti; ships with three lamps (two in the fore magazine and one the after) were to have six gallons of oil and twenty yards of tape cotton wicks, and the other ships in proportion. The gunner was to keep a log of every time the magazine was opened, with the reason why (action, exercise, cleaning, etc.) and the expenditure of oil and wick, and each time the ship returned to port he was to demand oil and or wick to keep his store to the establishment.[24]

It is easy to forget just how unused to a mass of artificial light people were in the Georgian period. Peter Cullen travelled from Edinburgh to London in November 1789 and 'was struck with astonishment' as he approached 'in a long, dark winter's night, when all the shops, stalls and streets were lighted', and when the *Endeavour* was at Rio de Janeiro in 1768, Joseph Banks saw the boys of one of the parishes walk through the streets, each carrying

> a lanthorn hung on the end of a pole about 6 or 7 feet long, the light caused by this (for there were always at least 200 lights) is greater than can be imagind; I myself who saw it out of the cabbin windows call[ed] together my mess mates and shewd it to them imagining that the town was on fire.[25]

---

† A First and Second Rate's top lantern was the same size as a Fourth Rate's middle lantern, a Third Rate's top lantern as a Fifth Rate's poop lantern and a Fourth Rate's top lantern as a Sixth Rate's poop lantern.

APPENDIX 3
The stores of the *Milford* (74)

On 1 November 1809, Captain Bayntun of the *Milford*, then in Basque Roads three days out from Plymouth, compiled a report for the Admiralty entitled 'An estimate of every Article used in the Equipment of His Majesty's Ship *Milford* when Victualled and Stored for Channel Service'. The *Milford* had been designed by Jean-Louis Barrallier, a royalist émigré from Toulon, and Captain Bayntun had found her in some aspects very unsatisfactory; she was 3ft 6in by the stern, even after ballast had been landed, instead of the intended 1ft 9in, carried a slack helm, sailed very much to leeward and was 212 tons short of capacity when fully stored. He proposed that to make her sufficiently stiff her 32 tons of limestone ballast should be thrown out and replaced by 80–90 tons of 'good shingle' in the fore and main holds, and her fore yards should be shortened.

Barrallier had attributed the *Milford*'s alleged failures, in particular being too low in the water, to her being overstored, but Captain Bayntun observed that 'The information which Mr Barrallier says he got from the Navy Office of the usual weights put on board ships of the *Milford*'s class appears to be very erroneous, it must have been derived from an old date, at a time when the stores and provisions allowed for Channel Service were perhaps calculated for three, or at most four months'. He dismissed Barrallier's suggestion that 10 tons of bread, 30 tons of coal and 25 tons of wood be landed, since this was thirty-five days' bread for 640 men and more than half her fuel for the stoves, and the idea that he land 20 tons of shot from the after locker 'makes me smile'. His report therefore had two purposes: to list the quantities of all the stores and equipment in the *Milford* as she was equipped for Channel Service, and to supply their weights, since even in that his figures differed from Barrallier's. His calculations showed that the whole weight of the ship on 1 September was 3,006 tons (the totals in each table are Captain Bayntun's).

The information, Captain Bayntun wrote, was 'procured with infinite labour ... yet will be found tolerably correct'. It provides a unique insight into the workings of a 74-gun ship after fifteen years of near-continuous war.

1. Tonnage of provisions etc on board His Majesty's Ship *Milford* at her leaving Cawsand Bay

This table records the provisions taken on board and the casks and containers in which they were supplied.

Provisions	Tons	Cwt	Qrs	Lbs	Packages	Tons	Cwt	Qrs	Lbs
89,600 pounds of bread	40	0	0	0	800 [canvas] bags, 1½lb each	0	10	2	24
3,234 pieces of beef, 8lb each	11	11	0	0	77 barrels, 79lb each	2	14	1	7
6,446 pieces of pork, 4lb each	11	10	0	24	94 foreign cask, 55lb each 15 hogsheads, 109lb each	3	0	1	27
19,655 pounds flour	8	15	1	27	40 hogsheads, 90lb each	1	12	0	16
1,640 pounds suet	0	14	2	16	7 barrels, 91lb each	0	5	2	21
3,262 pounds raisins	0	16	1	18	10 barrels, 44lb each	0	4	0	0
1,838 pounds butter	0	13	3	20	15 firkins, 15lb each	0	2	0	1
3,800 pounds cheese	1	8	2	8	31 half-hogsheads, tare	0	8	1	4
2,800 pounds sugar for butter	1	5	0	0	5 hogsheads, 109lb each	0	4	3	13
3,197 pounds cocoa for cheese	1	5	2	8	2 hhds, 11 barrels, & 1 half hogshd	0	5	3	16
5,032 pounds sugar for oatmeal	2	4	3	24	9 hogsheads, 109lb each	0	8	3	1
5,608 pounds [sic] lime juice	2	10	0	8	65 cases, 115lb each 1 barrel, 91lb	3	8	0	18
5,600 pounds sugar for lime juice	2	10	0	0	10 hogsheads, 109lb each	11	9	2	23
5,401 pounds tobacco	2	8	0	25	5 foreign cask, 136lb each	11	6	0	7
372 bushels of pease	10	12	2	8	37 puncheons, 100lb each	1	4	0	12
300 bushels of oatmeal	8	11	1	20	25 hogsheads, 90lb each	1	2	2	0
2,012 pounds pot barley	0	17	3	24	4 hogsheads, 90lb each	0	3	0	24
827 gallons vinegar	2	19	0	8	13 hogsheads, 109lb each	0	12	2	17
2,849 gallons rum	10	3	2	7	33 puncheons, 100lb each	1	6	3	0
5,685 gallons wine	20	6	0	8	20 puncheons, 100lb each 30 pipes, 120lb each	0 1	15 12	0 0	8 8
40 chaldron coals	51	9	1	24					
40 chord wood	50	0	0	0					
1,329 pounds candles	0	11	3	13	tare of boxes	0	2	2	5
108 gallons oil	0	7	3	12	3 half-hogsheads, 77lb each	0	2	0	7
64,350 gallons water	229*	16	1	10	504 butts, 184lb each 32 puncheons, 129lb each 21 hogsheads, 109lb each 31 barrels, 91lb each 28 half-hogsheads, 77lb each	41 1 1 1 0	8 16 0 5 19	0 3 1 0 1	0 12 21 21 0
Total	474	13	3	10		67	12	3	16
NB. Having only 32 tons shingle ballast in the ship, a greater quantity of wood is necessary for stowing the ground tier casks.					**Total provisions etc**	474	13	3	10
					Total weight	542	6	2	26

---

* Probably a slip of the pen for 292 tons.

The water was stowed in four tiers, ground, second, third, and upper:

Butts	Puncheons	Hogsheads	Barrels	Half-hogsheads	
90	10	4	18	26	Ground tier
117	16	10	11	2	Second tier
142	4	7	2	–	Third tier
155	2	–	–	–	Upper tier
504	32	21	31	28	**Total**[1]

2. TONNAGE OF SLOP CLOTHING

Slop clothing was issued by the dockyards to the pursers of ships in commission, to be supplied to the men at standard costs. Kersey was coarse ribbed wool, intended for use in cold weather; duck was strong untwilled linen or cotton, intended for summer wear. Frocks were close-fitting garments worn instead of a shirt. One blanket was supplied with each bed (mattress). Captain Bayntun estimated that the total weight of 'bags and chests with clothes' was 7 tons 10cwt 1qr 8lb, of hammocks (at 44lb each) was 2 tons 2cwt 2qr 0lb and the men themselves (at an average weight of 150lb) was 42 tons 17cwt 0qr 16lb.

Kersey jackets	3 bales	115lb each	0	3	0	9
Kersey trousers	5 bales	126lb each	0	3	2	14
Duck frocks	6 bales	168lb each	0	9	0	0
Duck trousers	4 bales	143lb each	0	5	0	12
Shirts	4 bales	100lb each	0	3	2	8
Shoes	7 bales	162lb each	0	10	0	14
Stockings	5 bales	66lb each	0	2	3	22
Hats	8 bales	84lb each	0	6	0	0
Blankets	3 bales	105lb each	0	2	3	7
Flannel waistcoats	3 bales	66lb each	0	1	3	2
Flannel drawers	2 bales	38lb each	0	0	2	20
Guernsey frocks	3 bales	80lb each	0	2	0	16
Boys' linens	2 bales	45lb each	0	0	3	6
Boys' hats	2 bales	57lb each	0	1	0	2
Boys' woolens	1 bale	57lb	0	0	2	1
		Total	2	15	0	21

3. RIGGING, BLOCKS, ETC.

The component parts are individually detailed, but since these tables are printed elsewhere they are not reproduced here. The total of the rigging was 31 tons 7cwt 1qr 27lb, including 10,841 fathoms of rope (more than twelve miles) from 1½in to 17in circumference, and the total of the 962 blocks (with tackle hooks, futtocks and thimbles) was 10 tons 13cwt 3qr 32lb.

4. 'AN ACCOUNT SHOWING THE QUANTITY OF CANVAS AND THE WEIGHT OF EACH SAIL'

Thirty-three sails are listed, with one or two of each allowed. The weight is 9 tons 16cwt 3qr 2½lb.

5. BOATSWAIN'S STORES

Present use stores are used in fitting out the ship, and sea stores are for use at sea.

Sea store and present use	Tons	Cwt	Qrs	Lbs
Black varnish	0	5	2	0
Brushes, large	0	0	1	17
Brushes, tar	0	0	0	26
Buntin	0	0	0	4
Canvas awnings, old	0	0	0	7
New canvas, sorts	0	3	3	22
Old canvas	0	1	0	14
Boats' covers [canvas]	0	3	0	20
Cots	0	1	3	20
Hoses	0	0	0	20
Hammock covers [painted canvas]	0	11	0	0
Ensigns, jacks and pendants	0	1	2	15
Hammocks, old and new	1	15	2	21
Kersey [supplied in red and green and used for tablecloths, etc]	0	0	1	19
Compasses, cards, and chest	0	1	0	8
Copper kettles, large and small	0	1	1	0
Machine for sweetening water	0	0	0	25
Cordage of sorts	2	1	1	1
Main tacks, spare, and fore do.	0	3	3	4
Wheel rope, spare	0	2	3	27
Junk [old rope for various uses in the ship]	1	13	0	0
Lines of sorts	0	1	2	22
Marline	0	0	0	25
Rope netting	0	1	2	6
Old rope for spunyarn	0	2	3	0
Spunyarn	0	9	0	0
Twine	0	0	0	5
Thread	0	0	0	1
Glasses, watch	0	0	0	18½
Grindstone	0	0	2	0
Hides in hair	0	3	3	14
Axes, junk	0	0	0	12
Bilbow bolts and shackles	0	1	0	0
Boom irons on the yards	0	4	0	0
Top chains	0	5	0	0
Creepers [small grapnels for recovering items lost overboard in harbour]	0	10	1	25
Cringles	0	0	3	20
Crows	0	1	0	0
Grapnels of sorts	0	2	1	0
Hand and chain	0	1	2	0

Sea store and present use	Tons	Cwt	Qrs	Lbs
Hammers, fid [wooden hammers with pointed peens used to open strands of rope in splicing]	0	0	0	14
Hatchets	0	0	0	12
Hooks, boat	0	0	0	14
Hooks, can [used to sling casks]	0	0	0	20
Hooks, fish	0	1	3	20
Hooks, puttock [futtock]	0	0	2	0
Hooks, tackle	0	0	1	21
Hooks, travellers jib	0	0	2	7
Hooks, boat [sic]	0	0	1	18
Locks, hanging	0	0	0	6
Marline spikes	0	0	1	18
Mauls for topmasts [iron hammers for driving the iron fids in and out of topmasts when raising or striking them]	0	0	2	0
Pots	0	0	1	0
Puttock plates	0	1	1	0
Scrapers [for cleaning the decks]	0	0	3	12
Thimbles of sorts	0	0	3	14
Lanthorns, hand	0	0	0	5
Leads, deepsea	0	0	2	0
Leads, hand	0	0	2	0
Leather buckets	0	1	2	5
Tallow	0	1	3	14
Tar	0	16	2	7
Vinegar	0	11	0	0
Smoke sail [a small sail used to allow the galley smoke to rise and prevent it blowing on the quarterdeck]	0	0	1	17
Ballast baskets	0	0	2	20
Blocks, spare, cat	0	2	3	6
Blocks, deadeyes of sorts	0	3	3	1
Blocks, different sorts	0	9	0	11
Nails, woolding	0	0	0	18
Boat hook, spare	0	1	2	12
Brooms	0	7	1	4
Buckets, iron-bound	0	2	2	20
Buoys, nun [used to mark where the anchors lie]	0	2	1	12
Buoys, wood	0	1	3	10
Commanders [large wooden mallets used when metal ones would be dangerous]	0	0	1	10
Fids, splicing	0	0	1	6
Handspikes	0	4	2	14
Oars, barge and pinnace	0	6	1	20
Oars, launch	0	3	1	0
Oars, cutter	0	3	3	15
Ship sweeps [very long oars used to manoeuvre the ship in a calm]	0	3	3	9
Parrel topsails	0	0	0	16

Sea store and present use	*Tons*	*Cwt*	*Qrs*	*Lbs*
Pins for blocks	o	o	o	4
Oil	o	o	o	16
Leather, liquored	o	o	1	2
Scoops	o	o	o	18
Serving mallets	o	o	1	2
Shovels, iron	o	1	o	18
Shivers for blocks	o	o	o	16
Trucks for flag staves	o	o	1	26
Shrouds	o	o	o	28
Shrouds, vanes	o	o	o	1
Windsail hoops	o	o	o	5
Canvas, old, painted	o	2	2	14
Massey's sounding machines [propeller-driven ballasted machine for recording the depth of water and the nature of the sea bed]	o	o	o	5¼
— lead	o	o	o	23
— line	o	o	o	12
Materials for swabs	o	17	o	o
Rope for signal halyards	o	1	1	o
Junk for guard netting	o	9	o	o
Signal flags	o	o	2	o
Signal pendants	o	o	o	16
Signal vanes	o	o	o	6
Cables	30	16	1	12
Anchors, 74cwt 0qrs 14lbs	7	8	1	o
Anchors, 73cwt 0qrs 0lbs	3	13	o	o
Anchors, 74cwt 2qrs 0lbs	3	14	o	o
Anchors, 17cwt 0qrs 14lbs	o	17	o	14
Anchors, 8cwt 1qrs 14lbs	o	8	1	14
Total	**62**	**12**	**o**	**6**

6. *Milford*, WEIGHT OF BOATS

	Tons	*Cwt*	*Qrs*	*Lbs*
32 feet pinnace	1	10	o	o
28 feet pinnace	1	5	1	6
25 feet cutter	o	14	2	14
[second] 25 feet cutter	o	14	2	14
18 feet cutter	o	9	3	o
31 feet launch	3	16	1	10
Slide and chocks	o	4	o	o
NB. Oars, masts, and sails not included in the above.				
Total	**8**	**14**	**2**	**16**

(Although barge oars are listed in Table 5, a barge is not listed here.)

7. Estimate of the weight of masts, and yards for a ship of 74 guns (of the *Leviathan*'s class) from experiments made by Mr Ratcliffe, master mast maker at Portsmouth Dock Yard

The *Leviathan*, launched 1790, was 172ft 3in on the gundeck and 1703²¹/₉₄ tons; the *Milford* was 181ft 0in and 1906³⁹/₉₄ tons. The total is 85 tons 9cwt 0qr 27lb.

8. Carpenter's stores

Present use stores are used in fitting out the ship, and sea stores are for use at sea.

Present use and sea store	Tons	Cwt	Qrs	Lbs
Copper nails	0	0	0	12
Rove and clinch	0	0	0	8
Cabin bells	0	0	0	21½
Watch bells	0	2	1	20
Brushes, tar	0	0	0	23¼
Canvas, new	0	0	2	7
Canvas, old	0	0	1	2
Bed bottoms	0	0	1	2
Coats for masts [tarred canvas nailed to the mast to prevent water running down between the decks]	0	0	1	22
Coats for helm	0	0	1	0
Coats for apron	0	0	0	14
Hawse bags [canvas bags filled with oakum that plugged the hawseholes in heavy seas to stop water coming in]	0	0	1	12
Tarpaulins	0	1	2	21
Fearnought [strong woollen cloth, used to line the magazine passage and elsewhere as a fire preventer]	0	0	2	0
Ditto for screens [such as in hatchways]	0	1	3	0
Copper nails [*sic*]	0	0	0	12
Copper sheet	0	0	2	0
Rope, remanufactured	0	0	0	18
Ditto, 1½	0	0	2	16
Twine	0	0	0	3
Glass	0	0	0	26
Glue	0	0	0	2
Grindstone	0	0	2	0
Anchor stock bolts	0	0	0	25
Anchor stock hoops	0	0	3	10
Auger bitts	0	0	0	16
Ballast	180	0	0	0
Bars, hatch	0	1	1	9
Rudder irons	0	0	1	13
Tillers	0	0	0	5¾
Bolts, chain plate	0	1	3	24
Bolts, drawn	0	0	1	16
Bolts, drive [to drive out old bolts]	0	0	1	4
Bolts, eye [to secure ropes and tackle]	0	0	0	26
Bolts, ring [to secure the guns]	0	0	2	4

Present use and sea store	Tons	Cwt	Qrs	Lbs
Bolts, sett [to bring planks together]	o	o	o	14
Bolts, starting [also used to drive out old bolts]	o	o	o	4
Boom irons for lower yards and hoops	o	4	3	6
Chain plates with shackles	o	6	2	o
Shank painter	o	1	o	o
Rudder	o	3	2	21
Chisels, cold	o	o	o	6
Drivers for hoops on masts [used with a hammer to force a hoop into position]	o	1	3	o
Esses for shrouds [S-shaped hooks]	o	2	1	2
Fids for topmasts	o	9	o	16
Fire hearth complete	6	7	3	14
Furnace bars, spare	o	2	2	10
Hammers, clench [used to secure the ends of bolts by burring (flattening) them]	o	o	o	13¾
sets	o	o	o	7
Spare cast iron beck	o	3	1	23
Brass cock, spare	o	o	o	14
Cot frames	o	1	o	o
Camp forge, slice [?], hearth staff	o	4	2	o
Anvil	o	2	1	o
Hammers, sledge	o	o	1	20
Hammers, uphand [two-handed hammer used at the forge]	o	o	1	o
Hammers, hand	o	o	o	8
Hammers, bench	o	o	o	1
Hammers, riveting	o	o	o	1
Hammers, nail tool	o	o	o	3
Chisels, cold [sic] and hot	o	o	o	3
Rimer stock [reamers, used by caulkers to open planks when applying oakum]	[blank]			
Bellows, double	o	1	o	12
Files and rubbers	o	o	o	16
Smiths' tongues	o	o	o	16
Hasps and staples	o	o	o	3
Hinges, sorts	o	2	o	15
Hooks, nail	o	o	o	8
Hoops for yard arms	o	o	3	o
Iron, new, of sorts	o	6	o	26
Locks	o	o	o	9
Locks, sorts	o	o	1	9
Loggerheads	o	o	2	o
Mauls, double headed	o	o	o	23
Nails of sorts	o	6	o	20
Pins and chains for bars	o	o	o	12
Pitch ladles	o	o	o	9
Pots	o	o	1	7
Port shackles	o	o	o	24

Present use and sea store	Tons	Cwt	Qrs	Lbs
Staples	0	0	0	6
Pumps	0	13	1	9
Ditto gear	0	10	0	32
Pumps, hand	0	17	1	8
Ditto gear	0	1	0	22
Saw gear	0	0	1	13
Shivers brass for topmasts	0	3	1	24
Iron pins for topmasts	0	0	3	6
Staples, large	0	0	0	2½
Lanthorns, hand	0	0	0	5
Lanthorns, poop	0	0	3	0
Lanthorns, braces	0	0	0	21
Lead scuppers	0	2	3	16
Lead sheet	0	1	0	2
Leather hoses for p. ropes	0	0	0	10
Leather, liquored	0	0	2	2
Leather, scupper	0	0	1	12
Ocham, black	0	5	1	12
Oil for smoke jack	0	0	0	4
Pitch	0	6	0	0
Plates, single	0	0	0	14
Tallow	0	2	0	22
Tar	0	3	1	7
Anchor stocks	2	19	2	27
Ballast baskets	0	0	0	19
Bars, capstan, half	0	13	3	10
Bittacles	0	1	2	0
Board, elm [board was timber 14–18ft long, 8–9in wide, and less than 1½in thick]	0	5	1	12
Board, oak	0	3	2	11
Board, wainscot [Continental oak for panelling and joinery work, bought by the Navy Board in 1¼in 1in, and ¾in thicknesses]	0	3	2	10
Booms, fire [long spars used to fend off vessels on fire]	0	7	2	19
Buckets	0	0	1	19
Hawse plugs	0	10	2	27
Caps, spare	0	13	2	25
Mess tables	0	15	0	0
Stools for ditto	0	19	2	0
Iron scuttle fastenings	0	0	3	0
Caulking tools	0	0	1	27¼
Chests of sorts for stores	0	13	0	0
Davids [davits], and quarter davids	0	12	2	8
Dead eyes, iron bound	0	1	3	14
Deals, ordinary [deals were 6–14ft long, 9in wide and not more than 3in thick]	0	15	1	2
Filling troughs	0	0	1	0
Hen coops	0	6	0	0

Present use and sea store	Tons	Cwt	Qrs	Lbs
Log board	0	0	0	14
Long boats masts	0	3	1	14
Long boats yards	0	0	1	8
Long boats bowsprit	0	0	1	23
Long boats out rigger	0	0	0	25
Other boats masts etc	0	2	3	6
Moving pantry	0	3	3	0
Plank, elm, sorts [planks were 18ft long or more, 9–10in wide, and 1½–4in thick]	0	5	1	12
Plank, oak	0	5	2	18
Plank, oak, sorts	0	14	1	16
Reels, log and deep-sea	0	0	0	20
Screws, wood, with bolt	0	2	0	28
Tables, small	0	4	3	12
Tables, wainscot	0	7	1	0
Tables, sideboard	0	0	2	0
Tillers, spare	1	8	3	10
Topmast cross trees	0	8	3	20
Topmast stumps	0	7	3	25
Treenails	0	3	0	24
Water engine [for firefighting]	0	2	2	0
Leather pipe	0	0	1	0
Paint	0	2	0	15
Brushes	0	0	0	1½
Oil	0	1	0	8
Black varnish	0	5	0	0
Rulers	0	0	2	0
Lime, bushels [for making whitewash to use in the sickbay and elsewhere]	0	5	2	24
Ditto brushes	0	0	0	4
Steering index [a dial on the helm showing the rudder's position]	0	0	1	20
Vats for steward room	0	6	1	0
Brushes, tar, present use	0	0	0	5½
Canvas, old, present use	0	1	1	0
Fearnought, present use	0	0	2	10
Twine, present use	0	0	0	3
Nails of sorts, present use	0	0	2	19
Leather scuppers, present use	0	0	1	0
Tar, present use	0	3	1	7
Ballast baskets and buckets [, present use]	0	0	1	20
Board, elm, present use	0	0	2	10
Deals, ordinary, present use	0	6	0	12
Turn pins, present use	0	0	0	7
Baulks, present use	0	12	1	3
Wedges, present use	0	1	3	23
Total	211	13	3	18½

9. IRONWORK

The ironwork comprises stanchions, bolts, hooks, cranks, straps, etc., totalling 12 tons 5cwt 2qr 16lb.

10. ORDNANCE STORES

This includes the gunner's tools, and there are 218 entries, totalling 295 tons 17cwt 3qr 14lb.

A selection is printed below; long guns and carronades are listed separately.

	Tons	Cwt	Qrs	Lbs
32pdrs, twenty-eight in number	77	14	0	0
18pdrs, thirty in number	59	19	0	0
Shot, round, 32pdr, 2,940 in number	42	0	0	0
Shot, round, 18pdr, 2,730 in number	22	0	1	8
Shot, double-headed, 32pdr, 84 in number	1	7	3	0
Shot, double-headed, 18pdr, 96 in number	7	4	0	0
Shot, grape, 32pdr, 84 in number	1	4	0	0
Shot, grape, 18pdr, 224 in number	1	16	0	0
Shot, tin case, 32pdr, 124 in number	1	15	1	22
Shot, tin case, 18pdr, 222 in number	1	15	2	20
Paper cartridges with flannel bottoms, 32pdr, 924 in number*	0	2	3	6
Paper cartridges with flannel bottoms, 32pdr, 924 in number	0	3	1	24
Paper cartridges with flannel bottoms, 18pdr, 1,392 in number	0	2	2	26
Paper cartridges with flannel bottoms, 18pdr, 1,392 in number	0	3	0	26
Wadhooks with rammer, heads, and staves complete, 32pdr, fourteen in number	0	1	1	0
Wadhooks with rammer, heads, and staves complete, 18pdr, sixteen in number	0	1	1	4
Sponges with staves, 32pdr, old pattern, four in number	0	0	1	12
Sponges with staves, 32pdr, patent, ten in number	0	0	3	26
Sponges with staves, 18pdr, patent, sixteen in number	0	1	0	16
Sponges with ropes, 32pdr, old pattern, nine in number	0	1	3	11
Sponges with ropes, 18pdr, old pattern, ten in number	0	1	2	2
Sponges with ropes, 32pdr, patent, nineteen in number	0	3	3	17
Sponges with ropes, 18pdr, patent, twenty-two in number	0	3	1	10
Match	0	6	0	0
Quill tubes, 2,600 in number	0	0	0	5
Boxes and straps for ditto, forty-three of each	0	0	1	15
Blue lights, thirty-six in number	0	0	0	15
Signal rockets with stocks, 1lb, six in number	0	0	0	6
Signal rockets with stocks, ½lb, eighteen in number	0	0	0	9
Bayonets, 100 in number	0	9	3	8
Swords, scabbards, and belts, 200 each	0	8	3	20
Strong pikes, 100 in number	0	2	2	20

* This is confusingly laid out, but two dotted lines in the original probably indicate ordinary paper cartridges first then those with flannel bottoms, used particularly for grape and case shot, as the second entry in each case, since they weighed about a fifth more.

	Tons	Cwt	Qrs	Lbs
Pole axes, sixty in number	0	1	0	8
Shot, musket	0	4	0	0
Shot, pistol	0	1	0	0
Shot, tin case, 32pdr, 124 in number [for carronades]	1	15	1	20
Shot, tin case, 18pdr, 88 in number [for carronades]	0	14	0	12
Shot, 32pdr grape, in tin cases, 124 in number [for carronades]	1	15	1	20
Shot, 18pdr grape, in tin cases, 48 in number [for carronades]	0	7	2	24
Flannel cartridges, 32pdr, 1,512 in number [for carronades]	0	1	0	9
Flannel cartridges, 18pdr, 588 in number [for carronades]	0	0	0	24
Sponges, 32pdr, patent, 18 in number [for carronades]	0	0	3	24
Sponges, 18pdr, patent, 7 in number [for carronades]	0	0	1	0
Powder, 295 barrels	13	3	1	4
Powder for priming, 4 half-barrels	0	2	0	0
Musket ball cartridges, 7,000 in number†	0	5	2	4
Pistol ball cartridges, 2,000 in number	0	0	2	26

† 1,000,000 musket cartridges weigh 50 tons exactly (WO 55/1843, *sv* Tonnage, 20 April 1807).

NOTES

INTRODUCTION

[1] **Firepower**: Napoleon had 151 guns firing shot totalling 1,356lb at Austerlitz (1,462lb in British measure) and used only about 139 of them; a standard 74-gun ship had when equipped with carronades 1,852lb. Abercromby had twenty-four 6pdrs, sixteen 12pdrs, and six 5.5in howitzers. Wellington only had nine 6pdrs, nine 3pdrs and two 5.5in howitzers. **74-gun ship**: Lavery, *Bellona, passim*, and figures from ADM 95/69, 70 and 71. **Geese**: in 1813, NRS 82, p. 39. **Armageddon**: Michael Duffy, 'World-Wide War and British Expansion, 1793–1815', in *The Oxford History of the British Empire*, vol. II, *The Eighteenth Century* (ed. P. J. Marshall) (Oxford: Oxford University Press, 1998), p. 203.
[2] Rodger, *Command of the Ocean*, p. 562.
[3] NRS 146, pp. 397, 399.
[4] NRS 82, p. 28.
[5] Tracy (ed), *Naval Chronicle*, vol. IV, p. 331. **Disposition of ships**: ADM 7/50, his orders of 14 May, and especially 15 May to the *Nautilus*. **Gibraltar**: '1799 to 1803 Tank at Gibraltar papers relative thereto', in ADM 106/3546 part one. **Royal Sovereign**: ADM 7/50, 31 May 1810. **Bandol**: Laird Clowes, *The Royal Navy*, vol. V, pp. 288–9; James, *History*, vol. V, pp. 217–21.
[6] Cotton to Edward Fellowes, captain of the *Conqueror*, dated off Toulon, 31 May 1810, ADM 7/50, ff. 64–5.
[7] *Conqueror*'s log, ADM 51/2219; ADM 7/50, f. 81. The water was taken on by the launch, in eight days: 6½ tons, 59 tons, 30 tons, 32½ tons, 65½ tons, 23 tons, 28½ tons, 2½ tons. The total of the dry provisions was 50 tons 16cwt 7lb, plus the pease, and the bullocks and their fodder.
[8] Robinson, *Jack Nastyface*, pp. 31–2. **Defiance**: c/m of William Ferrier, ADM 1/5343. **Professional seamen**: eg Nagle, *Nagle Journal*, pp. 228–9, 240. Glascock relates an anecdote of a sailor of the *Surprise* who received prize money for that and other ships of nearly £80, and applied to her captain, Sir Edward Hamilton, for a fortnight's leave. Told he could only have a week, the sailor said: 'Well, sir, I'll try what I can do – must only work double tides – get an extry watch or so – take three or four more fiddlers in tow nor I intended – a couple of extry coaches for my *she*-messmates, 'sides one for Poll and one for myself; and if it comes to the worst I must only get *another* for my *hat!*': Glascock, *Naval Sketch-book*, vol. II, p. 112.
[9] C/m of Thomas Hubbard and George Hynes, ADM 1/5355.

Chapter 1
THE SHIP-OF-THE-LINE, ORGANISATION AND ROUTINE

[1] Hoffman, *A Sailor of King George*, p. 4.
[2] **Medical examination**: from 1808, pressed and volunteer men were required to be examined again on arrival on board the ship in which they would serve.
[3] Hay, *Landsman Hay*, pp. 41–5.
[4] NRS 12, p. 10.
[5] *St Domingo*: NRS 119, p. 353. **Bellerophon**: NMM: LBK/38, in Cordingley, *Billy Ruffian*, pp. 5, 210–12.
[6] Richardson, *Mariner of England*, p. 114. Her muster book lists no Orla Hou, but has an Oloss Hocq from Gottenburg (ADM 36/13327).
[7] **Two-deckers**: Gardiner, *Warships of the Napoleonic Era*, pp. 17, 18. **Foudroyant**: Nelson to Earl Spencer, 26 September 1799, asking that she be given to Troubridge, his favourite,

Nicolas, *Dispatches and Letters of Lord Nelson*, vol. IV, p. 30.

[8] The figures for 1793 are current before that date, and exist in many locations; 1802 is in ADM 1/4352 (there is no category for First Rates); 1808 is in the 'Scheme for Manning His Majesty's Ships of the Different Classes', 30 April 1808, in ADM 1/4335.

[9] **France**: Glete, *Navies and Nations*, vol. I, p. 265. **Slade**: Glete, *Navies and Nations*, vol. I, p. 268. Many readers take at face value Glete's use of the word 'tons' throughout his text; however, he states at vol. II p. 528 that his figures are 'metric tons of 1,000 kilograms', and so here the British English spelling 'tonnes' is used throughout for clarity. **36pdrs**: converted to British measure, the nominal weight of the French balls was 38lb 14oz and 19lb 7oz, and of the Spanish 24lb 5½oz and 18lb 4oz.

[10] Marmaduke Stalkaart, *Naval Architecture*, pp. 135–6, in Lavery, *Nelson and the Nile*, p. 108.

[11] *Bellona*: Lavery, *Bellona*, table 2. British First Rates carried 42pdrs until the last were replaced by 32pdrs in 1798; see for example Admiral Keppel to Sandwich, First Lord, 10 March 1778, in Hodges and Hughes, *Select Naval Documents*, pp. 156–7. *Bellerophon*: James, *History*, vol. I, p. 132. *Bellona*: Lavery, *Bellona*, table 2. *Northumberland*: NRS 96, p. 231.

[12] **More than two hundred**: Blake and Lawrence, *Illustrated Companion*, p. 29 and Lyon, *Sailing Navy List*, passim. Two more had been cut down to frigates. **Three to five years**: MacDougall, *Royal Dockyards*, p. 97. **Cost**: £43,820 and £20,380 in 1789. See Blake and Lawrence, *Illustrated Companion*, p. 30.

[13] **Statistics**: Glete, *Navies and Nations*, vol. I, p. 276; vol. I, p. 275; vol. II, table 23:53. **Foundry technology**: Glete, *Navies and Nations*, vol. I, p. 283, n50; Lambert, *War at Sea in the Age of Sail*, p. 113. **Launch details**: Lyon, *Sailing Navy List*, passim.

[14] *Kent*: Blake and Lawrence, *Illustrated Companion*, p. 30; Gardiner, *Warships of the Napoleonic Era*, pp. 26–7. **French service**: 'I never saw vessels sail as they; everything is calculated for the Mediterranean, light sails, small ropes, prodigious masts and yards': Captain Lord Cochrane to Lord Keith, 26 July 1801, NRS 90, p. 376 and Rodger, *Command of the Ocean*, p. 419. **Seppings**: R. Seppings, 'A New Principle of Constructing His Majesty's Ships of War' (1814), in Peter Goodwin, 'The Influence of Iron in Ship Construction: 1660 to 1830', *Mariner's Mirror*, vol. 84, no. 1 (February 1998), p. 38.

[15] *Hercule*: James, *History*, vol. II, p. 110; Brian Lavery, 'Guns and Gunnery', in Gardiner (ed), *The Line of Battle*, p. 153. See also Gardiner, *Warships of the Napoleonic Era*, pp. 104–5 where there is a plan of the *Hercule* as fitted at Plymouth in 1801.

[16] **Jervis**: the *Courageux* was the same length but measured as 1,720³⁰⁄₉₄ tons when taken. See his letter of 30 June 1797 to Earl Spencer, then First Lord, on his thoughts for the peace, in NRS 46, p. 212.

[17] **Rope ladders**: NRS 97, pp. 156–7. Other details from Lavery, *Bellona*.

[18] **Mess-room**: NRS 91, p. 58. *Tartar*: ADM 1/1549, Capt. B640.

[19] **1757**: ADM 106/2508, no. 445, 24 June 1757, and ADM 95/17, f. 248 ¶ 3rd., where this version comes from. **Curtains**: NMM POR/A/51, 24 October 1808, in Lavery, *Arming and Fitting*, p. 176.

[20] **1843**: they were now appointed by Admiralty commission, *Cockburn and the Navy in Transition*, p. 271; ARS 3, p. 64. **Cloacina**: I am indebted to Don Seltzer of the Marine History Information Exchange Group for this. NRS 91, pp. 52, 53.

[21] **Three tables**: ADM 106/2511, no. 568, 12 June 1797. Wainscot is 'A superior quality of foreign oak imported from Russia, Germany, and Holland, chiefly used for fine panel-work' (OED, sb.1). **Arranged**: NRS 91, p. 11. **Substantial**: in the *Milford* (74) on 1 November 1809, ADM 1/1548, Capt. B2; but the sideboard is recorded as weighing 2qrs. **Space**: c/m of Lt George Dentatus Haynes, ADM 1/5331.

[22] **Gunner**: Lavery, *Nelson's Navy*, p. 88. **Mizzen mast**: Lovell, *From Trafalgar to the Chesapeake*, p. 22; in all ships when entered for repair, by Admiralty order of 26 January 1807, McGowan, *Victory*, pp. 24 and 81.

[23] NRS 91, pp. 10–12.

[24] **Refuge:** c/m of the *Defiance* and *Terrible* mutineers, ADM 1/5346 and 1/5333.

[25] Hoffman, *A Sailor of King George*, p. 21.

[26] *Queen:* NRS 31, p. 87; Burton, *Adventures of Johnny Newcome*, p. 245n. Hoffman, *A Sailor of King George*, pp. 63–4.

[27] **Crawford and Chamier:** Tom Wareham, 'The Duration of Frigate Command', *Mariner's Mirror*, vol. 86, no. 4 (November 2000), p. 420.

Chapter 2
WASHING THE WEATHER DECKS

[1] **Tied their hammocks:** in the *Indefatigable* in 1812, for example, each man in the watch coming on deck was to 'settle the lanyard of one end of his hammock to give more air and room', NRS 138, p. 188. **Poop:** the list of decks to be washed in the middle watch is from the order book of the *Mars* (74), 'The Trafalgar general order book of H.M.S. Mars', in *Mariner's Mirror*, vol. 22, no. 1 (1936), p. 97.

[2] **St Vincent:** NRS 138, 25 September 1797, p. 217. **Keith:** NRS 90, pp. 412–13, Standing Order No. 17. **Dr Snipe:** Dr Snipe to Nelson, 23 November 1803, Wellcome Western MS 3680 (vol. 14), in Jane Bowden-Dan, 'Diet, Dirt and Discipline: Medical Developments in Nelson's Navy. Dr John Snipe's Contribution', *Mariner's Mirror*, vol. 90, no. 3 (August 2004), p. 268.) **It is a fact:** Trotter, *Medicina Nautica* (1804), in NRS 107, p. 274. **Regulations:** R&I, 1808, p. 138 art. VI. The 1790 edition had stated the captain was 'to take care' that the decks 'be well washed and swabbed once a day, and the air let into the hold as frequently as may be' (p. 28 art. XXVII). Thus Jack Nastyface takes it as standard that the middle watch is taken up with washing the deck (Robinson, *Jack Nastyface*, p. 32).

[3] **Buckets:** ADM 49/121. They cost 12s and 18s the dozen with wooden hoops, and £1 the dozen with two iron hoops. **Brooms:** The figures were

Guns	8 months	add for 12
100	400	160
90	386	140
80	374	140
74	360	120
70	348	120
64	348	120
60	320	120

(ADM 106/2511, no. 607, 14 October 1797. At this date, 'eight months' and 'twelve months' were the Navy Board's formulas for Channel and Foreign service: this was reformed in 1814.) In the summer of 1806 the Navy Board received several applications for an increase in the allowance of brooms to small ships, and consequently gunbrigs were increased from twelve for eight months to fifty for eight months and cutters to sixty (ADM 106/2517, no. 450, 14 July 1806 and no. 570, 19 August 1806). A similar request was received from Chatham for prison ships in 1807, and the allowance was increased to twelve dozen per month in winter and ten dozen per month in summer for the *Sandwich*, and the others eight dozen per month year-round (ADM 106/2518, no. 891, 17 December 1807). The previous winter Falmouth was paying 3s per dozen (ADM 106/2518, no. 44, 9 January 1807). The *Splendid*'s use is calculated rather arbitrarily from the boatswain's accounts in *Britannia* (100) in 1805: ten wooden buckets in 'keeping the ship clean' in August, fifty in September, and six in October, as well as a total of 155 brooms, eight large brushes, and six shovels, and twelve yards of canvas to make draw buckets (NRS 138, pp. 593–602). Dimensions are from ADM 49/121, ff. 92 and 140. They cost 2s or 2s 3d the dozen in the 1780s, 1s 4d in 1792, 1s 10d in 1795. **Weight**: WO 55/1747. **Brushes**: an example from HMS *Invincible*, shown in McGuane, *Heart of Oak*, p. 184. **Brooming parties**: in 1801, Captain Keats in the *Superb* (74) gave orders to brooming parties that accompanied watering parties, 'When there is a brooming party employed, the broomstuff may be sent off in such small quantities in the boats as not to render it inconvenient to row' (ADM 80/141 out-letters f. 138), and William Mark, captain's clerk in the *Hydra*, described brooming parties at Tetuan, where the Mediterranean Fleet watered, that cut the 'beautiful myrtle of which the country thereabouts is covered' (Mark, *At Sea with Nelson*, p. 94). **Pitched buckets**: ADM 106/2514, no. 197, 4 November 1803; **canvas buckets**: as recorded in the boatswain's accounts in *Britannia*, 1805, in NRS 138, pp. 593–602. Ships in the Indian Ocean were not issued with leather buckets, and were expected to make their own iron-bound buckets on board (ADM 106/2517, no. 230, 25 April 1806, to Madras). Also Admiral Smyth, *sv* buckets. **Seawater in buckets**: general testimony, c/m of Captain John Bowen, ADM 1/5353.

[4] NRS 91, p. 254.

[5] Captain's order no. XLVII in the *Amazon*, 1799 (NRS 138, pp. 154–5). In the *Amazon* the head was cleaned by 'two forecastle men and two waisters under the particular direction of the captain of the forecastle'; a 'Table for Watching the Ship's Company of every Rate' of 1807 shows the captain of the head (Lewis, *Social History*, p. 274). Unlike the captains of the other parts of the ship, this was a job title not a formal rate.

[6] *Splendid's* **rails**: Lavery, *Bellona*, drawing A. **Used to wash the decks**: Lavery, *Arming and Fitting*, p. 79. **Lead pipes**: these and their 'wash-deck' suction pumps were first fitted in 1807, Lavery, *Arming and Fitting*, p. 79, and *Ship of the Line*, vol. II, p. 119, where there is a better reproduction of the Navy Board's plan of 1807; that diagram shows winches on the upper deck, but in January 1795, Richard Poole, a seaman of the *Fortitude* (74), testified that he and some other sailors were 'leaning over the winch handles, looking down' through the main hatchway on the starboard side of the lower gun deck, to see who was causing a disturbance below (c/m of John Connor, ADM 1/5332), which matches plan F16 in Lavery, *Bellona*. **Cisterns**: ADM 106/2508, 9 April 1779, no. 831; a warrant of 13 April, no. 833, extended this down to all ships and sloops as far as 300 tons. **Elm-tree pumps**: Walter Rose, *The Village Carpenter* (Cambridge: Cambridge University Press, 1937, repr. Stobart Davies, Hertford, 1995 and 2001), pp. 77–93; Winfield, *50-Gun Ship*, p. 101; ADM 49/121, f. 122; fir or pitch-pine when there was not enough elm, ADM 106/2518, no. 881, 30 December 1807, and ADM 106/2518, no. 896, 30 December 1807. An order of 1771 (ADM 106/2508, no. 578, 6 September 1771) discontinued the old system established in 1758 (ADM 106/2508, no. 455, 11 February 1758): 'It being represented that [these] pumps by being hung over the sides of His Maj ships for washing their decks whilst they are in chace is a hindrance to their sailing these are to direct and request you to cause a leaden pump to be fixed in the heads of His Maj ships of 40 guns and upwards as you may have time and opportunity for doing the same without the cheek, or parts of the head being taken off for that purpose.' At least one officer, Commodore Johnstone, thought they were 'extremely useful', and he successfully petitioned to have them installed in the *Romney* in 1777 (George Johnstone to the Admiralty, ADM 1/387, printed as 'Commodore Johnstone's Improvements, 1779', in *Mariner's Mirror*, vol. 16, no. 1 (1930), p. 86. **Elm pumps**: 'no hand pumps being now supplied to ships except the common sort for washing ships decks', ADM 106/2517, no. 187, 18 March 1806. **Scuppers**: Lavery, *Arming and Fitting*, p. 66; *Ship of the Line*, II, p. 121. **Coamings**: ADM 106/2511, no. 34, 8 June 1795.

[7] **Sheep and cow pens**: c/m of Jonah alias Joshua Thomas, ADM 1/5354. The *Glory* was in port at the time, and that this was not universally followed is shown by the recommendation that the pens be fitted in the waist, Report of Committee of Sea Officers of Navy Board on

stores etc drawn up in 1814, ADM 106/5347, f. 110. Pens were in the care of the carpenter (ADM 106/2508, no. 1024, 21 September 1788). **Hencoops**: Captain Pasley, 21 February 1780 (*Private Sea Journals*, p. 63). They had formerly been on the poop (*e.g.* in the *Cumberland* (74) in 1802, testimony of Abraham Wade, c/m of James Pearce, ADM 1/5360); they were moved to the fore capstan in 1808 (Lavery, *Arming and Fitting*, p. 201). In 1814 they were moved back to the poop again, with additional coops by the fore capstan if desired, 'or either as most convenient' (Report of Committee of Sea Officers of Navy Board on stores etc drawn up in 1814, ADM 106/5347, original f. 110 and stamped f. 89). The quoted clause applied to line-of-battle ships only; in frigates it was to be fitted under the sheep pen in the waist. Lavery, *Arming and Fitting*, p. 201, prints a plan and profiles for the new design, but there is no scale in the original. It is clear, however, that it was supplied with drawers to make cleaning easier. **Rabbits**: ADM 95/17, f. 156 and NRS 91, p. 234. Janet Macdonald found no examples in her study of the Mediterranean Fleet of 1804–1805.

[8] Lever, *Sea Anchor*, p. 81; Marquardt, *Rigs & Rigging*, p. 197; Harland, *Seamanship*, p. 169; Lavery, *Bellona*, Table 15; ADM 1/1548, Capt. B2, Report on the *Milford*.

[9] These events are based on the c/m of Robert Nelson, ADM 1/5348. The narrative has been compressed and some details altered to be appropriate for a 74: Carson was Edward Lloyd, who did not report the incident for a week because he was so scared of the three or four men (he later named four, Thomas Weller, 'a Black man Thomas something', Matthew Welsh and Nelson) and that 'they would do some hurt to me', but he became 'uneasy in my mind' and went to George Foster, the master's mate. Why he went to him rather than the mate of the watch is not stated. Nelson's alibi was that he was lying on the cook's table, and his witness placed him there about three o'clock because he dropped a blue handkerchief from his hammock and Lloyd handed it up to him, but he was standing up and this may have influenced the court: the verdict was proved in part, 250 lashes round the fleet and two years' solitary confinement. Robert Wilson of the *Unité* relates a similar incident in his memoirs: the ship was in the Bay of Biscay in October 1805, nine gun-tackle falls were cut, all hands were called aft to hear 'a speech on the dreadful consequences that might arise from the guns being adrift in bad weather' from Captain Ogle, several men came forward and identified the three responsible, and the culprits were punished severely. One of the three threw himself overboard and drowned the following January (NRS 91, pp. 133, 136).

[10] *Marlborough*: testimony of George Langton (the sentinel), c/m of Charles Moore, ADM 1/5346. *Unité*: NRS 91, p. 144. **Instructions**: R&I, 1808, p. 227 art. VI. **Cranston**: c/m of the *Bellerophon* mutineers, ADM 1/5333. **Cumby**: 'The highly improper practice of what is called starting the men, is most peremptorily forbidden; punishment shall only be inflicted by order of the captain, to whom alone the Lords Commissioners of the Admiralty have thought proper to delegate that power.' Lavery, *Jack Aubrey Commands*, p. 125. **Pole**: c/m of Lieutenant Horace Pine, ADM 1/5330. **Superb**: Lavery, *Jack Aubrey Commands*, p. 125.

[11] Robinson, *Jack Nastyface*, pp. 147–8. The first passage is printed in Lavery, *Nelson's Navy*, p. 219, but he quotes an inaccurate transcription from Henry Baynham, *From the Lower Deck* (London: Hutchinson, 1969).

[12] Raigersfeld, *Life*, p. 17.

[13] C/m of Martin Brooke, ADM 1/5342.

[14] 7 March 1794, ADM 1/100, ff. 137–8, and 139.

[15] *Tickler*: report of Sir William Sydney Smith into the charges alleged by the crew of the *Tickler*, ADM 1/2498 Capt. S108, enc. no. 8. **London**: Richardson, *Mariner of England*, pp. 68, 70.

[16] C/m of Charles Moore, ADM 1/5346.

[17] C/m of Patrick Gallahan, ADM 1/5351. The charge was proved in part: he was sentenced to fifty lashes.

[18] Testimony of John Line, c/m of John Rowe, ADM 1/5329, and summary in ADM 12/26, ff. 158–9.

[19] **1808**: R&I, 1808, p. 375 art. VI. *Achille*: ADM 1/2498, Capt.S270 enclosures, and turnover.
[20] **Berth**: 1 July 1798, NRS 138, p. 219. *Defiance*: testimony of John McKenna, c/m of the *Defiance* mutineers, ADM 1/5346.
[21] C/m of St Leger Beville, ADM 1/5333.
[22] R&I, 1808, pp. 121–2 art. XVI; this article also applied to the sailmaker, caulker, ropemaker, armourer, armourer's mate and cook, and formally any change of rate was until the 'pleasure of the Admiralty or Commander in Chief shall be known'. Examples of marines and midshipmen: Sergeant John (alias James) Andrew of the marines of the *Quebec* (32) was doing duty as ship's corporal, his c/m, ADM 1/5351; Sergeant William Roberts of the marines was doing duty as a ship's corporal in the *Carnatic* (74) in November 1799, his c/m, ADM 1/5351; Sergeant James Russell of the marines was doing duty as master at arms in the *Hebe* (36), in Plymouth Sound, on 3 September 1795, his testimony as a witness, c/m of James Anderson, ADM 1/5333. Sergeant William Thompson of the 95th Foot was doing duty as master at arms aboard the *Tromp*, in December 1797, c/m of the *Tromp* mutineers, ADM 1/5343. Richard Loyd, midshipman on board the *Captivity* prison ship, promoted to master at arms on board the *Jason* at his request, ADM1/2498, Capt. S335, 24 August 1798. *Montagu*: testimony of Lieutenant Harford, c/m of William Holsby, ADM 1/5338.
[23] C/m of Charles King and James Dooley, ADM 1/5347.
[24] **Lookouts**: Lavery, *Nelson's Navy*, p. 200; Falconer, *sv* 'Look-out'; Smyth, *sv* 'Lookout'. Calling out and the mate's inspection are order 91st in the *Indefatigable*, 1812 (NRS 138, p. 200). **Midshipmen**: Hall, *Fragments*, vol. I, p. 223.
[25] **Trawl net**: Boteler's account of his service in the *Sceptre* (74) in 1812 and 1813 includes an account of fishing with a trawl net 'while backing and filling off the Texel'; Captain Duff likewise records fishing with a trawl net in the *Mars* (74) on 2 December 1804 ('A Captain's Life and Death at Sea: Captain George Duff's Last Correspondence', in Tracy (ed), *Naval Chronicle*, vol. III, p. 186 – Macdonald (*Feeding Nelson's Navy*, p. 39) places the *Mars* off Cadiz, but she was still in the Channel Fleet, blockading Brest and Rochefort). A line-of-battleship's trawl net was 24ft, and was supplied with 10lb of twine (ADM 106/2511, no. 25, 7 May 1795, gives numbers and dimensions, but this warrant is for ships on home service (i.e. in the Channel and North Sea) only: no. 582, 3 August 1797, changes seine nets for 100- to 80-gun ships inclusive to two nets each, referring to the printed establishment, which usually applied to ships both on home and on foreign service). Warrant no. 25 also provided 40 forty-fathom cod-fish lines and 120 hooks, 50 fifty-fathom whiting lines and 300 hooks, and 20 bait lines. Mark, *At Sea with Nelson*, p. 81. **Some smaller ships**: eg c/m of William Harris, ADM 1/5347. He was serving in the *Sandfly* (4) off St Marcou when he was captured by a French privateer while on a fishing/exchange expedition. **Seine nets**: line-of-battle ships, ADM 106/2517, no. 307, 13 May 1806, with the further order 'Trawls are not allowed to Ships on Foreign Service' (ADM 106, no. 438, 10 June 1806); sloops 'employed out of the North Seas', and 'any smaller vessels allowed trawls altho cruizing in the North Sea' were forbidden them by ADM 106/2517, letter, no. 611, 23 August 1806. Seine nets in the Royal Navy had had cods fitted 'for the purpose of obtaining a more ample supply of fish' since 1804, and ships that already had seine nets were supplied with twine to make the change (ADM 106/2515, no. 123, 4 July 1804). Twine was also supplied to repair nets, and the yards were not to receive damaged nets from ships in commission if they were repairable (ADM 106/2517, no. 632, 23 September 1806). Dimensions are not given, but Raigersfeld, whose description is quoted below, says 'the seine is a large net about fourteen feet deep, and in length fifty fathoms or upwards, with a large purse in the middle of it for the fish to go into'. In 1799 the *Renown* (74) was in Vigo bay, and was 'in the habit of hauling the seine on the Bayonne islands, and we were generally pretty successful', but in Orestana bay in 1802 fish 'were scarce – although, had we taken the right method, more perhaps might have been caught' (Lovell, *From Trafalgar to the Chesapeake*, pp. 12 and 28). **Boats launched by pipes**: Lieutenant

Charles Pollard of HM Sloop *Hope* testified in the court martial of William Robson that on the evening of 20 March 1814 he was so drunk that 'he piped in such a way, that was of no use, the captain and myself were obliged to hoist the boat in by word', ADM 1/5442. **Hove to:** Harland, *Seamanship*, p. 283.

[26] Raigersfeld, *Life*, pp. 19–20. He is describing fishing with a seine net in the West Indies in the *Mediator* (44) in the 1780s.

[27] **Tubs:** Boteler, NRS 82, pp. 30–31. **Sick first:** the surgeon was directed to give the captain, when fish are caught for the ship's company, 'a list of the men who stand most in need of such refreshment, that they may be the first attended to', R&I, 1808, p. 272 art. XV. The 1790 Regulations required the captain to employ 'some of the company in fishing', if his ship was equipped with fishing tackle and the ship was in fishing grounds (R&I, 1790, p. 55 art IV: it is possible that article IV can be read to mean that all ships have fishing tackle: there is an ambiguous comma); any fish caught were treated as an addition to the official allowance, distributed to the sick first, 'then by turns amongst the messes of the officers and seamen, without favour or partiality' (R&I, 1790, p. 55 art. IV): the disappearance of the former article can be taken to express the increased use of fish (both caught and bought) in the economy of ships on blockade. **Fish kettles:** in 1806 Woolwich Dockyard sent in an excessive demand, and was told that the proper number for frigates and sloops was four each – the number for ships of the line is not mentioned, but would probably be six or eight; the demand was for small copper fish kettles, implying large ones were also issued (ADM 106/2517, letter, no. 53, 27 January 1806), and stores to be removed from the establishment at Jamaica in 1803, presumably because they could be got locally cheaper than in England, included fish kettles (ADM 106/2514, no. 528, 2 July 1803).

[28] **Hammocks, bags and haversacks:** captain's order no. 50th in the *Indefatigable*, NRS 138, p. 192, requires that 'Whenever the hammocks are ordered to be scrubbed, every bag is likewise to be scrubbed. No excuse will be taken if either is dirty.' **Brush:** captain's order no. 19th in the *Indefatigable*, NRS 138, p. 185. **Gantlines:** captain's orders aboard the *Superb*, 'It is my direction that haversacks and hammocks are cured or dried after scrubbing, that you pay particular attention to see they are made properly fast to the gantlines in order, that no loss or expence may in future occur from their blowing away' (ADM 80/141, out-letters f. 282). Gantlines were synonymous with girtlines (or girdlines), defined by Steel as 'a rope reeved through a single block, occasionally lashed to mast and sheer heads, to hoist up rigging, etc' (*Art of Rigging*, p. 14). **1804:** 1 December 1798, letter and turnover, ADM 1/2497; **1814**, Report of Committee of Sea Officers of Navy Board on stores etc drawn up in 1814, ADM 106/5347, para 105. The frequency varied with the ship: in the *Pegasus*, for example, in 1786–88, they were scrubbed on the first Monday of the month if in port, and 'a few every other morning when the weather will permit' if at sea (NRS 138, p. 97).

[29] Harland, *Seamanship*, 'The Technique of Reefing', and Lever, *Sheet Anchor*, p. 83.

[30] **Inelastic particles:** John Hammond, Surgeon of the *St George*, to Admiral James Steuart, Portsmouth, 25 April 1747, NRS 120, pp. 149–52. Hammond thought bad air was the second most important cause of scurvy, after the salt diet, which constitutes a 'viscid inert chyle'; what was needed was 'something endowed with balsamic and saponaceous qualities', ideally spruce beer, and fruits and vegetables, but since that was impossible for the Western Squadron, 'at least a quart' of 'good sound cider' per man per day. Wine was also of great service. **Collingwood:** NRS 98, p. 228n; undated but 1807?, and 10 December 1807, p. 230. **Sutton's pipes:** Lavery: *Arming and Fitting*, p. 184; according to Dr Trotter, they worked on the principle that hot dry air weighs less than cold wet air: 'by communicating with the fire-place, where the air was rarified by heat, a column from below rushed up to restore the equilibrium' (NRS 107, p. 282), but Captain Barrington, in the *Crown* (44), reported that 'they do not cause the least suction', even when repaired. They were to be replaced by one of Webber's machines, whose details are obscure (NRS 77, pp. 105–6 and note). **Hales' pumps:**

Arming and Fitting, p. 184. Some ships had a ventilator by the manger: when the two-decked *Mediator* (44) was in the West Indies in the 1780s there was a 'hand pump that was called the ventilator, fixed abaft the manger board upon the lower gun deck', and was 'continually worked by the sculkers in the middle watch for a couple of hours' (Raigersfeld, *Life*, p. 21); Captain Pasley in the *Jupiter* (50) kept 'the air pump under the forecastle constantly worked' to ensure fresh air for his sick and convalescents. Pasley, *Private Sea Journals*, p. 163. Sir James Watt records that the French 'made half-hearted attempts to install Sutton's pipes and Hales's ventilators' ('Surgery at Trafalgar', *Mariner's Mirror*, vol 91, no. 2, 2005, pp.269–70). **Brodie's stove**: Macdonald, *Feeding Nelson's Navy*, p. 106; ADM 49/121. **Lukin's ventilator**: ADM 49/105, especially Simon Goodrich to the Navy Board, 16 & 20 February 1810.

[31] **Sheep pens**: testimony of several boys of the *Prince* (90), c/m of David Jenness, ADM 1/5346. **Water casks**: had she been in the Channel, beer casks would have stood available as well. *Achille*: Q: 'Was the Galley perfectly dry?' A: 'The galley was wet; the people go into the galley to piss, where tubs are placed for them.' Testimony of Richard Cunningham, c/m of Francisco Falso and John Lambert, ADM 1/5346. **Galley**: Mr Ross's plan. See p. 181. **Carpenter's mates**: question by Captain O'Brien Drury to Charles Grey, her first lieutenant, c/m of John Bigelston, ADM 1/5334.

[32] **Little fire**: as in the *Achille* (74), testimony of Thomas Ellis, c/m of Francisco Falso and John Lambert, ADM 1/5346. **Regulated family**: Collingwood to Admiral Pole, undated, NRS 108, p 82n; he was describing the men of the *Ocean*. **Smoking club**: testimonies of John Price and Henry Park, c/m of the *Defiance* mutineers, ADM 1/5346. **Many other ships**: Report of Committee of Sea Officers of Navy Board on stores etc drawn up in 1814, ADM 106/5347, original f. 116.

[33] **Galley area**: captain's order no. XLVII in the *Amazon*, 1799 (NRS 138, pp. 154–5). The sequence is from R&I, 1808, p. 379 art. VII, which merely states 'morning'; the timing is based on Macdonald, *Feeding Nelson's Navy*, pp. 106 and 108.

[34] For the use of fresh water, see Morning Watch, n. 17 below, at 'hot water'.

[35] *Culloden*: c/m of the *Culloden* mutineers, ADM 1/5331. *Terrible*: c/m of the *Terrible* mutineers, ADM 1/5333.

[36] **Sliding lid**: Lavery, *Arming and Fitting*, p. 139. **Illuminators**: ADM 106/241, no. 16, 28 July 1809; NRS 107, p. 185. The army figures are for 1795. See Appendix 2.

[37] *Defiance*: after supper was between 4 and 5pm. C/m of John Sutherland and Edward Milson, ADM 1/5428. *Splendid*: these events took place on 16 July 1798 in the *Excellent* (74), off Cadiz. Charles Kent was Henry Gillespie. When the assault was brought to a court martial, Mr Smith, the surgeon, said that he had known the prisoner about a month and 'He always appeared to me to labour under mental affliction if not derangement' (which did not prevent him being 'at all times' employed in the care of the sick and in administering medicines), and even Gillespie's friend said he had thought him 'deranged in mind' for about a year: he had seen him 'sitting in the berth in a very melancholy manner, he would immediately start up and say, "Damn it, never mind," and would take his flute down and play upon it and whistle and sing seemingly in great agitation of mind'; he always wanted to know what was spoken in the berth when he was not there'. Gillespie was dismissed the service and sentenced to be imprisoned in the Marshalsea in London for a year (c/m, ADM 1/5345).

[38] This is borrowed from Captain Hall's extracts from his diary in the *Leander* (50), off Bermuda, Sunday 22 April 1804 (Hall, *Fragments*, vol. I, p. 211).

[39] **Landmen**: Anon., 'Proposals to increase seamen', in NRS 119, p. 12. **Regulations**: R&I, 1790, Additional Instructions, p. 200 art. XI. *Prince George*: NRS 5, p. 74. This mephitic air was later identified as carbonic acid, known as choke-damp in mines, and now called carbon dioxide (Trotter, *Medicina Nautica* (1804), in NRS 107, pp. 285–6). **Hutchinson**: *Treatise on Practical Seamanship*, p. 2. **Ventilators**: there were two in ships of 70, 74 and 80 guns, three

in those of 98 and four in those of 100; they were all 10ft long and 4ft 6in wide, and 1ft 10in, 1ft 8in and 1ft 8in deep respectively, 'exclusive of the trunks for conveying the air', ADM 95/17, f. 299. **Half an hour in each watch**: Admiralty order 4 April 1757, NRS 77, p. 165, and again in R&I, 1790, Additional Instructions, p. 215 art. XXVIII, which noted that the regulation was imperfectly understood: 'Whereas His Majesty's Ships are ordered to be furnished with ventilators, at a very great expence, in order to keep the ships free from foul air, and the captains in the navy, in general, not understanding the proper use of them, they are hereby strictly required and directed to cause them to be made use of, at least one half hour in every watch; and the mate of the watch to note in the log-book the time of its being made use of.' **Splendid**: as in the *Mars*: 'Trafalgar general order book', p. 91. In the 1806 and 1808 Regulations they were to be worked 'continually' (NRS 138, p. 54 and R&I, p. 138 art. VI). By this time the navy was supplying a new machine, the White's extractor, described in the warrant as 'more useful than the ventilators now in general use'; to be supplied to all ships 'as fast as they can be provided, giving the preference to the ships of the largest class', but about which details are scarce, other than that it was included in the stores removed from the very smallest vessels as too bulky to be stored, in 1807, when they were removed from brig-rigged sloops of 264 tons (ADM 106/2510, no. 224, 5 Apr 1794, and ADM 106/2518, no. 303, 10 May 1807). **Windsail**: Falconer, *Marine Dictionary*, from <http://southseas.nla.gov.au/refs/falc/1515.html>. The *Tigre* (74) had five fit for survey in July 1810, ADM 7/50, ff. 143–4. **Boteler**: NRS 82, pp. 30–31.

[40] **Sweeten the ship**: in 1795, the usual time for pumping the *Powerful* (74) was 'in the middle watch, when washing the decks in fine weather; and when blowing hard, the two hand pumps were kept going for the four hours, it only blew once so, to occasion us to do so, but they were very bad pumps' (c/m of John Bigelston, ADM 1/5334); 16in is stated in the captain's order no. 57th in the *Indefatigable* (NRS 138, p. 193); no time is specified, but I have inferred from 'following morning' and 'carpenter to report' that this was done to conclude with his report at seven bells in the morning watch. **Boys and idlers**: NRS 91, 254. **Vertical pipe**: ADM 106/2514, no. 35, 2 March 1803. **Men stationed**: captain's order no. XLVII in the *Amazon*, 1799 (NRS 138, p. 155). **Jupiter**: Pasley, *Private Sea Journals*, p. 153. **Drained separately**: Lavery, *Bellona*, p. 15. The Report of Committee of Sea Officers of Navy Board on stores etc drawn up in 1814 (ADM 106/5347, original f. 116) considered 'the present pump dales are greatly in the way on the lower deck. There should be two cast-iron pump dales, one for each cistern.' The Navy Board's remarks considered that the working of the ship would make them leak, and an experiment was to be made.

Chapter 3
HOLYSTONING THE WEATHER DECKS

[1] **Splendid's holystone**: Edgar K Thompson, 'Holystone', *Mariner's Mirror*, vol. 58, no. 2 (1972), p. 182, and Pope, *Life in Nelson's Navy*, p. 167. Thompson states that the navy's holystones came from Malta, 'as the island had large deposits of soft yellow sandstone which made excellent scouring material. Visiting men-of-war generally laid in large quantities of this most useful stone.' Pope states that the holystones were pieces of Portland stone, which is limestone, which weighs 140lb to the cubic foot. This is supported by, for example, http://www.soton.ac.uk/~imw/portnew.htm; limestone, however, is much less coarse than sandstone, and would clog too quickly. (The navy was certainly buying blocks of Purbeck stone 'not less than 5in deep', at 18s the ton in 1781, but this was for construction (ADM 49/121, f. 23).) Sandstone is more widely recorded than limestone, and not just by those who may be supposed to be recording an unusual variant on the standard practice, for example, Joseph Bates, a pressed American seaman in the *Rodney* (74), who wrote his *Memoirs* after he

became an American minister, wrote that a mountain in Minorca supplied the holystones: 'The stone of this mountain is a kind of sandstone, much harder than chalk, called "holy-stone", which is abundant on the island, and made use of by the British squadron to scour or holy-stone the decks with every morning to make them white and clean.' Admiral Smyth, in his *Sailor's Word Book*, thought the name came from 'being originally used for Sunday cleaning, or obtained by plundering church-yards of their tombstones, or because the seamen have to go on their knees to use it.' The vocabulary may not have been so fixed as these accounts imply: according to Leech, who served in the *Macedonian*, 'These larger stones are called holy bibles; the smaller hand ones are also called holy-stones, or prayer-books, their shape being something like a book' (*Voice from the Main Deck*, p. 46). Thompson continues: 'Ladders were never holystoned but were scrubbed with canvas and sand and were never scraped except to remove stains of paint and tar. Sand buckets were never pushed along the deck but [were] passed from hand to hand. Quarter-gunners always placed wash deck chocks under all guns before the deck was washed down'. The supposition that a single holystone was used comes from Gardner's account, below, and from the letter written to Admiral Hotham by the mutineers in the *Windsor Castle* (98) in 1794, who complained that among other things 'yesterday morning the scouring stone was not to be found, all the maintop men was call'd up to know what was become of it, every man said he knew nothing of the matter, a brick was immediately put in the hands of every main top man in the ship, we was in three watches and all hands of them was made to scour the Qr and Main deck' (ADM 1/5331). For practical details of holystoning I am indebted to the correspondents of the Marine History Information Exchange Group. **33 tons**: the *Milford* (74), stored for Channel service, carried 22 tons on 1 November 1809 (ADM 1/1548, Capt. B2) and I have made the *Splendid* restock at Mahon; it is not recorded in the *Conqueror*'s log but other ships did restock that summer.

[2] **Jack Nastyface**: Robinson, *Jack Nastyface*, pp. 32–3. **Eight bells**: Edgar K Thompson, 'Holystone', *Mariner's Mirror*, vol. 58, no. 2 (1972), p. 182.

[3] NRS 31, p. 90 and p. 88. It is possible that by 1810 holystoning was not done every day: captain's order no. 52nd in the *Indefatigable* directs that the decks 'are to be well scrubbed and washed every morning', with sand and brushes, but 'on Sundays and Thursdays the holy and hard stones' (NRS 138, p. 192): the distinction between holy and hard stones is also not well attested, but hard stones may simply be an error for handstones.

[4] This sequence from the *Conqueror*'s log, and procedure from Lever, *Sheet Anchor*, p. 82 and 84; Harland, *Seamanship*, pp. 169 and 130; Lavery, *Ship of the Line*, p. 76. **Weights**: for ships of the *Leviathan* class, from ADM 1/1548, Capt. B2, citing experiments made by Mr Ratcliffe, master mast maker at Portsmouth. **Lengths**: based on Marquardt, *Rigs & Rigging*, pp. 39–40.

[5] **Four bells**: Robinson, *Jack Nastyface*, p. 33. **Thrums**: Admiral Smyth says these were particularly used for cabins. The navy paid 5d per cwt for them (ADM 49/121). **Swabs**: these had traditionally been made out of junk (lengths of old worn-out rope or cable worked for the purpose), but when ships stayed on blockade for unprecedented periods, junk was turned back into rope on board ship, and substitutes had had to be found, such as worn hammocks and old canvas (as recorded by Captain Keats in the *Superb* (74), ADM 80/141, out-letters ff. 36–7). In 1807 the Navy Board issued a table of equivalences, so that eight hammocks, or 36lb canvas, or eighty strands of rope, or 36lb old fearnought, or 20lb old buntin was sufficient for making four swabs, and was equal to 1cwt of junk (ADM 106/2518, no. 906, 4 December 1807). **Swabber**: this was one of the 'obsolete or unnecessary ratings' whose abolition was proposed in 1816 (Memorial from the Admiralty to the Prince Regent in council, 25 November 1816; the Admiralty's foul proof is in ADM 1/4539 and this passage is on p. 27). **Swab-washers**: from the *Culloden* (74); Rowland Johnstone said during his testimony against Cornelius Sullivan in 1794, 'I do my duty at the present time as what they call a swab washer', c/m of the *Culloden* mutineers, ADM 1/5331. Head is from Admiral

Smyth, *sv* swab, who notes that now the decks were clean, cleaning the cleaning equipment had to be done in the head. The boy is Landsman Hay, who when he was a boy in the *Culloden* (74) was given the duty in November 1805 and thought it was because one of the lieutenants had taken against him: 'I was compelled to wash swabs, sweep decks, turn spits, and every other duty which required hard labour, or to which a degrading idea was attached' (Hay, *Landsman Hay*, p. 120).

[6] This sequence from the captain's order no. XLVIII in the *Amazon*, 1799 (NRS 138, pp. 155–6); swabs from Admiral Smyth, *sv* head.

[7] **Between 5 and 6am**: the testimony of James Phillips of the bread room of the *Gibraltar* (80), c/m of Richard Parke (ADM 1/5336), was that at 5am Parke sent for him to get his clean clothes, and to send the steward to begin cutting up the beef. **Mess pieces**: beef had been cut into 8lb pieces from 1778, then 4lb by 1790. The Victualling Board assumed a wastage of 12lb per cwt of salted beef while in cask, and 8lb per cwt of pork. 'If 100 pounds of beef were cut into 28 pieces, they wd. turn out about 3½ pounds each, but the fact is, that it is not practicable to cutt beef in this manner, and if it was it would not be proper, as some of the pieces must be mostly bone, and it is a meer chance whether in cutting beef in such manner as to answer the said standard, any two pieces in 28 may happen to be exactly of the same weight … The uncertainty of cutting beef in such manner even as that every 28 [4lb] pieces on an average may weigh 100 pounds averdupoise [*sic*] is implied by the 5th Article of the Instructions [in the section 'Of the Provisions'], which was formed expressly to prevent the seamen from suffering by that uncertainty, and it affords an effectual, and the only remedy that can be had for this relief.' (The fifth article directed the captain to order the purser to issue beef or pork to make up the deficiency, the purser's accounts credited accordingly. It is present in the 1790 edition, but not in the 1808.) Victualling Board's note, ADM 30/44, ff. 60–61. **Six oxen**: for convenience I have used six oxen with the weights given in the worked examples in R&I, 1808, but six was perfectly plausible: the *Superb*'s weekly report of cattle slaughtered for the week ending 7 November 1802, for example, shows she received six oxen on board on 5 November and killed them on the 6th; the produce of beef was 1,401lb, with no tallow or suet recorded (ADM 80/141, out-letters f. 159). The 1808 Regulations' column for live weight was not required in 1802. In the form reproduced here, the mutton issued as eighty beef pieces on 17 February must be a printer's error and should be in the next line, for the 23rd.

[8] **Harness tub**: *Director*, c/m of William James and Robert Willis, ADM 1/5337; *Rota*, c/m of William Clear, ADM 1/5406. **Cisterns**: ADM 106/2514, no. 121, 24 June 1803; Hall, *Fragments*, vol. III, p. 141; **Regulations** R&I, 1808, p. 343 art. XXXI. **Scuir or skewer pieces**: Pope, *Life in Nelson's Navy*, p. 160; Admiral Smyth, *sv* skewer-pieces. **1813**: Admiralty Order 4 November 1813, p. 46 art. XXVI, in ADM 7/972.

[9] Robinson, *Jack Nastyface*, p. 132.

[10] This account is adapted from the testimony of Lieutenant Gardiner Henry Guion of the *Diomede*, c/m of John Parker, ADM 1/5347. The ship was cutting up a cask of salt meat, and the narrative has been modified as if for fresh; punctuation has been added and Parker's name substituted for 'the Prisoner'. The court established that the cask contained seventy-five double pieces, made into 149 single pieces, and Parker was sentenced to sixty lashes.

[11] **Credit**: also ADM 30/44, f. 104. **Used on board**: Glascock, *Naval Sketch-book*, vol. I, p. 153n1; NRS 138, pp. 593–602 passim; NRS 91, p. 209.

[12] This is actually Captain Keats's in the *Superb* (74), ADM 80/141, out-letters f. 195, undated but August 1803. In this respect he was probably unusual (cf. Macdonald, *Feeding Nelson's Navy*, p. 91), but Glascock, writing in 1826, added 'Men-of-war have continually, at sea, hides towing overboard in soak'. A letter from Captain Keats of 25 November 1803 recorded that fourteen hides were thrown overboard 'being a nuisance in the ship', but they were part of the supply from the *Belleisle*. **Sold**: the *Superb* resold her hides for at 1¼ dollars each in

March 1804, for example (ADM 80/141, out-letters f. 251 and f. 263); the Victualling Board's precedent book records that it paid £334 16s 8d for its forty Belle Isle oxen, plus £107 0s 0d for the hides and offal; it then spent £1 3s 4d on salt for to preserve the hides, and resold the unused portion for £16 12s 6, and the tallow for £5 4s 6d (ADM 30/44 f. 101). The hides were not made into stock, as one French admiral has speculated (*Mariner's Mirror*, vol. 89, no. 2 (May 2003), p. 208). The note at the end of the order is supported by records in the Office of Stores of hides in the hair supplied to the fleet for use on board (for example, 18 August 1796, twelve hides in the hair to be delivered to the fleet at Falmouth as part of a large consignment of stores, ADM 106/2822), and in the Office of Bills for hides in the hair bought at Buenos Aires, 'dried with the hair on', from 1782 at 7½d per cwt (ADM 49/121, f. 28).

[13] **502**: ADM 80/141, in-letters, f. 48. **Tallow**: The 18 August 1796 consignment included 4cwt, ADM 106/2822. In 1806 the Navy Board was paying 8d per lb for hides averaging 29lb, and from £61 15s 0d to £63 5s 0d at the time (the previous contract, of an average of 32lb, subjected the contractor to losses), ADM 106/2517, letter, no. 690, 30 September 1806 and ADM 106/2516, no. 9, 7 January 1805. The 1808 Regulations changed this slightly: 'nor is it at any time to be delivered to the Boatswain, as has been formerly practised, unless the Captain and Master certify that he has no grease or tallow remaining in charge, nor can be supplied with any', p. 336 art. XXIII). **Boatswain's stores**: ADM 106/2508, 10 December 1771, no. 589.

[14] **As daylight approached**: this sequence is order 89th in the *Indefatigable*, 1812 (NRS 138, p. 199).

[15] **At daylight**: this sentence is Captain Pasley's, 16 November 1781: 'At daylight agreeable to custom and orders I was called by the Officer of the Watch, who acquainted me that the wind was moderate and favorable. I desired him to set what sail he could with safety, and continued to lay lolling in bed contrary to my allmost invariable custom, for I did not get up till near six' (Pasley, *Private Sea Journals*, p. 199). Similar captains' orders exist for many ships at later dates: for example, in the *Indefatigable* in 1812, order 88th ends 'I am to be … always to be made acquainted at daylight with the situation of the ship and state of the weather, etc' (NRS 138, p. 199). **Entering the cabin**: this is inferred from the courts martial of Lieutenant Grey (ADM 1/5348) and Lieutenant-Colonel Desborough (ADM 1/5349); Grey followed exactly this procedure, but his character witness testified that while he was 'very respectful of his superiors', it was 'with more ceremony than is commonly used in our service', and Desborough, who was serving as captain of Marines aboard the *Princess Royal* (98), came into Captain Dixon's cabin 'without previously sending any message for permission or that he wished an interview and wanted to have some conversation', but when questioned by the court Dixon admitted that others had come into his cabin without a message and there were no orders to the contrary. In the *Barfleur* (98), Gardner sent a note to the captain to ask whether he was 'at leisure' to speak with him, in 1790, but only after the captain had told him he was disgraced and had dismissed him the ship; while they were talking, the first lieutenant came into the cabin, apparently without any ceremony (*Above and Under Hatches*, p. 97), from all of which I conclude it was still familiar enough to be practised for a purpose but not for ordinary daily behaviour between men on good terms. *Victory*: Nicolas, *Dispatches and Letters of Lord Nelson*, vol. IV, p. 386. Pocock, *Terror Before Trafalgar*, pp. 170–71, citing John Ruskin, *Praeterita and Dilecta*, p. 586. **Custom of the service**: Hall, *Fragments*, vol. I, p. 229. *Britannia*: *Wynne Diaries*, vol. II, p. 108, 15 July 1796. *Samnite*: *Wynne Diaries*, vol. II, p. 208, 7 March 1798.

[16] **Brodie's stove**: William N Boog Watson, 'Alexander Brodie and his Firehearths for Ships', *Mariner's Mirror*, vol. 54, no. 4 (1968), p. 410. **6cwt**: in the *Milford* (74) on 1 November 1809, almost certainly gross weight, ADM 1/1548, Capt. B2. **Suffren**: Hickey, *Memoirs*, vol. III, p. 54. *Endeavour*: Pasted from <http://southseas.nla.gov.au/journals/cook/17680901.html>. *Spartan*: ADM 1/1548, Capt. B56 and B227. **Boteler**: NRS 82, pp. 135–6.

[17] **Casks**: this is an inference from the c/m of Peter Richieu, ADM 1/5428, where there certainly was such a cask; there is no evidence that it was generally so, but it would have been useful. The cask could have been a harness cask, as in the c/m of William Clear, ADM 1/5406. Macdonald, *Feeding Nelson's Navy*, p. 116. **Hot fresh water**: the captain's orders to the marines in the *Blenheim* (74) in 1796 included an instruction that the marine sentinel at the wardroom door was to permit the officers' servants 'to take one jug every morning for their master's use' (NRS 138, pp. 224–5), but that the water was taken to the galley and heated is supposition, as is that officers washed and shaved daily. That fresh water was generally used when available is supported by a complaint made by Marmaduke Wybourn, in the *Isis* (50), returning from Holland in 1799, that 'the last four days we had no fresh water allowed us to wash in' (*Sea Soldier*, p. 28).

[18] **Daylight**: captain's order no. 46th in the *Indefatigable*, 1812 (NRS 138, p. 191). **Uniform**: captain's order no. 145 in the *Pegasus* (28), 1786–88 (NRS 138, p. 117). It is not clear how much, if at all, formality in uniform in the navy as a whole increased by 1815: captain's order no. 12th in the *Indefatigable* directs that an officer leaving the ship on duty will be 'dressed in his uniforms and with side arms', meaning full-dress uniform (NRS 138, p. 184), but working dress is not mentioned. In 1798 Anthony Brompton, first lieutenant of the *Daedalus* (32), appeared at a punishment in 'a blue coat half lapelled with a lieutenant's uniform button', a 'striped waistcoat' and 'brownish corduroy breeches'; Captain Henry Ball ordered him to put on his uniform coat, and he was going down the gangway apparently to do so when he was ordered to his cabin under arrest, but it had been his usual dress on the quarterdeck since joining the ship six weeks or two months before and there were no standing orders to that effect: he was reprimanded (c/m of Anthony Brompton, ADM 1/5345). Breeches were more formal than trousers. For washing officers' clothes, see p. 158. The boatswain's, carpenter's and gunner's duties are from captain's order no. 46th in the *Indefatigable* (NRS 138, p. 191), with additions as shown.

[19] **Boatswain**: R&I, 1808, p. 227, arts III and IV. **After the decks were cleaned**: captain's order no. LIV in the *Amazon*, 1799 (NRS 138, p. 157).

[20] **Carpenter**: R&I, 1790, p. 113, arts I and II; R&I, 1808, p. 234, arts III and IV; captain's order no. 46th in the *Indefatigable*, 1812 (NRS 138, p.191). **Gratings**: Nicol, *Life and Adventures*, p. 157. **Half-ports**: Steel, *An Explanation of the Terms Used in Ship Building* (1805).

[21] **Six boats**: boatswain's stores in ADM 7/579, f. 11. **Barge**: captains were allowed to exchange the barge for a cutter. **Launch**: the establishment supplied a longboat or a launch, but since 1780 the yards had been directed to replace longboats in all ships repairing or building (ADM 106/2508, no. 1036, 7 November 1780), and in 1804 their watering capacity had been improved ('Launches at present supplied to ships are not properly calculated for watering them', and launches of First and Second Rates should floor 14 butts and Third Rates should floor 12 butts, ADM 106/2515, 30 August 1804, no. 163). Carronades had been supplied for the launches since 1795 (James, *History*, vol. I, p. 306; cf. Sidney Smith's designs, NRS 46, pp. 36–7), and the launches had been specifically fitted for carronades, and all necessary equipment, so that they may be ready 'at a moment's notice', since 1803 (ADM 106/2514, no. 153, 10 August 1803 and no. 155). **Cutter**: the establishment supplied a pinnace or a cutter, but once eight-oared cutters had been introduced, pinnaces were not to be built henceforth without instructions from the Navy Board (ADM 106/2511, no. 330, 12 July 1796). The establishment notes that per warrant of 7 November 1799 a yawl of 26ft could replace a cutter on the captain's application, 'provided the cutter is worn out'; and a warrant of 1808 states that a yawl of Captain Brenton's design is to be furnished, in lieu of the cutter (ADM 106/241, no. 1, 1 April 1808: not, apparently, the launch, as stated by Lavery, *Arming and Fitting*, pp. 224 and 232, whose source is ADM 2/272, 15 March 1810, which is impossible since ADM 2/272 is Lords' out-letters, 17 February to June 1794). Admiral Smyth notes that the large cutter is especially used for anchor work. The terms 'four-oared (Deal) cutter' and

'jolly boat' were synonyms, indicated by a comma in the establishment (Smyth, *sv* cutter; May, *Boats of Men-of-War*, p. 45). **Stowage**: ADM 106/2512, no. 194; May, *Boats of Men-of-War*, p. 49. In 1808 ships were allowed a yawl of Captain Brenton's design, one in lieu of the cutter (ADM 106/241, no. 1, 1 April 1808: they were not successful, and a warrant of 19 March 1810 (ADM 106/2521, no. 97) directs the dockyard 'to issue only such of the said boats as are already on hand'). **Quarter davits**: ADM 106/2512, no. 194; May, *Boats of Men-of-War*, p. 49; Lavery, *Arming and Fitting*, pp. 235–6. Exactly what the carpenter was checking for is supposition: the regulations state that he is to 'keep the boats, ladders, and gratings in as good condition as possible, always repairing every damage they may sustain as soon as he discovers it' (R&I, 1808, p. 234 art. VI). **Old canvas**: *eg* on 12 September 1804 the *Superb* recorded carpenter's stores discharged to the Mediterranean Fleet, including 240 yards old canvas for two boat's covers into the *Leviathan* (ADM 80/141, out-letters). **Booms**: captain's order no. LII in the *Amazon*, 1799 (NRS 138, pp. 156–7).

[22] **Gunner**: R&I, 1790, p. 104 art. XIV. R&I, 1790 and 1808, gunner's instructions passim; and 1808, captain's instructions, p. 175 art. XI. Guns' weight from Lavery, *Bellona*, table 19.

[23] Office of Ordnance, Portsmouth, 27 March 1813 to the Admiralty, in ADM 7/226.

[24] **Sixty live bullocks**: this is based on the experiences of the *Superb* (74), which under Captain Keats was frequently dispatched for live animals, onions, lemons and wine for the fleet. On 30 August 1803 Captain Keats ordered his purser to buy sixty live bullocks and their food for five days at 18lb per head per day, forty pipes of 'good and sound wine', twelve tons of onions for the fleet, with the master 'to see that the bullocks are good and fit for His M. Service', following an order from the *Victory* dated Naples Bay, 20 July 1803 (ADM 80/141, out-letters f. 199). On 5 September the bullocks were to be distributed as follows: *Victory*, 12; *Kent*, 8; *Canopus*, 8; *Superb*, 7; *Triumph*, 6; *Renown*, 6; *Belleisle*, 6; *Gibraltar*, 6; *Raven*, 1; and on 6 September the onions as follows: *Victory*, 1968lb; Kent, 1410lb; *Canopus*, 1610lb; *Superb*, 1610lb; *Triumph*, 1350lb; *Renown*, 1350lb; *Gibraltar*, 1770lb; *Raven*, 242lb (ADM 80/141, in-letters f. 132). **Tied**: this follows the practice in the *Amazon* in 1804, and other examples given in Macdonald, *Feeding Nelson's Navy*, p. 89–90. **Fodder**: ADM 80/141, out-letters ff. 239–41.

[25] These are the words of Alexander Campbell, captain of the mast of the *Queen Charlotte*, in the court martial for her loss, ADM 1/5353. **Jack-in-the-box**: NRS 91, p. 199. **Breadroom**: as in the *Gibraltar* (80), testimony of George Reynolds, c/m of Richard Parke, ADM 1/5336. **2lb**: Keats' order in the *Superb* (74), 9 December 1803, was 2lb hay, ½ pint oats and ½ pint bran for each sheep per day (ADM 80/141, out-letters ff. 239–41: bullocks had 14lb straw, 1 pint oats, 1 pint bran as above).

[26] **Visit daily**: R&I, 1790, p.113 art. II. **To examine**: R&I, 1808, p.234 art. III. **Air scuttles**: cut in every other gundeck port of line-of-battle ships, ADM 106/2508, no. 770, 28 November 1778; changed to alternate ports, no. 1161, 6 May 1782; changed to every gundeck port of all two-deck ships, ADM 106/2509, no. 600, 7 May 1789.

[27] **Royal Dockyards**: the terms used are new and old work; new work required a specified mixture of white and black oakum; caulking the bottom required white and black oakum and hair (ADM 106/2509, no. 238, 5 December 1783). Cooper's tools were allowed to pursers of ships victualled for Foreign service: '1 brick iron, 1 bung borer, 1 hammer, 2 drivers, 2 punches, 2 chisels, 2 bolsters, 500 rivets' – the set is £1 0s 4¼d, and ships victualled for the East Indies had two sets (ADM 30/44, f. 190). **Caulkers**: ADM 2/124, ff. 257–8, 1 July 1793, repeated to the Channel Fleet the same date; and to Keats in the *Galatea*, 24 May 1794, ADM 80/136. **Caulker's mate**: ADM 2/125, f. 316, 23 January 1794. **Pitch**: ships of the line now had two barrels for eight months (*ie* Channel service) and three for twelve months (Foreign service), ADM 106/2511, no. 357, 10 October 1796. **Tools**: armourers also had tools supplied, but by the Ordnance Board. **At sea**: R&I, 1808, p. 235 art. VIII.

[28] ADM 2/124, ff. 257–8, dated 1 July 1793, repeated to the Channel Fleet the same date; and to Keats in the *Galatea*, 24 May 1794, ADM 80/136.

[29] R&I, 1808, p. 235 art. VIII, and p. 258 art. II.

[30] **Tools:** four sets to each line-of-battle ship and two to each frigate; these to be supplied in addition to what the caulker supplies (ADM 106/2515, no. 70, 18 April 1804; ADM 106/2515, no. 82, 1 May 1804 orders that this allowance is inserted in the establishment of carpenter's stores. The 1816 report noted that carpenters and their crew were unique in providing their own tools, and recommended to continue the allowance of 7s per month for this purpose that had begun on 3 February 1814, Memorial from the Admiralty to the Prince Regent in council, 25 November 1816; the Admiralty's foul proof is in ADM 1/4359; this passage is on p. 27. The report said that this allowance is 'in fact already, though partially, made'; it was not at this stage paid to the carpenter himself. **Apprenticed:** Rodger, *Wooden World*, p. 23. **1802:** ADM 7/678, Admiralty Office to Navy Board, 12 November 1802. R&I, 1808, p. 86 art. XV. **Wallis:** C Knight, '"Carpenter" Master Shipwrights', *Mariner's Mirror*, vol. 18, no. 4 (1932), table. Provo Wallis was the father of Admiral of the Fleet Sir Provo Wallis, who served ninety-six years in the navy.

[31] **Brodie's stoves,** c/m of Ralph Thomson, ADM 1/5348. **Paint:** they replaced the former allowance of tar, red ochre, pitch, etc. ADM 106/2508, no. 1007, 18 July 1780. The proportions of the different colours for ships of each class varied frequently: for 'weatherwork' only, the paints were Venetian red, yellow, port red, and lamb black, with linseed oil (ADM 95/17, f. 249): a 70-gun ship required 7cwt 3qr 0lb. 5cwt of yellow English ochre was added, and 14cwt of Spanish brown changed to 10cwt on 29 January 1803 (ADM 106/2514, no. 235), and changed again to 3cwt of yellow English ochre and 3cwt of Spanish brown on 5 February 1803 (ADM 106/2514, no. 336). **Lightning conductors:** Admiralty orders of 19 and 28 November 1793; ADM 106/2510, no. 85, 11 January 1794. The sizes supplied are in no. 349, 17 March 1794: a 74's was 207ft long. On 15 July 1812 came a 'General order for all ships of the line to be supplied with conductors also 50 gun ships down to 32 gun frigates inclusive', ADM 7/710. **Stuff and nails:** ADM 106/2508, no. 1024, 21 September 1788. The location of the sheep pen seems not to have been fixed until 1808, when it was placed 'between the main hatchway and the capstan' (Lavery, *Arming and Fitting*, p. 200); in 1814 it was placed more generally in the waist (Report of Committee of Sea Officers of Navy Board on stores etc drawn up in 1814, ADM 106/5347, original f. 110 and stamped f. 89). *Victory:* ADM 95/17, ff. 150–56. *Mars:* 'General order book of HMS Mars', p. 102. **Buckets:** ADM 106/2517, no. 193, 12 March 1806.

[32] **1757:** ADM 95/17, ff. 247–53 and ADM 106/2508, no. 445, 24 June 1757. *Ça Ira:* testimony of Elias Alley in the c/m for her loss, 27 May 1796, ADM 1/5336. **Storerooms:** Lavery, *Bellona*, plan C2; McKay, *Victory*, plan A10. C/m of John Major, ADM 1/5350. *York:* ADM 51/2989, 25 July 1810. **Raigersfeld,** *Life*, p. 67. *Vanguard:* testimony of Mr Gill, c/m of Thomas McDowell, ADM 1/5363.

[33] Falconer, *Marine Dictionary*, from <http://southseas.nla.gov.au/refs/falc/0266.html>; Lavery, *Arming and Fitting*, pp. 141–2.

[34] **Bags:** ADM 106/2508, 12 October 1782, no. 1032. They were issued at 2s 8d each. Haversacks supplied at the same rate as they are supplied with hammocks, ADM 106/2511, letter, no. 288, 27 May 1795; they were to be charged to the men but the sum is not stated. The letter is addressed to Sir Peter Parker at Portsmouth, with another of 4 June to the Mediterranean, Jamaica, East Indies, Halifax and the Leeward Islands, so it may have been intended to apply to ships on Foreign service only. Fifty haversacks weighed 7cwt, or 15lb 11oz each (WO 55/1747). **Tidied:** captain's order no. 55th in the *Indefatigable* (NRS 138, p. 193). **Garlands:** Falconer, *sv* shelves: this is the *Blake* (74) at Christmas 1812, in Rodger, *Command of the Ocean*, p. 503; Macdonald (*Feeding Nelson's Navy*, pp. 110–11), doubts the existence of such racks, but her objection on the grounds that they would intrude into the hammock space is not relevant since hammocks were not slung so close to the ship's side, and her research is based on the period July 1803 to June 1804. Rodger notes that 'this domestic

sense seems to have been something new among the seamen'; Robert Wilson, who served in the *Unité* (38) from 1805 to 1809, says 'there are two shelves' in each berth (NRS 91, p. 256), but she was a notably smart frigate, so perhaps this was not yet universal. However, Rodger cites this from the *Macedonian* in 1811 or 1812, having refitted at Plymouth and ordered to sea: 'Most of the men laid out money in getting new clothing; some of it went to buy pictures, looking-glasses, crockery ware, &c to ornament our berths, so that they bore some resemblance to a cabin' (Leech, *Voice from the Main Deck*, p. 65).

[35] **Seven minutes**: captain's order no. 49th in the *Indefatigable* (NRS 138, pp. 191–2). In 1787, Prince William Henry in the *Pegasus* expected it to be done in fifteen minutes (NRS 138, p. 108); in 1814, Captain Dillon in the *Horatio* decided that the accustomed half an hour was too long, and quickly got them to do it in less than five minutes (NRS 97, p. 296).

Hammock cloths: for the present war, hammock- and quarter-cloths are not to be tarred but painted, 'when applied to by the captains for that purpose', ADM 106/2508, 4 March 1780, no. 958; and painted on one side only in future, 15 March 1782, no. 1139. A warrant of 1806 to the home yards directed hammock cloths to be made of new no. 4 canvas, ADM 106/2517, no. 626, 11 September 1806, and another that year to Plymouth established that 'it frequently occurs that hammock cloths and tarpawlins are ordered to be got ready for ships when at sea, and consequently the officers of such ships cannot attend to their being painted or tarred as usual, when the ships are in port' and directed the master shipwright's department to carry out this work (ADM 106/2517, no. 482, 29 July 1806). However, 'The present method of cutting the hammock cloths to fold completely round the hammocks is wasteful and unnecessary; because there are boards under the hammocks with render the cloths in that part useless', Report of Committee of Sea Officers of Navy Board on stores etc drawn up in 1814, ADM 1/3574, para 23: and paras 26 and 27 note that 'It happens, perhaps, six times out of ten in this yard [Plymouth], that a ship requiring new hammock covers, has to remain in port only a few days, in which time the old covers must be surveyed, new ones demanded, warranted, made, nailed to exposed walls, and painted; a process that is scarcely accomplished, with the utmost diligence, before it is time to take the cloths off to the ship. It is obviously impossible that cloths in this state can be fit for use, and the paint is presently [immediately] wiped off so as to render them perfectly unserviceable, by which the mens beds are constantly exposed to wet, and their health to injury, and thus the cloths, destitute of paint, become rotten, and again the same wasteful mode of supply is had recourse to.' This was an often-rehearsed complaint. The report, which estimated that 'the ships in commission have about three hundred and forty-five thousand yards of hammock covers in use', also suggested they should be rolled on board ships, not doubled as was the practice, which was adopted.

[36] NRS 138, p. 193; the exact procedure is an inference, as above p. 230.

Chapter 4
BREAKFAST IN THE WARDROOM

[1] **Pasley**: *Private Sea Journals*, p. 150. **Hickey**: *Memoirs*, vol. III. pp. 63 and 111-12. **Tench**: *Letters from Revolutionary France*, p. 11.

[2] **Breakfast cloth**: this is supposition, but likely since it would have been used on land and Collingwood, fitting out in May 1790 in the *Mermaid*, wrote to his sister in London asking for his sea kit, which included 'of linnen, 4 prs of sheets, and my sea table cloths and breakfast cloths, towels, etc.' (NRS 98, p. 24). **Guest**: Hall, *Fragments*, vol. I, pp. 228.
Breakfast: the details of breakfast in the Royal Navy are almost never recorded: this is from William Hickey's voyage in the *Held Woltemade* Dutch East Indiaman in 1780 (*Memoirs*, vol. II, pp. 228–9): Captain Christy-Pallière in Patrick O'Brian's *Master and Commander*, though

French, 'had a solid notion of what made a proper breakfast for a seafaring man: a pair of ducks, a dish of kidneys, and a grilled turbot the size of a moderate cartwheel, as well as the usual hams, eggs, toast, marmalade, and coffee.'
[3] Tench, *Letters from Revolutionary France*, p. 10.

Chapter 5
Drill, Slaughter, Punishment and the Sick

[1] **Mounting guard**: Captain's orders to the marine commanding officer in the *Mars* (74), 31 May 1799, 'by order of the Hon. George Berkeley, Rear Admiral of the Blue' (NRS 138, pp. 231–2); 'hair combed and tied' etc. is from the *Blenheim* (74), 1796 (NRS 138, p. 223). **Drill**: 'At 10 o'clock am went upon deck to inspect the guard, and superintended their drill for nearly an hour', wrote Captain Robert Clarke in the *Swiftsure* (74) on 3 January 1815, and again on the 4th, 7th, 10th and 21st – *ie*, most Tuesdays and Saturdays (NRS 138, pp. 466–77 passim). 'Awkward men' is from the *Blenheim*. In fleets under St Vincent's command they were particularised as a defence against mutiny by the seamen; in the Mediterranean Fleet he ordered that when ships were at anchor 'the whole party of marines in the respective ships of the fleet is to be kept constantly at drill or parade under the direction of the commanding officer of marines, and not to be diverted therefrom by any of the ordinary duties of the ship' (Lavery, *Nelson and the Nile*, p. 113). In 1810 this tension had long since relaxed.
[2] **Jolly**: ADM 1/5350. His sentence of death was commuted by Nelson at the request of Lady Hamilton 'till his Majesty's pleasure is known', which arrived as a pardon on 22 May 1800 (Nicolas, *Dispatches and Letters of Lord Nelson*, vol. III, pp. 401, 402 and vol. IV, p. 240). **Brightly**: his defence (which was traditional, though not necessarily untrue) was that he was 'decoyed into bad company, who kept me in a continual state of intoxication for near three days'. Guilty: fifty lashes, ADM 1/5329. **Patton**: NRS 46, p. 121n; Admiral Patton, *The Natural Defence of an Insular Empire*, in NRS 138, p. 634.
[3] **Prohibition**: R&I, 1790, p.46 art. III. Commissioned officers forfeited 1s for each offence, warrant officers 6d. The clause – indeed, the whole section – has gone by 1808, subsumed into the captain's instructions, where they properly belong. **Divine service**: R&I, 1790, art. II; 1808, p.160 art. XXXVII and p.248 art.III. **Mid-century**: Bulkeley and Cummins, *Voyage to the South Seas*, p. 45. Richardson, *Mariner of England*, pp. 233–4 and 205.
[4] Portsmouth Dockyard, 25 December 1788 (*sic*: Christmas Day was only a half-holiday), ADM 106/3546 part one, no. 26.
[5] ADM 1/2496.
[6] Percival Stockdale to David Garrick, in Rodger, *Command of the Ocean*, p. 393.
[7] ADM 12/59, Admiralty digests, 1793. Answered: 'He will not be called into active service.'
[8] R&I, 1808, p. 160 art. XXXVII, and pp. 247–9 arts III, II, IV, V. *Rippon*: c/m of John Blake, ADM 1/5297.
[9] *Autobiography of Joseph Bates*, chapter three.
[10] **1812**: Lavery, *Nelson's Navy*, p. 101 and Order in Council of 4 March 1812, in NRS 96, pp. 316–18. Applicants for a warrant had to be recommended by the Archbishops of Canterbury and York and the Bishop of London, through the Chaplain-General, created at the same time. **Mangin**: NRS 96, p. 315, and Lavery, *Nelson's Navy*, p. 209.
[11] George Price was in reality sent to the *Speedy*, and entered on her books on 1 March 1804 (Kennedy and Ellison, *Pressganged*, p. 18). As he says, ship's butcher was a job, not a rate, and as such he received no extra pay and was not entered as butcher in the ship's books (which is why Macdonald, *Feeding Nelson's Navy*, p. 91, can find no examples), though according to Kennedy and Ellison, butchers were entered as such in the East India Company's ships, as were poulterers. Poulterers in the Royal Navy were universally known as Jemmy Ducks

(Admiral Smyth, *sv*); despite their title they were the butcher's assistant and assisted him generally in the feeding and care of the livestock. According to Marryat in 1822, poulterer was one of the rates filled by landmen (NRS 119, p. 351). R&I, 1808, pp. 198–9 art. XX required all fresh meat to be delivered on board in quarters (beef) or carcasses (mutton), but the ships' boats frequently brought back live animals, from the port or from anchorages (*eg* Mark, *At Sea with Nelson*, p. 140).

[12] **540lb**: this is the stated average weight of the Calabrian cattle given in Macdonald, *Feeding Nelson's Navy*, p. 27, where she says the range of beef produced from oxen slaughtered by HM ships in the Mediterranean (in the period under review) was from 140lb to 675lb. This means the likely weight of the animals was probably 245lb to 1184lb (*Britannica*, 11th edn, *sv* cattle, and agriculture: 'A familiar practical method of estimating carcase weight from live weight is to reckon one Smithfield stone (8lb) of carcase for each imperial stone (14lb) of live weight'). The average weight of cattle sold at Smithfield in 1710 was 370lb, and in 1845, 800lb (*Microcosm*, p. 184); oxen bought at home markets are ideally 'good fat oxen of about six hundredweight', though on examination the oxen killed at Deptford last season were upwards of seven hundredweight (Victualling Board to Admiralty, 3 July 1745, NRS 120, p. 447); European cattle sent to Belle Isle in the 1770s weighed an average (mean) of 784lb each (ADM 30/44, f. 101). Foreign cattle were often smaller: when the *Culloden* was fitting out in Bombay harbour between 1 and 28 April 1805, for example, she took on board 12,831lb of beef, and was typically slaughtering four bullocks per day, yielding a daily mean of 534lb; the median yield was 540lb, and the mode 500lb. At Martinique in 1800 the beef issued from the dockyard to the *Tromp* (54) was 'like carrion; a man could bring up the side a whole quarter in his hand, it was so small and thin.' Richardson, *Mariner of England*, p. 177. **Microcosm**: text, p. 185; plate, p. 259. This is essentially the process described by Macdonald, *Feeding Nelson's Navy*, pp. 90–91. **Dr Trotter**: 'There is another very filthy practice in ships when in port of hanging their fresh beef under the half-deck, or under the booms in the waist … I think some plan might be fallen upon to hoist it up under the main yard and to cover it above with some sort of awning or safe' (*Medicina Nautica* (1804), in NRS 98, p. 286), but it seems to have been normal practice at sea as well, for example in the *Gibraltar* (80); and in the *Caesar* (80) the carcasses hung under the half-deck in the evenings, with sentries over them (defence of Bartholomew Duff, c/m of the *Caesar* mutineers, ADM 1/5346). This last detail I have copied into the *Splendid*. **Steak**: c/m of John Burrows et al., ADM 1/5333.

[13] *Conqueror's* log, ADM 51/2219.

[14] Robinson, *Jack Nastyface*, pp. 34–5.

[15] R&I, 1790, p. 46 art. IV; R&I, 1808, p. 163 art. XLII; letter to the Admiralty, dated *Niger*, at Spithead, 27 May 1798 7 o'clock, and turnover, ADM 1/2498.

[16] *Nagle Journal*, p. 65.

[17] Harland, *Seamanship*, pp. 132–3.

[18] *Conqueror's* log, ADM 51/2219, time not specified. R&I, 1790, p. 100 art. VIII.

[19] ADM 80/141, f. 281, 28 August 1804 (contractions expanded).

[20] *Eg*, ADM 106/2822 part one, 8 October 1796.

[21] NRS 141, p. 565.

[22] **Superb**: ADM 80/141, out-letters ff. 36–7, 30 April 1801. **St Vincent**: ADM 80/141, in-letters, ff. 2–3. **Since 1798**: ADM 106/2512, 22 March 1798, no. 188. **That winter**: ADM 106/2513, no. 10, 26 January 1801 and no. 12, 29 January 1801. **Nelson**: Nicolas, *Dispatches and Letters of Lord Nelson*, vol. V, Nelson to Nathaniel Taylor, 8 October 1803, pp. 235–6, and 5 November 1803, pp. 279–80.

[23] Captain's order no. 13th in the *Indefatigable*, 1812 (NRS 138, p. 184); the order was for the first lieutenant or lieutenant of the morning watch, so presumably the lieutenant of the forenoon watch reported to him.

[24] R&I, 1808, pp. 310–11 art. I and Appendix 23.

[25] **Regiment**: ARS 3, p. 22. **Dispensed with**: R&I, 1808, p. 133 art. XXIX. **Flinders**: ADM 1/1807, Capt. F215. This is part of a long sequence of letters in which he attempted to secure what he thought was his due: on applying for his personal and compensation pay during the time of his imprisonment he was granted the former but not the latter; he reapplied, the Lords asked Croker how much the compensation pay (for servants) came to, and on hearing it was £45 10s p.a. decided to 'allow him £500 with reference to the *very perilous* nature of his case, sufferings, and the works in which he had been employed,' (Capt. F224).

[26] ADM 7/55.

[27] ADM 80/141.

[28] ADM 80/142.

[29] **Paybook**: this was reduced to three by an order in council of 28 May 1800, ADM 106/2512, no. 546, 31 July 1800; changed again to four, ADM 106/2513, no. 14, 6 February 1801. The blank books and papers were supplied by the dockyard when the ship was fitting out. **Clerk**: R&I, 1808, p. 170 art. XLVII; NRS 77, p. 42; ADM 106/2515, no. 205, 14 November 1804 and no. 685, 1 December 1804.

[30] **Procedures**: General Thompson RM, personal correspondence. **Box**: c/m of George Crumpston, ADM 1/5363.

[31] Captain Dymond is borrowed from Captain Clarke in the *Swiftsure* (74) and Major Wybourn in the *Repulse* (74). The *Swiftsure* was taking a convoy to Barbados via Madeira, and Captain Clarke spent most of January 1815 reading: on the 4th 'a pretty interesting novel' entitled *The Clergyman's Widow and Family*, the 5th, *The Merchant's Widow* by the same author, the 6th, Scott's *Rokeby*, which he finished on the 7th after drilling the marines, the 10th, after losing two of the convoy to an American frigate and missing Madeira, *Jokeby*, a burlesque of *Rokeby*, and 'a couple of cantos in Marmion', which he finished on the 12th, and so on until the convoy arrived in Barbados. *Rokeby* was published in 1813; *Marmion* was published in 1808, so the same two-year gap (NRS 138, p. 467–77 passim.) The 500 volumes is borrowed from the *Gloucester* (74), NRS 91, pp. 24–5. In Hoffman's 74, one quarter gallery was fitted up as a library for the first lieutenant (*A Sailor of King George*, p. 29). **Cabin**: Wybourn, *Sea Soldier*, pp. 121 and 133; c/m of Lieutenant George Dentatus Haynes, ADM 1/5331 – though of course the reason is not given. Wybourn also recorded his reading. **Collingwood**: Wybourn, *Sea Soldier*, p. 131.

[32] Wybourn, *Sea Soldier*, p. 118.

[33] Wybourn, *Sea Soldier*, p. 116–17.

[34] **Poor men**: Thompson, *Royal Marines*, p. 35, citing personal correspondence with N A M Rodger. **To his wife**: Captain Alfred Burton, in the *Alfred* (50) in 1831: 3 January 1831, NMM BUR-1, in Bittner, *Officers of the Royal Marines*, p. 50. I am indebted to General Thompson RM for this point. To a certain extent this indicates the attitudes of the next generation – Captain Burton wrote in 1833, 'It is no recommendation now a days that an officer has seen service. The young men are only jealous of him, and affect to think that if he had any merit he would long ago have been promoted. If ever I go to another ship, I mean never to let it escape me that I was at Trafalgar' (p. 41) – but the general sentiment harmonises with Wybourn's. **Regulations**: R&I, 1808, p. 421 art. VI. **Unité**: NRS 91, pp.248–9.

[35] ADM 1/5333. NRS 46, pp. 135–6. R E R Robinson, *The Bloody Eleventh*, vol. I: *1685–1815* (Exeter, 1988), p. 261n. **War Office**: ADM 1/4352. Admiralty, ADM 1/4352. This was still being enclosed in orders to commanders of troop transports in 1812, as *eg* Melville to Captain David Patterson, appointed to command the *Fox*, 19 June 1812, ADM 1/4358. In 1804 bombardiers embarked refused to obey the orders of the commander of HM Bomb *Thunderer*, and their officers claimed to have no knowledge of the relevant Act of Parliament, but no serious consequences seem to have come of it. Nicolas, *Dispatches and Letters of Lord Nelson*, vol. VI, pp. 22, 230–4, 27. **Calpe**: ADM 80/141, out-letters f. 126. The Madras European Regiment were 'ordered to embark on English frigates, to act as marines', by the

Governor of Madras as a punishment, in 1809; they refused. Bayly, *Diary*, p. 209.

36 *Blenheim*: NRS 138, p. 226. *Mars*: NRS 138, pp. 228–30 passim. These orders were written by Captain John Manley to the commanding officer of the marines at the direction of Admiral Berkeley.

37 R&I, 1790, p. 132 art. V, p. 133 art. VII, and pp. 133–4 arts X–XI. In 1790 there were two journals, one of his 'physical practice in diseases', and one of 'his chirurgical operations in cases of wounds or hurts'; the first went to the Sick and Hurt Board, and second to the governors of the Surgeons' Company, who examined them and gave their judgement; in the 1808 edition the journal was tabular, and submitted to the Sick and Hurt Board annually with his accounts, and when he left the ship (pp. 282–1, art. XXXII), accompanied by a return of the expenditure of medicines, utensils and surgeon's stores (p. 283 art XXXIV). He also had to submit a return (weekly if the ship was in a British port, every two months if abroad, or at the end of a cruise), 'stating the effects of the weather and the climate on the health of the men' (pp. 282–3 art. XXXIII). Another bimonthly return was the list of wounded or injured men and marines 'entitled to relief from the Chest at Greenwich' to the Navy Board, and a cumulative list when he left the ship or applied for his pay (p. 281 art. XXXI).

38 Trotter, *Medicina Nautica* (1804), in NRS 107, p. 262. He supplies a draft, but the two dimensions for width do not agree. The original text has 'The walls of the sick-berth are either pannels [*sic*] of deal, or strong canvas, so closely put together as to exclude the smoke of the galley fire, and nicely whitewashed once a month', but canvas was abolished by an order of 1808 (Lavery, *Arming and Fitting*, p. 206). The sickberth had been moved to this position from the lower deck in 1798 in the Mediterranean Fleet and 1801 in all ships of the line (NRS 138, p. 206).

39 This was required by R&I, 1808, p. 275 art. XXI, but that states 'as often as possible', and that it was lit in the Mediterranean in June is supposition, but likely given the weather the *Splendid* was experiencing. The visitor is the Reverend Mangin in the *Gloucester* (74), in the summer of 1812, NRS 91, pp. 28–9.

40 Captain's order no. 97th in the *Indefatigable*, 1812 (NRS 138, p. 201).

41 This is James Ker, the surgeon of the *Elizabeth* (74), on passage to the West Indies in 1778. William N Boog Watson, 'Two British Naval Surgeons of the French Wars', *Medical History* XIII (1969), pp. 213–25, in Rodger, *Command of the Ocean*, p. 405.

42 R&I, 1790, p. 131 art. I and 1808, p. 265 art. II. *Blonde*: Hoffman, *Sailor of King George*, p. 5. *Mars*: 'General order book of HMS Mars', p. 92. The passage is noted as deleted, presumably by Captain Oliver when he took command from Captain Duff after Trafalgar. **Martin**: NRS 12, p. 7.

43 R&I, 1808, form for the surgeon no. 36.

44 Henry Bankes, 'Report From the Committee on Dr. Smyth's Petition, respecting his Discovery of Nitrous Fumigation, 10 June 1802': Mr Paterson of Forton Prisoner-of-War Hospital to the Sick and Hurt Board, n.d.(blank in the original); A. Bassan, surgeon of the *Union* hospital ship, Sheerness, to the Sick and Hurt Board, 6 February 1796.

45 Bankes, 'Report', appendix 13, Mr Glegg, surgeon of the *Defiance*, to J. Johnstone, 16 December 1798. The ship's company were aboard the *Elephant* (74) hulk at the time.

46 Bankes, 'Report', summary; appendix 8; appendix 7, from the Langstone Harbour hulks.

47 ADM 106/2509, 16 January 1784, no. 256. NRS 107, p. 253. R&I, 1808, form no. 33.

48 R&I, 1808, p. 269 art. VIII; pp. 418–19 arts I and II.

49 **Tables**: definition of deal from the *OED*. **Nailed together**: ADM 106/2514, 21 March 1803, no. 422. They were made on board, but in 1806 the home yards were directed to make and fit them if captains did not have enough men to do so themselves, ADM 106/2517, no. 552, 25 August 1806. Officers' tables were joiner-made of wainscot (oak), or bought by the officers. **Frigate**: see p. 96n, c/m of Solomon Nathan, ADM 1/5407. **Two messes**: Hall, *Fragments*,

vol. III, p. 143, and the c/m of Richard Potter, ADM 1/5428 (which refutes Macdonald, *Feeding Nelson's Navy*, p. 110). In the USS *Columbus* (74), launched 1816, there were 'two messes occupying the space between every two guns. There are between twelve and sixteen men in each mess' (Nordhoff, *Sailor Life*, p. 164). **Captain of the mess**: Hall, *Fragments*, vol. III, p. 143.

[50] **Burial**: Hall, *Fragments*, vol. III, p. 213. **Stiles**: C/m of William Stiles, ADM 1/5363. *Belliqueux*: testimony of Matthew Welsh, c/m of Robert Nelson, ADM 1/5348. **Griffiths**: NRS 138, p. 356. Captain Glascock noted that 'It has often been the practice aboard men-of-war to put all the mauvais sujets into one "mess" on the main-deck', but he disapproved of it (Glascock, *Naval Sketch-Book*, Book II, p. 16n.).

[51] **Freedom**: Hall, *Fragments*, vol. III, p. 162. **Procedure**: Hall, *Fragments*, vol. III, pp. 143–4. **Possible to join**: Richard Cole to Williams (2), c/m of Richard Cole, ADM 1/5347.

[52] NRS 98, p. 18.

[53] Raigersfeld, *Life*, p. 36. Hay, *Landsman Hay*, p. 70.

[54] Robinson, *Jack Nastyface*, p. 33. Janet Macdonald, in *Feeding Nelson's Navy*, pp. 110–11, doubts their existence, suggesting that the crockery shown in the well-known illustrations 'were an artistic shorthand for "this is where the men eat as well as drink" and that 'hammock space was cramped enough without such things as plate racks on the walls', but the first is not tenable and the second is answered by the fact that hammocks were inboard of the muzzles, and therefore of racks.

[55] Leech, *Voice from the Main Deck*, p. 65.

[56] Lady Bourchier, *Memoir of the Late Admiral Sir Edward Codrington*, vol. I, pp. 299–300, in Rodger, *Command of the Ocean*, p. 503.

[57] Raigersfeld, *Life*, pp. 11–12.

[58] **1806**: Macdonald, *Feeding Nelson's Navy*, p. 57. **Made**: Falconer, *Marine Dictionary* (1815 edn.), in Grossman and Thomas, *Lobscouse & Spotted Dog*, p. 101. Durand, *Life and Adventures*, p. 42. According to Admiral Smyth, when issued in hulks the water used had been used to boil the meat (*sv* skilly). **Acidity**: (*A Treatise on the Scurvy*, in NRS 107, p. 15). **Richardson**: *Mariner of England*, p. 28.

[59] **Peas**: testimony of Lieutenant Pringle, c/m of Moses Hawker, ADM 1/5333. **Water gruel**: McKinley questioning William Wallbank, purser, in the c/m of Captain Shield and Lieutenant McKinley, ADM 1/5331. **Lind**: NRS 107, pp. 34–5. **East India station**: Macdonald, *Feeding Nelson's Navy*; Trotter to Howe, ADM 1/102, ff. 51–2, 15 May 1795, forwarded by Howe to the Admiralty on 16 May (f. 50). **Rancid**: Jane Bowden-Dan, 'Diet Dirt and Discipline: Medical Developments in Nelson's Navy. Dr John Snipe's Contribution', *Mariner's Mirror*, vol. 90, no. 3 (August 2004), p. 265, citing C C Lloyd, 'Victualling of the Fleet in the eighteenth and nineteenth centuries', pp. 12–13, in J Watt, E J Freeman, and W F Bynum (eds), *Starving Sailors: The influence of nutrition upon naval and maritime history* (London: National Maritime Museum, 1981). **Lind**: NRS 107, p. 15.

[60] Testimony of Sergeant John Wilmot RM, c/m of Lieutenant Richard Hawkes, ADM 1/5385.

[61] **Ganges**: *Nagle Journal*, p. 73. Robinson, *Jack Nastyface*, p. 33

[62] His defence in his court martial, ADM 1/5297. *Swiftsure*: Lovell, *From Trafalgar to the Chesapeake*, pp. 95–6. **Bread bags**: captain's order no. LVIII in the *Amazon*, 1799, NRS 138, p. 160. These were distinct from the ship's bread bags, which each held 1cwt of biscuit each.

[63] R&I, 1808, p. 289 art. II.

[64] **Cocoa**: Macdonald, *Feeding Nelson's Navy*, p. 44; **Tea**: Rodger, *Command of the Ocean*, p. 503. **Bought their own**: for example the purser's steward's mess in the *Sheerness*, off Jamaica in 1798, took tea, supplied by John Ricket, master's mate, at his expense (testimony of John Ricket, c/m of Charles King and James Dooley, ADM 1/5347). **Blane**: 'On the Comparative Health of the British Navy', 1815, in NRS 107, pp. 191–2. **Teacups**: testimony of John

Snowden, c/m of William James and Robert Willis, ADM 1/5337.

[65] NRS 48, p. 480. *Splendid*: Robinson, *Jack Nastyface*, p. 33. R&I, 1810, p. 138 art. VI. In R&I, 1745, in NRS 138, p. 11, which survived verbatim as R&I, 1790, p. 28 art. XXVI, the captain was 'not to suffer the ship's decks or gratings to be scraped oftener than shall be absolutely necessary, but take care that they be well washed and swabbed once a day, and the air let into the hold as frequently as may be' – the battle against damp again. **Saturdays:** captain's order no. 54th in the *Indefatigable*, 1812, though there the deck was cleaned before breakfast (NRS 138, pp. 192–3). **Trotter:** *Medicina Nautica* (1804), in NRS 107, p. 286. **Surgeons' journals:** Henry Bankes, 'Report From the Committee on Dr. Smyth's Petition, respecting his Discovery of Nitrous Fumigation, 10 June 1802', appendix 36, journals of Mr Blair, surgeon of the *Formidable*, 29 October 1800 to 27 January 1801, and of Mr Butt, surgeon of the *Caesar*, 22 January 1800 to 21 January 1801. **Foul air:** Trotter, in NRS 107, pp. 285, 288.

[66] ADM 51/1130. This is a complete list for the range of dates in question. The great frequency of the early ones is possibly because of the mutiny, in which the men were not allowed on deck for five days and therefore presumably did not have access to the heads.

[67] **St Vincent:** NRS 138, 18 August 1798, p. 221.

[68] **Keith:** NRS 90, p. 413.

[69] **1783:** Lavery, *Arming and Fitting*, p. 184. He provides an illustration but there is no scale. **Brodie's:** they were described as 'A Stove, ordered and approved by the Honble. the Commissioners of His Majesty's Navy for AIRING of SHIPS, in a more expeditious safe Way than ever before adopted; having a Hasp, Staple, Padlock & Key to fasten up both Doors at Night, to prevent any Damage from evil disposed or careless Persons taking out the Fire' (William N. Boog Watson, 'Alexander Brodie and his Fire-Hearths for Ships', *Mariner's Mirror*, vol. 54, no. 4 (1968), p. 409), and were to be added to the establishment of dockyard stores by warrant no. 441, 3 August 1785 (ADM 106/2509: they were to keep six spares each). Admiralty orders of 19 and 28 November 1793 established the lamps in these proportions: First and Second Rates, six each; Third and Fourth Rates, four each; Fifth Rates, three each; Sixth Rates and sloops, three each; and cutters and small vessels, two each. They cost 9d each, and were part of the boatswain's stores (ADM 106/2510, no. 297, 11 January 1794). **Surgeon's instructions:** R&I, 1808, p. 276 art. XXIII. Real or suspected infections were dealt with by fumigation with nitrous acid. **Consumption:** In 1793 the allowance of coals for airing stoves was one chaldron (thirty-six bushels) per stove per year, and in 1808 was one chaldron per deck per year, but since the stoves were issued at one per deck it can be seen the allowance was nominally unchanged (ADM 2/123, f. 165, 2 February 1793, and R&I, 1808, p. 337 art. XXIV); however, as a result of a decision in King's Bench from 22 August 1803 these were to be Winchester bushels, reducing the volume from 2222 cu in to 2150.42 cu in (ADM 106/2514, no. 447). Daily consumption is calculated with figures drawn from a helpful court martial in 1798, in which a recent paper submitted to St Vincent by the pursers of the fleet (cited as evidence) stated that a year's consumption on the home station in a First or Second Rate was sixty chaldron of coals, and forty cord of wood; and that the *Leviathan* (74) was not burning more than three bushels a day in the Mediterranean Fleet: in the last ten months the *Powerful* (74) in the same fleet had burnt seventy-two and a half chaldron of coals and eighty cord of wood, or eight to nine bushels of coal per day, which the purser thought excessive (c/m of Walter Burke, ADM 1/5347; a chaldron occupied about 46 cu ft.). There was nothing to stop a captain ordering a purser to buy more, though he might have to justify it when his accounts were passed.

[70] Robinson, *Jack Nastyface*, pp. 32–4. R&I, 1808, pp. 138–9 art. VI. Lewis, *Social History*, p. 412. The details are from captain's order no. LVIII in the *Amazon* (NRS 138, p. 159).

[71] **Well secured:** R&I, 1790, p. 101 art. II. **Powder:** WO 55/1843, *sv* Gunpowder. R&I, 1790, pp. 101–2 art. IV. R&I, 1806, p. 225 art. XXXIII. **Turn:** R&I, 1808, p. 217 art. X. **Annual**

consumption: annual consumption in time of war was 43,000 barrels containing 100lb each, of which 76½lb or 77½lb was refined saltpetre (at £40 per ton in war, and £31 per ton in peace), WO 55/1843, *sv* gunpowder & salt petre; under gunpowder is stated that annual consumption in the American War was 'about 30,000 barrels', and that the annual average manufacture, King's and private, for 1776–82 inc. was 43,665 barrels of 100lb. **That summer**: on 28 June 1810 the storage capacity (inc. floating batteries) was 216,450 whole barrels; actual quantity stored was 129,705. The object was to maintain five years' supply, but this had never been achieved, and it was proposed to build new capacity for 100,000 barrels, WO 55/1843, *sv* magazines. **Captain's permission**: R&I, 1790, p. 102 art. VI; 1808, p. 216 art. VI.

[72] **Charges**: R&I, 1790, table on p. 174; p. 104 art. XIII. Richardson, *Mariner of England*, p. 121.

[73] Copy in ADM 80/136, 19 September 1793.

[74] **1801**: R M Crew at the Ordnance Office to the Admiralty, 29 April 1801, ADM 7/677: the Admiralty had agreed on 20 November 1800 with the Board's suggestion that the new powder be used, and Crew was reporting that 'there is a sufficient quantity of it in the King's magazines to commence upon a progressive exchange of the powder on board the ships of the Royal Navy'. **1808**: R&I, 1808, appendix 29. **Cartridge**: Lavery, *Arming and Fitting*, p. 135. **1804**: order issued by Congreve, WO 55/1843. **Two shots**: printed instructions accompanying Crew's letter in ADM 7/677, and repeated in R&I, 1808, appendix 29.

[75] Falconer, *Marine Dictionary*, *sv* cannon, <http://nla.gov.au/nla.cs-ss-refs-falc-0268>.

[76] Report by Captain Augustus S Fraser, Horse Artillery, 21 November 1810, in ADM 7/677.

[77] R&I, 1790, p. 106 art. XVIII, and p. 108, art. XXV. Only the direction concerning blocks is explicitly stated in 1808, p. 225 art. XXXII.

[78] W N Glascock, *Naval Officer's Manual* (2nd ed., 1848), in Harland, *Seamanship*, p. 209.

[79] The details are from captain's order no. LVIII in the *Amazon* (NRS 138, p. 159).

[80] **A Christ's Hospital youth**: Collingwood to Walter Spencer-Stanhope, MP, 24 September 1806, NRS 146, p. 195; the 'old schoolmaster died a short time since, a victim to the gaities of his youth'. Collingwood was 'almost unique as an admiral who took a personal care of the youths of his flagship' (the *Ocean*), Rodger, *Command of the Ocean*, p. 511. The regulations required the schoolmaster 'to be early every morning at the place of teaching', but left the location unspecified (R&I, 1790, p. 137 art. IV): in 1804, in the *Dreadnought* (98), Collingwood reported that 'little Cladius arrived here about a fortnight since … I will take the best care of him, and I hope he will turn out a good boy. He is in my cabin every morning soon after six, to read, and after breakfast goes to the school master who, I believe, is an able mathematician', Collingwood to Dr Alexander Carlyle, 27 August 1804, NRS 98, p. 155. R&I, 1808, merely require him to be 'extremely attentive' to his charges, p.371 art. II. **Many of the best captains**: Rodger, *Command of the Ocean*, p. 511. **The very best man**: Sir John Jervis to Mrs M. Parker, 22 February 1793, in Rodger, *Command of the Ocean*, p. 510. **Captains were**: Rodger, *Command of the Ocean*, p. 511. **Claude**: He was really Claude Crespigny, and the boys were midshipmen in the flagship, NRS 61, p. 261 and n. He was promoted commander on 31 March 1813.

[81] **Augustus Crespigny**: Collingwood to Mrs Stead, NRS 98, pp. 276, 278, 280–1.

[82] **Of any thing like**: Collingwood to Mrs Stead, his sister, 1 July 1807, NRS 98, p. 212. **It is a pity**: Collingwood to his brother, 12 September 1806, NRS 98, p. 191. **Hickey**: Hickey, *Memoirs*, vol. I, p. 13. **Even without**: Collingwood to Mrs Stead, 17 April 1806, NRS 98, pp. 179–80. **It is a great misfortune**: Collingwood to Walter Spencer-Stanhope, MP, 14 April 1806, NRS 146, p. 193. **He has bathed**: same to same, 24 September 1806, NRS 146, pp. 195–6. **Grows strong**: Collingwood to his sister, 1 June 1807, NRS 98, p. 207. **Read history**: Collingwood to Walter Spencer-Stanhope, MP, 16 May 1808 and 20 January 1806, NRS 146, pp. 202, 188. Crespigny was promoted lieutenant on 1 November 1811 and commander on 30 May 1825; both Crespignys died within a year of their final promotion, Claude on 30 July

1813 and Augustus on 24 October 1825. Stanhope eventually returned to England, after Collingwood's death in March 1810, then after a year's private study (Collingwood had recommended learning mathematics, drawing and French, and reading history and science, and in the evenings attending lectures 'which are always in some parts of London on Natural Philosophy and Mechanics' (NRS 146, p. 210), rejoined the service in the *Undaunted* (38), whose captain had been Collingwood's flag-captain since 1805; on 17 August 1812 he was promoted lieutenant into the *Berwick* (74), and after four years joined the *Impregnable* (98), but left the navy that year (NRS 146, p. 211n.). Raigersfeld, a generation earlier, was advised by Lord Hood to attend Mr de Roy's mathematical school in Old Burlington Street after his first cruise, of three and a half years, which he did for four months; then he attended an ex-employee of the Royal Observatory for a year, in Portsmouth, concentrating on spherical trigonometry, and 'other branches of calculation and science, which, though not immediately necessary to a sea officer, would occasionally be of infinite use to me in various ways'. He also learnt the guitar. He gave performances at a subscription concert held once a fortnight at Portsmouth run by his tutor, the organist at the dockyard, but 'the audience upon the evenings of the performance were generally outnumbered by the wooden benches'. At the end of the year he had learnt enough mathematics for a sea officer, and he joined the *Vestal* (28) (Raigersfeld, *Life*, pp. 37–8).

[83] R&I, 1790, pp. 136–7, 'The Schoolmaster'. An applicant had to produce two certificates: that he had been examined by the master, wardens and assistants of the Trinity House of Deptford Strand, and was 'well skilled in the theory and practice of navigation' (in 1808 this could be from the Royal Academy at Portsmouth); and that 'persons of known credit' testified to 'the sobriety of his life and conversation'. **Regulations**: July 1805, in ADM 7/412. Section 10 lays down that no person is to be examined for lieutenant or sub-lieutenant who has served as a warrant officer (except schoolmaster) or as acting second master or second master and pilot, even if they have their full time as well as time served in one or more of these capacities, and time served as captain's clerk or acting lieutenant did not count in the six years. R&I, 1808, p. 371 art. III, and p. 372 art. V. *Gloucester*: 1812 is NRS 91, pp. 20, 21; this was with the permission of the captain, but Mangin was unable to get him the pay, or a regular appointment; 1815 is NRS 82, p. 51. **Chaplains**: they received the Queen Anne bounty of £20, plus £5 a year from the pay of every midshipman and volunteer first class they taught (F B Sullivan, 'The Naval Schoolmaster during the Eighteenth Century and the early Nineteenth Century', *Mariner's Mirror*, vol. 62, no. 4 (1976), p. 322). They were relatively widespread – between 1712 and 1824 more than a thousand warrants were issued to at least 394 people, more than half of whom served more than one appointment, and ten of whom served over twenty years (pp. 311–12). 1712 is the date of the first warrant, but certificates were issued by Trinity House from 1702, when they were created by an order in council of Queen Anne; the total who served was probably 500–600 (p. 317).

[84] **Times**: captain's order no. 40th in the *Indefatigable* (NRS 138, p. 190). Both watches is a supposition, one answer to the problem identified by Macdonald (*Feeding Nelson's Navy*, p. 101), on which this section is based. **Cooper**: NRS 91, p.247; Nicol, *Life and Adventures*, p. 48. **Net**: NRS 138, p. 356; Macdonald, *Feeding Nelson's Navy*, p. 101. The ship's company of the *Suffolk* (74), in Colombo Roads, wrote to the Admiralty in 1798 that they had received intelligence from England (the *Bombay Courier*, 9 October 1797) that the grand fleet 'have received the indulgences granted by an Act of Parliament which was passed about the latter end of March or the beginning of April 1797. We therefore considering ourselves to be upon an equilibrium with those at home, wish to be, & have the same allowances as they enjoy.' The letter is undated but was written on 15 January; they were court martialled for it, on 5 and 6 June 1798, after five months' confinement.

[85] **Spencer**: Spencer to Jervis, 4 May 1797, NRS 48, p. 399.

[86] *Saturn*: c/m of Philip Le Verconte, ADM 1/5340. **Victualling Board**: ADM 30/44, f. 108.

Office of Stores: *eg*, 18 August 1796, 'small beams 2 No. with scales and weights complete' to be delivered to the fleet at Falmouth, ADM 106/2822. *Sunderland*: c/m of Henry Nelson, ADM 1/5297. **18 May:** ADM 2/133. This was slow in coming for ships on foreign stations. The ship's company of the *Suffolk* (74), in Colombo Roads, wrote to the Admiralty in 1798 that they had received intelligence from England (the *Bombay Courier*, 9 October 1797) that the grand fleet 'have received the indulgences granted by an Act of Parliament which was passed about the latter end of March or the beginning of April 1797. We therefore considering ourselves to be upon an equilibrium with those at home, wish to be, & have the same allowances as they enjoy'. The letter is undated but was written on 15 January; they were court martialled for it, on 5 and 6 June 1798, after five months' confinement. According to the master, when the captain asked their grievances, they answered 'they wanted the indulgence the ship had in Europe, additional allowance of beef & pork, liberty to go on shore, prize money to be paid & their own mode of punishing offenders.' The sentences were that they should be either hanged or flogged round the fleet with all pay due mulcted in favour of the hospital at Greenwich, as appropriate (ADM 1/5345).

[87] **2lb:** R&I, 1790, p. 127 art. XXXI. **Afterwards:** Testimony of Mr Maude, c/m of Captain George Hopewell Stephens, ADM 1/5342. **Shrinkage:** Bridport to Admiralty, 14 September 1797, NRS 141, pp. 269–70. *Jason* and *Garland*: letters and turnover of 11 January 1798 (*Garland*) and 14 February 1798 (*Jason*) in ADM 1/2498. R&I, 1808, p. 306 art. I, and pp. 308–9 arts VI and VIII.

[88] R&I, 1808, pp. 318–19 art. III.

[89] R&I, 1790, p. 115 art. I, and very similar wording in R&I, 1808, p. 316 art. I.

[90] R&I, 1790, p. 115 art IX; R&I, 1808, p. 322 art. VII.

[91] **Preservation:** ADM 30/44, f. 20; R&I, 1808, pp. 322–3 art. VI. **Custom:** Rodger, *Wooden World*, p. 91. **Waste of cask:** R&I, 1790, pp. 125–6 art. XXVIII; 1808, p. 349 art. XXXIX. **1770:** ADM 30/44, f. 181. **1808:** R&I, 1808, Purser's form no. 17.

[92] R&I, 1808, pp. 322–3 art. VI.

[93] **Necessary money:** and for ships with sixty men or under, 17d per man per month in sea victualling. R&I, 1790, p. 117, art. IX; 1808, p. 322 art. VII, with a table for ships of smaller complements. According to the Victualling Board, this was actually necessary money and extra necessary money, the former variable, the latter 8d per man per month whatever the complement (but not paid for supernumeraries) and only paid in sea victualling, ADM 30/44, f. 17. *Druid*: c/m of Charles Selwin Rann, ADM 1/5348. *Lion*: c/m of Moses Hawker, ADM 1/5333. Rodger, *Wooden World*, p. 89. **Other payments:** R&I, 1790, p. 117 art. IX, also in ADM 30/44, f. 17; R&I, 1808, pp. 324–5 art. VII. **Extras and poundage:** R&I, 1745, in NRS 138, p. 23 (which clause is confined to dead men's clothes); R&I, 1808, pp. 360–1 art. III (which extends it to all slop clothes and bedding) adds it did not apply to all slop clothes issued by him to supernumeraries borne for victuals only or those discharged to other ships, at the final settlement of accounts.

[94] This was by an order in council of 2 November, 'for the more regular preparation and transmission to the proper Department of [*sic*] Office, of the necessary muster books, quarterly accounts, and pursery accounts', and transmitted by Admiralty order. The main other changes were that on receipt of these orders a survey was to be taken on all pursery stores on board, and an account transmitted within a month; all substitutes had to be authorised by the captain, and the quarterly accounts were to contain the reason why; a victualling book was to be kept of all individuals on the ship's books; all reports of surveys and receipts were to be kept in triplicate, one copy to be sent immediately to the Victualling Office, one to be sent with his accounts and one to be kept by him as a backup; and all those who wanted to be pursers to be examined by three experienced pursers and a captain. A copy is in ADM 7/972.

[95] *Autobiography of Joseph Bates*, chapter three.

[96] **1812**: it followed a new set of regulations for chaplains, greatly improving their pay and status. NRS 96, p. 318n. **1815**: The books were to be issued gratis to the men and mustered at divisions with the clothes of the ship's company, and returned as ship's stores when the ship was paid off. Admiralty Office, 18 March 1815, in ADM 7/226.

[97] *Superb* (74), Rosier Bay, 26 November 1801: order to Lieutenant Gill, ADM 80/141, out-letters f. 133; a similar order is dated 16 July 1802, f. 148.

[98] Hall, *Fragments*, vol. III, pp. 138–9.

[99] 'with but after': since 28 September 1808 they had had the rank of lieutenant. **Duties**: R&I, 1790, pp. 95–8; 1808, pp. 182–98.

[100] Hall, *Fragments*, vol. III, pp. 139–45.

[101] **As Mr Male**: 'Journal of a Naval Surgeon', in Long, *Naval Yarns*, pp. 92–3. R&I, 1790, pp. 204–5; art. XVI directed the upper deck, to remove the danger of fire, and art. XVII directed the mixing and the officers of the watch. R&I, 1808, p. 300 art. XXI (also p. 137 art. IV) and pp. 301–2 art. XXII. **At least four times**: Macdonald, *Feeding Nelson's Navy*, p. 42. **A due proportion**: R&I, 1808, p. 301 art. XXI. The official daily allowance of spirits or wine was half a pint and a pint respectively, a substitution for the ration of a gallon of beer. Traditionally the regulations directed that spirits, wine and beer were stored aboard ships in Winchester gallons (277.25 cu. in.) and then issued to the ship's company in wine gallons (231 cu. in.); this was one of the practices abolished after the Great Mutinies of 1797, and thenceforward they were stored and issued to the men in wine gallons (25 April 1797; NRS 6, p. 334n. has the details mixed up; cf. R&I, 1808, p. 291 art. VII). **Raw**: Testimony of William Thurston, c/m of Lawrence Henderson, ADM 1/5348.

[102] C/m of Robert Nelson, ADM 1/5436.

[103] **In some ships**: for example aboard the *Royal William* (NRS 138, p. 387); and in the *Macedonian* the boys drew half the quantity of spirits and wine, and were allowed pay for the remainder (Leech, *Voice from the Main Deck*, p. 26). The credit for unused boys' wine in the *Superb*, 1 January 1804 to 31 March 1805, 1,022 gallons at 1s per gallon, was £51 2s 0d. (ADM 80/141, out-letters (unfolioed after 283).) *Unité*: NRS 91, p. 141. **Small town**: *eg, Royal William*, c/m of Captain David Hotchkiss, ADM 1/5342, and c/m of James Whitton in the *Sultan* prisonship ADM 1/5347.

[104] Hall, *Fragments*, vol. III, pp. 139–47. **Glass**: ADM 49/121, f. 59. The log-glasses were 5d each, the watch glasses were 1s 10 for the hour and 11d for the half hour.

Chapter 6
THE CAPTAIN DINES

[1] *Custom*: 'As I was entrusted with charge of a watch [as gunner of the *Prompte* (28)], it became my turn to dine with the captain', Richardson, *Mariner of England*, p. 149. *Gloucester*: NRS 91, p. 21.

[2] NRS 97, pp. 306, 194.

[3] NRS 97, pp. 119, 153, 154, 28, 285–6.

[4] The table and linen are Collingwood's, in the *Mediator* (44) in 1785 (NRS 98, pp. 17–18). The crockery is borrowed from an inventory of the 'necessaries received on board' the royal yacht *Augusta* in 1771 for the Lords Commissioners' use in their visitation of the dockyards, which is particularly interesting because it records not just the goods supplied but also what was lost or broken in the cruise, which lasted from 10 May to 26 November. The number of commissioners is not given, but that summer there were only seven in office.

Earthen Ware	Number and Quantity Received on Board	Broke and lost by Accident in the Voyage
Cream Coloured Dishes	32	6
Plates	7½ doz.	2 doz [and] 1
Tureens	2	
Baking Dishes	6	
Sauce Boats	10	
Small Plates	18	6
Salts	8	2
Fish Draners [sic]	2	1
Jug	1	
White Wash Hand Basons	12	2
Red Pans	12	8
China		
Blue and White Breakfast Cups and Saucers	18	3 Cups, 6 Saucers
Blue and White Cups and Saucers	18	5 Cups, 4 Saucers
Blue and White Basons and Plates	12	6 Basons, 3 Plates
Blue and White Cream Pots	5	
Sugar Dish	1	1
Blue and White China Pint Basons	12	3
Blue and White China half pint ditto	6	2
Blue and White China Bowls	2	1
Red Tea Pots	6	1
Black do.	2	1
Glass		
Wine decanters	6	2
Large Water decanters	2	1
Wine and Water Glasses	2 doz.	8
Wash Glasses	12	
Cut Wine Glasses	24	15
Champaign do.	24	5
Common do.	24	
Mustard Pots	3	1

The list continues with kitchen equipment including a fish and a turbot kettle, a Dutch oven, coffee and chocolate pots, single and double gridirons, a paste roller, twenty-four patty pans, and an oval mould, an apple corer, two turnip scoops, a case of larding and dobing pins and two jelly bags (it was a summer cruise), and their linen included forty-eight table cloths and seventy-two napkins (Inventory submitted by Charles Wray, in ADM 106/3546 part one). The Wedgwood tray is Dillon's, which he bought to impress his officers when fitting out the *Childers* brig, but which did not go entirely to plan: 'As time passed on, I invited my brother officers to come and dine with me. The tray which I depended on so much had not yet been used, but now was the time for displaying it. We were all seated in my cabin waiting the appearance of dinner, when my steward announced that the passage leading into it was so narrow that the tray could not be brought in. Here was a disappointment! The dishes were handed in separately' (NRS 97, pp. 79, 90). See also Macdonald, *Feeding Nelson's Navy*, pp. 123–4. *Spartan*: ADM 1/1548, Capt. B56. The total was $523 3q 4r; he was allowed £150, or $667 at the standard exchange rate.

[5] Hickey, *Memoirs*, vol. III, p. 116.

6 Pocock, *Terror Before Trafalgar*, pp. 170–1, citing John Ruskin, *Praeterita and Dilecta*, p. 586.
7 **Table money**: originally granted to captains as a recompense for their being forbidden to carry bullion without orders, in 1686, by 1790 it had become an essential part of any flag officer's economy (Rodger, *Command of the Ocean*, p. 124); ADM 7/911. Commodores with commissions as commanders in chief received it at the same rate. It was abolished by Admiralty order dated 10 December 1816, citing order in council of 25 November 1816, with effect from 1 January 1817, and replaced by an allowance, so that flag officers and commodores with a captain under them when commissioned as commanders-in-chief had a pay of £3 per day in lieu of table money, while the flag or broad pendant was flying within the limits of the station. **Nelson**: Lavery, *Nelson and the Nile*, p. 61. **St Vincent**: Matthew Sheldon, 'How to Re-fit an Old Admiral for Sea', *Mariner's Mirror*, vol. 87, no. 4 (November 2001), p. 479 and Macdonald, *Feeding Nelson's Navy*, p. 129; 'four gallons' is Sheldon, p. 479. **Kitchen equipment**: Sheldon, p. 481. He notes that this is only a sample of the invoices sent to St Vincent, and that St Vincent did not buy them himself, so it is not possible to know how exactly the material bought matched his taste. **An admiral's table**: essential details are from 'An account of the bedding' in ADM 95/17; this inventory lists pewter tableware, which was largely outdated by 1810. Diaper is 'a linen fabric (or an inferior fabric of "union" or cotton) woven with a small and simple pattern, formed by the different directions of the thread, with the different reflexions of light from its surface, and consisting of lines crossing diamond-wise, with the spaces variously filled up by parallel lines, a central leaf or dot, etc.' (OED) and appears in several Admiralty and Navy Board accounts, such as 'Plate and linen formerly used at Hill House, Chatham, and now at Sheerness for the lodgings of any commissioner who may occasionally reside there', also in ADM 95/17.
8 NMM, JOD/10. Other recipes from this notebook appear in NRS 138, pp. 616–21. See also Macdonald, *Feeding Nelson's Navy*, pp. 135–9 for *placement* and procedure.
9 **2pm**: Pope, *Life in Nelson's Navy*, p. 171. **Forecastlemen**: NRS 91, p. 245. **1808**: R&I, 1808, p. 186 art. XIII. **Indefatigable**: NRS 138, p. 194.
10 **Wooden barrels**: Lavery (*Arming and Fitting*, p. 190; *Bellona*, p. 19; *Nelson and the Nile*, p. 136) states that a butt for water is 108 gallons, measure not stated, but meaning beer measure (this can be demonstrated by calculation: beer and ale measure are synonyms). The Victualling Board's precedent book contains a table of tunnage that shows two butts make a tun/ton (ADM 30/44, f. 260), and there is various evidence that supports this in practice, for example a letter from the Victualling Board to the Admiralty in 1800 stating that 150 tons is equal to 300 butts of water (NRS 141, p. 481), and this is assumed at p. 496 of Rodger, *Command of the Ocean*, citing several statements of weights of provisions. These tons are weight not capacity. Macdonald (*Feeding Nelson's Navy*, p. 175) states that a butt is 108 gallons wine measure and 126 gallons beer measure, according to content, which is wrong; she also equates beer/ale measure with Imperial measure (*Feeding Nelson's Navy*, p. 174), which is incorrect for the period under discussion, being equated only in 1819, when the ale gallon was made to 'contain exactly ten pounds Avoirdupois of distilled water, at 62° of Fahrenheit, being nearly equal to 277.2 cubic inches', instead of the customary 282 cu. in. This standard gallon was redefined in 1834 as 277.274 cu. in., and the modern Imperial gallon was defined most recently (1985) as exactly 4546.09ml. Leaguers are even more problematic: they are not multiples of the successive sizes and were not always used (they are not given in the printed forms supplied to the dockyards to record the 'Account of the Draught of Water … and the Weight and Quantity of all Provisions' of ships sailing on Channel and Foreign service, and many ships sailed without any); Lavery claims in *Arming and Fitting* that a leaguer for water is 150 gallons and in *Bellona* that it is 189 gallons (Macdonald is certainly wrong in her belief that a leaguer meant a tun, English measure – this is based on a misreading of her source); John Edye's *Calculations relating to equipment and displacement of ships of war* (1832, at http://home.clara.net/rabarker/Barrels.htm), gives it as 190 wine gallons, containing water

weighing 1,592lb); Admiral Smyth, referring to the period before water tanks, gives it as 159 imperial gallons. Edye's figures work out to be correct to 4½oz per leaguer, equivalent to the product of rounding, and if Admiral Smyth's figure is a misprint and the *Arming and Fitting* figure an oversight, ships typically sailed from the Royal Dockyards with their barrels about 95 per cent full. In the Seven Years War ships only used the ground tier in an emergency (Rodger, *Wooden World*, pp. 91–2). During the French Revolutionary Wars they slowly became used to drawing on it, as is evident from a letter Admiral Bridport wrote to the Admiralty on 31 July 1798, advising them that 'keeping three deck ships cruizing nine weeks [blockading Brest] to occasion them to begin upon the ground tier of water causes great time and trouble in the refilling them' (NRS 141, p. 322). It was characteristic of the navy of the period, however, that as the war progressed and ships became expected to keep their station for months or even years this labour became part of the daily routine.

[11] Glascock, *Naval Sketch-Book*, vol. I, p. 56.

[12] **Started**: R&I, 1808, p. 186 art. XII. **On deck**: R&I, 1808, p. 188 art. IX. Macdonald, *Feeding Nelson's Navy*, p. 85. **Hydra**: Mark, *At Sea with Nelson*, p. 84. **Vocabulary**: J J Moore, *Midshipman's or British Mariner's Vocabulary*, cited in *OED*, sv Scuttlebutt. **Water whip stay tackle**: it was used to 'shift water casks', and was 'often kept rigged semi-permanently for lifting lighter articles in and out', Harland, *Seamanship*, p. 280. **Hoisted**: R&I, 1808, p. 300. *Duke of York*: NRS 90, p. 261. **Blane**: NRS 107, p. 184. *Dreadnought*: c/m of John Griffin, ADM 1/5297. ADM 1/1858, Capt. G331a.

[13] ADM 1/3174.

[14] ADM 1/1858, Capt. G331a; no turnover.

[15] *Culloden*: Hay, *Landsman Hay*, pp. 170–1. *Castor*: c/m of Solomon Nathan, ADM 1/5407.

[16] 'A cask': Moore, *British Mariner's Vocabulary*. **Cocks**: based on the *Queen Charlotte* (100): 'The cocks of the quarterdeck scuttle butts were turned, and water and wet swabs were brought from all parts of the ship as fast as possible' (testimony of Alexander Campbell, c/m for the loss of the *Queen Charlotte*, ADM 1/5352). **Marine sentinel**: captain's orders in the *Blenheim* (98) in the Mediterranean in 1796, NRS 138, pp. 224–5. **Pasley**: Pasley, *Private Sea Journals*, 72. **Carteret**: Wallis (ed), *Carteret's Voyage*, vol. I, pp. 21 and 151–2. He had been told by the Navy Board that an awning would be 'very improper to be built on the quarterdeck of a sloop' (*Voyage*, p. 21), but as recently as 16 February 1727/8 the Board had decided that it having been observed that sloops have awnings that hinder their sailing, they are for the future to have awnings 'not to exceed six feet in length, before the after cabin, to be covered with tarred canvas only so as that upon occasion it may be rolled up to the middle of the awning', NRS 120, p. 211). Awnings were supplied from 1784 (ADM 106/2509, 3 December 1784, no number; NRS 138, p. 11 notes that awnings were supplied for southern waters); the *Hannibal* (74) had both a poop and a quarter-deck awning in Jamaica in 1798. **Scoops**: ADM 49/121, f. 36. They cost 9s 6d a dozen in 1781, and 11s 11d in 1799. **Nelson**: Nicolas, *Dispatches and Letters of Lord Nelson*, vol. VII, p. 260. Bristol water is 'the water of warm springs at Clifton near Bristol, used medicinally' (*OED*); **Castle Eden**: Hickey, *Memoirs*, vol. IV, p. 373. Ranken, *Shipmates*, p. 68.

Petty officers: c/m of Solomon Nathan (ADM 1/5407), testimony of Robert Woodward. In the *Camilla* (20), men apparently stored water:

> Prisoner: Do you recollect whether in the early part of the passage [from England to Barbados, in summer 1807], I had ever given the Supernumerary Marines an additional allowance of water, upon the representation that they were not provided with conveniencies [*sic*] for containing their allowance of water at that time; and if I did order a cask to be given the supernumerary marines to keep their allowance of water separate from the ships companies [*sic*] at the request of Captain Gerrard.
> Answer [by Lt Frederick Waters, RM]: The first part they had an additional allowance,

the latter part their water was put in a tank separate from the seamens
(Testimony, c/m of Captain John Bowen, ADM 1/5353).

The *Camilla* was a very small ship, escorting a convoy, and her supernumerary marines had
had their berths removed when a sick bay was built under the half-deck, midway through the
passage, which is perhaps why the captain had to make special arrangements.
[17] **Weighing**: assuming that water was measured by the beer gallon, of 282 cu. in.; see n. 10
above and the arguments below.

All the standard-issue salt food was boiled. (Fresh meat was sometimes roasted, *eg*, c/m of
Captain Pakenham, ADM 1/5329 f.268.) To steep the meat and cook it in the Brodie's stove a
ship-of-the-line needed for its official complement 87½ to 190¼ gallons every pork day or 175
to 382½ gallons every beef day (between about 13¾ and 60 hundredweight of water) from the
hold. The volume of water to fill the boilers weighs about 39 to 62 hundredweight, but they
were not filled quite to the brim, because (for example) the cook had to scoop the slush from
the meat as it cooked, and from this volume must be deducted the volume of the meat itself,
and of any vegetables, pudding, etc. boiled alongside. I have not seen a statement of the
amount of water needed to cook the meat but a recipe by Soyer exists from the Crimean War
using War Office salt beef that calls for three (Imperial) quarts of water for two 3lb pieces of
salt beef, so on this basis (a pint per pound) a ship needed 62½ to 106¼ gallons on a pork day
and 125 to 212½ gallons on a beef day. The salt meat needed to be steeped before use, and
ships were equipped with steep tubs, later cisterns, but Robert Wilson, who served in the
Unité, states in his account of a ship's organisation that 'The salt meat is to be well steeped in
salt water, in proper steep-tubs or tanks' (NRS 91, p. 246). Since a floating body displaces its
own weight of water, it is possible to calculate, rather simplistically, the minimum volume
needed for each day's meat (assuming for convenience that the discrepancies in the weight of
the pieces recorded in the ships' logs would average out). The gallon used in the Navy Board
warrants is not specified, but it can be deduced that the 282 cu. in. beer gallon is used because
(a) this produces results closest to the stated capacities for warrants from 1757 onwards, and
(b) elsewhere, wine measure (*eg* the daily beer issue) or Winchester measure (*eg* the pease
issue) are always stated (the beer gallon was the 'default' gallon on land).

Figures in italics are calculated from dimensions in the warrants; the warrants do not state
whether they are internal or external, but external is more likely from the contexts.
'Contents of the Boilers' for Brodie's stoves, and the water needed to cook salt pork and salt
beef at the standard-issue sizes (per warrant no. 643, 28 February 1791, ADM 106/2509).

Gun-ships	Men	Contents of the Boilers, gallons	Water displaced and remaining on a pork day, gallons	Water displaced and remaining on a beef day, gallons	Water needed to cook the pork, gallons	Water needed to cook the beef, gallons	Total volume required, pork/beef, gallons
100	850	433	*85/348*	*170/263*	106.25	212.5	*191.25/382.5*
98 or 90	750	380	*75/305*	*150/230*	93.75	187.5	*168.75/337.5*
84	650	325	*65/260*	*130/195*	81.25	162.5	*146.25/292.5*
74	600	300	*60/240*	*120/180*	75	150	*135/270*
64	500	250	*25/225*	*50/200*	62.5	125	*87.5/175*

The capacities remained fairly constant from 1757, as the following tables show.

In 1757, the kettle was 'a single piece, divided into two unequal parts' (Lavery, *Arming and
Fitting*, p. 197). Four figures are given, 'whole length of both parts in the clear athwartship',
'breadth fore and aft', 'depth' and 'least part thwart ship'; the last was not used to calculate
the external volume.

Guns	Men	Whole length	Breadth	Depth	Least part	Large kettle, gallons	Small kettle, gallons	Total, gallons	External volume, gallons
100	850	78	51¼	30	29½	266	159	425	425.27
90	750	74⅛	49¼	29	27¾	235	140	375	375.42
80	650	69¾	47	28	26¼	202	122.5	324.5	325.5
74	580	64½	46½	27½	24	183	109	292	292.48
70	520	61¾	44	27	23¼	162	98	260	260.14
64	500	61	43½	26¾	22⅞	157	93	250	251.71
60	420	55¼	41	26?	21	129	81	210	212.87

(ADM 95/17, f. 267)

In 1777 it was still a single, divided copper.

1777

Guns	Length, ins	Width, ins	Depth, ins	External volume, gallons
100	78	51¼	30	425.27
90 & 84	74⅛	49¼	29	375.42
80 & 74	65½	47	27½	300.21
64	61	43½	26¾	251.71
60	55¼	41	26½	212.87

(ADM 106/2508, no. 716, 7 August 1777)

Each stove had two boilers (also called coppers, furnaces and kettles in various Navy Board documents) side by side, a large and a small. They were iron, but from 8 August 1800 ships going to the East Indies had been given copper boilers instead (ADM 106/2512, no. 428); ships had an extra copper for the use of troops when on board (ADM 2/137, 16 Apr 1799), but it's not clear how this was fitted. As noted in Macdonald, *Feeding Nelson's Navy* and McGowan, *Victory*, the replica Brodie's stove as fitted in the *Victory* has two boilers of 100 and 150 gallons, which contradicts this warrant; at present this contradiction is inexplicable, but Janet Macdonald suspects, for sound reasons, that the replica stove as fitted is not correct; Peter Goodwin's account of the *Victory* in July 1797, when she was on fresh not salt meat, notes that her galley needed about 400–500 gallons daily, of a total consumption of three tons, or 672 gallons (Goodwin, *Nelson's Ships*, p. 247 col. 1), and L. G. Carr Laughton's report on his search through the Admiralty papers for details of the *Victory's* construction and fitting notes that the Brodie's stove had a capacity of half a gallon for every man of the complement ('H.M.S. *Victory*. Report to the *Victory* Technical Committee of a search among the Admiralty records', *Mariner's Mirror*, vol. 10, no. 2 (1924), p. 202). The new Lamb and Nicholson stove began to be introduced in 1810, but the *Splendid* had been at sea throughout 1809 and 1810. According to Charles Nordhoff, who served in the USS *Columbus* (2,480 tons), there were three coppers for 700 men, each 6ft deep, 4ft wide and 5–6ft long, which works out as 1.05–1.26 English beer gallons per man; she had iron water tanks (Nordhoff, *Sailor Life*, p. 165).

[18] **Standard issue**: ADM 30/44, f. 7. 180 tons is 38,880 gallons beer measure. *Victory*: Goodwin, *Nelson's Ships*, p. 246 col. 1. St Vincent: two tons is four butts; he suspected that she was in fact using six due to the presence of unauthorised women aboard, who were notorious for washing their underwear in fresh water (NRS 141, p. 549). St Vincent complained to Spencer that he was 'very much hurt by the manner in which the ships of the line come to me so very deficient in water', alleging this was part of a conspiracy 'for the express purpose of short cruises and to avoid being sent on foreign service'. He claimed the *Edgar* ought to be able to stow 200 tons with four

months' provisions (NRS 141, p. 470); in fact she left Plymouth on 24 October 1799 with 200 tons 11cwt 2qr 20lb in 88 leaguers, 255 butts, 7 puncheons and 19 hogsheads for her 537 men (ADM 95/71). On 21 October he advised the Admiralty, 'I cannot too much applaud the conduct of Captain Hood of His Majesty's Ship the *Courageux* [74] who, by stowing a great quantity of water on his gun deck' brought out a great quantity of stores for the fleet (NRS 141, p. 570). **Osbridge's machine**: from 1765 all ships going on foreign voyages and from 8 June 1779 all ships, 6 November 1765, ADM 2/235 (in *Mariner's Mirror*, vol. 64, no. 4 (1978)); ADM 106/2508, 8 June 1779, no. 858. Transports on foreign service to be supplied, on the application of the agent for transports, ADM 106/2517, no. 647, 29 September 1806 (where it is Ottridge's machine), to Portsmouth and Plymouth. **It was made**: J C Beaglehole (ed), *The Journals of Captain James Cook* (Hakluyt Society, 1961), II, 10n, in T M Conway, 'Osbridge's Machine', *Mariner's Mirror*, vol. 89, no. 2 (May 2003), pp. 224–5. **Blane**: *Observations on Diseases Incident to Seamen*, 1785, pp. 311–12, in J A Sulivan, 'The Distillation and Purification of Water at Sea', *Mariner's Mirror*, vol. 65, no. 2 (1979), pp. 161–2. **Office of Bills**: ADM 49/121, f. 45. **Distilling**: Burney records in his *New Universal Dictionary of the Marine* several experiments in distilling sea water. Dr Irving, 'by whom distillation was generally introduced into the British navy', constructed a device tested in 1771 that used the fact that 'Every ship's kettle is divided into two parts, by a partition in the middle; one of these is only used when peas or oatmeal are dressed; but water is, at the same time, kept in the other to preserve its bottom', and 'by filling the spare part of the copper with sea-water, and fitting on the lid and tube, he has shewn that sixty gallons of fresh-water may be drawn off during the boiling of the above-mentioned provisions, without any additional fuel'. **Intrepid**: P K Crimmin, 'A Distilling Machine of 1772', *Mariner's Mirror*, vol. 52, no. 4 (1966), p. 392. **Pasley**: Pasley, *Private Sea Journals*, p. 61. **East India Company ships**: Hickey, *Memoirs*, vol. IV, pp. 8, 373, and 442 (the *Castle Eden*); Ranken, *Shipmates*, pp. 8–9 (the *Charlton*).

[19] ADM 30/44, f. 18 (a tun was calculated at two butts, or three puncheons, or four hogsheads, or six barrels, or eight half-hogsheads; three leaguers made two tuns); f. 236. These months are lunar months of twenty-eight days. R&I, 1808, pp. 349–50 art. XXXIX; pp. 293–4 art. XII.

[20] **Collingwood**: Collingwood to Rear Admiral Purvis, 1 December 1807, NRS 98, p. 229.

[21] **Whitewash**: ADM 106/2517, no. 783, 31 November 1806 and ADM 106/2517, no. 790, 21 November 1806 (the instructions for making it are given in ADM 106/2517, no. 852, 11 December 1806). **8cwt**: the *Milford* (74), stored for Channel service on 1 November 1809, carried 5cwt 2qr 24lb, ADM 1/1548, Capt. B2. **Ready-made stocks**: Lovell, *From Trafalgar to the Chesapeake*, p. 47. **York**: ADM 51/2989, 28 June. **Mars**: NRS 107, p. 264. **However**: Dr Snipe to Nelson, 7 November 1803, Wellcome Western MS 3680 (vol. 14), in Jane Bowden-Dan, 'Diet, Dirt and Discipline: Medical Developments in *Nelson's Navy*. Dr John Snipe's Contribution', *Mariner's Mirror*, vol. 90, no. 3 (August 2004), p. 267. **Proper procedure**: for example the *Vanguard* (74) in January 1796, Goodwin, *Nelson's Ships*, p. 169 col. 1.

[22] ADM 80/141, ff. 137–8.

[23] **Launch**: cutter-rigged, Lavery, *Arming and Fitting*, p. 219; mizzen sails, ADM 106/2514, no. 161, 25 August 1803; double-banked, ADM 106/2509, no. 6, January 1783. **1804**: ADM 106/2515, 30 August 1804, no. 163. The established lengths did not change.

[24] Raigersfeld, *Life*, p. 23.

[25] Wybourn, *Sea Soldier*, p. 73.

[26] NRS 31, pp. 132–3.

[27] Written defence, c/m of William Saunders, ADM 1/5345.

[28] R&I, 1808, p. 275 art. XIX, p. 276 art. XXII and p. 277 art. XXIV.

[29] NRS 9, p. 126.

[30] *Autobiography of Joseph Bates*.

[31] ADM 2/123, f. 85, 8 January 1793, Admiralty to the Victualling Board.

[32] **St Michael's**: ADM 80/141, out-letters f. 42. **Minorca**: 'I am now unmooring with very little

water in the ships, for this island does not afford much more than we drink', Keith to Nelson, 9 July 1799, Nicolas, *Dispatches and Letters of Lord Nelson*, vol. III, p. 415n. **Gibraltar**: Commissioner J N Inglefield to the Admiralty, 29 September 1797, '1799 to 1803 Tank at Gibraltar papers relative thereto', in ADM 106/3546 part one. **Ball**: Captain Ball to the Commissioners for Victualling HM Navy, ADM 7/55, 30 June 1797. The *Dolphin* was, according to David Lyon, a hospital ship.

[33] Keats to Rear Admiral Sir James Saumarez, 14 March 1802, ADM 80/141, out-letters ff. 140–2.

[34] '1799 to 1803 Tank at Gibraltar papers relative thereto', in ADM 106/3546 part one. Inglefield to the Admiralty, 29 September 1797, 17 November 1797, 30 December 1797. The estimate was £33,092 10s 9d, and the final cost was £33,097 3s 3d, less the cost of 300,000 bricks sent out from Woolwich (with a hundred barrows to move them with), and its construction involved the removal of 594,600 cubic feet of material at 5d per foot. (According to Ordnance Board figures, 1,000 bricks when embarked weighed 2.5 tons, and of 100,000 bricks shipped to Gibraltar, 73,105 were delivered whole, and 31,460 as bat – 'suppose two to a brick = 15,730; deficiency, 11,165'. WO 55/1843; WO 55/637, Orders Relating to Artificers, etc, f. 20.)

[35] Keats to Saumarez, 9 August 1801, ADM 80/141, out-letters f. 75.

[36] Lavery, *Arming and Fitting*, p. 190.

[37] NRS 141, p. 530.

[38] ADM 51/2910; *Sultan*, ADM 1/2860.

[39] Lavery, *Arming and Fitting*, pp. 191–2.

[40] **The mess cooks had been waiting**: this organisation uses some of the plausible sequence proposed by Janet Macdonald (*Feeding Nelson's Navy*, p. 114). She concludes that each net or bag was identified by a tally with the mess number, noting that it is 'pure conjecture, but would work', and suitable tally sticks have been recovered from the *Invincible* (McGuane, *Heart of Oak*, p. 45). However, the procedure I have adopted is that related by Robert Wilson, who served in the *Unité* (38) and others from 1805 to 1808 (NRS 91, p. 246). She also concludes that the mess cooks arrived at their messes before 'the general stampede', but this is contradicted by Captain Hall (*Fragments*, vol. III, pp. 147–8).

[41] **One o'clock**: this is possibly a little early in the day for 1810, but a change of dinner hour was more likely in a frigate than in a ship-of-the-line. **Lunch**: on 29 June 1815 the flag captain at Portsmouth 'called on board [the *Horatio*] to see me, and insisted upon my accompanying him to the Flagship to lunch with him.' Dillon left the *Horatio* at midday and was back at his lodgings at 1.30, where he found an invitation to dinner that day with friends at Havant; he was about to set off when he was interrupted (NRS 97, p. 335). **Wardroom table**: see p. 143 above. **Presidency**: testimony of Lieutenant Alexander Renny, c/m of Lieutenant Somerled McDonnell, ADM 1/5352. **It was now**: Hay, *Landsman Hay*, p. 68.

[42] **French service**: this lasted until the middle of the nineteenth century. **President**: or by a guest. Dillon tells a story of how, when dining with Lady Hamilton in 1813, he was asked to carve a bird, but had no knife or fork and had to use his fingers (NRS 97, p. 277). **To all**: Jane Grigson, *English Food* (1974, rev. edn 1992, Penguin, 1993), p. 3. **Examples**: see p. 127. **General Sir Alured Clarke**: Hickey, *Memoirs*, vol. IV, p. 167: 'to take salt with the point of a knife [instead of a salt spoon] deranged him beyond measure'. **William Holmes**: testimony of Peter Salmon, c/m of William Holmes, ADM 1/5346; Captain Smith to the Admiralty, 1 October 1798, ADM 1/2498 Capt. S220. He was dismissed the ship and rendered incapable of serving His Majesty, his heirs or successors as a chaplain in the navy; he left the ship at once, unobserved by any of the officers, but two hours afterwards met his former captain, John Smith, in Yarmouth market and called him a 'rascal and coward'.

[43] *Plassey*: Hickey, *Memoirs*, vol. I, p. 164. **Parsons**: Parsons, *Nelsonian Reminiscences*, p. 140. **Dillon**: NRS 97, p. 350. **Beaver**: c/m of Lieutenant Lord Cochrane, ADM 1/5348.

[44] **Purser**: this is based on the *Gibraltar*. For example, on 30 August 1803 Captain Keats ordered the purser of the *Superb* to buy sixty live bullocks and their food for five days at 18lb per head per

day, forty pipes of 'good and sound wine' and twelve tons of onions for the fleet, with the master 'to see that the bullocks are good and fit for His M. service', Naples Bay, 20 July 1803, ADM 80/141, out-letters f. 199.

[45] Wybourn, *Sea Soldier*, p. 65; Parsons, *Nelsonian Reminiscences*, p. 30 (and at a dinner commemorating the Battle of St Vincent, p. 130). **Blanche**: testimony of James Carpenter, sentry at the gunroom door in the *Blanche* (32), c/m of her purser, ADM 1/5337.

[46] Wybourn, *Sea Soldier*, pp. 153–4.

[47] Wybourn, *Sea Soldier*, p. 163.

[48] **Macedonian**: Leech, *Voice from the Main Deck*, pp. 51, 90. **Goliath**: *Wynne Diaries*, vol. II, September 1796, pp. 129 and 114. **Caesar**: Richardson, *Mariner of England*, p. 233. See also for example N A M Rodger, *Command of the Ocean*, p. 505, and Hickey, *Memoirs*, vol. II, pp. 282–3.

[49] **Noon**: it was 'always the etiquette in a squadron that the senior commanding officer should make the hours of breakfast and dinner', but the *Splendid* was a detached ship (NRS 138, p. 462). **Piping**: NRS 91, p.248. **Utensils**: Macdonald, *Feeding Nelson's Navy*, pp. 110–11. It must be remembered that her research is drawn from the period July 1803 to June 1804, and kit had become more sophisticated by 1810. That spoons, bowls and cups were the basics can be inferred from several letters to the Admiralty about misunderstandings when transporting troops, for example one from Horse Guards to the Admiralty dated 8 April 1799 complaining that the troops embarked do not have spoons, plates, bowls and cups issued to them; the Admiralty agreed to issue them in future (ADM 12/83). *Invincible* examples are from McGuane, *Heart of Oak*, pp. 38–45. **China**: thus Jack Nastyface, 'there are also basons, plates, etc., which are kept in each mess ... It sometimes happens that a lurch will dash all the crockery to pieces; they are then obliged to eat out of wooden or tin utensils, until they come into harbour, where they get another supply' (Robinson, *Jack Nastyface*, p. 33). **London**: testimony of William Hughes, c/m of Barnet Hughes, ADM 1/5352.

[50] The capacity of the boilers of Brodie's stoves, introduced in 1781, are in n. 17, p. 252

[51] **Still at work**: for example, the day the *Gibraltar* sailed from Leghorn in 1796 the purser and four men were stowing hay in the bread room that morning. **Trotter**: *Medicina Nautica* (1804), in NRS 107, p. 277. **Splendid**: captain's order no. 24th in the *Indefatigable*, 1812, NRS 138, p. 187. The regulation was also to prevent desertion.

[52] The official ration table was printed in the Regulations and Instructions. Janet Macdonald wonders whether 'those days of the week shown on the ration table' were 'meant to be absolute or merely advisory', *i.e.* the days when the food was issued or to be eaten (*Feeding Nelson's Navy*, p. 115), but while there was nothing to stop men saving food, either cooked or raw, the evidence is that the ration table was used as a template for the daily meals. *The Seaman's Vade Mecum* of 1756 is clear:

> Every Man to be allowed daily Provisions, as follows, viz.
> Sunday. One Pound of Biscuit, one Gallon of Small Beer, one Pound of Pork, and half a Pint of Pease.
> Monday. One Pound of Biscuit, one Gallon of Small Beer, one Pint of Oatmeal, two Ounces of Butter, and four Ounces of Cheese.
> Tuesday. One Pound of Biscuit, one Gallon of Small Beer, and two Pounds of Beef.
> Wednesday. One Pound of Biscuit, one Gallon of Small Beer, half a Pint of Pease, a Pint of Oatmeal, two Ounces of Butter, and four Ounces of Cheese.
> Thursday. The same as Sunday.
> Friday. The same as Wednesday.
> Saturday. The same as Tuesday.

Practical examples include the testimony of Lieutenant Pringle, who 'When the ship was at Blackstakes' asked the captain 'if he approved of the ship's company having pease on Monday at dinner, in the room of the oatmeal for breakfast on the banyan days, as was customary in many ships' (c/m of Moses Hawker, ADM 1/5333). **Pudding**: R&I, 1808, p. 292 art. VIII, 'for the better preservation of the health of the ship's company'; in 1790 it was issued one day a week (R&I, 1790, p. 63 art. VII). The proportion is not stated in either edition, but the Victualling Board's precedent book, compiled after 1790, gives as a substitute for one piece of beef 3lb flour, 4oz suet and 8oz raisins, bracketed together implying a pudding (ADM 30/44, f. 15). In 1793 it was decided that though suet was formerly issued for four months only for fear of it spoiling, it was now to be issued at six months' worth at a time (ADM 2/123, ff. 146–5, 28 January 1793); when this practice reverted is not clear. Macdonald speculates that half of each mess took the material for pudding when it was issued, 'so each beef day consisted of one pound of beef with suet pudding for each man' (*Feeding Nelson's Navy*, p. 18), which is plausible. There is a counter-example from the *Ganges* (74) in 1783: 'We arrived at Giberalter [29 October 1783], but purhaps it would be requeset to mention the situation of the poor raw soldiers that ware unaquainted on board of a man of war … They ware supplied with beds for the passage, and if not returned, they ware charged for them out of their wages. The sailors beds being small, they endeavoured to make them larger. In the night, they would crawl a long the deck and get holt of a blanket or rug. The sailors would pull, the soldier hold fast and hollow out, but 2 or three to on would gain the prize. Even in daylight, the hammocks being stowed on the booms, the topmen would send a hawling line down with a hook, and one standing by, hook on, away it would fly into the top, and whoever owned it was at a loss for his bed when night came on. By the same method, when the puddings ware nearly done, before dinner, in the coppers, they would send a line from the fore top, and one hook on a large pudding, and up it would fly in an instant, and in less than five minutes it would be devoured. When they piped to dinner, purhaps six in a mess come to look for there pudding, had nothing to eat, though if detected they would be punished' (*Nagle Journal*, p. 73) – but perhaps those acquainted with life on board would have divided their puddings as Macdonald suggests. Ingredients were supplied for puddings to men on the Ordinary establishment as well: biscuit, 14oz per man per day; loaf bread, 16oz per man per day; beer, 1 gallon wine measure per man per day; fresh beef, 20lb and 6lb flour and 2lb raisins per month; salt meat, 4 pieces of beef at 4lb and 4 pieces of pork at 2lb, per month; pease, 1 gallon, oatmeal, ¾ gallon, sugar, 1lb 8oz, butter, 1lb 8oz, cheese 2lb, per month (ADM 106/2517, no. 746, 13 October 1806). Canvas for making pudding bags was supplied at one ell per sixteen men (R&I, 1790, pp. 63–4 art. VII; 1808, p. 292 art. VIII). **Vegetables**: the saved pease were boiled for Monday's dinner. This was a custom of the service, formalised in R&I, 1808, pp. 299–300 art. XX. **Onions**: these were sometimes counted individually, sometimes recorded by weight, according to the method of delivery; in both cases they were 'aired and dried, and the damaged picked from the good every other day', as Captain Keats recorded in his account of onions for the fleet in 1803 (ADM 80/141, out-letters 2 August 1803, f. 192, on which date the *Superb* had forty-eight butts originally containing exactly 30,000lb, with contents ranging from 431lb to 747lb). **Carrots**: St Vincent to Sick and Wounded Board, 25 November 1800, asking them to buy forty bags, NRS 141, p. 588. Johnson and Trotter's proposed diet for the ship's companies in health, for the West Indian expedition under Admiral Christian, was half a pound of potatoes per man per day at dinner and half an ounce of white pickled cabbage, both with the salt meat, but pickled cabbage, like sauerkraut, was not often popular (25 September 1795, NRS 46, pp. 151–2). **Pumpkins**: Macdonald, *Feeding Nelson's Navy*, pp. 37–8; see also her pp. 36–8 for vegetables generally, though I am not convinced that the varieties available for sale in 1793–1815 were 'like those' found in the late nineteenth century, *i.e.* after a hundred years of intense and commercially rewarding specialisation and breeding.

[53] **Green**: for example, Captain Pasley's journal, 6 February 1782, in the *Jupiter*: 'Still calm with heavy rains; filled in the evening a ton and a half of [rain] water for the use of the cooks, being greatly superior to any other for breaking the pease' (*Private Sea Journals*, p. 229) and the many references to pease soup. **Yellow**: for example, any definition of dog's body, such as 'squeezed

pease, sometimes called Soldier's Joy', *Johnny Newcome*, p. 243n. Victualling Board contracts state 'peas' without reference to variety, as they do for other vegetables whose species and variety is of considerable significance, such as potatoes, and it's likely that it bought whatever was available at a sensible price. Grossman and Thomas come to a similar conclusion (*Lobscouse and Spotted Dog*, passim); see also Macdonald, *Feeding Nelson's Navy*, pp. 33–4, where she dismisses the *locus classicus*, NRS 31, p. 167. Brodie's stoves came with 'two brass cocks with set screws to plugs' for issuing soup.

⁵⁴ **Pineapple**: Hickey, *Memoirs*, vol. IV, p. 230; Ranken, *Shipmates*, p. 63 (3 November 1799). Jack Nastyface attributed deaths from Walcheren fever to agues caught while lying insensible after drinking too much gin brought on by an immoderate consumption of apples, but the apples themselves can hardly be blamed (Robinson, *Jack Nastyface*, pp. 119–20). **Forbidden**: R&I, 1790, p. 200 art. XI, in the 'rules for preserving cleanliness' rather than victualling. **Great cabin**: actually Sir John Jervis's in the *Victory* in 1797: Parsons, *Nelsonian Reminiscences*, p. 166. **Lisbon**: actually the *Macedonian* in 1810: Leech, *Voice from the Main Deck*, p. 31.

⁵⁵ **Captain's order**: no. 5th in the *Indefatigable*, NRS 138, p. 183. **One historian**: Macdonald, *Feeding Nelson's Navy*, p. 113; ADM 1/1548, Capt. B245. An hour and a quarter or an hour and a half was usual. **Silent ship**: *eg*, the *Cumberland* (74) in 1802 ('Q: Is it the constant order of the ship that there shall be perfect silence kept and generally understood. A: Yes there is [*sic*]', testimony of Abraham Wade, c/m of James Pearce, ADM 1/5360; or the *Unité* in 1805 ('no man dare at his peril speak above his breath, so strictly was the order of silence enforced', NRS 91, p. 130). It is a commonplace in published memoirs that conscientious officers did not disturb men at their meals except in an emergency: Captains Hall and Dillon wrote, respectively, 'Every good officer makes a point of conscience, as far as he possibly can, not to order any evolution, or otherwise to interfere with the people at their meals – especially at dinner', and 'It was a regular established system not to interfere with the seamen whilst at their meals, except in a case of the utmost urgency' (Hall, *Fragments*, vol. III, p. 163; NRS 97, p. 302), but the former was presenting an idealised picture of the navy 'for the use of Young Persons' and the latter was a relentless self-propagandist: Dillon's remark is occasioned by Captain Talbot, who served under Nelson and Collingwood, signalling the *Horatio* to make all sail. *Rodney*: *Autobiography of Joseph Bates*, chapter three. *America*: testimony of the first lieutenant, c/m of William Holmes, ADM 1/5346: the chaplain had complained to him that the butcher had insulted him.

⁵⁶ **Midshipmen**: 'The midshipmen in most ships dine at 12 o'clock, the lieutenants at 2', noted Captain Clarke RM in the *Gibraltar* in 1811 (NRS 138, p. 462). As late as 1825 the midshipmen in the *Ganges* (84) were told that dining at two was 'not the custom of the service', and they reverted to noon (Admiral of the Fleet Sir Alexander Milne, then a midshipman in the *Ganges* (84), to his brother, 'I saw Capt Inglefield yesterday morning[.] He appears to be a very pleasant man, but very particular[.] Directly he heard that we dined at two, he said it was not the custom of the service & we should dine at 12', NRS 147, p. 28n.). The dinner hour in society slipped later in the afternoon throughout the eighteenth century, and most memoirs contain an instance of the author being surprised by it. The *locus classicus* is Aspinall-Oglander, *Admiral's Widow*, p. 74. **Supplies**: these belong to William Mark, captain's clerk in the *Hydra*, who messed with the midshipmen, for a cruise in 1801 (Mark, *At Sea with Nelson*, pp. 87, 88), and Basil Hall (*Fragments*, vol. I, pp. 213), respectively.

⁵⁷ Burton, *Johnny Newcome*, pp. 106–7.

⁵⁸ Brodie's stove: ADM 106/2509, no. 479, 23 January 1787.

⁵⁹ C/m of James Fennigan, ADM 1/5333.

⁶⁰ C/m of the *Defiance* mutineers, ADM 1/5346.

⁶¹ Richardson, *Mariner of England*, p. 168.

⁶² Lady Bourchier, *Memoir of the Late Admiral Sir Edward Codrington*, vol. 1, pp. 299–300, in Rodger, *Command of the Ocean*, pp. 502–3.

Chapter 7
WASHING CLOTHES AND REEFING TOPSAILS

[1] **Wash and mend clothes**: *Expedition*, testimony of Henry Paulett St John, c/m of John Fose, ADM 1/5347; *Glory*, c/m of the *Glory* mutineers, ADM 1/5347; *Mars*, 'Trafalgar general order book'; *Indefatigable*, NRS 138, p. 183. Bates, *Autobiography*.

[2] Bates, *Autobiography*, chapter three. Conditions were not much better aboard American ships, however; Charles Nordhoff, who was a boy in the USS *Columbus* (74) a few years later, wrote in his memoirs that 'A bucket of clean salt water, a lump of soap, and plenty of hard rubbing, are the only means used for the renovation of a sailor's soiled linen ... Not half of those desiring to wash were able to obtain buckets, and of course many were obliged to wait, while many others had to do without altogether' (Nordhoff, *Sailor Life*, pp. 112–13).

[3] **Fresh water**: inferred from several remarks about salt water, *eg* NRS 91, p. 75: 'this ship's company altogether were ordered to be kept on short allowance, and old ropes were obliged to be used for fuel to dress the victuals which were breakfast and dinner only, and sea water for washing the linen etc.' **Soap**: testimony of Mr Maude, c/m of Captain George Hopewell Stephens, ADM 1/5342; Stephens said 'it has been the custom of the service long before my time, not only for sugar but soap, or other articles to be issued in that manner [at 1s per lb] when by their own desire', and indulged because it was conducive to health. The purser of the *Victory* (100) bought fourteen cases (3,258lb Italian measure) on 9 June 1796 (NRS 138, p. 568). **Women**: Mordecai M Noah, *Travels in England, France, Spain, and the Barbary States in the Years 1813, 14, and 15* (New York: Kirk and Mercein; London: John Miller, 1819), in Stark, *Female Tars*, p. 60, and Rodger, *Command of the Ocean*, p. 505. William Callicut, washerman, was one of those who elected to stay behind in Patagonia and not proceed with the *Speedwell*, in November 1741, but 'washerman' may be a description (Bulkeley and Cummins, *Voyage to the South Seas*, p. 88). There is no guarantee he washed clothes, but the *OED* gives washerman as 'A man whose occupation is the washing of clothes', and includes this example in its illustrative quotation. Washerman was a formal rate aboard hospital ships: *Le Caton* at Plymouth was to have four washermen or women and one nurse to every fourteen sick men at 19s per month in 1794 (ADM 2/125, f. 268, 9 January 1794). **Line**: in the *Mars*, 'Trafalgar general order book', p. 91.

[4] Hall, *Fragments*, vol. I, pp. 73–5.

[5] C/m of Robert Paton, ADM 1/5352. **Names and numbers**: Samuel Hayley fell overboard from the *Tromp* prison-ship in Martinique in 1800, and was eaten by a shark; when the body was recovered the only reason they knew it was him was because of the name on the inside of the waistband (Richardson, *Mariner of England*, p. 184). In the *Petrel* sloop in 1801 the men's clothes were numbered, which allowed her commander to identify a wounded mutineer by a set of discarded clothes with blood on (NRS 40, p. 376), and when Landsman Hay was caught by the press gang in London in 1811 he had a pair of numbered stockings in his bag (Hay, *Landsman Hay*, p. 217). On the other hand, captain's order no. 65th directed that 'whenever knives, shirts, trousers etc are found in betwixt decks, they are to be brought on the quarterdeck to be owned' (NRS 138, p. 194). **Sultan**: 17 July 1810, ADM 51/2860. **Warrior**: Andrew Lambert, *Warrior* (London: Conway Maritime Press, 1987), pp. 160, 163, 168.

[6] **Queen**: testimony of Thomas Ridings, c/m of James Morgan, ADM 1/5346. **Director**: testimony of John Cast, Richard Tonk and John Moore, c/m of William James and Robert Willis, ADM 1/5337. **Ardent**: Woodman, *Victory of Seapower*, p. 133.

[7] 'The Trafalgar general order book of H.M.S. *Mars*', in *Mariner's Mirror*, vol. 22, no. 1 (1936), pp. 89–90; NRS 138, p. 164; NRS 138, p. 185 (great coat is not in his list but is in the table to be followed by the officers of the divisions). General Orders issued at the Adjutant General's Office, 14 January 1792. The soldiers were also provided out of their pay with 'Soleing and Heelpiecing', 4s per year, pipe clay and whiting, 42s 4d per year, and 'Black Ball', 2s per year; washing was 4d per week. The gratis necessaries included 2s 6d for 'Altering his Clothing, to make it fit him', 1s

towards watch coats, a worm, turnscrew, picker and brush, every five years, at 3d per year, and emery, brickdust, and oil, at 2s 6d per year. The totals were £3 5s 5d and 16s 11½d respectively.
[8] C/m of John de Cruize, ADM 1/5406. The marine had a rather different version: 'He offered me a watch and a pair of pantaloons if I would let him fuck me.'
[9] R&I, 1808, pp. 424, 425 and 427 arts XV, XVI and XX. Their uniforms, if serviceable, were to be sent to the commanding officer of Portsmouth, Plymouth, Chatham or Woolwich, with their arms and accoutrements.
[10] On his submitting a letter from the surgeon they relented. ADM 1/2498, Capt. S115 et seq. Despite this, flock beds supplied with washed not new blankets were to be issued at 11s not 13s, ADM 106/2517, no. 172, 24 March 1806.
[11] *Macedonian*: Leech, *Voice from the Main Deck*, p. 31. *Isis*: Wybourn, *Sea Soldier*, p. 24. *Leopard*: NRS 97, p. 220. *Centaur*: Rodger, *Command of the Ocean*, p. 454. *Endymion*: Hall, *Fragments*, vol. III, pp. 122–3.
[12] Parsons, *Nelsonian Reminiscences*, pp. 30 and 127.
[13] Lovell, *From Trafalgar to the Chesapeake*, pp. 30–31 and 33.
[14] Ranken, *Shipmates*, p. 21.
[15] *Nagle Journal*, p. 198.
[16] **Hoffmann**: NRS 31, p. 61. **Cornwallis**: testimony of William Augustus Reaver, c/m of Charles King and James Dooley, ADM 1/5347. **Bayly**: *Diary of Colonel Bayly*, p. 29.
[17] Hickey, *Memoirs*, vol. III, pp. 51–2 and 62; Rodger, *Command of the Ocean*, p. 356; Hickey, *Memoirs*, vol. IV, p. 370.
[18] *Conqueror's* log, ADM 51/2219.
[19] This closely follows the c/m of William Mason, Stephen Rolls and John McCarthy, ADM 1/5430, with details from the muster book (ADM 37/3287). In real life the whole event takes place while the topsails are reefed, and Jameson is a man called Driskill; the next scene is invented, so his name is changed. The conversation follows Mason's written defence, except that he claimed to have offered the pacific 'I shall not play-act with you' instead of 'I can act a play that would astonish you'. Only Mason says Driskill was encouraged to resume the fight. The last sentence and the description of Driskill as a quarrelsome man are from the testimony of David Roberts, seaman. The court martial acquitted the accused.
[20] **Jolly boat**: Pasley, *Private Sea Journals*, p. 70. The method for recovering a drowned man follows that of Dr Lind, in 1779 (NRS 107, p. 46). He discounts the traditional practice of hanging the patient by his heels. The College of Surgeons ruled against the tobacco remedy in 1811 on the advice of Dr Brodie; variations included onions (Goodwin, *Nelson's Ships*, p. 133 col. 2, where they were unsuccessful). The quart of blood is based on the experiences of Major George Simmons of the Rifle Brigade, who was shot through the back at Waterloo; the ball was extracted and a quart of blood taken from his arm, and another when he returned to his billet: 'In four days I had six quarts of blood taken from me', as well as that removed by at least eighty leeches (Simmons, *British Rifle Man*, pp. 367–9). I am indebted to Tim Binding for the inspiration for this scene.
[21] This is based on the testimony of Lieutenant Henry Montresor, c/m of Richard Parke, ADM 1/5336.
[22] Captain's orders in the *Blenheim* (74), 1796, NRS 138, p. 226.

Chapter 8
WRANGLESOME AND QUARRELSOME

[1] Testimony of Henry Montresor, c/m of Richard Parke, ADM 1/5336.
[2] **Edwards**: 'A Captain's Life and Death at Sea: Captain George Duff's Last Correspondence', in Tracy (ed), *Naval Chronicle*, vol. III, p. 185. The tragedy of *Douglas* is by John Home,

1722–1808, first performed in Edinburgh in 1756, and at Covent Garden in 1757. On the 10th he reported: 'This is a proper gloomy November day, but not much wind. I went to the theatre last night, and I can assure you it was no bad performance. Between the play and the farce we had a most excellent Irish song, from one of the sailors. The music indeed was very good, and the entertainment for the night concluded with God save the King. The whole was over a quarter before eight o'clock. They had several scenes not badly painted. The ladies' dresses were not very fine, but did credit to their invention. Lady Randolph was all in black, made out of silk handkerchiefs; and I believe Anne's dress was made of sheets: but upon the whole they looked remarkably well.' **Wheeler:** *Letters*, p. 48. His account is particularly interesting because his time in the *Revenge* overlapped with that of William Robinson (Jack Nastyface), and his letters, such as the one dated at Lisbon, 10 March 1811, 'I am now half a sailor, having stood all the bad weather without seasickness, indeed I never enjoyed better health and spirits in my life', are a valuable correction. *Aboukir:* NRS 12, p. 188; Wingle is a slip for Mingle; the play is '*The Bee-Hive*, a Musical Farce, in Two Acts; As Performed at the Theatre Royal, Lyceum', in January 1811. See also Rodger, *Command of the Ocean*, p. 505, for earlier examples, including, 'In the Mediterranean in 1807 the *Royal George* had not less than three acting companies performing on alternate nights, nicely graded by social rank: the wardroom officers doing Shakespeare's *Henry IV*; the midshipmen producing the "genteel comedy" *The Poor Gentleman*; while the lower deck played Foote's "broad farce" *The Mayor of Garrett*'.' It was not only in the Royal Navy: in 1805 the *Leander* (50) captured the *Ville de Milan* (44), and 'The French midshipmen were actually playing at cards in our birth on the very evening they were taken; and, next day, there was a proposal made by them to get up a set of private theatricals in the cock-pit!' (Hall, *Fragments*, vol. II, p. 35). There was a long and respectable tradition for theatrical performances on board ships: the first recorded performance of *Hamlet* aboard ship was in the *Red Dragon*, off Sierra Leone, on 5 September 1607, and the ship's company also performed *Richard II*; these plays, put on for local rulers, were the first performances of Western drama in sub-Saharan Africa. (I am indebted to Hugh Gazzard and Professor Anthony Graham-White respectively for this point.) *Caesar:* Richardson, *Mariner of England*, p. 255.

[3] Captain's order no. 82nd, NRS 138, p. 198. This was required by R&I, 1808, p. 149 art. XIX. Leech, *Voice from the Main Deck*, p. 23. **Regularly arranged:** NRS 91, p. 339. **Retreat:** in the *Triumph* in 1802. Testimony of Robert Stupart, c/m of Lieutenant Thomas F. Kennedy, ADM 1/5362. NRS 138, p. 462.

[4] Rodger, *Command of the Ocean*, p. 405. C/m of Harry Humphries, ADM 1/5345; NRS 138, p. 218; c/m of Lieutenant Colonel Desborough, ADM 1/5349.

[5] C/m of the *Culloden* mutineers, ADM 1/5331. Johnston was one of the accused. *Royal Yeoman:* ARS 3, p. 70.

[6] Captain's orders to the boatswain no. 6th, NRS 91, p. 345 and Harland, *Seamanship*, p. 299; to the carpenter, no. 5th.

[7] R&I, 1790, pp. 103–4 art. XI, and pp. 134–5 art. II. The second reference is to the master at arms' instructions, but this duty had become largely obsolete by 1790. *Mars:* 'Trafalgar order book', p. 96 and pp. 101–2. Captain Oliver, who succeeded him, changed this to the washing days. **Allowance:** R&I, 1808, pp. 141–2, arts X and XI.

[8] R&I, 1808, pp. 220–21 art. XXI.

[9] R&I, 1808, pp. 142–3 art. XI. In a standard complement of 640, there were 125 marines and 105 men who were not seamen. **Army ammunition:** WO 55/1843, *sv* Ammunition.

[10] R&I, 1808, section II chapter II. The 1790 edition is very similar; the number of guns is occasionally different, and there is an additional clause, forbidding merchant ships firing guns in roads or ports after the watch is set if any HM ships are present.

[11] NRS 6, pp. 313–14.

[12] Captain's order no. 61st in the *Indefatigable*, 1812 (NRS 138, p. 194). Supper was usually the occasion for issuing the second half of the day's ration: but in some ships the grog was served

separately. Captain Riou's orders in the *Amazon* in 1799, for example, were that the 'afternoon grog serving is never to be considered a meal, nor are the watch upon this occasion to be permitted to go off deck' (NRS 138, p. 151). **Eight bells**: Robinson, *Jack Nastyface*, p. 38. Supper was a much more moveable feast than dinner; the East Indies squadron took it at 5.30pm in 1805 (Macdonald, *Feeding Nelson's Navy*, p. 112). **Oil**: butter was issued at the home ports, and intended to last three months, then when it ran out it was substituted by either oil or cocoa and sugar for cocoa. See for example Nicolas, *Letters and Dispatches of Lord Nelson*, vol. V, p. 309; for oil and how it might have been used, see Macdonald, *Feeding Nelson's Navy*, pp. 32–3, where she instances 'a dish of hot pease with oil and chopped onion' described in *Roderick Random*. One of the many faults committed by Richard Parke in the *Gibraltar* was issuing wine in lieu of oil, half a pint per man per day, without orders, which was clearly prejudicial to good discipline (ADM 1/5336).

[13] C/m of Richard Potter, ADM 1/5428.

[14] Testimony of Sergeant William Burt, c/m of William Collins, ADM 1/5352.

[15] *Observations on Some Points of Seamanship*, in NRS 138, pp. 361–2.

[16] **St Vincent**: Nicolas, *Dispatches and Letters of Lord Nelson*, vol. IV, p. 288. **One member**: really James R Durand, in the *Narcissus* (32), Captain Aylmer, in 1810, Durand, p.59. The master at arms was the master of the band (p. 70). Durand was drafted into the *Fortune*, whose captain was not so fond of music, and so put him into the sailmaker's crew, and then into Aylmer's new frigate, the *Pactolus*, in 1814, where he resumed his place in the band (p. 73). ***Culloden***: Hay, *Landsman Hay*, p. 94. ***Merlin***: c/m of Captain Pakenham for various offences, ADM 1/5329, f. 72. ***Minotaur***: Hoffman, *Sailor of King George*, p. 108.

[17] Wheeler, *Letters*, p. 47 (also in Rodger, *Command of the Ocean*, p. 504). She was under the command of James Nash, described as a commander in *Command of the Ocean* but a post-captain since 29 April 1802 in the Navy List.

[18] Wheeler, *Letters*, pp. 24 and 46.

[19] **It is ridiculous**: an anonymous diarist in the *Gibraltar*, 1811, in NRS 138, p. 463. **Rivals**: ADM 21/23, f. 400. **Upon all occasions**: NRS 31, pp. 103, 104. **Wheeler**, *Letters*, p. 46 (this was on a Sunday), and NRS 91, p. 257. **Smith**: c/m of William Smith (2), ADM 1/5407. **Hay**: *Landsman Hay*, p. 72. ***Renown***: Lovell, *From Trafalgar to the Chesapeake*, p. 5.

[20] Defence statement, c/m of Barnet Hughes, ADM 1/5352. William Hughes, drummer, agreed with this testimony, except that he did not hear Perkins challenge the mess, though he was at the same table, and agrees that the ship had orders against card-playing and gambling, and that the master at arms would throw the cards overboard if he found anyone gambling. Verdict: guilty but in consideration of circumstances, fifty lashes.

[21] **Issued**: *Amazon*, NMM JOD/45, *Superb*, RUSI/110, in Macdonald, *Feeding Nelson's Navy*, p. 100. The *Mars* was slightly different: 'The ship's company are to be served their provisions between the hours of 7 and 9 in the morning; after which the steward room is to be [well cleaned,] locked … and not to be opened till sunset for the issuing candles etc and again locked up at eight o'clock'. *Mariner's Mirror*, vol. 22, no. 1 (1936), p. 93. **Merlin**: c/m of Captain Pakenham, ADM 1/5329. The figures are for May 1787 to June 1789. Acheson also said that in the service, bread and bread dust condemned as wet was calculated as 'a third weight more wet than when it was dry' if it could not be weighed.

[22] The events described here took place on 21 January 1799 in the *America* (c/m of Lieutenant Charles Grey, ADM 1/5348). The boatswain's mate's name was William Edwards and the captain's name was Smith. Except for the name changes, regularising the punctuation and changing 'bread butter & cheese' to 'bread, oil, and cheese', this testimony is quoted exactly, from 'William Patterson, boatswain's mate'. In reality, of course, he did lift his hand, and although the court accepted that the language and tone was not disrespectful, the verdict was proved in part; but in consideration of his good character, dismissed the *America*, put on half-pay and rendered incapable of serving in any of HM ships or vessels at sea. Grey had joined the

ship early in November and was a follower of Captain O'Brian Drury, under whom he had
served in the *Powerful* in 1795 (testimonies of Thomas Pye Bennet, first lieutenant, and Captain
Charles Lock of the *Inspector*). He became a superannuated commander in 1816 and died in
1826.
[23] C/m of William Holsby, ADM 1/5338.
[24] **Troubridge**: Lavery, *Nelson and the Nile*, p. 159. **Browne**: ARS 3, p. 123. Possibly he means the
officers of the regiment only. **Walking on deck**: for example, Thomas Brown and John Keller,
marines of the *Director*, 'sat until the bottle was drank and after walking about we went below',
testimony of Thomas Brown, private marine, c/m of John Keller, ADM 1/5347. John Shorrock
and John Cook, marines of the *Bellerophon*, were walking on the main deck 'talking of
Lancashire' (where Cook was from), c/m of Dennis Kelly *et al.*, ADM 1/5333.
[25] *Conqueror*'s log, ADM 51/2219. Lavery, *Ship of the Line*, vol. II, p. 90.

Chapter 9
SUPPER IN THE WARDROOM

[1] **Time**: Macdonald, *Feeding Nelson's Navy*, p. 121 is too dogmatic in her assertion of 6pm.
Sitting: c/m of Lieutenant Joseph Street, ADM 1/5344. **Indicator**: William Loyd, master of the
Hannibal, came on board about nine on 3 July 1793; he went to the wardroom for his supper and
told the servant to lay a cloth on the table, to which Lieutenant Grice objected, and told him to
take it to a side table, which he did, but after some words Grice came at him with a knife (c/m
of Harry Grice, ADM 1/5330).
[2] Testimony of George Smith, c/m of the lieutenants of the *Gibraltar*, ADM 1/5333.
[3] R&I, 1808, p. 374 art. IV.
[4] **Beams and carlines**: the lower deck beams in the *Bellona* were 16½in square and the
athwartships carlines on the upper deck were 8in by 6in; in the *Victory*, the lower deck beams
were 'approximately' 15in wide by 16½in deep and the carlines 6in wide by 5in deep (Lavery,
Bellona, B19 and C4; McKay, *Victory*, B12). **Clearance**: Falconer, *sv* Cannon; Lavery, *Bellona*, A3;
McKay, *Victory*, B2/3. **Housed and secured**: Steel, *Art of Rigging*, p. 117. Lavery, in NRS 138 p.
243, claims that 'Ross does not take any account of the guns in his calculations', and therefore
'the system as applied to a ship of the line was impossible', but this is apparently contradicted by
the text he prints, and by the fact that berthing plans, such as that of an unnamed mid-
eighteenth-century Third Rate (in Lavery, *Arming and Fitting* p. 181), or an undated plan of the
Victory (McGowan, *Victory*, pp. 210–11), traditionally showed hammocks slung over the guns, as
well as standard pictures of lower-deck life. In *Arming and Fitting* (p. 183) his objection is focused
on Ross's identification of berth number with mess number, but again the objection is overcome
when correlated with the fact that a mess in a line-of-battle ship could occupy one side of a table
only (NRS 138, p. 244, supported by the testimony of, for example, James Hancock, boy, of the
Duncan, c/m of Richard Potter, ADM 1/5428). **Layers**: testimony of Sergeant Thomas, c/m of
the *Glory* mutineers, ADM 1/5347; Lewis, *Social History*, p. 28. **Screens**: for example, the ship's
steward's berth in the *Culloden* (74) in 1794 (testimony of Samuel Grange against Cornelius
Sullivan, c/m of the *Culloden* mutineers, ADM 1/5331).
[5] C/m of Charles Coleman, ADM 1/5362. In his defence Coleman said: 'Old age [he was fifty-
two] as can easily be perceived has greatly overtaken me – and although I may be so fortunate as
to meet the indulgence of this Honble Court – still I shall always feel unhappy at what
happened on the evening alluded to', and in view of his good character, and perhaps the
provocation, he was given thirty-six lashes only. (ADM 36/15237 lists him as joined 1 July 1801,
born Castle Carey, age 51, AB. Burrows is listed as joined 25 June 1802, no other details.)
[6] **1799**: Mr Ross's plan to be used in all ships built or repaired in the King's yards, ADM
106/2512, 14 September 1799, no. 242. The plan is reproduced in NRS 138.

⁷ **Scuttles:** ADM 106/2508, 28 November 1778, no. 770; ADM 106/2508, 6 May 1782, no. 1161; ADM 106/2509, 7 May 1789, no. 600. **Riou:** *Nagle Journal*, p. 74.

⁸ **One hammock each:** Lavery, *Arming and Fitting*, p. 180. A few spares were carried: 'a First Rate of the 1790s was issued with 900 hammocks for a crew of 850 men, with 260 extra for a long voyage.' **Bed:** ADM 49/121, ff. 120 and 136. **Goat:** inferred from ADM 49/121, f. 85. **Blanket and pillow:** ADM 49/121, f. 120; ADM 106/2514, 17 Mar 1803, no. 51. **Superior:** a Navy Board warrant of 1804 restricted flock beds to troops' tenders, receiving ships, and prison ships (ADM 106/2515, 8 May 1804, no. 88). Dockyard-made beds cost £1 2s 1d each, and were made at the rate of four beds per man per day (ADM 106/2514, 1 October 1803, no. 179; from hair, ADM 106/2514, no. 51, 17 March 1803). **Washed beds:** half-price: ADM 106/2511, no. 159, 12 November 1795, repeated in ADM 106/2514, 2 April 1803, no. 82. **Sheets:** Hall, *Fragments*, vol. I, p. 248; Trotter, *Medicina Nautica* (1804), in NRS 107, p. 275.

⁹ **Deptford:** ADM 49/121, f. 63. They were 2s 10½d each in 1784 and 3s 7d in 1792. **June:** ADM 106/2517, no. 393, 12 June 1806; **October**, ADM 106/2517, no. 699, 23 October 1806: 'The cloth to be cut 6 feet 2 inches wide and each hammock when made to measure 5ft 10ins in length to be made with a line of 3 threads agreeable to the pattern and tabled round the line with 100 stitches at least in each yard; – the seam to have 200 stitches at least in each yard and the seam not to exceed ¾ of an inch in breadth and after it is sewed to be rubbed down flat – to have 13 holes at each end one of them to be in centre of the seam in the middle and to have at least 15 stitches in each hole two of them round the line and the holes to be well rounded after made. Each hammock to be 4 feet 2 inches broad the seam, tabling & holes to be sewed with the best two thread seaming twine worked double'. **1814:** Report of Committee of Sea Officers of Navy Board on stores etc drawn up in 1814, ADM 106/5347, para 102, and remarks on paras 102–4. They were to have twenty-five eyelet holes at each end instead of fifteen as at present (stamped f. 127). **Bales:** WO 55/1747. **Head forward:** in the *Delft* troopship most of the men slept with their heads aft; it seems from the context of the remark that this was contrary to the usual practice (testimony of Robert Broughton, c/m of John Warner, ADM 1/5352), and there are several other courts martial for murder in which the victim is saved only by hanging the wrong way round: but Basil Hall, describing the operation of cutting down a hammock in the midshipmen's berth, assumes that if the foremost lanyard is cut the occupant falls to the deck feet first (*Fragments*, I, p. 249). **Cots:** Lavery, *Arming and Fitting*, pp. 180 and 177.

¹⁰ **Leech:** Leech, *Voice from the Main Deck*, p. 24. Also Lavery, *Arming and Fitting*, p. 181, quoting *A Voice from the Middle Deck* (sic), 1844, p. 37. **James:** cross-examination, c/m of William James and Robert Willis, ADM 1/5337. **White:** c/m of James Holland and John Reilly, ADM 1/5361.

¹¹ *Marlborough*: c/m of William Read, ADM 1/5331.

¹² *Terrible*: c/m of Thomas Dundas, ADM 1/5345.

¹³ **Manning:** ADM 1/5362.

¹⁴ C/m of John de Cruize, ADM 1/5406.

¹⁵ *Wynne Diaries*, vol. ii, p. 209.

¹⁶ Kempenfelt to Middleton, 28 December 1779, in Hodges and Hughes, *Select Naval Documents*, p. 165. R&I, 1790, pp. 30–31 art. XXXV; 1808, pp. 143–4 art. XII and p. 179 art. XXII. NRS 91, p. 248.

¹⁷ **Lind:** in NRS 107, p. 48. *Macedonian*: Leech, *Voice from the Main Deck*, p. 47. **Durand:** Durand, *Life and Adventures*, p. 32. *York*: ADM 51/2989.

¹⁸ **Wilson:** NRS 91, p.131. *Princess Royal*: Henry Bankes, 'Report From the Committee on Dr. Smyth's Petition, respecting his Discovery of Nitrous Fumigation, 10 June 1802', appendix 36, journal of Mr Lara, surgeon of the *Princess Royal*, 7 February 1801 to 17 April 1802. *Adamant*: testimony of Thomas Hall, c/m of John Morris and William Savage, ADM 1/5343. (A partial transcript is printed in NRS 138, pp. 383–6.) **Stirling:** testimony of Joseph Proctor, c/m of John Stirling, ADM 1/5442; the *Leviathan* (74) was off Jamaica. **R&I:** 1808, p. 179 art. XXII. John Brady to John Coffee, and his answer, c/m of the *Defiance* mutineers, ADM 1/5346. *Sceptre*: c/m

of Captain Edward Scobell, ADM 1/5407. *Nereus*: c/m of Lieutenant William Fynmore RM, ADM 1/5407.
[19] **Mark**: Mark, *At Sea with Nelson*, p. 69. *Formidable*: Henry Bankes, 'Report From the Committee on Dr. Smyth's Petition', appendix 36, journals of Mr Allen, surgeon of the *Formidable*, 24 March to 28 April 1801, and of Mr Innes, surgeon of the *Belleisle*, 3 December 1800 and 1 September 1801. **Dillon**: NRS 97, p. 300n.
[20] C/m of the *Defiance* mutineers, ADM 1/5346.
[21] **Washing and shaving**: NRS 138, pp. 224–5; c/m of George Crumpston, ADM 1/5363; Richardson, *Mariner of England*, p. 260. **Merlin**: testimony of Mr Borthwick, c/m of Captain Pakenham for various offences, ADM 1/5329 f. 64. **Pasley**: *Private Sea Journals*, p. 216. **St Vincent**: NRS 61, p. 193. **Hoffmann**: Hoffmann, *Sailor of King George*, p. 150.
[22] C/m of John Grover and John Brown 3rd, ADM 1/5342.
[23] *Brunswick*: c/m of William Jordan, ADM 1/5338.
[24] **Seats**: Lavery, *Bellona*, table D9; *Arming and Fitting*, p. 202. *Caesar*: Richardson, *Mariner of England*, p. 305. **Gibraltar**: c/m of Lieutenant Edward Dillon, ADM 1/5406.
[25] C/m of Thomas Nelson, ADM 1/5353.
[26] Testimony of John Owen Wigley, midshipman, c/m of William Jacobs, ADM 1/5352.
[27] ADM 1/5349. Lieutenant Lys claimed that Thompson slipped, and was not sober at the time. This was repeated by Mr Jones, the boatswain's mate, who said that Thompson was broke for drunkenness and mutinous expressions, and Lys was acquitted. He died on 19 October 1830, still a lieutenant.
[28] ADM 106/2516, no. 51, 22 February 1805. This warrant coincided with the installation of water closets in several of the Navy Board's buildings in the dockyards, in 1806 and in 1807.
[29] Lavery, *Arming and Fitting*, p. 202.
[30] Testimony of Isaac Western, seaman, c/m of the *Defiance* mutineers, ADM 1/5346.
[31] C/m of Francisco Falso and John Lambert, ADM 1/5346.
[32] Lever, *Sea Anchor*, p. 87; J M Boyd, *Manual for Naval Cadets* (London, 1857), in Harland, *Seamanship*, p. 187, and Harland, *Seamanship*, pp. 188 and 191–5.
[33] *Conqueror*'s log, ADM 51/2219.

APPENDIX 1

[1] This was one of the rates proposed to be abolished in the 1816 report.
[2] The additional armourer's mate was to assist the marines in maintaining their arms. The regulations imply that the duty is shared, but William Richardson, in the *Caesar*, recorded: 'January 1, 1811.—Departed this life John Holman, the marine armourer, by a fall only from the forecastle to the main deck. He was a good inoffensive man.' (*Mariner of England*, p. 299.)
[3] Lavery, *Nelson's Navy*, p. 330.

APPENDIX 2

[1] *Druid*: c/m of Charles Selwin Rann, ADM 1/5348.
[2] Testimony of Sergeant Grimes, ADM 1/5297: 'Capt. Gardner afterwards examined both Grimes, and the Prisoner, in the ward-room, where the Prisoner again confessed his guilt, and said he came from Norfolk'.
[3] Grimes is Gramo and Grame and Graham in the *Rippon*'s muster book, and John Blake a private marine who joined 13 May 1758 and was discharged 12 October (ADM 36/6509).
[4] C/m of William White, ADM 1/5350. *Leopard*: NRS 97, p. 220.
[5] **Candles**: ADM 106/2512, no. 572, 25 September 1800, notes that the officers of the yard at

Antigua having favourably reported on the patent candlesticks that burned oil, the candles 'being too soft to stand the heat of the climate', twelve are being sent, with oil, and they are to demand more as required in lieu of candles, but they don't seem to have been supplied to ships: Captain Hall wrote in one of his letters home as a midshipman in about 1805 that it was so hot that the candles 'melted away by degrees, and often tumbled on the table by their own weight' (*Recollections*, vol. I, p. 187). **Regulations**: R&I, 1808, pp. 136–7 arts III and IV; 1790, p. 26 art. XXI is very similar. *Success*: testimony, c/m of Philip Faely, ADM 1/5348. John Trotman, marine, had similar orders. *Ça Ira*: the court martial for her loss, ADM 1/5336.

[6] Dale's court martial is in ADM 1/5344; Hawker's is in ADM 1/5333. Dale's defence, in addition to the claim of excessive use, was that the deficiency in the ship was due to the lieutenant not granting him the use of a boat to fetch off more. He was convicted but Hawker, who showed that the officers' accounts were muddled at best, was acquitted.

[7] ADM 51/1363.

[8] Testimony of John Douglas, and Rann's defence, c/m of Charles Selwin Rann, ADM 1/5348.

[9] *Victory*: accounts, NRS 138, p. 587, wardroom, McKay, *Victory*, table A8. **Commissioner**: ADM 106/2518, no. 888, 3 December 1807. *Edgar*: NRS 31, p. 72.

[10] C/m of Walter Burke, ADM 1/5347. Randolph Cock, in 'Lighting on Eighteenth-Century Ships', *Mariner's Mirror*, vol. 90, no. 2 (May 2004), p. 231, gives a figure of thirty-six 1½ cwt chests as a ship-of-the-line's annual consumption, but has no source; on the basis of the purser's claim that 10lb a day or 3,650lb per year is typical, his figure of 6,048lb per year seems exaggerated.

[11] *A Warrant for the Regulation of Barracks*, 1795, pp. 25–7.

[12] However, equipment and necessaries to barracks were supplied by Alexander Davison, who charged 2.5 per cent commission; but he sold his own goods to himself, for which he was eventually fined £8,883 and sent to Newgate for twenty-one months, so this might account for the relatively large amounts authorised to be supplied. Philip J Haythornthwaite, *The Armies of Wellington* (London: Arms and Armour Press, 1994; new edition, London: Brockhampton Press, 1998), p. 60.

[13] NRS 97, p. 419.

[14] ADM 7/358. The officers whose indents are listed but who recorded no candles used were the maître voilier, the maître charpentier, the maître calfat, the patron du chaloupe, the patron du grand canot, the patron du second canot, the capitaine d'armel, the armurier, the chirurgeon major, the boulanger, the aspirants and the lieutenant en pied.

[15] ADM 95/69, 95/70, 95/71. The averages are mean figures, and the mean per man is the total complement recorded divided by the total weight supplied for those ships and vessels, not the average of the weights per man in each ship or vessel. The figures include the ships and vessels with no candles. The lowest number recorded is for the *Staunch*, which sailed on 23 June 1798 with 4lb for her twenty men. The Victualling Board's collection of precedents notes that in 1776 it issued candles at the rate of 8,465 dozen pounds for 10,000 men for six months, or 0.891oz per man per day, in chests containing 120lb each, ADM 30/44, f. 205.

[16] **Necessaries**: this rate applied to all ships with a complement of more than 343 men. Ships with a smaller complement were supplied at the rate of 1s 5d per lunar month for 343 to 265 inclusive, increasing to 2s 6d for 67 and under. There was also an annual allowance paid when his accounts were passed, from £7 in vessels of under 15 men to £25 in ships of 800 and more, an allowance of 6d per man per lunar month for supernumeraries, and an allowance for top and poop lights if the ship bore a flag or broad pendant. R&I, 1808, pp. 323–5 art. VII. Tare of cask is recorded as a total, but tare of cask for the *Milford*'s 1,329lb of candles in November 1809 was 285lb [21 per cent], ADM 1/1548, Capt. B2. **Navy Board**: ADM 49/121, ff. 32 and 138 and enclosures. *Penelope*: Keats to Captain Broughton, 2 February 1807, ADM 80/142.

[17] *America*: testimony of Tomas Pye Bennett and William Miller, c/m of John Sleffito, ADM 1/5346. Unfortunately most of the witnesses in this trial contradict each other. *Druid*: testimony of John Douglas, c/m of Charles Selwin Rann, ADM 1/5348. *Warspite*: c/m of John Wardocks, ADM 1/5442.

[18] **Rodger**: Rodger, *Wooden World*, p. 45 and *Command of the Ocean*, p. 212, for the period 1689–1714. *Rippon*: testimony of Corporal Mansfield, c/m of John Blake, ADM 1/5297. *America*: c/m of John Sleffito, ADM 1/5346. *Monarch*: testimony of James North, c/m of Robert Nelson, ADM 1/5346.

[19] C/m of James Duckworth and Stephen Simpson, ADM 1/5342.

[20] C/m of John Wardocks, ADM 1/5442.

[21] ADM 95/18, 19 May 1803, f. 135.

[22] WO 55/1747; undated but 1800–1809; ADM 1/1548, Capt. B2 (and appendix 3).**Plates**: ADM 49/121, f. 81.

[23] **1784**: ADM 106/2509, 3 December 1784, no number. **1815**: ADM 7/579, 7/580 [both undated]; 7/581 [September 1815]. **Sizes**: ADM 49/121, f. 67. *Victory*: NRS 138, pp. 563–77 passim. **Oil**: ADM 49/121, f. 81.

[24] ADM 106/241, no. 87, 26 October 1815. Signal lanterns would in future be considered part of the ship's stores, as the signal flags, and placed in the charge of the carpenter or boatswain, but since they would contain glass it would preferably the carpenter; and the Navy Board was to propose the establishment, 'which must be regulated by the greatest number of lanthorns required to make any signal with one or two to spare'. ADM 106/241, no. 172, 9 January 1819; no. 189, 13 September 1819 modifies the plan to that of the *Bulwark*, with lamps in the light room, issued with spare glass chimneys, and a few wax candles if they should fall into disrepair; no. 196, 13 March 1820 replaces Congreve's lamps with Argand's, once Congreve's have been used up.

[25] *Courageuse*: c/m of William White, ADM 1/5350. *Leopard*: NRS 97, p. 220. **Cullen**: NRS 91, p. 48. **Banks**: 7 December 1768.

APPENDIX 3

[1] Captain Bayntun records this as 'Making 276½ tons' (including tare of cask). Unfortunately this raises as many questions as it solves. If this total is correct he is using an 8lb gallon; this is smaller than any of the three standard gallons, and I have not seen it used anywhere else: but later in the report he compares M. Barrallier's supplied weights with those he has found, and lists M. Barrallier's water and tare of cask as 280 tons exactly, implying the Navy Board used a standard 8lb gallon (which Captain Bayntun also uses for his vinegar, rum and wine, despite their different specific gravities and the fact that Navy Board contracts for the 1790s specify 252 gallons of vinegar to the ton (ADM 49/121 f. 54)); but in the same comparison table he lists his own water and tare of cask as 276 tons 6cwt 0qr 15lb, which gives a weight of water of 229 tons 0cwt 2qr 17lb, which is 64,136 gallons 1 pint exactly in 8lb gallons and 50,449 gallons ale measure. Further, the standard capacities for the casks he lists produces a total of 59,770 gallons (weighing in 8lb gallons 213 tons 9cwt 0qr 32lb, and in ale measure gallons 271 tons 7cwt 1qr 7lb). I have concluded elsewhere that water was issued in ale gallons, and using a modern conversion factor, 292 tons 16cwt 1qr 10lb has a volume of 64,492 gallons ale measure, and 64,350 gallons ale measure weighs 292 tons 3cwt 1qr 24lb (a difference between the inferred measure and Captain Bayntun's of 142 gallons or 0.22 per cent and 1,512lb or 0.23 per cent); since there are transcription and substitution errors elsewhere in the report, I have assumed one here and suggested 292 gallons, but it is impossible to be conclusive.

SELECT BIBLIOGRAPHY

This select bibliography is confined to unpublished works directly quoted, and to printed works of naval interest directly quoted or referenced in the notes. In the PRO sources, numbered entries can be found within the file; file names in inverted commas are as listed in the catalogue. Courts martial are by catalogue number then by date (place names are as given in the minutes).

NATIONAL ARCHIVES: PUBLIC RECORD OFFICE

1. Courts martial (by catalogue number and then by date)

ADM 1/5297

1. Court martial of Henry Nelson, purser of the *Sunderland*, for malpractice, specifically issuing tobacco at short measure, held on board the *Sunderland*, Spithead, 27 January 1758.
2. Court martial of John Griffin, 'for having been guilty of quarrelling and fighting, and accused of murder', held on board the *Marlborough*, Port Royal Harbour, Jamaica, 8 March 1758.
3. Court martial of John Blake, a seaman of the *Rippon*, for buggery, held on board the *Monarque*, Blackstakes, 11 August 1758.

ADM 1/5329

1. Court martial of Captain Edward Pakenham for embezzlement of stores, false muster, tyranny and oppression, unofficer and ungentlemanlike behaviour and false expenditure of stores, held on board the *Royal William*, Portsmouth Harbour, 18–12 July 1791.
2. Court martial of John Rowe, seaman of the *Culloden*, for neglect of duty and contempt of his superior officer, held on board the *St George*, 19 September 1791, Hamoaze.
3. Court martial of John Brightly alias John Brighty or Brighteye, of the *Bellerophon*, for desertion, held on board the *Royal William*, Portsmouth Harbour, 27 July 1791.

ADM 1/5330

1. Court martial of Lieutenant Horace Pine, for striking a captain of a gun for allegedly firing without permission, held on board the *Britannia*, at sea, 2 August 1793.
2. Court martial of Francis Richmond Batty, surgeon's first mate, of the *Illustrious*, held on board the *Britannia*, in the outer road of Toulon, 9 October 1793.
3. Court martial of Harry Grice for 'having been the occasion of frequent disturbances in the Wardroom by using reproachful and provoking speeches to several of the Officers, and for a repetition of very disorderly and irregular conduct', held on board the *Cambridge*, Hamoaze, 22 to 26 October 1793.

ADM 1/5331

1. Court martial of William Read, a seaman of the *Marlborough*, for mutinous expressions and contempt for his superior officer, held on board the *Marlborough*, Hamoaze, 31 December 1794.
2. Court martial of ten men of the *Culloden* for mutiny, held on board the *Caesar*, at Spithead, 13 to 20 December 1794.
3. Court martial of Lieutenant George Dentatus Haynes of the *Blenheim* for frequent reproachful and provoking speeches against Lieutenant Legard, held on board *Cambridge*, Hamoaze, 22 to 25 November 1794.
4. Court martial of Captain William Shield and Lieutenant George McKinley for cruelty and oppression in the *Windsor Castle*, held on board the *St George*, Fiorenzo Bay, 11 November 1794.

ADM 1/5332

1. Court martial of John Connor, landman, of the *Fortitude*, held on board the *St George*, Fiorenzo Bay, 12 January 1795.

ADM 1/5333

1. Court martial of Lieutenant George Fitzgerald of the 11th Regiment of Foot for behaving with contempt to Charles Tyler, captain of the *Diadem*, held on board the *Princess Royal*, San Fiorenzo Bay, Corsica, 3 July 1795.
2. Court martial of Christopher Clough, yeoman of the sheets of the *Princess Royal*, and boatswain's mate in the third watch, for striking John Broughton, a sergeant of the 30th Foot, then doing duty as a marine, held on that ship, San Fiorenzo Bay, 6 July 1795.
3. Court martial of John Burrows, 1st Lieutenant, Francis Lloyd, 2nd Lieutenant, John Smollett Rouet, 3rd Lieutenant, William Bissell, 4th Lieutenant, and Randolph McDonald, 5th Lieutenant, of the *Gibraltar* for cruel, oppressive and tyrannical treatment, held on board the *St George*, San Fiorenzo Bay, 20–23 July 1795.
4. Court martial of Dennis Kelly, corporal, Benjamin Rippington, John Shorrock, James Hawley, James Harris, James Smith, Peter Ackerly, Charles Newton, and Richard Gill, marines of the *Bellerophon*, for 'attempting to make a mutiny amongst the whole party on board' and being accessory to writing a public letter to the commanding officer on shore, Major General Wemyss (except James Smith, ill in Haslar), held on board the *Le Juste*, Portsmouth Harbour, 29 September 1795.
5. Court martial of Moses Hawker, purser of the *Lion*, for disobedience, neglect of the captain's orders, and not having supplied the ship with sufficient necessaries for three or four months preceding the trial, held on board the *Bellerophon*, Portsmouth Harbour, 13 and 14 October 1795.
6. Court martial of James Anderson, seaman of the *Hebe*, for insolence, contempt to and abuse of the boatswain held on board the *Le Juste*, Portsmouth Harbour, 15 September 1795.
7. Court martial of twelve seamen of the *Terrible* for mutiny, held on board the *Princess Royal*, San Fiorenzo Bay 25 September, to 3 October 1795.
8. Court martial of James Fennigan, sergeant of marines in the *Bellerophon*, for striking the gunner's servant, quarrelling with and using insolent and improper expressions to the gunner and catching hold of his coat and jostling against him in a mutinous manner, held on board *La Sybille* at Portsmouth, 21 November 1795.

ADM 1/5334

1. Court martial of St Leger Beville, gunner of the *Valiant*, for drunkenness, neglect of duty, and absenting himself from the ship without leave from Saturday 14 November to Wednesday 18 November, held on board the *Romney*, Portsmouth Harbour, 25 November 1795.
2. Court martial of John Bigelston, carpenter, for exaggerating the defects of the *Powerful* on 20 December 1795, thereby retarding His Majesty's service, held on board the *London*, Portsmouth Harbour, 7 January 1796.

ADM 1/5335

1. Court martial of Thomas Hubbard and George Hynes, seamen of the *St George*, for sodomy, held on board the *Gladiator*, Portsmouth Harbour, 10 December 1800.

ADM 1/5336

1. Court martial for the loss of the *Ça Ira*, held on board the *Egmont*, San Fiorenzo Bay, 27 May 1796.
2. Court martial of Richard Parke, purser of the *Gibraltar*, for seditious speeches and other offences, held on board the *Barfleur*, at sea, 17 and 18 June 1796.

ADM 1/5337

1. Court martial of William James and Robert Willis, seamen of the *Director*, for theft and 'disorderly behaviour when sharing money at a late hour of the night', held on board the *Repulse*, Yarmouth Road, 3 October 1796.
2. Court martial of George Nicolson, purser of the *Blanche*, for concealing mutinous designs, held on board the *Barfleur*, Mortilla Bay, 19 October 1796.

ADM 1/5338

1. Court martial of William Holsby, cook of the *Montagu*, then in Yarmouth Roads, for mutinous and seditious language, held on board the *Trent*, Little Nore, 6 January 1797.
2. Court martial on William Jordan, marine of the *Brunswick*, 13 March 1797, for attempting to stab a seaman, held on board the *Brunswick*, Cape Nicolas Mole, San Domingo.

ADM 1/5340

1. Court martial of Philip Le Verconte, purser of the *Saturn*, for issuing provisions at short measure, held on board the *Cambridge*, Hamoaze, 18 July 1797.

ADM 1/5342

1. Court martial of Captain George Hopewell Stephens, at his own request, for oppression and neglect of duty, held on board the *Sceptre*, Table Bay, Cape of Good Hope, 6–14 November 1797.
2. Court martial of James Duckworth, marine drummer, and Stephen Simpson, both of the *Atlas*, for sodomy committed on the evening of 1 May 1797, held on board the *Cambridge* in Hamoaze, 10 November 1797.
3. Court martial of Captain David Hotchkiss, of the *Puissante*, for making use of reproachful and provoking speeches against Captain Rickmore of the *Royal William*, for behaving in a scandalous manner by asserting that there were thirty licensed gin shops aboard the *Royal William*, and that Rickmore and his officers connived at this and took a share of the profits, held on board the *Britannia*, Portsmouth, 22 November 1797.
4. Court martial of Martin Brooke, 2nd Lieutenant of HM receiving ship *Puissante*, for cruelty and oppression, disobedience of orders and conduct disrespectful in words and letters to Captain David Hotchkiss of that ship, held on board *Britannia*, Portsmouth Harbour, 23 to 25 November 1797.
5. Court martial of John Grover and John Brown 3rd, seamen, of the *Ganges*, for mutinous expressions, held on board the *Ganges*, Yarmouth Roads, 15 to 16 December 1797.

ADM 1/5343

1. Court martial of the company of the *Tromp*, for mutiny, held on board the *Britannia*, Portsmouth Harbour, 3 January 1798.
2. Court martial of John Morris and William Savage, seamen, of the *Adamant*, for buggery, held on board the *Adamant*, Yarmouth Roads, 9 January 1798.
3. Court martial of William Ferrier, seaman, of the *Defiance*, held on board the *Duke*, Portsmouth Harbour, 21 March 1798.

ADM 1/5344

1. Court martial of Lieutenant Joseph Street of the *Carnatic* for wounding Lieutenant William Davies, causing his death, held on board the *Carnatic*, Mole St Nicholas, 4 May 1798.
2. Court martial of Robert Dale, purser of the *Lion*, for calling her commanding officer a scoundrel and not supplying her with pease and necessaries, held on board the *Prince* off Cadiz, 30 to 31 May 1798.

ADM 1/5345

1. Court martial of Harry Humphries, lieutenant, of the *Centaur*, for negligence in the performance of his duty on 29 April, and on Captain John Markham's questioning him on the subject, behaving with contempt towards him on the lower deck, held on board the *Prince*, off Cadiz, 1 and 2 June 1798.
2. Court martial of six seamen of the *Suffolk*, for mutiny, held on board the *Victorious*, Clappenberg Cove, Trincomalee Harbour, 15 June 1798.
3. Court martial of William Saunders, seaman, of the *Arrogant*, for absenting himself without leave with intention to desert, held on board the *Victorious*, Clappenberg Cove, Trincomalee Harbour, 15 June 1798.

4. Court martial of Anthony Brompton, 1st Lieutenant of the *Daedalus*, for appearing at a punishment not in uniform, held on board the *Royal William*, Spithead, 25 June 1798.

5. Court martial of James Hosken, gunner, for being materially concerned in the clandestine conveyance of two butts of gin from the Victualling Quay at Dover, 5 July 1798, aboard the *Alfred*, in the Downs.

6. Court martial of Thomas Dundas, of the *Terrible*, for having on the night of 1/2 May 1798 struck James Mackie a midshipman, and making use of disrespectful language to the officers who arrested him, held on board the *Royal Sovereign*, Cawsand Bay, 16 July 1798.

7. Court martial of Mr Henry Gillespie, surgeon's mate, for assault aboard ship, held aboard the *Prince*, off Cadiz, 18 to 19 July 1798.

ADM 1/5346

1. Court martial of John Whittorne of the *Zebra*, 'for drunkeness and insolence, making use of daring and provoking language, setting his Majesty's service at defiance and saying he did not care a damn for it, and by his conduct affording an example of mutiny and sedition', held on board the *Haerlem*, at the Nore, 3 August 1798.

2. Court martial of Charles Moore, seaman, of the *Marlborough*, for behaving in a riotous manner, making use of mutinous expressions, and knocking down the sentinel that had charge of him, held on board the *Prince*, off Cadiz, 15 August 1798.

3. Court martial of twenty-two seamen of the *Caesar* for mutinous assembly, eight as ringleaders and fourteen as aiders and abettors, held on board the *Cambridge*, Hamoaze, 16 to 23 August 1798.

4. Court martial of David Jenness, seaman, of the *Prince*, for buggery of James Lyons, Thomas Willis and Joseph Perry, three boys belonging to the ship, between 1 June and 23 August 1798, held on board the *Prince*, off Cadiz, 25 August 1798.

5. Court martial of twenty-four seamen and one private marine of the *Defiance* for mutinous assembly, held on board the *Gladiator*, Portsmouth Harbour, 8 to 14 September 1798.

6. Court martial on Francisco Falso and John Lambert, seamen of the *Achille*, for sodomy, held on board the *Admiral de Vries*, Blackstakes, 18 September 1798.

7. Court martial of Robert Nelson, captain of the forecastle of the *Monarch*, for having accused the steward of issuing grog for twenty men more than he mixed for, held on board the *America*, Yarmouth Roads, 25 September 1798.

8. Court martial of John Sleffito, sergeant of marines of the *America*, for secreting a quantity of purser's stores committed to his charge, held on board the *America*, Yarmouth Roads, 25 September 1798.

9. Court martial of William Holmes, chaplain of the *America*, for behaving in a scandalous and quarrelsome manner in endeavouring to sow dissensions among the officers aboard the ship, held on board the *America*, Yarmouth Roads, 28 September to 1 October 1798.

10. Court martial of James Morgan, midshipman, for killing Henry Cox, seaman, held on board the *Hannibal*, Port Royal, Jamaica, 28 September to 1 October 1798.

ADM 1/5347

1. Court martial of eleven men the *Glory* for mutiny held on board the *Cambridge*, Hamoaze, 1 to 9 October 1798.

2. Court martial of John Fose, private marine, for desertion, held on board the *Expedition*, Blackstakes, 17 October 1798.

3. Court martial of Richard Cole, seaman of the *London*, for mutiny, held on board the *Prince George*, held off Cadiz, 18–19 October 1798.

4. Court martial of John Keller, private marine, for sleeping on his post, on board the *Director*, Yarmouth Roads, 22 October 1798.

5. Court martial of Charles King and James Dooley, seamen, for theft and Charles Burton, boatswain, and Thomas Pollington, purser's steward, all of the *Sheerness* for accessory to

theft, held on board the *Valiant*, Port Royal Harbour, 22 to 25 October 1798.

6. Court martial of John Parker, seaman, of the *Vanguard*, for insolence, mutinous expressions and endeavouring to stir up a disturbance on a pretence of the provisions having been improperly cut up, held on board the *Diomede*, Sheerness, 25 October 1798.

7. Court martial of James Whitton, private marine, of the *Sultan* prison ship, for quarrelling with and disobeying the commands of his superior officer, held on board the *Gladiator*, Portsmouth, 1 November 1798.

8. Court martial of William Harris, seaman of the *Sandfly*, for 'having in company with six other persons deserted in the jolly boat to the enemy on 19 June 1796 [*sic*]', held on board the *Gladiator*, Portsmouth Harbour, 26 November 1798.

9. Court martial of Walter Burke, purser of the *Powerful*, for writing a letter to Captain Drury of the *Powerful* 'complaining of a wasteful expenditure of necessaries, he not having any just grounds for so doing, and by his exaggerated misrepresentations in the said letter, reflecting on his Captain Drurys, Conduct in the Regulations of His Majesty's Ship under his Command, and expressly imputing to him a disobedience of my [Sir Roger Curtis's] Orders, dated 6th May and 17th August last, directing the utmost frugality in the consumption of Fuel and Candles', held on board the *Foudroyant*, Gibraltar Bay, 24 December 1798.

ADM 1/5348

1. Court martial of Charles Selwin Rann, purser of the *Druid*, for having been often negligent of his duty to the hindrance of His Majesty's service, and for having absented himself without leave, the ship being ready for sea and wanting the necessary supplies, held on board the *Gladiator*, Portsmouth Harbour, 21 January 1799.

2. Court martial of Ralph Thompson, carpenter of the *Ramillies*, for disobeying the orders of Lieutenant Gore and treating Captain Henry Inman with disrespect, both on 10 January, and for being repeatedly drunk, held on board the *Cambridge*, Hamoaze, 28 January 1799.

3. Court martial of Robert Nelson, seaman of the *Belliqueux*, for 'having Cut the Breechings and Tackles of the Main Deck Guns on or about the 14th of November during a heavy Gale of Wind with an intent to destroy the Ship' and various other crimes, held on board the *Belliqueux*, Yarmouth Roads, 24 January to 29 January 1799.

4. Court martial of Lieutenant Charles Grey, of the *America*, for disrespect, held on board the *America*, Yarmouth Roads, 4 February 1799.

5. Court martial of the Right Honourable Lieutenant Lord Cochrane for disrespect to Lieutenant Ralph Beaver, held on board *le Souverain*, Gibraltar, 15 February 1799.

6. Court martial of Lawrence Henderson, a quarter master, of the *Agamemnon*, for murder, held on board the *Romney*, Sheerness, 6 March 1799.

7. Court martial of Philip Faely, 1st Lieutenant of the *Success*, for treating John Spinney, 1st lieutenant of marines, with disrespect and for other crimes, held on board the *Gladiator*, Portsmouth Harbour, 18 March 1799.

ADM 1/5349

1. Court martial of Lieutenant-Colonel Desborough, serving as captain of Marines aboard the *Princess Royal*, for disrespect and disobedience, held on board the *Barfleur*, Tetuan Bay, 8 April 1799.

2. Court martial of John Major, carpenter of the *Vengeance*, on charges of cruelty, oppression, disobedience of orders and mutinous and insolent expressions to Captain Thomas Macnamara Russell of that ship, and suspicion of embezzlement, held on board the *Invincible*, Port Royal Bay, Martinique, 9 to 11 April 1799.

3. Court martial of Lieutenant James Oades Lys of the *Brunswick* for the murder of Thomas Thompson, boatswain's mate, held on board the *Brunswick*, Port Royal Harbour, Jamaica, 21 May 1799.

ADM 1/5350

1. Court martial of John Jolly, marine of the *Alexander*, for striking Lieutenant Pearce of the Marines, held on board the *Leviathan*, Naples Bay, 6 July 1799.
2. Court martial of William White, boatswain's mate, of the *Gibraltar* but serving aboard the *Courageuse*, for mutiny, held on board the *Bellerophon*, Port Mahon, 15 October 1799.
3. Court martial of William McMaster, seaman, and John Callanghan, marine of the *Invincible*, for buggery, held on board the *Unité*, Fort Royal Bay, Martinque, 29 July 1799.

ADM 1/5351

1. Court martial of Patrick Gallahan, seaman of the *Excellent*, for striking or lifting a weapon against a superior officer, held on board the *Cambridge*, Hamoaze, 9 November 1799.
2. Court martial of Sergeant William Roberts of the marines in the *Carnatic* for being drunk and conducting himself in a riotous and disorderly manner, held on board the *Hannibal*, Port Royal Harbour, Jamaica, 20 November 1799.
3. Sergeant John (alias James) Andrew of the marines of the *Quebec*, for being frequently drunk, held on board the *Hannibal*, Port Royal Harbour, Jamaica, 21 November 1799.

ADM 1/5352

1. Court martial of Robert Paton, boatswain of the *Volage*, for having attempted to 'commit a crime unnatural and detestable', held on board the *Hannibal*, Port Royal Harbour, Jamaica, 4 February 1800.
2. Court martial of Lieutenant Somerled McDonnell, of the *Formidable*, for striking Lieutenant Richard Ottley in January, and for insulting him scandalously by pulling off his hat and following him into his cabin and calling him a blackguard, held on board the *Cambridge*, Hamoaze, 31 March 1800.
3. Court martial of John Warner, seaman of the *Delft*, for 'having on the morning of the 17th of March last cut down the hammock of James Lyon, a private in the 13th Regiment, in consequence of which the latter received a violent contusion on the back, and notwithstanding every medical assistance was given, he languished till noon and then died', held on board the *Gladiator*, Portsmouth Harbour, 1 April 1800.
4. Court martial for the loss of the *Queen Charlotte*, held on board the *Audacious*, Vado Bay, 11 April 1800.
5. Court martial of Barnet Hughes, private marine of the *London*, for reproachful and insulting expressions to Sergeant William Perkins, and 'making use of very contemptuous and threatening language' to Lieutenant Joseph Bradley Bague, held on board the *Windsor Castle*, Torbay, 15 April 1800.
6. Court martial of William Collins, marine of the 35th company serving on board the *Prince*, for 'behaving in a most irregular manner and for having, when Serjeant Burt ordered him on the quarter-deck, used threats and contemptuous menaces to him when in the execution of his duty', held on board the *Gladiator*, Portsmouth Harbour, 20 April 1800.
7. Court martial of William Jacobs, seaman of the *Trusty*, for desertion, held on board the *Gladiator*, Portsmouth, 26 May 1800.
8. Court martial of Thomas Hawkins, purser, of the *Retribution*, for riotous conduct, quarrelling with and insulting his superior officer Lieutenant Bountin when officer of the watch, held on board the *Carnatic*, Port Royal Harbour, Jamaica, 18 May 1800.

ADM 1/5353

1. Court martial of Captain John Bowen of the *Camilla* for 'conducting himself in a most partial, cruel and tyrannical manner towards several of the [marines]', held on board the *Ramillies*, St Thomas, 2 January 1808.
2. Court martial of Thomas Nelson, supernumerary seaman of the *Royal William*, for 'having

on or about the 14th of July instant, used reproachful and provoking speeches to a man who had given evidence before a court martial held for the trial of one of the mutineers of the *Hermione*', held on board the *Gladiator*, Portsmouth Harbour, 30 July 1800.

ADM 1/5354

1. Court martial of Jonah alias Joshua Thomas, seaman of the *Glory*, for attempted sodomy, held on board the *Cambridge*, Hamoaze, 4 August 1800.

ADM 1/5360

1. Court martial of James Pearce, marine of the *Cumberland*, for drunkenness, held on board the *Sans Pareil*, Port Royal Harbour, 30 January 1802.

ADM 1/5362

1. Court martial of Charles Coleman, seaman of the *Excellent*, for fighting, held on board the *Venus*, Port Royal Harbour, 6 July 1802.

2. Court martial of Carol Manning, seaman of the *Tremendous*, for drunkenness, held on board the *Lancaster*, Table Bay, Cape of Good Hope, 17 December 1802.

ADM 1/5363

1. Court martial of William Stiles, private marine, of the *Jupiter*, for mutinous expressions, held on board the *Lancaster*, Table Bay, Cape of Good Hope, 11 February 1803.

2. Court martial of Thomas McDowell, carpenter's crew, for a breach of the nineteenth article of war, held on board the *Ganges*, Port Royal Harbour, Jamaica, 5 March 1803.

3. Court martial of Lieutenant Charles Clarke Dobson for using improper language, and otherwise behaving in an ungentlemanlike manner to Captain Oliver Fitzgerald of the Marines, held on board the *Ganges*, 15 April 1803, Port Royal Harbour.

4. Court martial of George Crumpston, carpenter of the *Vanguard*, for drunkenness and neglect of duty, held on board the *Vanguard*, Port Royal Harbour, 21 May 1803.

ADM 1/5385

1. Court martial of Lieutenant Richard Hawkes, commanding the schooner *Arrow*, 'upon charges exhibited against him by the crew of the said schooner dated the 29th December 1807 vizt. Keeping the schooner in want of fuel, for cooking the provisions of the company, want of beer and water, or anything at times being four days without any thing to drink, excepting one pint of wine commencing the 26th of December 1807, and also of not attending to their frequent complaints on the subject', held on board the *Magnanime*, Sheerness, 12 January 1808.

2. Court martial of Lieutenant Samuel Graves Averell RM for kicking William Louffler and striking John Henderson, held on board the *Windsor Castle*, off Cadiz, 13 January 1808.

ADM 1/5406

1. Court martial of Lieutenant Edward Dillon, of the *Gibraltar*, for 'constant and repeated instance of neglect of duty particularly on the 3rd of April 1810', held on board the *Salvador del Mundo*, Hamoaze, 2 June 1810.

2. Court martial of William Clear, landsman of the *Rota*, for robbing John Broid, seaman, of a bag containing his clothes, held on board the *Gladiator*, Portsmouth Harbour, 14 June 1810.

3. Court martial of John de Cruize, supernumerary seaman of the *Namur*, for 'taking indecent and improper liberties with William Taylor a supernumerary boy of the second class in attempting to commit an unnatural crime' on 2 June, and for attempting to corrupt the sentinel over him on 21 June 'to allow him to commit the aforesaid abominable act', held on board the *Magnanime*, Sheerness Harbour, 27 June 1810.

ADM 1/5407

1. Court martial of Solomon Nathan, ship's corporal of the *Castor*, for a breach of the twenty-ninth article of war, and for uncleanness, held on board the *Dannemark*, at the Saintes, 9 to 11 July 1810.

2. Court martial of Lieutenant William Fynmore RM of the *Nereus* for cruelty, held on board the *Magnanime*, Sheerness Harbour, 16 to 19 July 1810.

3. Court martial of William Smith (2), able seaman of the *Niemen*, for robbery, held on board the *Salvador del Mundo*, Hamoaze, 20 July 1810

ADM 1/5428

1. Court martial of Richard Potter, a private marine, of the *Duncan*, for murder, held on board the *Duncan*, off West Capel, 15 July 1812.
2. Court martial of John Sutherland and Edward Millson, of the *Defiance*, for buggery, held on board the *Defiance*, off West Capel, 17 July 1812.
3. Court martial of Peter Richieu, landsman of the *Valiant*, for fighting, held on board the *Royal Oak*, off the Scheldt, 30 July 1812.

ADM 1/5430

1. Court martial of William Mason, Stephen Rolls and John McCarthy, seamen of the *Abercrombie*, for fighting, held on board the *Salvador del Mundo*, Hamoaze, 24 September 1812.

ADM 1/5442

1. Court martial of John Wardocks, seaman of the *Warspite*, for striking Philip Buckhawson, held on board the *Salvador del Mundo*, Hamoaze, 15 April 1814.
2. Court martial of John Stirling, late midshipman of the *Leviathan*, for his disrespectful and contemptuous conduct to Captain Drummond and Lieutenant Andae of that ship on 1 January 1814 and to Lieutenant Dains on the day preceding; for complaining to the Admiralty that Drummond had struck him publicly on the quarterdeck, 'a palpable falsehood'; for conducting himself in the most audacious and disrespectful manner to Drummond while he was investigating Stirling's alleged disobedience of orders from Lieutenant Williamson; for frequent neglect of duty; and for frequently speaking in his berth in the most indecorous manner of the captain and lieutenants of the ship, held on board the *Leviathan*, Port Royal Bay, Jamaica, 14 May 1814.
3. Court martial of William Robson, boatswain of the *Hope*, for drunkenness, held on board the *Gladiator*, Portsmouth Harbour, 18 April 1814

2. Other files (by catalogue number)

ADM 1/100
Letters from flag officers, Channel Fleet: 1794, nos. 1–240.
ADM 1/102
Letters from flag officers, Channel Fleet: 1795, nos. 1–280.
ADM 1/1548
Letters from captains, surnames B: 1810, nos. 1–300.
ADM 1/1549
Letters from captains, surnames B: 1810, nos. 301–642.
ADM 1/1858
Letters from captains, surnames G: 1811.
ADM 1/2498
Letters from captains, surnames S: 1798, nos. 201–392.
ADM 1/3174
Letters from lieutenants, surnames T: 1811.
ADM 1/4335
Letters from the War Office, 1804 to 1807.
ADM 1/4352
Miscellaneous secret letters, 1756 to 1800.
ADM 1/4358
Miscellaneous secret letters, 1812.
ADM 1/4359
Miscellaneous secret letters, 1813.

ADM 2/123
Admiralty Orders and Instructions, 8 December 1792 to 18 April 1793.
ADM 2/124
Admiralty Orders and Instructions, 18 April to 12 October 1793.
ADM 2/125
Admiralty Orders and Instructions, 14 September 1793 to 25 April 1794.
ADM 2/133
Admiralty Orders and Instructions, 1 March to 22 August 1797.
ADM 7/50
Admiral Sir Charles Cotton, Bart., Commander-in-Chief, Mediterranean. Orders to subordinates, April 1810 to February 1811.
ADM 7/55
Letter-Book of the commander of HMS *Alexander*, October 1796 to August 1801.
ADM 7/358
'Munitions and stores on the French covette *La Mutine*, 1796'
ADM 7/226
Admiralty instructions, various, 1805–1830.
ADM 7/412
'Miscellaneous Papers, &c., 1788–1809'.
ADM 7/579
'Establishment of Boatswains' Stores', 1815.
ADM 7/677
'Establishments of Ordnance, 1679–1810, compiled by William Pearce, 20 June 1807 [*sic*]'.
ADM 7/678
Sea officers' pay and half-pay, 1693–1806.
ADM 7/911
'Rate of the Pay of the Royal Navy from 1796 compiled in pursuance of Admiralty Minute of 21st October 1840. Officers Full Pay Division'.
ADM 7/972
Additional instructions to the flag officers, captains, commanders, commanding officers, and pursers of His Majesty's navy, relative to books and accounts, 1813.
ADM 12/59
Admiralty digests, 1793, 51–104.
ADM 12/83
Admiralty digests, 1799, 53–104.
ADM 30/44
'Precedents and exceptions for pursers' accounts'.
ADM 36/6508
Muster book of the *Rippon*, March to December 1758.
ADM 36/13327
Muster book of the *Prompte*, May 1795 to March 1796.
ADM 36/15237
Muster book of the *Excellent*, January to October 1802.
ADM 37/3287
Muster book of the *Abercrombie*, May to December 1812.
ADM 49/105
Papers relating to Mr Lukin's plan for ventilating ships, 1810–11.
ADM 49/121
'Stores: prices of. 1777–1800'.
ADM 51/1363
Captain's log, *Lion*, 20 July 1797 to 3 May 1800.

ADM 51/2989
Captain's log, *York*, 10 September 1807 to 30 June 1812.
ADM 51/2219
Captain's log, *Conqueror*, 28 December 1808 to 20 December 1810.
ADM 51/2860
Captain's log, *Sultan*, 16 October 1809 to 30 June 1814.
ADM 51/2910
Captain's log, *Tigre*, 1 September 1809 to 26 August 1815.
ADM 51/2189
Captain's log, *York*, 10 September 1807 to 30 June 1812.
ADM 80/136
Captain Keats' Letter-Book, 1793–1795.
ADM 80/141
Captain Keats' Letter-Book, 1801–1805.
ADM 80/142
Captain Keats' Letter-Book, 1806–1807.
ADM 95/17
1. 'An Account of the Bedding, Furniture, Linen, Plate etc on bd. His Majesty's Yacht *Charlot* in the Charge of Capt. C. Patten, Shewing also what has been supplied him, what was found remaining & delivered into the Custody of Capt. John Bentley his successor, with what is wanted or taken on Survey per Warrant 26 March 1755'.
2. 'Accommodations proposed for Officers on board Ships of War in the Royal Navy'.
3. 'Plate and linen formerly used at Hill House, Chatham, and now at Sheerness for the lodgings of any commissioner who may occasionally reside there'.
ADM 95/18
Orders as to stores, etc., 1801–8.
ADM 95/69
Ships: draught and qualities, 1792–1795.
ADM 95/70
Ships: draught and qualities, 1795–1799.
ADM 95/71
Ships: draught and qualities, 1799–1802.
ADM 106/241
Documents relating to flags and stores.
ADM 106/2508
Standing orders to the yards 1756–1782.
ADM 106/2509
Standing orders to the yards 1783–1791.
ADM 106/2510
Standing orders to the yards 1792–1794.
ADM 106/2511
Standing orders to the yards 1795–1797.
ADM 106/2512
Standing orders to the yards 1798–1800.
ADM 106/2513
Standing orders to the yards 1801–1802.
ADM 106/2514
Standing orders to the yards 1803.
ADM 106/2515
Standing orders to the yards 1804.

ADM 106/2517
Standing orders to the yards 1806.
ADM 106/2518
Standing orders to the yards 1807.
ADM 106/2822
Office for Stores, August to December 1796.
ADM 106/3546
'Miscellaneous papers, 1799–1803' (actually from the 1740s onwards).
ADM 106/5347
Report of Committee of Sea Officers of Navy Board on stores etc drawn up in 1814.
WO 55/637
Stores, 1794–1832, inc. Ordnance Board orders to artificers, 1806–11.
WO 55/1747
Proportions of Ordnance Stores for the Royal Navy 1818.
WO 55/1843
'Secretary's Book, commencing 1803', in alphabetical headings.

PUBLISHED SOURCES

Admiralty
Regulations and Instructions Relating to His Majesty's Service at Sea. Established by His Majesty in Council (13th edn: London: 1790).
Regulations and Instructions Relating to His Majesty's Service at Sea. Established by His Majesty in Council (London: 1808).

Army Records Society
ARS 3: *The Napoleonic War Journal of Captain Thomas Henry Browne, 1807–16* (ed. Roger Norman Buckley), 1987.
ARS 4: *An Eighteenth-Century Secretary at War. The Papers of William, Viscount Barrington* (ed. Tony Hayter), 1988.

Navy Records Society
NRS 5: *Life of Captain Stephen Martin 1666–1740* (ed. Clements R Markham), 1895.
NRS 6: *Journal of Rear Admiral Bartholomew James 1752–1828* (ed. John Knox Laughton with the assistance of James Young F Sulivan), 1896.
NRS 9: *The Journal of Sir George Rooke Admiral of the Fleet 1701–1702* (ed. Oscar Browning), 1897.
NRS 12: *Letters and Papers of Admiral of the Fleet Sir Thos. Byam Martin G.C.B.* vol. II (ed. Sir Richard Vesey Hamilton, G.C.B.), 1898.
NRS 19: *Journals and Letters of Admiral of the Fleet Sir Thomas Byam Martin*, vol. III (ed. Sir R Vesey Hamilton), 1901.
NRS 31: *Above and Under Hatches. Recollections of James Anthony Gardner* (ed. Sir R Vesey Hamilton and John Knox Laughton), 1906.
NRS 40: *The Naval Miscellany*, vol. II (ed. Sir John Knox Laughton), 1912.
NRS 46: *Private Papers of George, second Earl Spencer, First Lord of the Admiralty 1794–1801*, vol. I (ed. Julian S Corbett), 1913.
NRS 48: *Private Papers of George, second Earl Spencer, First Lord of the Admiralty 1794–1801*, vol. II (ed. Julian S Corbett), 1914.
NRS 58: *Private Papers of George, second Earl Spencer. First Lord of the Admiralty 1794–1801*, vol. III (ed. Julian S Corbett), 1924.
NRS 59: *Private Papers of George, second Earl Spencer. First Lord of the Admiralty 1794–1801*, vol. IV (ed. Rear Admiral H W Richmond), 1924.

NRS 61: *Letters of Admiral of the Fleet the Earl of St. Vincent whilst First Lord of the Admiralty 1801–1804*, vol. II (ed. David Bonner-Smith), 1927.
NRS 77: *The Barrington Papers. Selected from the Letters and Papers of Admiral the Hon. Samuel Barrington*, vol. 1 (ed. D. Bonner-Smith), 1937.
NRS 82: *Recollections of My Sea Life from 1808 to 1830 by Captain John Harvey Boteler, R.N.* (ed. David Bonner-Smith), 1942.
NRS 89: *The Sergison Papers* (ed. Commander R D Merriman), 1950.
NRS 90: *The Keith Papers*, vol. II (ed. Christopher Lloyd), 1950.
NRS 96: *The Keith Papers*, vol. III, *1803–1815* (ed. Christopher Lloyd), 1955.
NRS 97: *A Narrative of my Professional Adventures (1790–1839)*, by Sir William Henry Dillon, K.C.H., Vice Admiral of the Red (ed. Michael Lewis), vol. II, 1802–1839, 1956.
NRS 98: *The Private Correspondence of Admiral Lord Collingwood* (ed. Edward Hughes), 1957.
NRS 100: *Nelson's Letters to his Wife and Other Documents 1785–1831* (ed. George P B Naish), 1958.
NRS 101: *A memoir of James Trevenen* (ed. Christopher Lloyd and R C Anderson), 1959.
NRS 107: *The Health of Seamen. Selections from the Works of Dr. James Lind, Sir Gilbert Blane and Dr. Thomas Trotter* (ed. Christopher Lloyd), 1965.
NRS 119: *The Manning Pamphlets of the Royal Navy: Selected Public Pamphlets, 1693–1873* (ed. J S Bromley), 1974.
NRS 120: *Naval Administration 1715–1750* (ed. Daniel A Baugh), 1977.
NRS 129: *The Hawke Papers. A Selection: 1743–1771* (ed. Ruddock F Mackay), 1990.
NRS 138: *Shipboard Life and Organisation, 1731–1815* (ed. Brian Lavery), 1998.
NRS 141: *The Channel Fleet and the Blockade of Brest, 1793–1801* (ed. Roger Morriss), 2001.
NRS 146: *The Naval Miscellany VI* (ed. Michael Duffy), 2003.
NRS 147: *The Milne Papers. The papers of Admiral of the Fleet Sir Alexander Milne, Bt., KCB*, Volume 1 1820–1859 (ed. John Beeler), 2004.
Occasional Publications: David Syrett and R L DiNardo, *The Commissioned Sea Officers of the Royal Navy 1660–1815* (1994).

A
Aitchison, John, *An Ensign in the Peninsular War. The Letters of John Aitchison*, ed. W F K Thompson (London: Michael Joseph, 1981, paperback 1994).
Aspinall-Oglander, Brigadier General Cecil, *Admiral's Widow. Being the Life and Letters of the Hon. Mrs. Edward Boscawen from 1761 to 1805* (London: Hogarth Press, 1943).
Aspinall-Oglander, Cecil, *Admiral's Wife. Being the Life and Letters of The Hon. Mrs. Edward Boscawen from 1719 to 1761* (London: Longmans, Green, 1940).
Admiral's Widow. Being the Life and Letters of the Hon. Mrs. Boscawen from 1761 to 1805 (London: Hogarth Press, 1943)

B
Barrack Office, *A Warrant for the Regulation of Barracks* (London, 1795).
Bayly, Colonel, *Diary of Colonel Bayly, 12th Regiment* (1896: facs. repr. Naval and Military Press, n.d.).
Bittner, Dr Donald F, *Officers of the Royal Marines in the Age of Sail: Professional and Personal Life in His and Her Majesty's 'Soldiers of the Sea'* (Royal Marines Historical Society Special Publication no. 26, 2002).
Blake, Nicholas, and Lawrence, Richard Russell, *The Illustrated Companion to Nelson's Navy* (London: Chatham Publishing, 2000; 3rd edn 2002).
Bulkeley, John, and John Cummins, *A Voyage to the South Seas in His Majesty's Ship the* Wager *in the Years 1740–1741* (London, 1743: New York, Robert M McBride, 1927).
Burton, Alfred, *The Adventures of Johnny Newcome in the Navy. A Poem, in Four Cantos* (1818: London: Methuen, 1904).

C

Cordingly, David, *Billy Ruffian: The Bellerophon and the Downfall of Napoleon* (London: Bloomsbury, 2003).

D

De Jonnès, Moreau, *Adventures in the Revolution and Under the Consulate*, trans. Cyril Hammond (1929; London: Peter Davies, 1969).

Deane, Anthony, *Nelson's Favourite. HMS Agamemnon at War 1781–1809* (London: Chatham Publishing, 1996).

Durand, James R, *The Life and Adventures of James R. Durand. During a period of fifteen years, from 1801 to 1816: in which time he was impressed on board the British Fleet, and held in detestable bondage for more than seven years* (1920; Yale University Press, ed. George S. Brooks, 1926, repr. Sandwich, MA: Chapman Billies, 1995).

F

Frazer, Augustus Simon, *The Letters of Colonel Sir Augustus Simon Frazer, K.C.B. commanding the Royal Horse Artillery in the army under the Duke of Wellington written during the Peninsular and Waterloo Campaigns*, ed. Major-General Edward Sabine (London: Longman, Brown, Green, Longmans, & Roberts, 1859; facs. repr. Elibron Classics, 2003).

G

Gardiner, Robert (ed), *The Campaign of Trafalgar* (London: Chatham Publishing, 1997).

_____, *Fleet Battle and Blockade. The French Revolutionary War 1793–1797* (London: Chatham Publishing, 1996)

_____, *The Line of Battle. The Sailing Warship 1650–1840* (London: Conway Maritime Press, 1992).

Gardiner, Robert, *Warships of the Napoleonic Era* (London: Chatham Publishing, 1999).

Glascock, William Nugent, *Naval Sketch-book, or, The service afloat and ashore. with characteristic reminiscences, fragments and opinions. by an officer of rank* (2nd edn. London: H Colburn, 1826).

Glete, Jan, *Navies and Nations. Warships, Navies and State Building in Europe and America, 1500–1860*, 2 vols (Stockholm: Stockholm University, 1993).

Goodwin, Peter, *Nelson's Ships. A History of the Vessels In Which He Served 1771–1805* (London: Conway Maritime Press, 2002).

Grossman, Anne Chotzinoff, and Lisa Grossman Thomas, *Lobscouse & Spotted Dog* (New York: W W Norton, 1997).

H

Hall, Basil, *Fragments of Voyages and Travels* (3 vols: Edinburgh: R Cadell; London: Whittaker, 1831).

Harbron, John D, *Trafalgar and the Spanish Navy* (London: Conway Maritime Press, 1988).

Harland, John, *Seamanship in the Age of Sail. An Account of the Shiphandling of the Sailing Man-of-War 1600–1860, Based on Contemporary Sources* (London: Conway Maritime Press, 1984).

Hay, Robert, *Landsman Hay. The Memoirs of Robert Hay*, ed. M D Hay (London: Rupert Hart-Davis, 1953).

Herbert, Lord (ed), *Pembroke Papers (1780–1794). Letters and Diaries of Henry, Tenth Earl of Pembroke and his Circle* (London: Jonathan Cape, 1950).

Hervey, Augustus, *Augustus Hervey's Journal. The Adventures Afloat and Ashore of a Naval Casanova*, ed. David Erskine (London: W Kimber, 1953; facs. repr. London: Chatham, 2002).

Hibbert, Christopher, *Nelson. A Personal History* (London: Viking, 1994).

Hickey, William, *Memoirs of William Hickey*, ed. Alfred Spencer (4 vols: London: Hurst and Blackett, 1913, 1918, 1923, 1925).

Hodges, H W, and E A Hughes, *Select Naval Documents* (Cambridge: Cambridge University Press, 1927).

Hoffman, Captain Frederick, *A Sailor of King George. The Journals of Captain Frederick Hoffman RN, 1793–1814* (ed. A Beckford Bevan and H B Wolryche-Whitmore, London: John Murray, 1901; repr. London: Chatham Publishing, 1999).

Hutchinson, William, *A Treatise on Practical Seamanship* (1777; London: Scolar Press, 1979).

J

James, Willliam, *The Naval History of Great Britain, etc.* six vols. (London: Richard Bentley, 1837).

K

Kennedy, Alistair and Ellison, David, *Pressganged* (Orwell, Herts.: Elissons, 1984).

L

Laird Clowes, William, *The Royal Navy. A History from the Earliest Times to the Present* (1900; London: Chatham Publishing, 1997).

Lambert, Andrew, *War at Sea in the Age of Sail 1650–1850* (London: Cassell, 2000).

Lavery, Brian, *The Arming and Fitting of English Ships of War 1600–1815* (London: Conway Maritime Press, 1987).

——————, *Jack Aubrey Commands. An Historical Companion to the Naval World of Patrick O'Brian* (London: Conway Maritime Press, 2003).

——————, *Nelson's Navy. The Ships, Men and Organisation 1793–1815* (London: Conway Maritime Press, 1989).

——————, *Nelson and the Nile* (London: Chatham Publishing, 1998).

——————, *The 74-gun ship 'Bellona'* (London: Conway Maritime Press, 1985).

——————, *The Ship of the Line*: Vol 1: *The Development of the Battlefleet 1650–1850* (London: Conway Maritime Press, 1983); Vol 2: *Design, Construction and Fitting* (London, Conway Maritime Press, 1997).

Lawrence, Sergeant William, *The Autobiography of Sergeant William Lawrence, A Hero of the Peninsular and Waterloo Campaigns*, ed. George Nugent Bankes (London: Sampson Low, Marston, Searle, & Rivington, 1886; facs. repr. Naval & Military Press, n.d.).

Leech, Samuel, *A Voice from the Main Deck. Being a Record of the Thirty Years Adventures of Samuel Leech* (originally published as *Thirty Years from Home, or, A Voice from the Main Deck : being the experience of Samuel Leech, who was for six years in the British and American navies: was captured in the British frigate Macedonian: afterwards entered the American navy, and was taken in the United States brig Syren, by the British ship Medway* (Boston, Mass.: Tappan & Dennet, 1843; facs. repr. of the sixteenth edition of 1857, London: Chatham Publishing, 1999).

Lever, Darcy, *The Young Sea Officer's Sea Anchor* (1819: facs. repr. London: Constable, 1998).

Lewis, Michael, *A Social History of the Navy 1793–1815* (1960; London: Chatham Publishing, 2004).

Long, W H, *Naval Yarns of Sea Fights and Wrecks, Pirates and Privateers from 1616–1831 as told by Men of Wars' [sic] Men. Many now for the first time printed* (New York: Francis P Harper; London: Gibbings, 1899).

Lovell, Vice Admiral William Stanhope, *From Trafalgar to the Chesapeake. Adventures of an Officer in Nelson's Navy* (originally published as *Personal Narrative of Events, From 1799 to 1815, With Anecdotes*) (Annapolis, MD: Naval Institute Press, 2003).

Lyon, David, *The Sailing Navy List. All the Ships of the Royal Navy – Built, Purchased and Captured – 1688–1860* (London: Conway Maritime Press, 1993).

M

Macdonald, Janet, *Feeding Nelson's Navy: The True Story of Food at Sea in the Georgian Era* (London: Chatham Publishing, 2004).

MacDougall, Philip, *Royal Dockyards* (Newton Abbot: David and Charles, 1982).

McGowan, Alan, HMS *Victory. Her Construction, Career and Restoration* (London: Chatham Publishing, 1999).

McGuane, James P, *Heart of Oak. A Sailor's Life in Nelson's Navy* (New York: W W Norton, 2002).

McKay, John, *The 100-gun ship Victory* (London: Conway Maritime Press, 1987).

Mark, William, *At Sea with Nelson. Being the Life of William Mark, a Purser who served under Admiral Lord Nelson* (London: Sampson Low, Marston, n.d. but 1929).

Microcosm or, A Picturesque Delineation of the Arts, Agriculture, and Manufactures of Great Britain in a Series of above a Thousand Groups of Small Figures for the Embellishment of Landscape, Drawn and Etched by William Henry Pyne (London, 1806: facs. repr., New York; Benjamin Blom, 1971).

Marquardt, Karl Heinz, *Eighteenth-Century Rigs & Rigging* (London: Conway Maritime Press, 1992).

May, Commander W E, *The Boats of Men-of-War* (new edn, London: Chatham Publishing, 1999).

N

Nagle, Jacob, *The Nagle Journal. A Diary of the Life of Jacob Nagle, Sailor, from the Year 1775 to 1841*, ed. John C. Dann (New York: Weidenfeld and Nicolson, 1988).

Nicol, John, *The Life and Adventures of John Nicol, Mariner*, ed. Tim Flannery (1822; Edinburgh: Canongate, 2000).

Nicolas, Sir Nicholas Harris, *The Dispatches and Letters of Vice Admiral Lord Viscount Nelson*, 7 vols. (1844; London: Chatham Publishing, 1997).

Nordhoff, Charles, *Sailor Life on a Man of War* (1855: new edn., New York, Dodd, Mead, 1879).

O

O'Byrne, William R, *A Naval Biographical Dictionary: Comprising the Life and Services of Every Living Officer in Her Majesty's Navy, from the Rank of Admiral of the Fleet to that of Lieutenant, inclusive* (1849: 3rd edn, Polstead, Suffolk: J B Hayward & Son).

P

Parsons, Lieutenant G S, *Nelsonian Reminiscences. Leaves from Memory's Log*, ed. W H Long (Boston, Mass.: 1843; new edition, London: 1905: London: Chatham Publishing, 1998).

Pasley, Rodney M S (ed), *Private Sea Journals Kept by Admiral Sir Thomas Pasley when in command of H.M. Ships Glasgow (20), Sybil (28) and Jupiter (50)* (London and Toronto: J M Dent, 1931).

Pocock, Tom, *The Terror Before Trafalgar: Nelson, Napoleon and the Secret War* (London: John Murray, 2002).

Pope, Dudley, *Life in Nelson's Navy* (London: 1981; republished London: Chatham Publishing, 1997).

R

Raigersfeld, Jeffrey Baron de, *The Life of a Sea Officer*, ed. L G Carr-Laughton (Maidstone: J. Brown, c. 1840; republished London: Cassell, 1929).

Ranken, Agnes, *Shipmates* (privately published, 1967).

Richardson, William, *A Mariner of England. An Account of the Career of William Richardson from Cabin Boy in the Merchant Service to Warrant Officer in the Royal Navy [1780 to 1819] as told by himself*, ed. Colonel Spencer Childers (London: John Murray, 1908).

Robinson, William, *Jack Nastyface. Memoirs of an English Seaman* (first published as *Nautical Economy*, London: William Robinson, 1836; new edition, London: Chatham Publishing, 2002).

Rodger, N A M, *The Command of the Ocean: A Naval History of Britain 1649–1850* (London: Allen Lane, 2004).

———————, *The Wooden World. An Anatomy of the Georgian Navy* (London: Fontana, 1988).

S

Simmons, Major George, *A British Rifle Man. The Journals and Correspondence of Major George Simmons, Rifle Brigade, during the Peninsular War and the Campaign of Waterloo*, edited, with introduction, by Lieut.-Colonel Willoughby Verner (London: A & C Black, 1899).

Smith, Sir Harry, *The Autobiography of Sir Harry Smith 1787–1819* (1910: London: Constable, 1999).

Spavens, William, *The Narrative of William Spavens, a Chatham Pensioner by Himself* (1796: London: Chatham Publishing, 1998).

Stark, Suzanne J, *Female Tars. Women Aboard Ship in the Age of Sail* (London: Constable, 1996).

Steel, David, *Art of Rigging* (1818: repr. Gloucester: Fisher Nautical Press, 1974).

T

Tench, Watkin, *Letters from Revolutionary France. Letters Written in France to a Friend in London, between the month of November 1794, and the month of May 1795*, ed. Gavin Edwards (1796: Cardiff: University of Wales Press, 2001).

Thompson, Julian, *The Royal Marines. From Sea Soldiers to a Special Force* (Sidgwick & Jackson, 2000).

Tracy, Nicholas, *Nelson's Battles. The Art of Victory in the Age of Sail* (London: Chatham Publishing, 1996).

———————(ed), *The Naval Chronicle. The Contemporary Record of the Navy at War* (consolidated edition in five volumes, London: Chatham Publishing, 1999).

W

Walker, George, *The Voyages and Cruises of Commodore Walker*, with introduction and notes by H S Vaughan (1760; London: Cassell, 1928).

Wallis, Helen (ed), *Carteret's Voyage Round the World*, vol. 1 (Cambridge: Hakluyt Society, 1965).

Walters, Samuel, *Samuel Walters Lieutenant, R.N. His memoirs, edited, with an introduction and notes*, ed. C Northcote Parkinson (Liverpool: University Press, 1949).

War Office, *A List of all the Officers of the Army and Royal Marines on Full and Half-Pay: with an index*, 13 March 1815 (facs. repr. Uckfield: Naval and Military Press, n.d.).

Wheeler, William, *The Letters of Private Wheeler 1809–1802*, edited with a foreword by Captain B H Liddell Hart (London: Michael Joseph, 1951).

Winfield, Rif, *The 50-Gun Ship* (London: Chatham Publishing, 1997).

Woodforde, James, *The Diary of a Country Parson 1758–1802* (1924–1931; World's Classics edition, 1949).

Woodman, Richard, *The Victory of Seapower. Winning the Napoleonic War 1806–1814* (London: Chatham Publishing, 1998).

Wybourn, Major T Marmaduke, RM, *Sea Soldier. An Officer of Marines with Duncan, Nelson, Collingwood and Cockburn. The Letters and Journals of Major T. Marmaduke Wybourn RM, 1797–1813*, Collected and transcribed by his sister, Emily Wybourn; selected, edited and with notes by Anne Petrides and Jonathan Downs (Tunbridge Wells: Parapress, 2000).

The Wynne Diaries, ed. Anne Fremantle: vol. II, 1794–1798 (London: Oxford University Press, 1937).

INDEX